W9-BZG-790

Psychology
Basics

MAGILL'S CHOICE

Psychology Basics

Volume 1

Abnormality Defined—
Intelligence

edited by

FRANK N. MAGILL

SALEM PRESS, INC.
Pasadena, California
Englewood Cliffs, New Jersey

PJC WARRINGTON CAMPUS LRC

Copyright © 1993, 1998, by SALEM PRESS, INC.
All rights in this book are reserved. No part of this work may be
used or reproduced in any manner whatsoever or transmitted in any
form or by any means, electronic or mechanical, including photo-
copy, recording, or any information storage and retrieval system,
without written permission from the copyright owner except in the
case of brief quotations embodied in critical articles and reviews. For
information address the publisher, Salem Press, Inc., P.O. Box 50062,
Pasadena, California 91115.

Essays originally appeared in *Survey of Social Science: Psychology*, 1993; new material has been added.

∞ The paper used in these volumes conforms to the American
National Standard for Permanence of Paper for Printed Library Materials, Z39.48-1984.

Library of Congress Cataloging-in-Publication Data
Psychology basics / edited by Frank N. Magill.
     p.   cm. — (Magill's choice)
Includes bibliographical references and index.
ISBN 0-89356-963-1 (set : alk. paper). — ISBN 0-89356-964-X
(v. 1 : alk. paper). — ISBN 0-89356-965-8 (v. 2 : alk. paper)
    1. Psychology—Encyclopedias. I. Magill, Frank Northen, 1907-
1997. II. Series.
BF31.P765   1998
150'.3—dc21   97-39249
                                                 CIP

Third Printing

PRINTED IN THE UNITED STATES OF AMERICA

PUBLISHER'S NOTE

Psychology Basics is the third entry in the Magill's Choice series, the Salem Press imprint designed to meet the basic reference needs of all libraries, even those with the smallest reference collections. Its two volumes collect the most essential articles from the popular six-volume *Psychology* set in Salem Press's Survey of Social Science series.

Psychology Basics is broad in scope, its 110 articles supplying information in a quickly retrievable format and easy-to-understand style. It presents topics drawn from seventeen major areas of psychology: cognition, consciousness, developmental psychology, emotion, intelligence and intelligence testing, language, learning, memory, motivation, personality, psychological methodologies, psychopathology, psychotherapy, sensation and perception, social psychology, stress, and the biological bases of behavior. Within each of these fields is a range of articles selected to provide concise answers to the most-asked questions about psychology. For example, readers will easily be able to find information on Pavlovian (classical) and instrumental (operant) conditioning; short- and long-term memory; the anatomy and functioning of the nervous system; "IQ" testing; theories of personality, including those of Carl Gustav Jung, Sigmund Freud, Karen Horney, Erik Erikson, B. F. Skinner, and Alfred Adler; such psychopathologies as depression, bipolar disorder, and schizophrenia; clinical approaches such as cognitive behavior therapy and classic psychotherapy; smell and taste; crowd behavior; and stress-related diseases. In addition, four overview articles introduce and define the central concepts of behaviorism, cognitive psychology, neuropsychology, and psychoanalytic psychology.

The articles in *Psychology Basics* follow the familiar Magill format. Averaging six pages in length, they begin with ready-reference information that states the type of psychology and particular field of study to which the article's topic belongs. A brief, italicized summary describes the topic's significance; key terms are then listed and defined. To aid the reader in finding information, the main text of each article is divided into three sections: "Overview," "Applications," and "Context." The "Overview" section introduces and explains the topic. "Applications" then describes how the topic is put into practice, including examinations of laboratory or field experimentation as well as a look at how it may be applied to everyday life. "Context" locates the subject within the field of psychology as a whole, relates it to relevant historical or cultural currents, and notes its implications. An annotated "Bibliography" follows these sections; it directs the reader to sources that have been selected for their accessibility to the nonspecialist—the student and the general reader. The bibliographies have been updated to include citations through 1997. Finally, the "Cross-References" section lists related articles that appear elsewhere in *Psychology Basics*.

Readers can locate information on a particular topic in a number of ways. The set is arranged alphabetically by article title, so looking for "behaviorism" will bring the reader to the overview article "Behaviorism"; the cross-references at the end of that article refer the reader to related articles, such as "Learning," "Instrumental Conditioning," and "Radical

Behaviorism." Two other features that will aid the reader in understanding and locating information are found at the end of volume two. A glossary defines more than five hundred important terms, and a comprehensive, cross-referenced index directs the reader to personages, terms, and concepts.

Salem Press gratefully acknowledges the academicians and professionals who contributed their time, talents, and expertise to *Psychology Basics*. A list of these individuals and their affiliations appears on the following pages.

CONTRIBUTORS

Christopher M. Aanstoos
West Georgia College

Steven C. Abell
Loyola University of Chicago

Richard Adler
University of Michigan—Dearborn

Mark B. Alcorn
University of Northern Colorado

Jeffery B. Allen
University of Mississippi

Richard P. Atkinson
Fort Hays State University

Bryan C. Auday
Gordon College

Stephen M. Auerbach
Virginia Commonwealth University

Stephen R. H. Beach
University of Georgia

Donald G. Beal
Eastern Kentucky University

Brett L. Beck
Bloomsbury University

Susan E. Beers
Sweet Briar College

D. Alan Bensley
Texas Wesleyan University

T. L. Brink
Crafton Hills College

Joan Bartczak Cannon
University of Lowell

Paul J. Chara, Jr.
Loras College

Carl D. Cheney
Utah State University

Rebecca M. Chesire
University of Hawaii—Manoa

Allen L. Combs
University of North Carolina at Asheville

Richard G. Cormack
Independent Scholar

Lincoln G. Craton
Trinity University

Kenneth G. DeBono
Union College

James R. Deni
Appalachian State University

Thomas E. DeWolfe
Hampden-Sydney College

Carolyn Zerbe Enns
Cornell College

Lawrence A. Fehr
Widener University

Donna J. Frick
North Carolina A&T University

Lisa Friedenberg
University of North Carolina at Asheville

R. G. Gaddis
Gardner-Webb College

Virginia L. Goetsch
West Virginia University

Doyle R. Goff
Lee College

Laurence Grimm
University of Illinois at Chicago

Leonard W. Hamilton
Rutgers University

Jean S. Helgeson
Collin County Community College

Peter C. Hill
Grove City College

Robert A. Hock
Xavier University

David Wason Hollar, Jr.
Rockingham Community College

Sigmund Hsiao
University of Arizona

Timothy L. Hubbard
Eastern Oregon State College

Eugene R. Johnson
Central Washington University

Laura Kamptner
California State University, San Bernardino

William B. King
Edison Community College

Debra A. King-Johnson
Clemson University

Terry J. Knapp
University of Nevada, Las Vegas

R. Eric Landrum
Boise State University

Kevin T. Larkin
West Virginia University

Joseph C. LaVoie
University of Nebraska at Omaha

Leon Lewis
Appalachian State University

Deborah R. McDonald
New Mexico State University

David S. McDougal
Plymouth State College of the University System of New Hampshire

Salvador Macias, III
University of South Carolina at Sumter

Linda Mealey
College of St. Benedict

Laurence Miller
Western Washington University

Laurie S. Miller
University of Illinois at Chicago

John W. Nichols
Tulsa Junior College

Steve A. Nida
Franklin University

Annette O'Connor
La Salle University

Randall E. Osborne
Phillips University

Linda J. Palm
Edison Community College

Timothy S. Rampey
Victoria College

Cheryl A. Rickabaugh
University of Redlands

Loretta A. Rieser-Danner
Pennsylvania State University, Ogontz

John Santelli
Fairleigh Dickinson University

Rosemary Scheirer
Chestnut Hill College

Elliott P. Schuman
Long Island University

Michael F. Shaughnessy
Eastern New Mexico University

Marilyn N. Silva
California State University, Hayward

Sanford S. Singer
University of Dayton

Lesley A. Slavin
Virginia Commonwealth University

Sheldon Solomon
Skidmore College

Michael A. Steele
Wilkes University

Joseph E. Steinmetz
Indiana University Bloomington

Lori L. Temple
University of Nevada, Las Vegas

Harry A. Tiemann, Jr.
Mesa State College

Derise E. Tolliver
DePaul University

Susana P. Urbina
University of North Florida

Lois Veltum
University of North Dakota

Scott R. Vrana
Purdue University

Elaine F. Walker
Emory University

Daniel L. Wann
Murray State University

Jennifer A. Sanders Wann
Murray State University

Ann L. Weber
University of North Carolina at Asheville

Michael Wierzbicki
Marquette University

David A. Wilder
Rutgers University

Gregory L. Wilson
Washington State University

Stephen L. Wolfe
University of California, Davis

Karen Wolford
State University of New York, College at Oswego

Edelgard Wulfert
State University of New York at Albany

Frederic Wynn
County College of Morris

Taher Zandi
State University of New York

TABLE OF CONTENTS
Volume 1

Volume 2

Psychology
Basics

ABNORMALITY

Type of psychology: Psychopathology
Field of study: Models of abnormality

Abnormality means behavior, thinking processes, or feelings deemed undesirable and therefore subject to control or change. Differing points of view about theoretical orientation, tolerance for deviance, where to draw the line between normal and abnormal, and the use of labeling lead to differences in the criteria used for definitions. Important criteria include subjective discomfort, disability or inefficiency, and deviance, especially bizarre or reality-distorting deviance.

Principal terms

ANXIETY: a chronic fearlike state that is accompanied by feelings of impending doom and cannot be explained by a threatening object or event

BEHAVIORAL VIEW: a perspective that emphasizes understanding a person in terms of his or her objectively measured behavior; normal, in this view, is functioning well

DEVIANCY: the quality of having a condition or engaging in behavior that is different from the typical in a social group and is considered undesirable

DISTORTIONS OF REALITY: beliefs that distort universally accepted assumptions such as those about time, space, cause and effect, or life and death; delusions

MEDICAL MODEL: a view in which abnormality consists of a number of diseases which originate in bodily functions, especially in the brain, and have defined symptoms, treatments, and outcomes

NEUROSIS: a mild abnormality accompanied by moderate discomfort and impairment in functioning; a consequence of anxiety and rigid, play-it-safe behavior

PHENOMENOLOGICAL VIEW: a perspective that emphasizes understanding a person from his or her own viewpoint; normal, in this view, is feeling satisfied with oneself

PSYCHODYNAMIC VIEW: a perspective that emphasizes understanding a person in terms of how he or she copes with unconscious feelings and conflicts; normal, in this view, is understanding and controlling the feelings and conflicts

PSYCHOSIS: a severe abnormality accompanied by distortions in reality and breakdown of functioning

STATISTICAL DEFINITION: a definition of abnormality as a condition that is different from the average or mean of the characteristic or trait

Overview

Abnormality is a term applied to behaviors, thinking processes, or feelings that are viewed by the individual and/or by society as undesirable and requiring control or change, and viewed as deficits which may or may not have a clear etiology but which should be compensated for by the individual and society. Psychologists or other mental health professionals are enlisted to test and/or interview individuals to determine whether a condition is abnormal, and to facilitate change or advise in delineating compensation. There are three typical standards, or criteria, that are used by mental health professionals to decide whether the condition is abnormal: discomfort, disability, and deviance.

The first two of these criteria have some similarity to the general indicators of a physical disease. Just as physical disease may be marked by pain, the major symptom that brings most private patients to a psychotherapist is a chronic psychological pain or discomfort. Just as a physical impairment, such as a broken leg, usually leads to problems in daily living, so the second condition that defines abnormality is some sort of difficulty in functioning, a disability or impairment. Both discomfort and disability are often evaluated by one's personal standards. One is feeling discomfort because of problems one knows best oneself, or one is inefficient compared to what one expects of oneself.

The third major criteria for abnormality, deviance, is based not on personal standards but on the standards of society. Deviance is behavior that is undesirably different from social expectations; such behavior is most likely to be considered psychologically abnormal if it is unpredictable, bizarre, or dangerous.

Each of these three major criteria that collectively define psychological abnormality can range greatly in quality and degree, and each summarizes a large number of symptoms and conditions. Any deviancy or discomfort is more likely to be defined as abnormal if disability or impairment in function is present. The impairment can be judged based on the typical performance of others, or it can be judged based upon the individual's own potential or subjective expectation. The impairment may sometimes be based on a physical condition such as retardation or brain injury. Even if the condition itself cannot be changed, a psychologist can help determine the degree of the problem and help facilitate useful compensations.

Although one can catalog the suggested criteria for abnormality, there are broad theoretical disagreements about which of these criteria should be emphasized in practice. For example, there are phenomenologists who argue that problems do not exist unless they are perceived by the individual and reflected in personal distress. There are behaviorists who argue equally vehemently that only overt behavior should be treated. Such theoretical differences are a primary reason for differences in definitions.

A second core issue is the quantitative one, the question of how much deviance, bizarreness, inefficiency, or distress constitutes "abnormality." Many of those who use the medical model assume a dichotomy between those who have a specific mental disease and the vast majority of normals who are disease free. An alternative view is that the dimensions defining illness are continuous ones ranging from abnormality through mere adequacy to equally rare degrees of supernormality.

Defining categories of deviancy as "abnormal" presents the particularly thorny problem of the relativity of cultural standards. The actions society considers deviant seem limited to particular cultures at particular times. For example, in Victorian times, young women who had children out of wedlock were sometimes committed to hospitals for the "morally insane." Such deviant actions of one generation may later be ignored or even approved by society. A common solution to this dilemma is to distinguish deviancies requiring correction and treatment from others. Deviancies that are dangerous, harmful to others, or accompanied by personal distress are examples.

A final issue pertains to the value placed on the defining process itself. According to the medical model, the definition of abnormality is all-important, central to understanding the cause of the disease and to planning treatment. Any disease should be diagnosed as soon as possible. A sharply contrasting view, held by some sociologists, is that defining, or labeling, has mostly harmful effects. Not only does labeling a person as abnormal relegate him or her to the stigma of being undesirably different, but the label itself creates a self-fulfilling prophecy as others pay particular attention to symptoms of the person's deviancy. The process is also challenged because it focuses on symptoms of the individual that may really result from difficulties in the family, the community, or even the society.

Applications

Each criterion for abnormality referred to above can be applied to many varieties of abnormality, differing in quality and degree. One important feeling of discomfort is sadness, which is called "depression" when it is considered abnormal. Another typical feeling of discomfort is anxiety: a chronic, vague, fearlike feeling of impending doom. When depression or anxiety is chronic, intense, and interferes with functioning, it is much more likely to be considered abnormal than when it is the temporary or mild feeling everyone has from time to time. These feelings are also much more likely to be considered abnormal if there is no real-life stress or crisis to explain them.

Another major criterion of abnormality is deviance, characterized by a condition or behavior that is undesirably different from that of the significant cultural group. This is not necessarily the same as being statistically different from the average of the group, as one can be statistically different in unimportant or even desirable ways. (Wolfgang Amadeus Mozart and Albert Einstein were statistically different from the average.) Rather, deviance is always different in some significant way and is undesirable.

To classify conditions as psychologically abnormal simply because they are deviant is an expansive use of the concept of abnormality that is highly controversial. There are, nevertheless, particular types of deviants that are practically always thought of as abnormal, particularly those that seem bizarre.

The key discriminator, bizarreness, involves behavior, thoughts, or feelings that do not seem consistent with any recognized social role. The deviant individual may distort reality in that he holds beliefs that violate universal assumptions about time, space, selfhood, and cause and effect. Belief in bizarre plots, seeing things that are not there, or hearing imaginary voices are all examples of such distortions. It should be pointed out that this sort of behavior seems to be accepted as abnormal in practically every known culture, although some cultures have valued such bizarreness as religious experiences.

Definitional questions are involved whenever a psychologist considers the question of whether a patient is suitable for treatment and, if so, what sorts of treatment are appropriate. Typical cases sometimes involve the referral of a case that fits only one of the criteria above. A successful lawyer, married, with an attractive family, sees his career as one of only playing silly games. Adequate and conforming, he is abnormal only by the standard of subjective discomfort. A student promoted to the fourth grade seems conscientious and hardworking, but cannot seem to do much more than first-grade work. A psychologist finds that she tests within the retarded range of intelligence. Her problem is an impairment in functioning. A youth who has wounded an owner of a jewelry store during a robbery is interviewed by a psychologist in a detention center. He explains that he did not do anything wrong, really, because the store owner could have simply collected from his insurance company and should have minded his own business. This young man, who can easily rationalize almost any behavior, feels good about himself. He is abnormal in the sense of being deviant and dangerous.

Psychodynamic or phenomenologically oriented psychologists would consider the first patient ideal; behavioral psychologists might help the second develop useful compensations. The approach to the deviant would be largely a matter of external controls.

Most cases seen by psychologists would be abnormal by more than a single criterion. A young man who cannot start the day without a couple of shots of vodka begins developing family problems and staying away from work. He is both a deviant (alcoholic) and shows an impairment in functioning. A woman in a deep depression considers herself worthless and feels she is guilty of unforgivable sins. She also moves very slowly and has stopped eating. She experiences discomfort, shows impairment, and her feelings of guilt seem to distort reality. A middle-aged accountant becomes preoccupied with the fact that he feels estranged from his wife. He thinks so much about this that his performance ratings drop. Like most of the milder cases seen by mental health professionals, subjective discomfort here results in an impairment in efficiency.

Many symptoms that could be diagnosed from a psychiatric manual may not really be considered significant or abnormal if they do not interfere with the individual's functioning. A phobia concerning flying would not be significant for those who never travel; such a phobia might be highly significant for someone who has to travel in work.

Definitional questions are also involved in collective decisions of the American Psychiatric Association (APA) when they revise their *Diagnostic and Statistical Manual of Mental Disorders* (DSM), first published in 1952. At each revision, new syndromes are proposed and borderline ones discussed. As the third edition was being prepared, homosexuality became the focus of a major controversy. Some psychodynamically oriented psychiatrists argued that homosexuality involves an impairment in mature sexual functioning, and so is inherently abnormal. The argument that homosexuals function adequately and sometimes extremely well in important areas of life and that any discomfort is largely the result of discrimination, however, prevailed. Homosexuality was removed from the DSM-III (1980) as a mental disorder.

Context

Modern mental health professionals deal with an enormously varied assortment of problems. Definitions of abnormality offer a guideline as to what conditions should be treated in whom. In contrast, the pioneers of the mental health professions served limited groups of dramatically different populations in different settings.

One such limited group was the hospitalized psychotic population on which the medically oriented Emil Kraepelin, about 1900, commenced his work of classifying the behavior of patients. He hypothesized discrete diseases, each of which presumably had a specific course, outcome, and cause within the brain. Advocates of the medical model still hold that real abnormalities are brain conditions. Even in cases of such real brain impairment, it is usually behavior that reveals the abnormality.

Sigmund Freud, a pioneer of psychodynamic theory and a contemporary of Kraepelin, saw ambulatory middle-class patients who were suffering from anxiety and irrational rigidity in their behavior. Freud identified the causes as impulsive desires with various defensive strategies to keep these from awareness. The defining symptoms that brought the patients to Freud, however, were the anxiety (subjective discomfort) and the rigid, defensive behavior (impairment).

Around the middle of the twentieth century, phenomenologist Carl Rogers identified the basic problem of many of his bright young college students as a lack of self-esteem. This was caused, he believed, by the client's adopting of the artificial, unrealistic standards of others. Rogers paid attention to the client's subjective comfort, or inner attitude toward self. To the phenomenologist, a person, however deviant, who knows and likes himself, is normal. Rogers, like Freud, had faith in insight into oneself and the world "as it really is" as the key to normality.

About the same time in mid-century, the behavioral psychology of B. F. Skinner developed in the animal laboratory, and was applied to the treatment of humans. To Skinner, abnormality consisted of adjustive behavior that had not been learned (impairment) and maladjustive behavior that had been learned (deviance). Inner torment was not, to the behaviorist, a problem.

Definitions of abnormality allowed the practitioner to know the conditions appropriate for treatment and clarified the differences among practitioners. In the late twentieth century, criticism from several sources has led to a fine-tuning of these definitions. The tendency to extend the illness model to many conditions when there is no hard evidence of brain pathology and to assert medical control over these conditions was challenged by Thomas Szasz. Sociologists pointed out the negative effects of labeling as well as the relevance of family and community problems that are defined by psychologists as individual abnormality. In contrast to widely held assumptions, research by Shelley Taylor and associates suggested that the most robust, altruistic people were not the most "realistic" and open to experience, but were rather biased toward a belief in their own good traits and good fortunes. Research and new technology in the field of medical psychology has led to an understanding of genetic or physiological components in conditions previously known only by behavior.

The mental health professions have begun to absorb this research and technology to extend an understanding of abnormalities outward to the community and inward toward underlying genetic or brain pathology. Criteria for the conditions which they define within the domain of psychology will remain the same: discomfort, disability, and deviance.

Bibliography

Altrocchi, John. *Abnormal Behavior*. New York: Harcourt Brace Jovanovich, 1980. Practically every textbook of abnormal behavior contains a discussion of the definitional problem. Altrocchi's chapter 1 offers a particularly thorough discussion, put in the historical context of alternative nonmedical approaches to abnormal conditions. Written on the introductory college level.

Archer, D. "Social Deviance." In *Handbook of Social Psychology*, edited by Gardner Lindzey and Elliot Aronson. 3d ed. Hillsdale, N.J.: Lawrence Erlbaum, 1985. Chapter 26 presents a general review of deviance from the perspective of several sociologists. A discussion of the variety of conditions which are defined as deviant at different times and places, and the negative consequences of labeling. Puts the issue in a sociological perspective. Heavy going but worth it.

Jahoda, Marie. *Current Concepts of Positive Mental Health*. New York: Basic Books, 1958. Reviews and classifies the many different views of mental health, with an emphasis upon those offered by psychotherapists. Argues for attention to "psychological health," which Jahoda views as a "positive striving," not the mere absence of illness. Good as a review of the early literature on the specific problem of definition. Thorough, but some knowledge of personality theories helps.

Lazarus, Arnold A., and Andrew M. Colman, eds. *Abnormal Psychology*. New York: Longman Group, 1995.

Phares, E. Jerry. *Clinical Psychology: Concepts, Methods, and Profession*. 3d ed. Homewood, Ill.: Dorsey Press, 1988. Chapter 4 of this text for college psychology students contains a thorough description of standards for judging normality. These are discussed from the viewpoint of famous psychologists and applied to problems in psychological diagnosis. Cases of the sort found in clinical practice illustrate and help the reader comprehend the issues. Quite readable by the introductory-level student.

Wechsler, Henry, Leonard Solomon, and Bernard M. Kramer, eds. *Social Psychology and Mental Health*. New York: Holt, Rinehart and Winston, 1970. Each of the first ten papers in this edited volume consists of arguments for one of the alternative definitions of abnormality, each by a leading proponent. The papers, particularly those for and against the medical model, are classics. One would otherwise have to comb many journals to find so many important papers from a variety of perspectives.

Widiger, T. A., and T. J. Trull. "Diagnosis and Clinical Assessment." In *Annual Review of Psychology* 42. Stanford, Calif.: Annual Reviews, 1991. This article applies a consideration of definitions of abnormality to the continuing problem of specifically what sorts of disabling or distressful conditions should be included in the APA's revised diagnostic manual. Shows that psychiatrists take the definitional issue seriously.

Wilson, G. Terence, et al. *Abnormal Psychology: Integrating Perspectives*. Boston: Allyn & Bacon, 1996.

Thomas E. DeWolfe

See also:

ACHIEVEMENT MOTIVATION

Type of psychology: Motivation
Fields of study: Motivation theory; personality theory; social motives

The study of achievement motivation examines crucial ingredients in the accomplishment of desirable goals. Studies have included a wide variety of domains, and new insights have been gained into factors involved in areas of accomplishment such as academic achievement, economic and other work-related achievement, gender differences regarding achievement orientation, and individual personality differences.

Principal terms

ACHIEVEMENT MOTIVE: the tendency to strive for success or attain a desired end
EXPECTANCY-VALUE THEORY: the perspective that achievement motivation is predicted by expectancy of success in relation to expectancy of failure, with consideration of values associated with each expectancy
EXTRINSIC MOTIVATION: engaging in activities for external reward
INTRINSIC MOTIVATION: engaging in activities for internal reward such as enjoyment or satisfaction
PSYCHOANALYTIC THEORY: a set of theories conceived by Sigmund Freud which see the roots of human behavior in unconscious motivation and conflict
TRAIT THEORY: a way of conceptualizing personality in terms of relatively persistent and consistent behavior patterns manifested in a wide range of circumstances
UNCONSCIOUS BEHAVIOR: an activity in which an individual engages without knowing the reason or motive for the action

Overview

Achievement motivation can be understood simply as the tendency to strive for success or the attainment of a desirable goal. Embedded within this definition are a number of important implications. First, it is suggested that achievement motivation involves an inclination on the part of the individual. Usually, this includes a consideration of the individual's personality and how that personality influences a motivational state given the presence of certain environmental factors. Second, achievement usually involves a task-oriented behavior that can be evaluated. Third, the task orientation usually involves some standard of excellence that may be either internally (by the person) or externally (by others) imposed.

Henry A. Murray, in his influential book *Explorations in Personality* (1938), conceived of personality as a series of needs which involve a "readiness to respond" in certain ways under specific conditions. Largely influenced by Sigmund Freud's psychoanalytic theory of personality, Murray considered these needs to be primarily unconscious. One of these needs is the need for achievement. Because these needs are largely unconscious, Murray decided that he could not use standard techniques such as questionnaires to measure them directly. He therefore developed the Thematic Apperception Test (TAT). The test involves relatively ambiguous pictures that should evoke from individuals, when asked to provide interpretations, themes reflecting underlying personality needs or characteristics.

With regard to achievement, four pictures are used (for example, one shows a boy looking into space with a violin on a table in front of him). Some interpretations are indicative of a high need for achievement (for example, "The boy is taking a break from his usual hard work of becoming an accomplished violinist"), while others indicate a low need for achievement (for example, "The boy wishes he were outside playing with his friends instead of having to practice"). The test itself, however, is not a particularly valid and reliable indicator of need for achievement and has therefore been frequently replaced by other techniques of measurement.

John Atkinson refined the concept of achievement motivation in 1957 by proposing the expectancy-value theory. This theory maintains that the strength of the achievement motive is determined by two opposing inclinations: a tendency to approach success and a tendency to avoid failure. The first tendency is manifested by engaging in achievement-oriented activities, while the second tendency is manifested by not engaging in such activities. Atkinson further specifies on what basis the strength of these two opposing tendencies can be determined. He suggests, first, that the expectancy, or perceived probability, of success or failure of the action is important. Second, he suggests that the incentive value of success and failure must be taken into account. By this, he means that the degree of pride in accomplishment versus the degree of shame in failure must be considered.

Several modifications were subsequently offered by Atkinson and others. For example, an important distinction between extrinsic motivation (engagement in a task for an external reward, such as a school grade or a pay raise) and intrinsic motivation (engagement in a task as a pleasure in its own right, with some standard of performance as a goal in itself) was developed to explain why some people may still engage in achievement activities, such as attending school or accepting a demanding job, even when their tendency to avoid failure is greater than their tendency to approach success. Though modifications have been necessary and some detailed predictions of the model have not been supported, the general expectancy value model has been helpful in understanding the achievement motive.

The concept of intrinsic motivation has particularly interested psychologists and has been the focus of work by Janet Spence and Robert Helmreich. They were concerned that the earlier work of psychologists on achievement motivation was too unidimensional, and suggested that intrinsic achievement motivation may be something more complex than simply a striving toward excellence for its own sake. Their thinking, based upon some initial research involving statistical analyses of collected data, was that achievement motivation is best conceptualized in terms of three dimensions: work orientation, mastery, and competitiveness. Spence and Helmreich also developed the Work and Family Orientation Questionnaire (WOFO) to measure each of these factors. Work orientation, the first factor, refers to the amount of effort one is willing to put in on a task to do a good job. People who strongly agree with statements such as "There is satisfaction in a job well done" or "It is important for me to do my work as well as I can, even if it isn't popular with my coworkers" from the WOFO would score high on this dimension. The mastery factor reflects a preference for an internally prescribed standard of performance and for difficult, challenging tasks. A person who would strongly disagree with statements on the WOFO such as "I would rather learn easy, fun games than difficult thought games" would score high in achievement motivation on this factor. The competitiveness dimension describes the enjoyment in interpersonal striving, such as the desire to be "number one."

Like Murray had in the 1930's, Spence and Helmreich reflected the mind-set of many psychologists in suggesting that the achievement motive should be considered in terms of general personality traits. Unlike Murray, however, who maintained that the need for achievement was a single need (or trait), Spence and Helmreich thought that achievement motivation consists of three traits (work orientation, mastery, and competitiveness). The idea that these are general personality traits is an important one because it means that the person should somewhat consistently reflect these traits regardless of the situation. Also, if these are personality traits, then people will normally not show sudden changes or major shifts as they grow older.

Applications

Achievement motivation is an important psychological concept and is useful in explaining why some people are more successful in attaining goals than are others. In general, people with a higher need for achievement do better than their counterparts with a low need for achievement.

With regard to academic achievement in college students, it has been found that people with higher need for achievement have higher grade point averages (GPAs). In terms of the three dimensions of achievement recommended by Spence and Helmreich, the correlation between achievement motivation and GPA is a function of the work orientation and mastery factors. In one study, high-GPA students scored high on these two dimensions but surprisingly low on the competitiveness factor. Low-GPA students scored low on all three factors. The same pattern of results was found with fifth- and sixth-grade students in another study. Those with higher standardized achievement test scores were also higher on work orientation and mastery, but lower on competitiveness. Thus, it appears that, at least in relation to academic achievement, not all components of a high need for achievement correspond to better performance.

David McClelland and his associates have studied the relation of achievement motivation to vocational performance. His conclusion is similar to what is commonly found in much of the achievement literature: High achievement is generally a desirable trait that leads to more successful performance. In particular, it appears that entrepreneurs require a high need for achievement to function successfully. Again, however, a broad conclusion such as this may need to be qualified. Spence and Helmreich again question whether a competitive spirit is necessary or even helpful in attaining goals. For example, they found that highly competitive individuals, especially if they are also high in work orientation and mastery, make lower salaries than less competitive colleagues. While salaries may not be a complete measure of success, these results further imply that a competitive characteristic may actually result in lowered performance. Whether discussing academic or vocational performance, one must draw conclusions such as these cautiously since the underlying causes for this relationship are not yet fully understood.

One of the most interesting applications in the study of achievement motivation has involved gender differences. Achievement motivation in women may be a considerably different experience than it is for men. Most of the research conducted by McClelland and Atkinson during the 1950's and 1960's was with men only, in part on the basis of the belief that men need success and women need approval. With women's changing roles in society, however, the study of achievement motivation in women has flourished since the late 1960's.

Early research indicated that women show less need for achievement than do men. One explanation was derived from Atkinson's expectancy-value model, which suggested that women fear success out of concern for the negative social consequences they may experience if they achieve too much. An example would be a girl who lets her boyfriend win when they play tennis. In part, she may be concerned about his feelings, but she may also believe that she will be better accepted (by him and others) if she loses. While it is clear that some people, especially some women, may not find as much delight in winning as do others, subsequent research has suggested that some of the original conclusions may have been overstated. In fact, in terms of Spence and Helmreich's three-factor model of achievement motivation, it appears that the structure of men's and women's achievement motives are more similar than they are different. When sex differences do emerge, women tend to be slightly higher than men in work orientation, while men seem to be slightly higher in mastery and considerably higher in competitiveness.

McClelland has also attempted to demonstrate the potential benefits of increasing achievement motivation in certain populations. Through various educational programs, increasing achievement motivation has helped raise the standard of living for the poor, has helped in the control of alcoholism, and has helped make business management more effective. McCelland has also developed, with apparent success, an elaborate program designed to increase achievement motivation among businesspeople, especially in Third World countries.

Context

The study of achievement motivation grew out of two separate perspectives in the study of personality. The first perspective is the psychoanalytic tradition of Sigmund Freud. Henry Murray was a committed Freudian in his theory of personality, stressing an unconscious dynamic interaction of three personality components: the id, the ego, and the superego. Psychoanalytic thought stresses the similarity of motives among all people by focusing on these driving forces from the unconscious domain of the personality. Murray's contribution to the psychoanalytic tradition is the concept of need, which is understood as an entity that unconsciously organizes one's perception of and one's action orientation toward the world. One of these needs is the need for achievement.

The second major perspective is the trait, or dispositional, tradition in personality theory. This perspective assumes that there are measurable individual differences between people in terms of their needs and motives; that these individual differences are relatively stable over time and manifest themselves in a wide variety of behaviors; and that motives (including the achievement motive), as dispositions within people, provide the basis of behavior. Thus, the emphasis within the trait tradition is on individuals' differences of motives. The psychoanalytic and trait approaches intersect in Murray's theory, which is one reason why his theory is so important in psychology.

In addition, developments in industrial and postindustrial twentieth century societies made the time ripe for the study of achievement. McClelland has suggested that achievement motivation may explain economic differences between societies. In his book *The Achieving Society* (1961), McClelland attempted to predict the economic growth of twenty-three countries from 1929 to 1950 on the basis of images of achievement found in children's stories in those countries in the decade of 1920 to 1929. He found that those societies which emphasized achievement through children's stories generally experienced greater economic growth. While direct cause-and-effect relationships could not be established in a study such as this, subsequent research using experimental studies provided some support for McClelland's position.

Finally, developments in academic achievement testing and vocational performance testing since the early part of the twentieth century have provided a natural setting for measuring attainment in these domains. As more and more tests were developed, and as they became increasingly sophisticated in measuring achievement, it became readily apparent that a conceptual model of achievement was necessary.

Bibliography

Alschuler, Alfred S., Diane Tabor, and James McIntyre. *Teaching Achievement Motivation: Theory and Practice in Psychological Education*. Middletown, Conn.: Education Ventures, 1970. An immensely practical book that briefly discusses achievement motivation and psychological growth, and then describes in considerable detail the ten sessions of an achievement motivation workshop for teachers. The final chapter discusses achievement motivation training for students as well. Can easily be read by individuals at the high school level.

Atkinson, John William, and D. Birch. *An Introduction to Motivation*. 2d ed. New York: Van Nostrand, 1978. Very readable; does an effective job of discussing motivational concepts in general. Because of the first author's interest and research, a heavy emphasis is placed on achievement motivation, focusing particularly on elaborations of the expectancy value model.

Atkinson, John William, and Joel O. Raynor, eds. *Motivation and Achievement*. New York: Halsted Press, 1974. Reprints some of the most important research on achievement motivation. Many of the articles are too technical for the nonprofessional, but chapters 1, 2, 15, 19, and 20 are readable for the college student and are outstanding reviews of prior theory and application to academic achievement and career striving.

DeCharms, Richard. *Enhancing Motivation in the Classroom*. New York: Irvington, 1976. Designed primarily for teachers, with applications at all levels. Nicely incorporates prior research on achievement motivation. More than a how-to book; provides a challenge to the reader to think about factors involved in differing levels of achievement motivation in students.

Fletcher, Jerry L. *Patterns of High Performance: Discovering the Ways People Work Best*. San Francisco: Berrett-Koehler, 1993.

McClelland, David Clarence. *The Achieving Society*. Princeton, N.J.: Van Nostrand, 1961. Considered by many a classic. Applies the methods of the behavioral sciences to provide a psychological basis for evaluating economic, historical, and sociological explanations of the rise and fall of civilizations. The achievement motive is a key to McClelland's theory. Readable by the general reader at the college level and beyond. Highly recommended.

Spence, Janet T., ed. *Achievement and Achievement Motives: Psychological and Sociological Approaches*. San Francisco: W. H. Freeman, 1983. Applies theoretical developments in achievement motivation to topics such as gender differences, children from one-parent households, social mobility, and cultural differences. Though scholarly and thorough, this excellent book is readable by the general audience at a college level, but not without effort.

Peter C. Hill

See also:

Drive Theory, 218; Instinct Theory, 303; Motivational Constructs, 404.

ADOLESCENCE
Cognitive Skills

Type of psychology: Developmental psychology
Fields of study: Adolescence; cognitive development

Adolescence brings the capacity for logical and theoretical reasoning, systematic problem solving, and acquisition of abstract concepts; adolescent cognitive skills are reflected in social and personality development as well as in learning and problem-solving behavior.

Principal terms

CONCRETE OPERATIONS STAGE: the stage, according to Piaget's theory, between ages seven and twelve, during which children acquire basic logical rules and concrete concepts

EGOCENTRISM: the inability to see things from the perspective or point of view of another person

FORMAL OPERATIONS STAGE: the stage, according to Piaget's theory, corresponding to adolescence, during which children acquire sophisticated logic and abstract concepts

IMAGINARY AUDIENCE: the belief that the self is constantly being watched and critiqued by other people

INFORMATION-PROCESSING APPROACH: the study of how people perceive information, remember information, think, and solve problems

PERSONAL FABLE: the belief that one's own experiences are unique and different from anyone else's

PSEUDOSTUPIDITY: the appearance of stupidity resulting from seeing problems and situations as much more complicated than they really are

PSYCHOMETRIC APPROACH: the study of cognition through intelligence testing

Overview

Psychologists approach the study of adolescent cognitive skills from three perspectives: the psychometric, the developmental, and the information-processing. The psychometric approach focuses on defining and measuring intellectual skills. Psychometric research typically involves studies of performance on intelligence tests. The developmental approach seeks to identify the types of cognitive skills which are unique to the adolescent years. This approach has been heavily influenced by the cognitive stage theory of Swiss psychologist Jean Piaget. The information-processing approach examines the characteristics of memory and problem solving. It views adolescent cognitive skills as parameters that determine how the brain stores and analyzes information.

In the psychometric view, adolescence is a period of cognitive stability. Intelligence test (IQ test) scores show little change during adolescence. Although IQ scores often fluctuate during early childhood, scores generally stabilize about age eight. It is not uncommon to find temporary periods of instability in IQ scores after age eight, such as at the onset of puberty or during other stressful times, but dramatic and long-term score changes are rare. According to this perspective, adolescence does not bring significant changes in cognitive skills.

This statement may be confusing. Clearly, sixteen-year-olds must "know more" than eight-year-olds, and adolescents have the capacity to learn school subjects beyond the grasp of elementary school children. The psychometric approach, however, is not designed to contrast the nature of cognitive skills at different ages. Intelligence tests are scored by comparing a specific person to other people of the same age. A score of 100 at age eight means that a person performs similarly to the average eight-year-old; a score of 100 at age eighteen means that a person performs similarly to the average eighteen-year-old. IQ score is expected to remain the same if the person matures at a relatively normal rate.

The developmental approach, centered on the work of Piaget, seeks to identify the cognitive skills of adolescence and to contrast them with the skills found at other ages. Two of Piaget's stages are of particular importance to the study of adolescence: the concrete operational stage (ages seven to twelve) and the formal operational stage (age twelve and up). During the concrete operational stage, children acquire basic logical concepts such as equivalence, seriation, and part-whole relations. Children also master reversibility, a skill allowing them mentally to restore a changed object or situation to its original state. With reversibility, children can recognize that a small glass of juice poured into a taller and thinner glass may look like more juice but is actually the same amount.

The formal operational stage supposedly begins at adolescence. During this stage, thinking becomes more logical, more abstract, more hypothetical, and more systematic. Unlike their concrete operational counterparts, formal thinkers can study ideologies, generate a variety of possible outcomes to an action, and systematically evaluate alternative approaches to a problem. Formal thinkers also are better able to adopt a new course of action when a particular strategy proves unsuccessful.

Research has called into question the link between adolescence and the stage of formal operational thought, however; most adolescents show some evidence of formal thinking but fail to demonstrate the consistency necessary for this stage to be aligned specifically with adolescence. Performance does not necessarily improve with age. Adults also show variability in formal thinking, implying that people may become only partially formal operational. Many psychologists are beginning to question whether formal operational thought is a coherent stage of cognitive development. In addition, research indicates that cultural background affects performance on problems requiring formal thinking. Perhaps experience determines the extent of formal operational thinking.

In spite of the controversy surrounding the stage of formal operations, there is evidence that cognitive skills change as children enter adolescence. The information-processing approach provides additional information about these child/adolescent contrasts. According to John Flavell, cognitive growth is the acquisition of increasingly sophisticated and efficient problem-solving skills. For example, adolescents can hold more information in memory than children, which enhances their ability to solve complex problems. Improvements in memory reflect more than changes in capacity. Adolescents are better able to develop associations between words and ideas, which in turn facilitates remembering them. Part of their improvement is a result of the fact that adolescents know more than children. Adolescents also are better able to think abstractly and develop hypotheses. These skills in part reflect improvements in generalization, identifying similarities between previous situations and new ones. Changes in thinking and hypothesizing also enable adolescents to generate a wider variety of problem-solving strategies, which also enhances their performance. Finally, adolescents know more about the nature of thought and memory. This metacognition, or ability to "think about thinking," increases the planning in their problem-solving behavior.

Applications

The research on adolescent thinking has been applied to the study of learning, personality, and social behavior during adolescence. For example, research on adolescent cognition has influenced the development both of curricula and teaching methods at the middle-school and high-school levels. As individuals who are entering the stage of formal thinking, adolescents are better equipped to handle abstract topics such as geometry and physics. Their emerging ability to consider systematically the effects of several factors when solving a problem make adolescents good candidates for laboratory science courses.

Some applications of research on adolescent cognitive skills are the subject of much debate, however; ability tracking is a case in point. Psychometric research indicates that intellectual functioning becomes relatively stable in preadolescence. From this point onward, children continue to perform at the same level relative to their age-mates on standardized measures such as IQ tests. The stability of test performance has been used to support the creation and maintenance of ability tracks beginning in the middle-school years. Proponents of tracking maintain that ability grouping or tracking enables teachers to challenge more able students without frustrating less capable students. Opponents of tracking maintain that less able students benefit from both the academic challenges and the competent role models provided by superior students in ungrouped classrooms. In fact, critics of tracking charge that the level at which performance stabilizes actually results from subtle differences in how teachers interact with their students, differences often based on inaccurate assumptions about student potential. Perhaps students with low test scores, many of whom are poor or minority students, perform poorly because people expect them to be less capable.

David Elkind sees the emergence of features of formal thinking reflected in adolescent personality characteristics. According to Elkind, the ability to think abstractly and hypothetically enables adolescents to develop their own idealistic, theoretical views of the world. The ability to distinguish between reality and theory, however, can lead to disillusionment and the recognition that adolescents' idols have "feet of clay." Elkind identifies three somewhat bizarre ways of thinking that result from cognitive growth in combination with a lack of experience. In personal fable, young adolescents see themselves as unique and special. Personal fable may lead adolescents to take unnecessary risks because they believe they are so different from others: "I can drink and drive." "Only other people get pregnant." Personal fable also makes adolescents believe that no one else can understand how they feel or offer any useful suggestions: "No one has ever had a problem like mine."

In imaginary audience, adolescents believe that "everyone" is watching them. Elkind sees this self-consciousness as an application of hypothetical thinking: "If my characteristics are so obvious to me, they must also be obvious to everyone else." In pseudostupidity, newly acquired cognitive skills prove difficult to control, causing adolescents literally to think too much and unnecessarily complicate the problems they face. As a result, they often appear "stupid" rather than mature.

Cognitive changes also affect social behavior by inducing changes in social cognitive development. Social cognition refers to an individual's understanding of people and of interactions between people. According to Piaget, changes in cognition are reflected in the way we think about ourselves and other people. The thinking of preadolescents (seven to eleven years) begins to focus less on the obvious features of objects, events, and people. They are better able to translate patterns of behavior into psychological characteristics, such as concluding that a particular person is "nice" or "rude." They are becoming less egocentric, better able to appreciate that people have different points of view. It is not surprising, then, that they are better able to see the world from the perspective of another person. As they enter formal operations (eleven or twelve years and older), adolescents are able to think in more logical and abstract ways. These changes are reflected in their ability to describe people in abstract terms, such as "cooperative" or "uncoordinated," and compare people along psychological dimensions.

Robert Selman has observed that changes in social cognition occur in stages that closely parallel Piaget's stages of cognitive development. According to Selman's research, most concrete operational preadolescents (ages ten to twelve) recognize the existence of different points of view. Many of them, however, have difficulty evaluating conflicting perspectives or understanding how perspectives relate to membership in different social groups. As adolescents become more fully formal operational (twelve to fifteen years and older), they become able to understand the relationship between another person's perspective and their membership in social systems. For example, the difference between two people's points of view may reflect their membership in different racial or ethnic groups. Progress through Selman's stages also is influenced by social experiences. In other words, it is possible for a person to mature intellectually and to become less egocentric without becoming skillful at adopting others' points of view.

Context

Theory and research on cognitive skills began with the development of modern intelligence tests, such as Alfred Binet's 1916 test; however, the intelligence-testing, or psychometric, approach has contributed little to an understanding of adolescent cognitive skills. Intelligence tests are best suited to the study of individual differences, or how people compare to others of their age. It is difficult to use intelligence testing to compare and contrast cognitive skills at different ages.

Intelligence tests also are used to study the stability of intellectual level and the likelihood it will change in later years. Research indicates, however, that intelligence test scores in adolescence generally are similar to scores during childhood, although scores may fluctuate during childhood as a function of changes in factors such as diet, socioeconomic status, and education. Again, the psychometric approach seems poorly suited to the study of adolescent cognitive skills.

Psychometric (IQ score) research also contributes little to understanding the process of cognitive development. The developmental approach addresses both the qualities of thought and the process of change. In 1958, Piaget and his coworker, Barbel Inhelder, published *The Growth of Logical Thinking from Childhood Through Adolescence*, a detailed account of his four stages of cognitive development. In addition to proposing that specific cognitive skills emerge in each stage, Piaget proposes that the move from one stage to the next is largely maturational.

Piagetian theory has been notoriously difficult to evaluate. Research indicates that performance on Piagetian tasks depends on understanding the instructions, being able to attend to the relevant aspects of the problems, and being interested in the problems themselves. Adolescents who perform best on formal operational tasks are often those with interests in the natural sciences—an unlikely finding if cognitive change is largely maturational.

Although the popularity of Piagetian theory has declined, it remains one of the most influential theories in developmental psychology. In fact, it was Piagetian theory that led information-processing psychologists to become interested in cognitive development. Although disputing Piaget's proposals about cognitive stages, many of these psychologists noted parallels between Piaget's descriptions of cognitive skills and their own. Information processing began to devote increasing attention to age-related changes in cognitive processes.

Information-processing research has helped explain some of the inconsistencies that appear in Piagetian research. According to Piagetian theory, people are located within particular cognitive stages and will reason at those levels of maturity in all problem-solving situations. Why, then, do most people show features of several stages, depending on the type of problem presented? According to information-processing research, variability in performance across different problem types is to be expected. The more one knows, the easier it is to use efficient cognitive processes. People will appear more cognitively mature performing tasks about which they are knowledgeable.

Understanding cognitive skills during adolescence requires some familiarity with all three perspectives, in spite of the weaknesses of the psychometric and Piagetian approaches. Each has made a unique historical contribution to current views of cognition.

Bibliography

Ashby, Deborah. "Can Iron Supplementation Improve Cognitive Functioning?" *The Lancet* 347 (October 12, 1996): 973.

Bervonsky, M. "Formal Reasoning in Adolescence: An Alternate View." *Adolescence* 13 (1978): 280-290. A review of the research on formal thinking. Suggests that formal thinking typically emerges at eleven to fifteen years but that the ability to utilize this thinking varies among individuals.

Elkind, David. *The Child's Reality: Three Developmental Themes*. Hillsdale, N.J.: Lawrence Erlbaum, 1978. Discusses the ways in which adolescent cognitive skills are reflected in personality and in social behavior. Excellent presentations on egocentrism, ideologies, personal fable, imaginary audience, and pseudostupidity.

Flavell, John. *Cognitive Development*. Englewood Cliffs, N.J.: Prentice-Hall, 1985. Presents theory and research on cognitive development from an information-processing approach. Discusses relationship between information processing and Piagetian theory. An excellent effort to compare and contrast these two perspectives.

Ginsburg, Herbert, and Sylvia Opper. *Piaget's Theory of Intellectual Development*. Englewood Cliffs, N.J.: Prentice-Hall, 1988. In its latest edition, this now classic work contains an updated presentation of Piaget's theory of cognitive development, including a detailed analysis of formal operational thinking.

Muuss, R. E. "Social Cognition: Robert Selman's Theory of Role Taking." *Adolescence* 17, no. 67 (1982): 499-525. Discusses the relationship between adolescent cognitive skills and the ability to adopt another person's point of view. Includes an overall summary of Robert Selman's model of social cognitive development.

Lisa Friedenberg

See also:

Adolescence: Sexuality, 19; Cognitive Development Theory: Jean Piaget, 135; Gender-Identity Formation, 254; Generativity in Adulthood, 260; Identity Crises, 284; Moral Development, 399; Trust, Autonomy, Initiative, and Industry, 633.

ADOLESCENCE
Sexuality

Type of psychology: Developmental psychology
Field of study: Adolescence

Adolescent sexuality examines the physical, psychological, and behavioral changes that occur as the individual leaves childhood, acquires sexual maturity, and incorporates the various aspects of sexuality into his or her identity. This emerging sexuality may cause adjustment problems, which can be severe.

Principal terms

ADOLESCENCE: the period extending from the onset of puberty to early adulthood
ADOLESCENT GROWTH SPURT: a rapid increase in height and weight that begins at about eight or nine in girls and ten or eleven in boys
MENARCHE: the term for a female's first menstrual period
PRIMARY SEX CHARACTERISTICS: the physiological features of the sex organs
PUBERTY: the stage of development when the individual reaches sexual maturity and becomes capable of reproduction
SECONDARY SEX CHARACTERISTICS: physical features other than genitals that distinguish women and men
SEXUAL SCRIPT: a stereotypic pattern that defines how individuals should behave sexually

Overview

Perhaps no single event during the adolescent years has as dramatic or widespread effects as the realization of sexuality. The lives of both males and females become wrapped in this new dimension. Adolescence is a time of sexual exploration and experimentation, of sexual fantasies and sexual realities, of incorporating sexuality into one's identity. It is not surprising, then, that the adolescent's emerging sexuality causes adjustment problems.

Adolescence is the life stage between childhood and adulthood. Its age limits are not clearly specified, but it extends roughly from age twelve to the late teens, when physical growth is nearly complete. Puberty, a term often confused with adolescence, occurs at the end of childhood and lasts from two to four years. It is the period of adolescence during which an individual reaches sexual maturity.

Human beings grow most rapidly at two times during their lives: before they are six months old and again during adolescence. The second period of accelerated growth is often referred to as the adolescent growth spurt. Adolescents grow both in height and weight, with the increase in height occurring first. As they gain weight, the amount and distribution of fat in their bodies change, and the proportion of bone and muscle tissue increases. In girls the adolescent growth spurt usually begins between the ages of nine and eleven and reaches a peak at an average of twelve-and-a-half years. Then growth slows and usually ceases completely between the ages of fifteen and eighteen. The growth spurt in boys generally begins about two years later than it does in girls and lasts for a longer time. It begins between the ages of eleven and fourteen, reaches a peak at about age fifteen, and slowly declines until the age of nineteen or twenty.

The teenager's body grows at differing rates, so that at times adolescents look a bit awkward. Big feet and long legs are the early signs of a changing body, but even these changes do not occur at the same time. First the hands and feet grow, then the arms and legs; only later do the shoulders and chest grow to fit the rest of the developing body. Changes in body proportion become obvious. The trunk widens in the hips and shoulders, and the waistline narrows. Boys tend to broaden mostly in the shoulders, girls in the hips.

Puberty is chiefly characterized by sexual development. Sexual development can be best understood by examining the maturation of primary and secondary sex characteristics. Primary sex characteristics are the physiological features of the sex organs. For males, these organs are the penis and the testes; for females, they are the ovaries, uterus, clitoris, and vagina. Secondary sex characteristics are not directly related to the sexual organs but nevertheless distinguish a mature male from a mature female. Examples of secondary sex characteristics are the male beard and the female breasts.

In girls, the onset of breast development is usually, but not always, the first signal that puberty has begun. This typically occurs between the ages of ten and eleven, but can occur as late as ages thirteen and fourteen. There is simultaneous development of the uterus and vagina, with enlargement of the labia and clitoris. Menarche (the first menstrual period), although perhaps the most dramatic and symbolic sign of a girl's changing status, occurs relatively late in puberty, after the growth spurt has reached its peak velocity. The first menstrual periods tend to be irregular, and ovulation (the release of a mature egg) does not usually begin until a year or so after menarche.

The first noticeable change in boys is usually growth of the testes and scrotum. The growth of the genitals begins, on average, about the age of twelve and is completed, on average, by about the age of fifteen. Boys generally become capable of ejaculation about a year after the penis begins to grow. These first emissions may occur as a result of nocturnal emissions, the ejaculation of semen during sleep. Nocturnal emissions are a normal phase of development and are frequently caused by sexual excitation in dreams or by some type of physical condition, such as a full bladder or even pressure from pajamas.

As adolescents' bodies become more adultlike, their interest in sexual behavior increases sharply. They must learn the necessary behavior to satisfy that interest, and they must face the issue of a mature gender identity. This includes the expression of sexual needs and feelings and the acceptance or rejection of sex roles. The onset of dating and the beginning of physical intimacies with the opposite sex can provoke frustration and anxiety. As this unfamiliar territory is explored, the adolescent is often very underinformed and overly self-conscious. Conflicting sexual values and messages are frequently encountered, accentuating the problem of integrating sexual drives with other aspects of the personality.

Applications

Adolescents are acutely aware of the rapid changes taking place in their bodies. How they react to such changes greatly affects how they evaluate themselves; it is in this manner that physical and psychological development are related.

Physical changes may cause psychological discomfort. Adolescents are particularly concerned about whether they are the "right" shape or size and whether they measure up to the "ideal" adolescent. Rapid growth, awkwardness, acne, voice changes, menarche, and other developments may produce emotional distress. Therefore, it is not surprising that the timing of physical and sexual maturity may have an important influence on psychosocial adjustment. Adolescents are generally concerned about anything that sets them apart from their peers. Being either the first or last to go through puberty can cause considerable self-consciousness.

In general, boys who mature early have a distinct advantage over those who mature late. They tend to be more poised, easygoing, and good-natured. They are taller, heavier, and more muscular than other boys their age. They are also more likely to excel at sports, achieve greater popularity, and become school leaders. In contrast, late-maturing boys not only are smaller and less well developed than others in their age group, but they also are not as interested in dating. When they do become interested in girls, they often lack social skills; they are more likely to feel inadequate, anxious, and self-conscious. These personality characteristics tend to persist into early adulthood, although they become less marked and often disappear as time goes by.

For girls, early maturation appears to be a mixed blessing. Girls who mature early grow taller, develop breasts, and go through menarche as much as six years before some of their peers. Their larger size and more adult physique may make them feel conspicuous and awkward, while at the same time they may be popular with boys and experience more dating opportunities. They also may have to deal with parents and other caregivers who have reacted to their early sexual development by being overly restrictive. For these reasons, the late-maturing girl often finds adolescence a little easier than her early-maturing peer. As with boys, the consequences of early and late maturation decrease over time.

Sexual maturation has other psychological consequences as well. In particular, patterns of sexual behavior change tremendously with the arrival of sexual maturity. As adolescents' bodies become more adult, their interest in sexual behavior increases sharply; as they explore their sexual identities, they develop a sexual script, or a stereotyped pattern for how individuals should behave sexually.

The sexual script for boys is frequently different than the sexual script for girls. As a result, males and females generally think differently about sex. This discrepancy can cause problems and confusion for adolescents as they struggle with their sexual identities. For males, the focus of sexuality may be sexual conquest, to the point that young men who are nonexploitative or inexperienced may be labeled with negative terms such as "sissy." Males are more likely than females to see intercourse as a way of establishing their maturity and of achieving social status. As a consequence, boys are more likely to have sex with someone who is a relative stranger, to have more sexual partners, and to disassociate sex from love and emotional intimacy.

Adolescent girls are much more likely than adolescent males to link sexual intercourse with love. The quality of the relationship between the girl and her partner is a very important factor. Most females would agree that sexual intercourse is acceptable if the two people are in love and is not acceptable if the two people are not in a romantic relationship. Consequently, females are less likely than males to list pleasure, pleasing their partner, and relieving sexual tension as reasons for having sex.

Given their different sexual motives, boys generally expect sex sooner in a relationship than girls. Since girls usually want to wait until an emotional commitment and intimacy have developed, they may feel pressured into having sex before they are ready. Therefore, girls may be somewhat uncomfortable with a decision to engage in sexual intercourse.

During the past several decades, attitudes toward sexual activity have changed dramatically. Views regarding premarital sex, extramarital sex, and specific sexual acts are probably more open and permissive today than they have been at any time in recent history. Young people are exposed to sexual stimuli on television and in magazines and motion pictures to a greater extent than ever before. Effective methods of birth control have lessened the fear of pregnancy. All these changes have given the adolescent more freedom. These changes also produce more conflict, however, since guidelines for "appropriate behavior" are less clear-cut than they were in the past. In some families, the divergence between adolescent and parental standards of sexual morality is great.

Context

Sexual behavior as a subject for scientific investigation has traditionally met with much resistance; historically, the majority of individuals in the fields of medicine and psychology have not considered sex to be an appropriate topic for investigation. As a result, knowledge regarding this important dimension of life has been slow to develop. Only since the 1940's have researchers been able to explore the physical and psychological aspects of human sexuality objectively.

Sigmund Freud, the father of psychodynamic theory, was one of the first scientists to demonstrate the influence of sexuality in human life. He clearly described the existence of sexuality in infants and children and developed a detailed theory of psychosexual development. Although his theory has been criticized, his rich observations and concepts have had a great impact on psychological thinking. At about the same time that Freud was developing his ideas, Havelock Ellis was publishing a seven-volume series called *Studies on the Psychology of Sex* (1897-1928). Ellis, an English physician, devoted much of his life to sexual research. He focused on the varied nature of human sexual behavior and challenged ideas commonly held at the time. For example, he did not agree that women were basically asexual, and he recognized the common occurrence of masturbation in both sexes.

Alfred Kinsey was another sexologist who has been instrumental in furthering understanding of human sexual behavior. Although severely criticized for his work, Kinsey paved the way for detailed, objective research. He and his colleagues conducted extensive face-to-face interviews with twelve thousand people from all segments of the population. This research produced a large amount of detailed data, resulting in the publication of two major works: *Sexual Behavior in the Human Male* (1948) and *Sexual Behavior in the Human Female* (1953).

The research of Kinsey and others focused on interviews and case histories. The goal was to discover how people behaved sexually, addressing such issues as how often and when they engaged in sexual activity as well as specific behaviors involved. It was not until the 1950's that William Masters and Virginia Johnson began to study what people actually did. Masters was trained as a gynecologist, and Johnson received her training in social work and psychology. Working as a team, they began to study sexual anatomy and physiology as well as psychological and sociological data. Under laboratory conditions, they observed and recorded the details of human sexual activity. In 1966, their findings were published in a report titled *Human Sexual Response*.

Research specifically directed toward the exploration of adolescent sexuality was not seriously undertaken until the 1950's and 1960's. Even then, the few studies that were conducted handled the topic delicately and focused on attitudes rather than behavior. When behavior was emphasized, age at first intercourse was generally selected as the major variable. Later studies have been more detailed and expansive; however, a paucity of research in this area still exists.

Jeanne Brooks-Gunn and Frank Furstenberg, in the book *Adolescent Behavior and Society* (4th ed., 1990, edited by Rolf E. Muuss), suggest that numerous issues have received little or no exploration. Included in their list of "research omissions" are the following: frequency of behaviors other than intercourse, pubertal education aimed at boys on topics such as ejaculation and condom use, the relation of sexual behavior to other adolescent behavior, the meaning of eroticism in adolescents' sex lives, and differences between younger and older adolescents.

Social concerns such as teenage pregnancy, sexually transmitted diseases, and sex education have focused attention on the need to understand clearly the dynamics of adolescent sexuality. This awareness should encourage broader perspectives for the study of teenage sexual behavior and produce detailed knowledge of sexuality as it occurs in the adolescent experience.

Bibliography

Bell, Ruth, et al. *Changing Bodies, Changing Lives: A Book for Teens on Sex and Relationships*. New York: Random House, 1987. A comprehensive book that includes information on various aspects of adolescent sexuality. Written specifically for a teenage audience. Teens from around the United States were surveyed in order to determine the book's contents, and they share their unique perspectives on sexuality. This is perhaps one of the best resources available for teens.

Bowe-Gutman, Sonia. *Teen Pregnancy*. Minneapolis: Lerner, 1987. An excellent book which discusses values involving sexuality, health issues for adolescent mothers and their babies, contraception, parenting readiness, and the economics of raising a child. The book includes five case studies of pregnant teens and offers advice for teens who think they may be pregnant.

Gullotta, Thomas P., Gerald R. Adams, and Raymond Montemayor, eds. *Adolescent Sexuality*. Newbury Park, Calif.: Sage Publications, 1993.

Johnson, Eric W. *Love and Sex in Plain Language*. Philadelphia: J. B. Lippincott, 1985. This book was originally written in 1968; this fourth revision remains an excellent resource for the study of human sexuality. It is concise and comprehensive. The author discusses the development of male and female reproductive systems in an understandable manner. Illustrations, a glossary, and an index make the information readily accessible.

Leeming, Frank C., William O. Dwyer, and Diana P. Oliver, eds. *Issues in Adolescent Sexuality: Readings from the Washington Post Writers Group*. Boston: Allyn & Bacon, 1996.

McCoy, Kathy, and Charles Wibbelsman. *The New Teenage Body Book*. Los Angeles: Body Press, 1987. An excellent resource, the book is concerned with the overall health of adolescents. Included is an excellent section on sexually transmitted diseases. Provides addresses of nationwide agencies that assist adolescents with health and sexual concerns.

Comprehesive and readable, with illustrations and an index to complement the text.

Madaras, Lynda, with Area Madaras. *The What's Happening to My Body? Book for Girls: A Growing Up Guide for Parents and Daughters*. Rev. ed. New York: Newmarket, 1987. Written especially for adolescents and their parents. The author is a leading sex educator, and she is joined by her daughter. The primary focus is on female puberty; however, topics such as sexual feelings and sexual intercourse are also discussed. Well written, with illustrations that enhance the text.

Madaras, Lynda, with Dane Saavedra. *The What's Happening to My Body? Book for Boys: A Growing Up Guide for Parents and Sons*. 2d rev. ed. New York: Newmarket, 1987. Written by a leading sex educator with the assistance of an adolescent male. The book deals primarily with male puberty but includes information about sexual feelings and sexual intercourse. A very useful and informative book, written in a conversational style which makes complicated information available to teens. Illustrations and an index are included.

Doyle R. Goff

See also:

AFFILIATION AND FRIENDSHIP

Type of psychology: Social psychology
Fields of study: Interpersonal relations; social motives

Affiliation is the tendency to seek the company of others; people are motivated to affiliate for several reasons, and affiliation also meets many human needs. Friendship is an important close relationship based on affiliation, attraction, and intimacy.

Principal terms

AFFILIATION: the tendency to seek the company of others and to be with one's own kind
ATTRACTION: the preference for contact with specific individuals
COMMUNAL RELATIONSHIP: a long-term relationship based on common investments rather than balanced exchange
COMPLEMENTARITY: the possession of qualities that complete or fulfill another's needs and abilities
CONSENSUAL VALIDATION: the verification of subjective beliefs by obtaining a consensus among other people
EXCHANGE RELATIONSHIP: a short-term relationship based on balance of benefits given and received
PROPINQUITY: proximity or nearness to others
PROSELYTIZE: to preach or convert with propaganda
SOCIAL COMPARISON: the comparison of oneself to others to judge the appropriate way to behave

Overview

Affiliation is the desire or tendency to be with others of one's own kind. Many animal species affiliate, collecting in groups, flocks, or schools to migrate or search for food. Human affiliation is not controlled by instinct but is affected by specific motives. One motivation for affiliation is fear: People seek the company of others when they are anxious or frightened. The presence of others may have a calming or reassuring influence. Research in 1959 by social psychologist Stanley Schachter indicated that fear inducement leads to a preference for the company of others. Further work confirmed that frightened individuals prefer the company of others who are similarly frightened, rather than merely the companionship of strangers. This preference for similar others suggests that affiliation is a source of information as well as reassurance.

The value of obtaining information through affiliating with others is suggested by social comparison theory. Social comparison is the process of comparing oneself to others in determining how to behave. According to Leon Festinger, who developed social comparison theory in 1954, all people have beliefs, and it is important to them that their beliefs be correct. Some beliefs can be objectively verified by consulting a reference such as a dictionary or a standard such as a yardstick. Others are subjective beliefs and cannot be objectively verified. In such cases, people look for consensual validation—the agreement of others—to verify their beliefs. The less sure people are of the correctness of a belief, the more they rely on social comparison as a source of verification. The more people who agree with one's opinion about something, the more correct one feels in holding that opinion.

Beyond easing fear and satisfying the need for information or social comparison, mere affiliation with others is not usually a satisfactory form of interaction. Most people form specific attractions for other individuals, rather than being satisfied with belonging to a group. These attractions usually develop into friendship, love, and other forms of intimacy. Interpersonal attraction, the experience of preferring to interact with specific others, is influenced by several factors. An important situational or circumstantial factor in attraction is propinquity. Propinquity refers to the proximity or nearness of other persons. Research by Festinger and his colleagues has confirmed that people are more likely to form friendships with those who live nearby, especially if they have frequent accidental contact with them.

Further research by social psychologist Robert Zajonc indicated that propinquity increases attraction because it increases familiarity. Zajonc found that research subjects expressed greater liking for a variety of stimuli merely because they had been exposed to those stimuli more frequently than to others. The more familiar a person is, the more predictable that person seems to be. People are reassured by predictability and feel more strongly attracted to those who are familiar and reliable in this regard.

Another important factor in attraction and friendship is physical attractiveness. According to the physical attractiveness stereotype, most people believe that physically attractive people are also good and valuable in other ways. For example, physically attractive people are often assumed to be intelligent, competent, and socially successful. Attraction to physically attractive persons is somewhat modified by the fear of being rejected. Consequently, most people use a matching principle in choosing friends and partners: They select others who match their own levels of physical attractiveness and other qualities.

Matching implies the importance of similarity. Similarity of attitudes, values, and background is a powerful influence on interpersonal attraction. People are more likely to become friends if they have common interests, goals, and pastimes. Similar values and commitments are helpful in establishing trust between two people. Over time, they choose to spend more time together, and this strengthens their relationship.

Another factor in interpersonal attraction is complementarity. Research has failed to confirm that "opposites attract," since attraction appears to grow stronger with similarities, not differences, between two people. There is some evidence, however, that people with complementary traits and needs will form stronger relationships. For example, a person who enjoys talking will have a compatible relationship with a friend or partner who enjoys listening. Their needs are different but not opposite—they complete each other, hence the term "complementary."

Friendship begins as a relationship of social exchange. Exchange relationships involve giving and returning favors and other resources, with a short-term emphasis on maintaining fairness or equity. For example, early in a relationship, if one person does a favor for a friend, the friend returns it in kind. Over time, close friendships involve shifting away from an exchange basis to a communal basis. In a communal relationship, partners see their friendship as a common investment and contribute to it for their mutual benefit. For example, if one person gives a gift to a good friend, he or she does not expect repayment in kind. The gift represents an investment in their long-term friendship, rather than a short-term exchange.

Friendship also depends on intimate communication. Friends engage in self-disclosure and reveal personal information to one another. In the early stages of friendship, this is immediately reciprocated: One person's revelation or confidence is exchanged for the other's. As friendship develops, immediate reciprocity is not necessary; long-term relationships involve expectations of future responses. According to psychologist Robert Sternberg, friendship is characterized by two experiences: intimacy and commitment. Friends confide in one another, trust one another, and maintain their friendship through investment and effort.

Applications

Theories of affiliation explain why the presence of others can be a source of comfort. In Stanley Schachter's classic 1959 research on fear and affiliation, university women volunteered to participate in a psychological experiment. After they were assembled, an experimenter in medical attire deceived them by explaining that their participation would involve the administration of electrical shock. Half the subjects were told to expect extremely painful shocks, while the others were assured that the shocks would produce a painless, ticklish sensation. In both conditions, the subjects were asked to indicate where they preferred to wait while the electrical equipment was being set up. Each could indicate whether she preferred to wait alone in a private room, in a large room with other subjects, or had no preference.

The cover story about electrical shock was a deception; no shocks were administered. The fear of painful shock, however, influenced the subjects' preferences: Those who expected painful shocks preferred to wait with other subjects, while those who expected painless shocks expressed no preference. Schachter concluded that (as the saying goes) misery loves company. Further research gave subjects the choice of waiting with other people who were not research subjects. In this study, subjects who feared shock expressed specific preference for others who also feared shock: Misery loves miserable company.

The social comparison theory of affiliation explains the appeal of group membership. People join groups such as clubs, organizations, and churches to support one another in common beliefs and to provide one another with information. Groups can also be a source of pressure to conform. One reason individuals feel pressured to conform with group behavior is that they assume the group has better information than they have. This is termed informational influence. Cohesive groups—groups with strong member loyalty and commitment to membership—can also influence members to agree in the absence of information. When a member conforms with the group because he or she does not want to violate the group's standards or norms, he or she has been subjected to normative influence.

Studies of interpersonal attraction and friendship have documented the power of circumstances such as propinquity. In their 1950 book *Social Pressures in Informal Groups*, Leon Festinger, Stanley Schachter, and Kurt Back reported the friendship preferences of married students living in university housing. Festinger and his colleagues found that the students and their families were most likely to form friendships with others who lived nearby and with whom they had regular contact. Propinquity was a more powerful determinant of friendship than common background or academic major. Propinquity appears to act as an initial filter in social relationships: Nearness and contact determine the people an individual meets, after which other factors may affect interpersonal attraction.

The findings of Festinger and his colleagues can be applied by judiciously choosing living quarters and location. People who wish to be popular should choose to live where they will have the greatest amount of contact with others: on the ground floor of a high-rise building, near an exit or stairwell, or near common facilities such as a laundry room. Zajonc's research on the power of mere exposure confirms that merely having frequent contact with others is sufficient to predispose them to liking.

Mere exposure does not appear to sustain relationships over time. Once people have interacted, their likelihood of having future interactions depends on factors such as physical attractiveness and similarity to one another. Further, the quality of their communication must improve over time as they engage in greater self-disclosure. As friends move from a tit-for-tat exchange to a communal relationship in which they both invest time and resources, their friendship will develop more strongly and satisfactorily.

Research on love has identified a distinction between passionate love and companionate love. Passionate love involves intense, short-lived emotions and sexual attraction. In contrast, companionate love is calmer, more stable, and based on trust. Companionate love is strong friendship. Researchers argue that if passionate love lasts, it will eventually calm down and become transformed into companionate love.

Researcher Zick Rubin developed a scale to measure love and liking. He found that statements of love involved attachment, intimacy, and caring. Statements of liking involved positive regard, judgments of similarity, trust, respect, and affection. Liking or friendship is not simply a weaker form of love, but a distinctive combination of feelings, beliefs, and behaviors. Rubin found that most dating couples had strong feelings of both love and liking for each other; however, follow-up research confirmed that the best predictor of whether partners were still together later was how much they had liked—not loved—each other. Liking and friendship form a solid basis for love and other relationships that is not easily altered or forgotten.

Context

Much early research on affiliation and friendship developed from an interest in social groups. After World War II, social scientists were interested in identifying the attitudes and processes that unify people and motivate their allegiances. Social comparison theory helps to explain a broad range of behavior, including friendship choices, group membership, and proselytizing. Festinger suggested that group membership is helpful when one's beliefs have been challenged or disproved. Like-minded fellow members will be equally motivated to rationalize the challenge. In their 1956 book *When Prophecy Fails*, Festinger, Henry Riecken, and Schachter document the experience of two groups of contemporary persons who had attested a belief that the world would end in a disastrous flood. One group was able to gather and meet to await the end, while the other individuals, mostly college students, were scattered and could not assemble. When the world did not end as predicted, only those in the group context were able to rationalize their predicament, and they proceeded to proselytize, spreading the word to "converts." Meanwhile, the scattered members, unable to rationalize their surprise, lost faith in the prophecy and left the larger group.

Research on propinquity combined with other studies of interpersonal attraction in the

1960's and 1970's. Friendship and love are challenging topics to study since they cannot be re-created in a laboratory setting. Studies of personal relationships are difficult to conduct in natural settings; if people know they are being observed while they talk or date, they behave differently or leave the scene. Natural or field studies are also less conclusive than laboratory research, since it is not always clear which factors have produced the feelings or actions that can be observed.

Friendship has not been as popular a topic in relationships research as romantic love, marriage, and sexual relationships. Some research has identified gender differences in friendship: Women communicate their feelings and experiences with other women, while men's friendships involve common or shared activities. Developmental psychologists have also identified some age differences: Children are less discriminating about friendship, identifying someone as a friend who is merely a playmate; adults have more complex ideas about friendship forms and standards.

As research on close relationships has gained acceptance, work in communication studies has contributed to the findings of social psychologists. Consequently, more is being learned about the development and maintenance of friendship as well as the initial attractions and bonds that encourage people's ties to others.

Bibliography

Cherry, Andrew L., Jr. *The Socializing Instincts: Individual, Family, and Social Bonds.* Westport, Conn.: Praeger, 1994.

Duck, Steve. *Friends, for Life: The Psychology of Close Relationships.* New York: St. Martin's Press, 1983. Duck, an influential theorist in the field of close relationships, explains the value of friends, the strategies by which friendships are developed, and the ways in which friendships can be assessed and strengthened. Readable and engaging.

Festinger, Leon, Stanley Schachter, and Kurt Back. *Social Pressures in Informal Groups.* Stanford, Calif.: Stanford University Press, 1950. This classic work documents the authors' research on housing and friendship preferences and ties work on friendship to theories of group structure and function.

Fletcher, Garth J. O., and Julie Fitness, eds. *Knowledge Structures in Close Relationships: A Social Psychological Approach.* Hillsdale, N.J.: Lawrence Erlbaum, 1996.

Hendrick, Clyde, and Susan Hendrick. *Liking, Loving, and Relating.* Monterey, Calif.: Brooks/Cole, 1983. The Hendricks provide a thorough review of the processes of affiliation and interpersonal attraction. They include a discussion of issues in contemporary relationships, such as separation and divorce, blended families, changing sex roles, and dual-career couples.

Huston, Ted L., ed. *Foundations of Interpersonal Attraction.* New York: Academic Press, 1974. This edited volume brings together chapters by major researchers in close relationships. Most chapters emphasize theory and are directed at the college student and graduate student.

Rubin, Lillian B. *Just Friends: The Role of Friendship in Our Lives.* New York: Harper & Row, 1985. A very accessible popular work examining a much-neglected topic. Considers gender differences in friendships and how friendships coexist with other close relationships in people's lives.

Ann L. Weber

See also:

Attraction Theories, 77; The Contact Hypothesis, 170; Crowd Behavior, 182; Self: Definition and Assessment, 524; Self-Esteem, 530.

AGGRESSION

Type of psychology: Social psychology
Field of study: Aggression

Aggression is conceptualized as a diverse category of behaviors that are intended to injure or harm another. Psychological theories of aggression seek to explain, and ultimately to control, people's hostile or antisocial behaviors. Generally, psychological theories address the relative influences of biological factors (such as aggressive instincts or physiological arousal) and situational factors associated with aggression in animals and humans.

Principal terms

CATHARSIS: a reduction of psychological tension and/or physiological arousal

DEFENSE MECHANISM: according to Sigmund Freud, a psychological strategy by which an unacceptable sexual or aggressive impulse may be kept from conscious thought or expressed in a disguised fashion

DISPLACEMENT: according to Freud, a defense mechanism by which a person redirects his or her aggressive impulse onto a target that may substitute for the target that originally aroused the person's aggression

FRUSTRATION: a psychological state of arousal that results when a person is prevented from attaining a goal

HOSTILE AGGRESSION: aggressive behavior that is associated with anger and is intended to harm another

INSTINCTIVE AGGRESSIVE BEHAVIOR: aggressive behavior that does not result from learning experiences; such behavior is expressed by each member of a species with little variation in its expression

INSTRUMENTAL AGGRESSION: aggressive behavior that is a by-product of another activity; instrumental aggression occurs only incidentally, as a means to another end

OBSERVATIONAL LEARNING: learning that results from observing other people's behavior and its consequences

SUBLIMATION: according to Freud, a defense mechanism by which a person may redirect aggressive impulses by engaging in a socially sanctioned activity

THANATOS: the instinctive aggressive instinct located in the human unconscious

Overview

Aggression is any antisocial behavior that is harmful or injurious to another. This may include overt physical and verbal behaviors (for example, firing a gun or screaming at someone in anger) as well as nonverbal behaviors, such as the display of obscene gestures. Psychologists consider aggression to be a category of diverse behaviors under which two subordinate categories of behaviors can be subsumed. The first category, instrumental aggression, consists of aggressive behaviors that are simply a means to another end. Hence, the primary goal of instrumental aggression is not necessarily to injure another person; aggression is used to attain a desired outcome. For example, a soccer player might knock her teammate down as they both run to tackle a ball. The girl's aggressive behavior was not intended to harm her teammate; rather, her goal was to gain possession of the ball and to score. The second category, hostile aggression, is often the result of anger, and its sole purpose is to injure or harm its target. Hostile aggression includes cases of physical assault, verbal abuse, and other antisocial behaviors. Most of the theoretical perspectives and empirical studies of aggression in psychology are concerned with hostile aggression.

There are three major psychological perspectives on aggression. The first perspective adopts a strongly biological stance on the development and maintenance of aggression in the human species. The second perspective takes the position that aggression is a result of the buildup of psychological frustration. The third perspective argues that aggression is a learned social behavior.

The first theoretical perspective, instinct theories, adopts the position that human nature includes an inborn drive for aggression. The ethologist Konrad Lorenz studied the instinctive nature of aggression in animals and humans. According to his work, aggression is a species-specific impulse that builds within the body and is eventually released by specific stimuli that elicit aggression. For example, an aggressive impulse might be unleashed by the presence of one's enemy. In some cases, however, the expression of this instinct may be inhibited by certain stimuli (for example, a parent may become angered by a child's behavior but not strike the child). Ethologists argue that the "babyish" facial characteristics of infants and young children serve as stimuli that inhibit the expression of aggressive behavior by adults.

Another instinct theory, psychoanalytic theory, posits that the seeds of aggression lie in the human personality. According to Sigmund Freud, a significant portion of one's unconscious psychological processes are governed by Thanatos. Thanatos, or the death instinct, is a reservoir of aggressive, and often self-destructive, tendencies that Freud considered to be part of the human species' evolutionary heritage. The psychic energy dedicated to Thanatos is thought to build over time until it is released in aggressive behavior. Periodic discharge, or catharsis, of this psychic energy is necessary for psychological health. Catharsis can occur either directly through overt aggression or indirectly through a number of disguised avenues. Many of Freud's defense mechanisms allow for a safe outlet of a person's aggressive impulses. For example, a man might be angered by his abusive employer's demands. Instead of accosting his employer directly, however, he might drive to his health club and "blow off steam" by sparring with a boxing partner. His aggressive urge is thus reduced through displacement of his aggressive impulse. As another example, an angry and sarcastic young girl may become a prosecuting attorney upon reaching adulthood. By aggressively prosecuting accused criminals and interrogating defense witnesses, a necessary part of her profession, this woman may be sublimating her aggressive tendencies.

The second theoretical perspective was introduced by John Dollard and his colleagues' early work investigating S-R (stimulus-response) theory. Their theory of aggression consisted of two simple propositions. First, aggression must always result from frustration. Second, frustration always leads to aggression. Thus, aggression was thought to be attributable to the thwarting of one's purpose or being prevented from attaining a valued goal. This theory, the frustration-aggression hypothesis, was later revised by Leonard Berkowitz, who argued that the frustration-aggression relationship was not quite so clear-cut. He posited that frustration simply makes a person ready to be aggressive. Aggression will result from frustration if, and only if, a cue for aggressive behavior is present. Aggressive cues are social stimuli, such as potential weapons, that have been associated with aggression in the past. Thus, the revised frustration-aggression hypothesis posits that aggressive tendencies will accumulate as a response to frustration. Catharsis is likely to occur when situational cues support an aggressive response.

The final perspective, social learning theory, emphasizes the role of social and situational factors in the learning and expression of aggressive behaviors. According to Albert Bandura, aggressive behaviors can be learned through two primary avenues, direct experience and observational learning. Learning by direct experience involves the actual enactment of aggressive behavior. If aggression is rewarded, then it is likely to recur. If aggression is punished, then it is likely to be suppressed, especially in the presence of the punishing agent. Observational learning, on the other hand, involves a process whereby people attend to the behaviors of people in their environment and the consequences of these behaviors. Bandura stated that people are most likely to attend to, and thus learn from, the behaviors of three salient model categories: families, subcultures, and the media. For example, a young boy may observe the aggressive behavior exhibited by the fellow members of his neighborhood gang. This modeling by other gang members not only may teach him novel behaviors but also may lower his inhibitions to be aggressive. Thus, when this boy becomes aroused by an aversive event, such as a taunt from a rival gang member, he will be likely to respond in an aggressive manner.

Applications

Much of the psychological research investigating the nature of aggression has been focused on the control of aggression. Of particular interest to researchers is the notion that allowing limited expression of low levels of aggression (catharsis) might play an important role in controlling the expression of high levels of aggression and antisocial behavior. The concept of catharsis is a central component of both psychoanalytic theory and the frustration-aggression hypothesis. Further, the idea of catharsis is intuitively appealing to many people who feel that periodically "blowing off steam" is important to positive mental health.

Psychologists Russell Geen, David Stonner, and Gary Shope designed a laboratory study to define the role that catharsis plays in aggression. In this study, male college students were angered and then administered electric shock by a confederate of the experimenters. When these subjects were allowed to retaliate against the confederate, they experienced a drop in their blood pressure (defined by the experimenters as a cathartic release). At this point in the experiment, the role of catharsis in moderating physiological arousal was supported. The experimenters, however, also wanted to know the effect of catharsis on subjects' subsequent behavior, so they next provided subjects with an opportunity to administer shocks to the confederate. Geen and his colleagues found that the subjects who had experienced catharsis (reductions in blood pressure) actually delivered higher levels of shock to the confederate. Thus, while catharsis was reflected in decreased physiological arousal, it was associated with higher, not lower, levels of actual aggression. These researchers concluded that they were unable to find support for psychoanalytic theory or the frustration-aggression hypothesis, both of which would predict that catharsis would reduce subsequent aggression.

Laboratory studies have been subjected to a number of criticisms because they isolate people from their natural social environments and perhaps encourage the expression of artificial behavior. Laboratory studies of aggression are particularly vulnerable to such criticism, because they may provide subjects with a safe arena within which they may be encouraged to behave in an unnaturally aggressive manner. In response to these critics, many psychologists have studied the aggressive behavior of adults and children in typical social environments. Leonard Eron and his associates investigated the role that television might play in modeling aggressive behavior for a sample of elementary school children. First, the children's viewing habits were observed, to establish the nature of the programming they preferred and the amount of time they spent watching television. These children were followed up twenty-two years later to observe the effect their television viewing habits might have had on their behavior. Eron and his colleagues found that the amount of television these children had watched was significantly related to their level of aggressive behavior in young adulthood. The criminal records of certain children revealed that the more serious crimes were committed by the children who had been the heaviest consumers of violent television programming. The researchers interpreted these results to support social learning theory; that is, the media may be effective models of aggression, both immediate and long-term.

Proponents of handgun legislation point to studies such as these to argue for the control of privately owned firearms. They point to violent models in the media that may be related to the high rate of homicides in the United States. Additionally, they argue that the presence of a handgun itself may serve as a cue that elicits aggression and that the use of a handgun allows the aggressor to distance himself or herself physically from the victim. At firing range, the cues that elicit empathy and inhibit aggression are not so readily apparent. The influence of gun control on homicide rates was studied by a group of physicians led by John Henry Sloan. This team selected two cities for comparison. One city, Vancouver, British Columbia, had adopted restrictive handgun regulations. The comparison city, Seattle, Washington, was similar to Vancouver on a number of important demographic variables, but had no handgun control. The crime rates for both cities were compared for six years (1980 through 1986). Although the rates in both cities for burglary, robbery, and assault were not significantly different, the homicide rate was significantly higher in Seattle. They found that the citizens of Seattle had a 4.8 times higher risk of being killed with a handgun than did the citizens of Vancouver. These researchers concluded their report with the suggestion that handgun control legislation might reduce community homicide rates.

Context

Early psychological theories of aggression were quite pessimistic in the inferences they made about human nature. Much of Sigmund Freud's writings about the nature of Thanatos and the expression of aggression in humans occurred against the backdrop of the two world wars that he experienced in Europe. Becoming increasingly pessimistic about human nature and civilization, he revised his theory of the libido to include not only the sexual instinct, Eros, but also the aggressive instinct, Thanatos. Other theorists of that time entertained similar views of aggression as an instinct. For example, social psychologist William McDougall included aggression in his taxonomy of innate human instincts.

During the 1930's John Dollard and his colleagues at Yale attempted to reformulate psychoanalytic theory by use of S-R theory. These researchers were concerned with the mentalistic nature of Freud's theory, and they attempted to test his propositions by reconceptualizing libidinal impulses as biological drives. The frustration-aggression hypothesis grew out of this research program and generated a considerable amount of empirical research for a number of years. Interest in this concept then flagged, for the most part, until the 1960's, when Berkowitz published his revised frustration-aggression hypothesis that acknowledged the important role of social cues in the instigation of aggression.

Berkowitz's revision of the frustration-aggression hypothesis reflected the increased focus of American psychologists on social learning theory. Albert Bandura's classic studies of the social learning of aggressive responses, published in the early 1960's were influential in two ways. First, they generated considerable empirical research. Second, they provided a theoretical framework and methodology by which the effects of a relatively new social phenomenon, television, could be studied. Since then, more than two thousand studies have looked at the role of television in the modeling and maintenance of aggression in adults and children.

That is not to say that the instinct theories have fallen into disfavor. Konrad Lorenz's influential book, *On Aggression*, published in 1966, again brought instinct theories into the public eye. His book captured the interest not only of the comparative psychologists who studied aggression in other species but of the general reading public as well.

Bibliography

Bandura, Albert. *Aggression: A Social Learning Analysis*. Englewood Cliffs, N.J.: Prentice-Hall, 1973. Bandura presents a thorough overview of his social learning theory of aggression. He outlines the important antecedents of aggression and the critical factors in the instigation and maintenance of aggressive behavior. He also describes relevant social learning principles and applies those principles that are useful techniques for behavioral change. Accessible to the college-level reader.

Berkowitz, Leonard. *Aggression: A Social-Psychological Analysis*. New York: McGraw-Hill, 1962. This classic volume presents the frustration-aggression hypothesis. Contrasts the frustration-aggression hypothesis with instinct theories of aggression and discusses situational factors implicated in the expression and inhibition of aggression. The role of catharsis in aggression is also discussed.

. "Biological Roots: Are Humans Inherently Violent?" In *Psychological Dimensions of War*, edited by Betty Glad. Newbury Park, Calif.: Sage Publications, 1990. This is an excellent, easy-to-read critique of instinct theories of aggression. Berkowitz presents the frustration-aggression hypothesis and applies this theory to an analysis of international conflict. The role of aggression in the human condition and international relations is thoroughly discussed.

Denfeld, Rene. *Kill the Body, the Head Will Fall: A Closer Look at Women, Violence, and Aggression*. Foreword by Katherine Dunn. New York: Warner Books, 1997.

Geen, Russell G. *Human Aggression*. Pacific Grove, Calif.: Brooks/Cole, 1990. The author, a prominent researcher in the field, provides a solid empirical and theoretical discussion of the concept of aggression. Individual differences in aggression are discussed as well as interpersonal and environmental factors that mediate the actual expression of aggressive behavior.

Groebel, Jo, and Robert A. Hinde, eds. *Aggression and War: Their Biological and Social Bases*. New York: Cambridge University Press, 1989. This edited volume presents a lively discussion of the biological, psychological, and cultural factors in human aggression. Physiological and individual differences in aggression are presented in addition to social and situational forces that are useful in the control of aggression and the encouragement of pro-social behaviors. Cultural and political issues relevant to aggression are discussed.

Lorenz, Konrad. *On Aggression*. New York: Methuen, 1966. This easy-to-read classic is a comparative study of aggression in a number of species. Lorenz documents the evolutionary significance of aggression and describes its expression in fish, animals, and humans. He argues that aggression plays an important social role in same-species interactions.

Luschen, Gunther. "Psychological Issues in Sports Aggression." In *Sports Violence*, edited by Jeffrey H. Goldstein. New York: Springer-Verlag, 1983. Describes the cathartic role of sports in both athletes' and spectators' aggressive behaviors. The author summarizes the central role that catharsis plays in several psychological and philosophical perspectives on aggression, then presents the results of empirical studies investigating the links between sports and aggression.

Segall, Marshall H. "Cultural Roots of Aggressive Behavior." In *The Cross-Cultural Challenge to Social Psychology*, edited by Michael Harris Bond. Newbury Park, Calif.: Sage, 1988. Segall presents a summary and critique of important cross-cultural studies of aggression. His presentation focuses on the manner in which gender roles, biology, and cultural forces interact in the socialization of aggression across the globe. An intriguing and quite accessible article.

Cheryl A. Rickabaugh

See also:

Affiliation and Friendship, 25; Attraction Theories, 77; The Contact Hypothesis, 170; Crowd Behavior, 182; Emotion: Definition and Assessment, 242; Instinct Theory, 303; Self-Esteem, 530; Social Learning: Albert Bandura, 559.

AGING
Cognitive Changes

Type of psychology: Developmental psychology
Fields of study: Aging; cognitive processes

Psychologists study cognitive changes across the life span in order to assist individuals with the aging process and in order to comprehend the secrets of brain-behavior interrelationships and aging.

Principal terms

COGNITIVE ABILITIES: psychological capabilities including attention, learning, intelligence, memory, language and speech, perception, concept formation, and problem solving

CRYSTALLIZED INTELLIGENCE: the form of intelligence that reflects knowledge acquired through education and everday life experiences across time and maturity

FLUID INTELLIGENCE: the form of intelligence that reflects speed of information processing, reasoning, and memory capacity

INFORMATION PROCESSING: cognitive capabilities that involve processing memories

NEURON: a brain cell specialized for the transmission of information in the nervous system

Overview

Behavioral scientists have become increasingly interested in studying the cognitive changes that occur in the elderly across time. These studies have been conducted in order to assist individuals in their adjustment to aging as well as to unlock the secrets of the aging process itself. Cognitive changes refer to those changes which occur in overall mental functions and operations. Cognition encompasses all mental operations and functions, including attention, intelligence, memory, language and speech, perception, learning, concept formation, thought, problem solving, spatial and time orientation, and motor/behavior control. Psychologists have worked hard to define and measure various areas of cognitive functioning, even though there has been no consensus about these areas. Understanding the progression of cognitive functioning requires an understanding of brain structure and those human functions emanating from the brain and its fullest human potentiality, the mind. There is considerable debate within the scientific community about what type of cognitive functions actually exist as well as the nature of the mental mechanisms that are necessary to understand cognitive functioning.

There is a common belief that cognitive abilities decline markedly in older individuals. More and more, however, this idea is being shown to be exaggerated. Studies have shown that the diminishment of cognitive skills with age may not be significant, especially before the age of about seventy-five. Aging has been found to have different effects on long-term and short-term memory processes. The capacity of short-term memory (which is quite limited in all age groups) remains essentially the same for older people. Long-term memory, however, does show a decline. This decline can be minimized by various strategies; the use of mnemonic devices is very effective, as is taking extra time in learning and remembering.

Both biological and environmental factors have been studied in regard to aging and cognition. An environment that induces apathy or depression has been found to have a lowering effect on cognitive abilities. Environments that provide stimuli to interest the individual can reduce cognitive decline. Moreover, at least one study has found that providing challenging stimuli can even reverse cognitive declines that have been observed. There is a tremendous range of aging effects from individual to individual, with some showing virtually no changes and others showing serious decay of functions. It should be noted that this discussion concerns cognition in healthy individuals; diseases, such as Alzheimer's disease and Parkinson's disease, and events such as strokes (cardiovascular accidents) have effects on memory that are considered separately from the normal effects of aging.

Contemporary research on cognitive changes caused by aging emphasizes the information-processing capabilities of individuals as reflected in memory capacities. Memory is a basic psychological function upon which higher-level psychological processes such as speech, learning, concept formation, and problem solving are based. Lester Sdorow describes the brain's information-processing capacities as the human being's active acquisition of information about the world. Sensory stimuli are transmitted to the brain, where replicas of the external world are stored briefly in the sensory registry (one second for visual stimuli and four seconds for auditory memory). Information is then transferred to short-term memory (STM) for about twenty seconds, unless it is actively rehearsed, then into long-term memory (LTM), where it is potentially retained for a lifetime.

Information processing is a view of cognitive development that is based on the premise that complex cognitive skills develop as the product of the integration of a hierarchy of more basic skills obtained through life experience and learning. According to this view, prerequisite skills are mastered and form the foundation for more and more complex skills.

Information-processing theories emerged as psychologists began to draw comparisons between the way computers operate and the way humans use logic and rules about the world as they develop. Humans use these rules for processing information. New rules may be added and old rules modified throughout childhood and adulthood as more information is obtained from interactions with the world. The cognitive changes that occur throughout adult life, as more useful and accurate rules are learned, are every bit as important as the cognitive advances that occurred during childhood, as long as the basic rules acquired in childhood were not distorted by aberrant experiences. Each advance refines the ability to process information. Elizabeth F. Loftus points out that the terms "cognition" and "information processing" have supplanted the term "thinking" among contemporary cognitive scientists. Similar efforts have been made to redefine other human abilities such as problem solving (by H. A. Simon) and intelligence (by Robert Sternberg) in order to describe greater specificity of function.

Researchers have spent much time and effort defining and redefining memory constructs, although theorists remain in the early stages of understanding memory. Much debate has focused on naturalistic versus laboratory methodologies, with few resolutions as to how the results of both can contribute to a permanent knowledge base of memory.

The mediation school of thought suggests theoretical mechanisms of encoding, retention, and retrieval to explain memory functioning. Consequently, concerted efforts have been made to attribute memory changes across the life span to the specific deterioration of such mechanisms. Researchers continue to debate the importance, even existence, of such constructs. Similarly, the dichotomy of long-term versus short-term memory continues to be debated. In order to test the empirical validity of such theories, constructs must be able to be disproved if false, and these metaphorical constructs have proved difficult or impossible to test because of their abstract nature.

The greatest controversy in memory research focuses on laboratory versus naturalistic experiments; some researchers, such as M. R. Banaji and R. G. Crowder, state that naturalistic experiments have yielded no new principles and no new methods of memory research and should be abandoned. Others, such as H. P. Bahrick, however, claim that the naturalistic approach has provided in ten years what the laboratory has not in a hundred years. Banaji and Crowder criticize naturalistic experiments for their lack of control and thus their lack of generalizability. Yet confining a study to a specific population in a contrived laboratory setting does not seem to generalize any further. S. J. Ceci and Urie Bronfenbrenner emphasize the need to focus on the process of understanding, whatever that process might be. As Endel Tulving notes, the polemics that have ensued from this debate are not going to advance the science of memory. He concludes that there is no reason to believe that there is only one correct way of studying memory.

Applications

In examining cognitive changes in aging populations, aside from the theoretical debates, researchers have reported that cognitive processes progressively decline as chronological age advances. Studies have tended to describe the cognitive declines as gradual and general, rather than being attributable to discrete cognitive losses in specific areas of functioning.

Psychologists who have studied memory change identify diminished memory capacity in the elderly as attributable to a number of processes, such as slowed semantic access and a reduced ability to make categorical judgments. Other researchers concluded that older subjects were slower in mental operations but were not less accurate. Some researchers hypothesized that slower speed tied up processing functions, resulting in apparent memory impairment. Still others have hypothesized that older adults have more trouble with active memory tasks because of an increased competition for a share of memory processing resources, whereas others have linked the aged's poor performance on working memory tasks to an actual deficiency in processing resources. Finally, some researchers have concluded that older adults might simply have less mental energy to perform memory tasks. These studies accept gradual memory decline, or a slowing of processing, as a normal by-product of aging.

R. A. Hock, B. A. Futrell, and B. A. Grismer studied eighty-two elderly persons, from sixty to ninety-nine years of age, who were living independently in the community. These normal adults were tested on a battery of eight tasks that were selected to reflect cognitive functioning, particularly measuring primary and secondary memory, memory for nonverbal material, span of attention, the capacity to divide attention between competing sources of stimulation, and two motor tasks requiring psychomotor integrity. This study found a gradual, progressive decline in cognitive functioning but found that the decline did not reach statistically significant levels. The decline was general, suggesting that it may have been a function of reduced attention, rather than more discrete losses. This finding appears to be consistent with the notion that crystallized intellectual or abstract processes are well maintained across time. There were suggestions that speed of information processing is a sensitive measure of the aging process.

It is possible, however, that the tasks selected for this study did not discriminate between younger and older aging adults because the tasks may be more reliable for assessing brain injuries and psychologically impaired persons, which were not included in the population studied. Consequently, further studies on the same cognitive tasks with impaired aged adults would be necessary to see if the same relationships and conclusions would apply. Individuals with impaired cognitive functioning offer a unique opportunity to determine if the brain continues to show the same propensity to function as a unitary, global system as is observed with individuals who experience the normal aging process.

Although the brain does exhibit localization of functions, with specialization of certain brain cells for specific functions, its overall mode of operation is as a total unit. The brain has an exceptional capacity to compensate for the loss of some specific functions and continue the rest of its mental operations. This capacity or flexibility in brain function has been termed equipotentiation. Further studies of individuals with brain impairments will help to show how the brain attempts to carry out its overall functions when more specific impairments have been sustained. When cognitive disorders result in faulty information processing, actual observable changes may occur in a person's daily behavior. The previously neat person, for example, may neglect personal hygiene. The person who previously exhibited exceptional verbal abilities may speak in a socially inappropriate manner. The staid conservative businessperson may act impulsively or even make unreasonable decisions about personal finances, and may show impaired social judgment.

Context

Studies of cognitive changes across the life span must distinguish between normal gradual change in the elderly and change that is associated with disordered functioning. Studies must also respect the complexity of the human brain. Morton Hunt notes that cognitive scientists have concluded that there may be 100 billion neurons in the interior of the brain. Each of these neurons may be interconnected to hundreds of others by anywhere from one thousand to ten thousand synapses, or relay points. This may enable the average healthy person to accumulate five hundred times as much information as is contained in the entire *Encyclopædia Brittanica*, or 100 trillion bits (10^{14}) of information. The circuitry in one human brain is probably sixty times the complexity of the entire United States telephone system. Given this complexity, even the daily estimated loss of 100,000 brain cells from the aging process may leave human beings capable of sound cognitive functioning well into old age.

Paul Baltes notes that it used to be considered "common knowledge" that cognitive abilities decline with age, but today this view is highly debatable. When the effects of disease and injury are separated out in studies of the healthy elderly, no drastic decline in cognitive ability is found. This conclusion may be one reason that studies of cognition and aging have begun to make a distinction regarding intelligence. The distinction is between crystallized intelligence, involving the accumulation of facts and knowledge, which holds up with age, and fluid intelligence, which is the rapid processing of new information, a function that appears particularly associated with the young and vulnerable to the effects of age or disease. Studies of neurologically healthy aging adults have revealed no consistent evidence of a reduced ability to learn. Studies have further shown that very little practice may be required to improve substantially an elderly person's ability to perform some cognitive tasks, reflecting a motivational factor. Studies of mentally active persons in their eighties have concluded that loss of cognitive ability stemmed more from intellectual apathy or boredom than from actual physical deterioration.

John Darley and his colleagues concluded that on average, the decline of intellectual capability with age is slight and probably does not occur before age seventy-five. When declines do occur, they do not occur equally across cognitive functions. Vocabulary and verbal skills may actually improve with age, whereas skills involving spatial visualization and deductive reasoning are more likely to diminish. In general, verbal skills and accumulated knowledge are maintained with aging, while tasks that require quick responses are more susceptible to aging.

Bibliography

Bahrick, H. P. "A Speedy Recovery from Bankruptcy for Ecological Memory Research." *American Psychologist* 46, no. 1 (1991): 76-77. This article addresses the controversy between those who favor naturalistic memory studies and those who favor strict experimental studies; Bahrick favors the naturalistic approach.

Banaji, Mahzarin R., and Robert G. Crowder. "The Bankruptcy of Everyday Memory." *American Psychologist* 44, no. 9 (1989): 1185-1193. This article addresses the controversy between naturalistic and experimental research; the authors favor more controlled experimental approaches.

Ceci, S. J., and Urie Bronfenbrenner. "On the Demise of Everyday Memory." *American Psychologist* 46, no. 1 (1991): 27-31. Addresses the naturalistic versus experimental memory study issue, offering a balanced perspective and inviting scientific inquiry regardless of the type of methodology.

Darley, John M., Samuel Glucksberg, and Ronald A. Kinchla. *Psychology.* 3d ed. Englewood Cliffs, N.J.: Prentice-Hall, 1986. This introductory text summarizes the findings of studies of cognitive change with aging adults.

"Do 'Smartness Drugs' Boost Cognition in the Old?" *Patient Care* 28 (March 15, 1994): 18.

"Giving the Elderly the Time of Day." *Science News* 144 (September 18, 1993): 188.

Hunt, Morton M. *The Universe Within.* New York: Simon & Schuster, 1982. Hunt's book discusses the findings of the scientific specialty called cognitive science, arguing for a greater appreciation for the humanity of the human mind than detractors have allowed.

Launer, Lenore J., et al. "The Association Between Midlife Blood Pressure Levels and Late-Life Cognitive Function: The Honolulu-Asia Aging Study." *The Journal of the American Medical Association* 274 (December 20, 1995): 1846-1852.

Loftus, Elizabeth F. *Memory: Surprising New Insights into How We Remember and Why We Forget.* Reading, Mass.: Addison-Wesley, 1988. Loftus discusses the development of the cognitive sciences in seeking greater specificity for human abilities such as thinking and memory.

Sternberg, Robert J. *Intelligence, Information Processing, and Analogical Reasoning: The Componential Analysis of Human Abilities.* Hillsdale, N.J.: Lawrence Erlbaum, 1977. Focuses on a redefinition of human abilities by redescribing intellectual processes in more accuracy than the historical view of intelligence as a static capacity to learn.

Robert A. Hock

See also:

Adolescence: Cognitive Skills, 13; Cognitive Development Theory: Jean Piaget, 135; Dementia, Alzheimer's Disease, and Parkinson's Disease, 188; Generativity in Adulthood, 260; Intimacy in Adulthood, 340; Trust, Autonomy, Initiative, and Industry, 633.

AMNESIA, FUGUE, AND MULTIPLE PERSONALITY

Type of psychology: Psychopathology
Fields of study: Anxiety disorders; models of abnormality; organic disorders

Amnesia, fugue, and multiple personality form a group of mental disorders that are typically referred to as the dissociative disorders; they are called dissociative because some area of memory is split off, or dissociated, from conscious awareness.

Principal terms

AMNESIA: total or partial memory loss, which is often acute and follows an emotional or physical trauma

BIOGENIC DISORDER: an illness that is attributable primarily to some type of physiological trauma or sickness

DIAGNOSIS: the classification or labeling of a patient's problem within one of a set of recognized categories of abnormal behavior

DISSOCIATIVE DISORDERS: disorders that occur when some psychological function, such as memory, is split off from the rest of the conscious mind

FUGUE STATE: a flight from reality in which the individual leaves his or her present situation, travels to a new location, and establishes a new identity

MULTIPLE PERSONALITY: a rare mental disorder characterized by the development and existence of two or more relatively unique and independent personalities in the same individual

PSYCHOGENIC DISORDER: an illness that is attributable primarily to some psychological conflict or to emotional stress

Overview

Amnesia, fugue, and multiple personality are considered by most mental health professionals to be the three major types of dissociative disorders—disorders in which some important area of memory is split off (dissociated) from the individual's conscious awareness.

Like all the dissociative disorders, amnesia has long fascinated both mental health professionals and the general public. Most professionals define amnesia as the sudden inability to recall important personal information, such as one's name, occupation, or family. Amnesia victims, or amnesiacs, suddenly wonder who they are and why they are in their present circumstances.

In some cases, amnesia is caused by biological factors. A variety of physical traumas, such as a blow to the head, gunshot wound to the brain, stroke, or history of chronic alcoholism, can cause an individual to suffer from impaired memory. When amnesia is caused by such physical problems, the amnesia is said to be biogenic. A person who suffers from biogenic amnesia will typically experience the loss of both personal and general knowledge. For example, a concert pianist with biogenic amnesia not only will lose personal information such as name and family history but also will lose such general information as knowledge of music and the ability to play the piano. If physicians are able to treat the physical causes of biologically based amnesia in a successful manner, the afflicted individual's memory often tends to return slowly—over a period of weeks, months, or even years.

When amnesia is caused by emotional factors, the individual's situation is somewhat different. In these cases, the person is said to have psychogenic amnesia. This person will typically suffer the loss of personal, but not general, information. For example, the concert pianist with psychogenic amnesia may forget such personal information as his or her name and address but will still be able to play difficult pieces of music and recall the complexities of music theory. Such a case of psychogenic amnesia will typically occur when a person is suffering from numerous emotional stressors, such as marital, financial, or career problems, or when the person receives a severe emotional shock, such as the unexpected death of a loved one. The amnesia may thus help the person escape such unpleasant circumstances. Many theorists believe that psychogenic amnesia victims forget in order to avoid the unbearable anxiety that is associated with their problems or traumatic experiences.

A few cases of psychogenic amnesia have continued for the rest of the victim's life. In most cases, however, the afflicted individual will regain his or her memory anywhere from a day to several years after the syndrome's onset; no one knows why many amnesiacs are suddenly able to regain their memory. Psychogenic amnesia will often come and go in a rapid manner.

Like amnesia, a fugue syndrome tends to begin and end abruptly. Fugue (also known as psychogenic fugue) occurs when the afflicted individual takes an unexpected trip or excursion, forgets his or her identity, and assumes a new identity. The term fugue is derived from the Latin word *fuga*, meaning flight. This is an appropriate name, since the fugue victim is usually in a state of flight, fleeing some intolerable situation. While amnesiacs may wander about in a confused manner, fugue patients tend to travel in a way that appears both purposeful and deliberate. Fugue patients also tend, unlike amnesiacs, to manufacture a new identity. This new identity allows these individuals greater freedom and an escape from their troubles.

The length of fugue states varies considerably. In most cases, the person travels for little more than a day or two and goes no farther than the next town. A small group of fugue patients, however, will travel hundreds of miles, create new identities, and pursue their new lives for months or even years. During the fugue state, the patient will appear normal to other people. When the person finally "wakes up," he or she will have no memory of what took place during the fugue state. Like amnesia, fugue states seem to occur when a person has numerous troubles or has experienced an unbearable psychological trauma. For this reason fugue states, which are normally quite rare, are more common in wartime or after natural disasters.

While fugue patients travel to a new place to be someone else, individuals with multiple personality disorder stay in one place as they experience the existence of two or more separate personalities. Each personality will have a unique set of habits, tastes, and learned behaviors. Only one personality will dominate the person's thoughts and consciousness at a given time, and the shifts from one personality to the next will be quite abrupt and dramatic. While cases of multiple personality are very rare, this disorder has received considerable attention from the popular media because of its bizarre and fascinating nature.

Most individuals with multiple personality disorder have one primary personality, as well as one or more secondary personalities. The primary personality is the individual who is known to most people. This personality is often quiet, meek, and obedient, while the secondary personalities tend to be more aggressive, irresponsible, and pleasure seeking.

Though it is not entirely clear how an individual comes to have more than one personality, many professionals now believe that this disorder stems from a history of extreme emotional, physical, or sexual abuse during one's childhood. If a small child is severely beaten or molested, he or she may attempt to cope by pretending that the abuse is happening to someone else. The child may even give a name to this "other" person. As the child comes to rely repeatedly on this other person to cope with the abuse, the secondary personality eventually takes on a life of its own.

Applications

Like all psychiatric diagnoses, the dissociative disorders are useful when they help mental health professionals understand the experience of a disturbed individual. If it is known that someone suffers from a particular syndrome, such as amnesia, the knowledge may facilitate the individual's treatment. Diagnostic categories also enable psychologists to place individuals in groups, so that their problems and potential treatment can be studied by research scientists. One way to understand how knowledge of dissociative disorders can help professionals make sense of an individual's problems is to review some of the well-known case studies in this field.

In 1967, Henry Laughlin published the story of a patient named Robert who joined the Army and served for a year during a fugue state. Laughlin reports that Robert was a fifteen-year-old boy who was attending high school in a small New Jersey town. At the onset of his fugue state, Robert was beset by numerous problems. He was unusually large for his age and was frequently teased by peers. He was also engaging in a number of quarrels with his parents and was making poor grades at school. Robert was apparently quite upset by these problems, and he had begun to believe that his current situation was hopeless. One afternoon Robert came home and, with a sense of utter despair, threw his school books on the front porch.

Robert then remembered nothing more until approximately one year later. At that time, Robert, who was successfully serving under another name in the Army, suddenly recalled his life as a high school student. The last thing he remembered was throwing his books on the front porch. Robert had no idea why he was on an Army base, and he could remember nothing of his military career. His family was eventually contacted, and he was discharged for being underage.

Robert's fugue state was typical in that he had been experiencing considerable stress before the onset of his illness. Like most fugue patients, he temporarily escaped his troubles by creating a new identity in a new locale. Robert was also like most fugue patients in that he regained his memory rapidly and was then unable to recall what had transpired during his travels and military career. Although Robert's fugue state did last for an unusually long time, his case is in many ways a classic example of psychogenic fugue.

A case that is perhaps even more sensational than Robert's is the story of Eve White, a multiple personality patient described by Corbett Thigpen and Hervey Cleckley. Thigpen and Cleckley indicate that Eve White was a young woman who sought medical assistance because of severe headaches and occasional blackouts. This woman was described as "demure, retiring, in some respects almost saintly." Eve White was a devoted mother who worked extremely hard to support and rear a young daughter. Friends and coworkers found Eve White to be quiet, sensitive, and at times a little too serious.

One day as Eve White was describing her problems to her therapist, she was seized by a sudden headache and put both hands to her head. Thigpen and Cleckley report that "after a tense moment of silence, her hands dropped. There was a quick, reckless smile and, in a bright voice that sparkled, she said, 'Hi there, Doc!' " The patient began to talk about Eve White in a casual and carefree manner; she referred to Eve White as "her" and "she." When asked her name, the patient stated, "Oh, I'm Eve Black." As time went on, the therapist began to discover that Eve Black was "a party girl, shrewd, childishly vain, and egocentric." While Eve White was suffering from blackouts, Eve Black would attend parties, flirt with men in bars, and engage in wild spending sprees. Eve Black would then retreat and force Eve White to deal with the consequences of her reckless behavior. Eve White had no awareness of Eve Black. Eve Black was, however, typically conscious of Eve White and her troubles. Eve Black was also able to remember a number of painful childhood memories that Eve White was completely unable to recall. For example, as treatment progressed, it was Eve Black who was able to tell the therapist how Eve White was severely beaten by her parents as a child.

Eventually a third personality emerged from this young woman. This personality, named Jane, was aware of both Eve White and Eve Black. Jane was described as more mature, thoughtful, and balanced than either Eve White or Eve Black. The emergence of Jane may thus have represented an attempt on the part of this patient to integrate aspects of Eve White and Eve Black into one cohesive personality.

As the three personalities became better known, Thigpen and Cleckley eventually published a popular account of them in a book entitled *The Three Faces of Eve* (1957). Eve's case history serves as a clear example of how an individual can develop multiple personalities, each of which can take on a life of his or her own.

Context

Mental health professionals have known about the existence of dissociative disorders for many years. Sigmund Freud and his followers began to study psychogenic amnesia around the beginning of the twentieth century, and the first widely publicized case of multiple personality was reported by Morton Prince in 1905. Since the time of this early work, both professionals and the general public have been fascinated with the dissociative disorders.

Despite the widespread interest in psychogenic amnesia, psychogenic fugue, and multiple personality, these disorders are actually quite rare. Many experienced psychiatrists and clinical psychologists have never encountered a patient with one of these dissociative disorders in their practice. Because of the extreme rarity of these conditions, the dissociative disorders are not a major mental health problem in the United States.

Many social scientists, however, continue to believe that these disorders merit further study. It is difficult to conduct large-scale research projects on the dissociative disorders, simply because it is so hard to obtain an adequate number of subjects. Carefully conducted case studies, however, will continue to further understanding of the disorders. These case histories may be able to teach some important lessons about human nature. Although most individuals do not experience the dramatic memory problems of amnesia or multiple personality patients, the dissociative experience should not be seen as completely foreign to the ordinary person. Expressions that suggest dissociative reactions are commonly used to describe ordinary individuals. One might say that someone is "running away from his problems," is "not quite herself today," or "has become a different person." All these expressions suggest that the person has somehow disavowed a part of his or her conscious experience or personality style. It is possible that the dissociative disorders of psychogenic amnesia. psychogenic fugue, and multiple personality may thus be nothing more than a very extreme and dramatic exaggeration of a common human experience.

Bibliography

Bliss, Eugene L. "Multiple Personalities: A Report of Fourteen Cases with Implications for Schizophrenia and Hysteria." *Archives of General Psychiatry* 37 (December, 1980): 1388-1397. This journal article is written by a leading scholar in the field of multiple personality. In clear language, the author describes his controversial theory, which suggests that multiple personality disorders develop when children use self-hypnosis as a coping mechanism. Recommended for the reader who is interested in the causes and diagnosis of multiple personality.

Bootzin, Richard R., and Joan Ross Acocella. *Abnormal Psychology: Current Perspectives.* 5th ed. New York: Random House, 1988. This textbook contains an excellent chapter on the dissociative disorders that describes relevant case studies and explains how different psychological theorists view the dissociative diagnoses. The author's discussion of psychogenic amnesia and psychogenic fugue is particularly informative. Clear, easy to read, and understandable by the high school or college student.

Braude, Stephen E. *First Person Plural: Multiple Personality and the Philosophy of Mind.* Rev. ed. Lanham, Md.: Rowman & Littlefield, 1995.

Cohen, Lewis M., Joan N. Berzoff, and Mark R. Elin, eds. *Dissociative Identity Disorder: Theoretical and Treatment Controversies.* Northvale, N.J.: Jason Aronson, 1995.

Davison, Gerald C., and John M. Neale. *Abnormal Psychology.* New York: John Wiley & Sons, 1990. Contains a very readable chapter on somatoform and dissociative disorders. The authors give a well-organized overview of the topic and enhance their discussion with a number of lively examples. Recommended for the high school student, college student, or casual reader.

Greaves, G. B. "Multiple Personality: 165 Years After Mary Reynolds." *Journal of Nervous and Mental Disease* 168 (1980): 577-596. This article provides the reader with a solid understanding of the ways in which a history of sexual or physical abuse during one's childhood can lead to the development of multiple personality disorder. Recommended for college students who wish to know more about the causes of multiple personality.

Hacking, Ian. *Rewriting the Soul: Multiple Personality and the Sciences of Memory.* Princeton, N.J.: Princeton University Press, 1995.

Keyes, Daniel, *The Minds of Billy Milligan.* New York: Random House, 1981. A journalistic account of a young man's illness with multiple personality disorder. Especially helpful to readers who are interested in the relationship between mental illness and the criminal justice system, since the story's protagonist was convicted of raping several women. An interesting discussion of the insanity defense is included.

Sackheim, H., and W. Vingiano. "Dissociative Disorders." In *Adult Psychopathology and*

Diagnosis, edited by Samuel M. Turner and Michael Hersen. New York: John Wiley & Sons, 1984. Provides the reader with a scholarly overview of the dissociative disorders. Relevant diagnostic issues are discussed, in conjunction with a thorough review of the major research studies that have been conducted on amnesia, fugue, and multiple personality. Ideal for the student who seeks a detailed and challenging discussion of the dissociative disorders.

Schreiber, Flora Rheta. *Sybil*. New York: Warner Books, 1974. This popular account of a young woman's struggle with multiple personality disorder reads like a well-written novel. The author provides a fascinating description of both the development and treatment of multiple personality. This book will be especially helpful to individuals who are interested in the psychotherapy process.

Weiskrantz, Lawrence. *Consciousness Lost and Found: A Neuropsychological Exploration*. New York: Oxford University Press, 1997.

Steven C. Abell

See also:

Abnormality, 1; Anxiety Disorders, 65; Bipolar Disorder, 104; Dementia, Alzheimer's Disease, and Parkinson's Disease, 188; Depression, Clinical, 194; Depression: Theoretical Explanations, 200; Obsessions and Compulsions, 427; Phobias, 459; Schizophrenia: Theoretical Explanations, 517.

ANALYTICAL PSYCHOLOGY
Carl G. Jung

Type of psychology: Personality
Field of study: Psychodynamic and neoanalytic models

Analytical psychology is one of the most complex theories of personality. It attempts to improve on Sigmund Freud's work by deemphasizing sexual instincts and the abnormal side of human nature. Three of its more significant contributions are the notions of psychological types, the concept of the collective unconscious, and the depiction of the unconscious self as the most critical structure within the psyche.

Principal terms

ANIMA and ANIMUS: major archetypes that represent the feminine aspects of males (anima) and the masculine aspects of females (animus)

ARCHETYPES: structures contained within the collective unconscious that determine behaviors and ways of interpreting the environment

COLLECTIVE UNCONSCIOUS: memory traces that have been passed down to all humankind as a function of evolutionary development; includes inherited tendencies to behave in certain ways

CONSCIOUS EGO: the conscious mind; it represents one's identity from a conscious perspective and is therefore at the center of consciousness

ENTROPY: a concept maintaining that aspects of a person's psychic energy that are not in balance will tend to seek a state of equilibrium

EQUIVALENCE: a principle stating that an increase in energy or value in one aspect of the psyche is accompanied by a decrease in another area

PERSONA: a major archetype representing one's public personality; it is the mask that one wears in order to be acceptable to society at large

PERSONAL UNCONSCIOUS: items removed from the consciousness of the individual; this can occur through forgetting or unconscious repression, and the items may be remembered at a later time

SELF: the most important psychic structure in Jung's theory; it is the archetype which provides the whole psyche with a sense of unity and stability

SHADOW: the archetype indicative of the animal side of human nature; the shadow represents unsocial thoughts that are typically not overtly expressed by the person

Overview

Analytical psychology is perhaps the most complex major theory of personality. It includes the presentation and analysis of concepts and principles based on numerous disciplines within the arts and sciences. Because this complexity is combined with Carl Gustav Jung's often awkward writing, the task of mastering his theory is a challenge even for experts in the field of personality.

Jung's theory can best be understood by examining the key structures he proposes and the dynamics of personality. Jung divides the personality, or psyche, into three levels of consciousness. At the conscious level, there is the conscious ego. The conscious ego lies at the center of consciousness. In essence, it is the conscious mind—one's identity from a conscious perspective. It is particularly important to the person whose unconscious self is not yet fully developed. As the unconscious self begins to develop, the importance of the conscious ego will diminish.

Beneath the conscious ego (in terms of consciousness) is the personal unconscious. This involves material that has been removed from the consciousness of the person. This information may leave consciousness through forgetting or repression. Because the personal unconscious is close to the surface which is consciousness, items in it may be recalled at a later date. This is similar to Sigmund Freud's notion of the preconscious. Material within the personal unconscious is grouped into clusters called complexes. Each complex contains a person's thoughts, feelings, perceptions, and memories concerning particular concepts. For example, the mother complex contains all personal and ancestral experiences with the concept of mother. These experiences can be both good and bad.

The deepest level within the unconscious is called the collective unconscious. This contains the memory traces that have been passed down to all humankind as a function of evolutionary development. It includes tendencies to behave in specific ways, such as living in groups or using spoken language. While people have their own personal unconscious, they all share the same collective unconscious. The key structures within the collective unconscious that determine how people behave and respond to their environment are labeled archetypes. Each archetype enables people to express their unique status as human beings.

Archetypes are divided into major and minor archetypes. The major archetypes include the persona, animus, anima, shadow, and self. The persona is one's public personality, which one displays in order to be accepted by society. One's goal is to balance the needs of the persona with the desire to express one's true self. In contrast to the persona, the shadow represents the dark side of the psyche. It includes thoughts and feelings which the person typically does not express because they are not social. These cognitions can be held back on either a conscious or an unconscious level. The anima represents the feminine aspects of males, while the animus represents the masculine aspects of females. These archetypes have come about as a function of centuries of interactions between males and females. They have the potential to improve communication and understanding between males and females. Finally, the self is the most important archetype. It provides the psyche with a sense of unity, harmony, and stability. The major goal of each person's life is to optimize the development of the self.

In an effort to optimize the development of the self, each person develops his or her own psychological type. Each type (Jung conceived of eight types) consists of a combination of a person's basic attitude and basic function. Jung's two attitudes are extroversion and introversion. These terms follow societal stereotypes, with the extrovert being outgoing and confident and the introvert being hesitant and reflective. These attitudes are combined with four basic functions, or ways of relating to the world. These functions are thinking, feeling, sensing, and intuiting, which are consistent with a general societal view of these terms. Jung used the possible combination of the attitudes and functions to form the eight possible psychological types. Each person is thought to have dominance within one of the available types.

In addition to providing key psychic structures, Jung provides personality dynamics. He claimed that each person is endowed with psychic or libidinal energy. Unlike Freud, however, Jung did not view this energy as strictly sexual. Rather, he perceived it as life-process energy encompassing all aspects of the psyche. According to Jung, this energy operates according to two principles of energy flow: equivalence and entropy. The principle of equivalence states that an increase in energy within one aspect of the psyche must be accompanied by a decrease in another area. For example, if psychic energy is increasing in the unconscious self, it must decrease elsewhere, such as in the conscious ego. The principle of entropy states that when psychic energy is unbalanced, it will seek a state of equilibrium. For example, it would not be desirable to have the majority of one's psychic energy located in the conscious ego. The energy needs of the other levels of consciousness must also be met.

Jung's psychic structures, along with his views on the dynamics of personality, have provided psychologists with a wealth of information to consider, many complexities to address, and numerous possible ways to apply his ideas to human development and personality assessment.

Applications

Carl Jung made significant contributions to knowledge of areas such as human development and personality assessment. In terms of human development, Jung emphasized that person-ality development occurs throughout the life of the person. This was critical in that Freud's theory, the dominant theory at that time, emphasized the first five years of life in examining personality development. The overall goal of the person in Jung's approach to development is the realization of the self, which is a long and difficult process. Unlike Freud, Jung was particularly interested in development during the adulthood years. He emphasized the changes that occur beginning at the age of thirty-five or forty. He believed that this was often a time of crisis in the life of the person. This notion of a midlife crisis (which Jung experienced himself) has continued to be the source of significant theoretical and empirical claims.

Jung believed that the concept of a crisis during middle age was necessary and beneficial. Often, a person has achieved a certain level of material success and needs to find new meaning in life. This meaning can be realized by shifting from the material and physical concerns of youth to a more spiritual and philosophical view of life. The person seeks gradually to abandon the emphasis on the conscious ego which is dominant in youth. A greater balance between the unconscious and conscious is pursued. If this is successfully achieved, the person can reach a state of positive psychological health that Jung labels individuation. Perhaps the key to the midlife years in Jung's theory is that these are the years in which the person is attempting to discover the true meaning of life. Finally, Jung stated that religion can play an important role in life during the midlife and old-age years. During the midlife years, a sense of spirituality rather than materialism is important in personality development; looking at the possibility of life after death can be positive for the older adult.

Jung made use of several interesting assessment techniques in addressing the problems of his patients. Like Freud, Jung was an advocate of the case-study method. He believed that much could be learned through an in-depth analysis of the problems of his patients. In his cases, Jung made extensive use of dream analysis. Jung maintained that dreams serve many purposes. They can be used to address and resolve current conflicts or to facilitate the development of the self. Dreams can therefore be oriented toward the future. While Freud focused his analysis on individual dreams, Jung would examine a group of dreams in order to uncover the problems of the patient. This examination of multiple dreams was viewed by Jung as a superior approach to gaining access to the deeper meanings of dreams, which could often be found in the collective unconscious.

Another important assessment device used by Jung which continues to have applications today is the word-association test. In this test, a person responds to a stimulus word with whatever comes to mind. Jung originally worked with a group of one hundred stimulus words and would focus on issues such as the response word given by the patient, the length of time it took the patient to respond, the provision of multiple responses, the repetition of the stimulus word, and the absence of a response. These and other factors could be used to establish the existence of an underlying neurosis as well as specific conflicts and complexes.

Applications of Jung's theory are too numerous to mention. In many ways, his key contribution was taking the study of psychology beyond the claims made by Freud. Jung's emphasis on adult development and personality types and his willingness to break with strict Freudian teachings were major contributions within the history of psychology in general and personality in particular.

Context

The development of Carl Jung's analytical psychology can be traced to the development of his relationship with Sigmund Freud and the subsequent split that occurred between the two theorists. In 1906, Jung published a book which concerned the psychoanalytic treatment of schizophrenia. He sent a copy of this book to Freud, who was thoroughly impressed by Jung's work. Jung became one of the strongest Freudian advocates from 1907 to 1912. During this time he collaborated with Freud and was viewed by many within psychoanalytic circles as the heir apparent to Freud. Jung had in fact been elected president of the prestigious International Psychoanalytic Association. In 1913 and 1914, however, he abandoned Freud and his psychoanalytic theory. Three basic problems led to this split. The first was Freud's emphasis on sexuality. Jung believed that while sexual instincts did exist, they should not be emphasized at the expense of other relevant aspects of the psyche. Second, Jung believed that Freud overemphasized abnormality. He maintained that Freud appeared to have little to say about the normal aspects of human nature. Finally, unlike Freud, Jung wished to emphasize the biology of the species rather than the biology of the individual.

The split between Freud and Jung was important for practical as well as theoretical reasons. Jung was rejected for a period of time by other analytically oriented thinkers because of his split with Freud. In addition, the break with Freud led Jung to experience a mental crisis which lasted for several years. This combination of factors eventually led Jung to conclude that he must develop his own view of the psyche, along with appropriate treatment techniques.

While the challenges encountered by Jung in his life were difficult to overcome, they clearly played a major role in his ability to develop the most complex theory of personality ever formulated. His key concepts and psychic structures, including the collective unconscious, personal unconscious, archetypes, self, and personality typology, continue to be among the most interesting theoretical contributions in the history of personality psychology.

Bibliography

Brome, Vincent. *Jung: Man and Myth*. New York: Atheneum, 1981. This is a sound biography of Jung and discussion of his work. Perhaps its main advantage is that it provides an analysis which is fair to both Jung and his critics.

Hannah, Barbara. *Jung: His Life and Work*. New York: Putnam, 1976. This positive biographical view of Jung is provided by a Jungian analyst who was a friend and colleague of Jung for three decades. While it may not be as objectively written as other accounts, it has the advantage of being written by a scholar who had firsthand knowledge of many of Jung's ideas.

Homans, Peter. *Jung in Context: Modernity and the Making of a Psychology*. 2d ed. Chicago: University of Chicago Press, 1995.

Jung, Carl Gustav. *Memories, Dreams, Reflections*. New York: Pantheon Books, 1963. Jung's autobiography. It thoroughly portrays the evolution of Jung's thinking, including all those factors that were critical to his theoretical conceptions. Essential reading for anyone interested in gaining further insights into Jung and his work. It should be remembered, however, that Jung's writing is often difficult to follow.

_____. *Psychological Types*. Translated by Richard and Clara Winston. New York: Harcourt Brace, 1923. Provides both an overview of the basic principles of Jung's theory and an analysis of the derivation of the attitudes and functions that yield his psychological types. Particularly important to those who are interested in the derivation of Jung's view of typology.

McGuire, William, ed. *The Freud/Jung Letters*. Princeton, N.J.: Princeton University Press, 1974. Provides a unique analysis of the development of the relationship between Freud and Jung. Accurately portrays the promise of unity and collaboration within the relationship in its early years, beginning around 1907, and exposes the problems that eventually led to the Freud/Jung split, which was complete by 1914. Provides a context for examining the remainder of Jung's work and the personal problems that he was to encounter following his split with Freud.

Stein, Murray. *Practicing Wholeness: Analytical Psychology and Jungian Thought*. New York: Continuum, 1996.

Lawrence A. Fehr

See also:

Analytical Psychotherapy, 54; Dream Analysis, 206; Dreams, 212; Personality Theory: Major Issues, 453; Psychoanalytic Psychology and Personality: Sigmund Freud, 478.

ANALYTICAL PSYCHOTHERAPY

Type of psychology: Psychotherapy
Field of study: Psychodynamic therapies

Analytical psychotherapy is associated with the theory and techniques of Carl Gustav Jung. Similar to other psychodynamic therapies, it stresses the importance of discovering unconscious material. Unique to this approach is the emphasis on reconciling opposite personality traits that are hidden in the personal and collective unconsciouses.

Principal terms

COLLECTIVE UNCONSCIOUS: memories and emotions of which people are usually unaware but which are shared by all humanity

COMPENSATORY FUNCTION: displaying denied aspects of one's personality; a characteristic of dreams

CONFESSION: the first stage of Jungian psychotherapy, in which the patient relates conflicts in an emotional fashion

EDUCATION: the third stage of Jungian psychotherapy, in which the therapist communicates the danger of one-sided personality development

ELUCIDATION: the second stage of Jungian psychotherapy, in which the patient acts toward the therapist as toward some significant person from the patient's past

METHOD OF ACTIVE IMAGINATION: the process of discovering unconscious material from the patient's artistic productions

METHOD OF AMPLIFICATION: a Jungian technique for dream analysis in which the patient makes multiple associations to the contents of the dream

PERSONAL UNCONSCIOUS: a structure of personality that contains thoughts and emotions that are too anxiety-provoking for conscious awareness

TRANSFERENCE: acting toward the therapist in a similar way as to some significant person from the patient's past

TRANSFORMATION: the fourth stage of Jungian psychotherapy, in which the patient seeks self-discovery through reconciling opposite personality traits

Overview

Analytical psychotherapy is an approach to psychological treatment pioneered by Carl Gustav Jung (1875-1961), a Swiss psychoanalyst. A follower of Sigmund Freud, Jung was trained in the psychoanalytic approach, with its emphasis on the dark, inaccessible material contained in the unconscious mind. Freud was fond of Jung and believed that he was to be the heir to the legacy he had begun. Jung began to disagree with certain aspects of Freud's theory, however, and he and Freud parted ways bitterly in 1914.

Jung's concept of the structure of personality, on which he based his ideas of psychotherapy, was obviously influenced by Freud and the psychoanalytic tradition, but he added his own personal and mystical touches to its concepts. Jung believed that the personality consists of the ego, which is one's conscious mind. It contains the thoughts, feelings, and perceptions of which one is normally aware. Jung also proposed a personal unconscious that contains events and emotions of which people remain unaware because of their anxiety-provoking nature. Memories of traumatic childhood events and conflicts may reside in the personal unconscious. Jung's unique contribution to personality theory is the idea of a collective unconscious. This consists of memories and emotions that are shared by all humanity. Jung believed that certain events and feelings are universal and exert a similar effect on all individuals. An example would be his universal symbol of a shadow, or the evil, primitive nature that resides within everyone. Jung believed that although people are aware of the workings of the conscious ego, it is the unavailable material contained in the personal unconscious and collective unconscious that has the greatest influence on one's behavior.

Jung believed that emotional problems originate from a one-sided development of personality. He believed that this is a natural process and that people must constantly seek a balance of their traits. An example might be a person who becomes overly logical and rational in her behavior and decision making while ignoring her emotional and spontaneous side. Jung believed this one-sided development eventually would lead to emotional diffi-culty and that one must access the complementary personality forces that reside in the unconscious. Even psychotherapists must be aware that along with their desire to help others, they have complementary darker desires that are destructive to others. Jung believed that emotional problems are a signal that one is becoming unbalanced in one's personality and that this should motivate one to develop more neutral traits.

The process of analytical psychotherapy, as in most psychodynamic approaches, is to make the patient conscious or aware of the material in his or her unconscious mind. Jung believed that if the conscious mind were overly logical and rational, the unconscious mind, to balance it, would be filled with equally illogical and emotional material. To access this material, Jung advocated a free and equal exchange of ideas and information between the analyst and the patient. Jung did not focus on specific techniques as did Freud, but he did believe that the unconscious material would become evident in the context of a strong, trusting therapeutic relationship. Although the patient and analyst have equal status, the analyst serves as a model of an individual who has faced her or his unconscious demons.

Analytic psychotherapy proceeds in four stages. The first stage is that of confession. Jung believed that it is necessary for the patient to tell of his or her conflicts and that this is usually accompanied by an emotional release. Jung did not believe that confession is sufficient to provide a cure for one's ills, however, nor did he believe (unlike Freud) that an intellectual understanding of one's difficulties is adequate. The patient must find a more neutral ground in terms of personality functioning, and this can only be accomplished by facing one's unconscious material.

The second stage of psychotherapy is called elucidation, and it involves becoming aware of one's unconscious transferences. Transference is a process in which a patient transfers emotions about someone else in his or her life onto the therapist; the patient will behave toward the therapist as he or she would toward that other person. It is similar to meeting someone who reminds one of a past relationship; for no apparent reason, one might begin to act toward the new person the same way one did to the previous person. Jung believed that these transferences to the analyst give a clue about unconscious material. A gentle, passive patient might evidence hostile transferences to the therapist, thus giving evidence of considerable rage that is being contained in the unconscious.

The third stage of analytic psychotherapy consists of education. The patient is instructed about the dangers of unequal personality development and is supported in his or her attempts to change. The overly logical business executive may be encouraged to go on a spontaneous vacation with his family with few plans and no fixed destinations. The shy student may be cajoled into joining a debate on emotional campus issues. Jung believed in the value of experiencing the messages of one's unconscious.

The final stage of psychotherapy, and one that is not always necessary, is that of transformation. This goes beyond the superficial encouragements of the previous stages and attempts to get the patient to delve deeply into the unconscious and thereby understand who he or she is. This process of understanding and reconciling one's opposites takes considerable courage and exploration into one's personal and cultural past. It is a quest for one's identity and purpose in life that requires diligent work between the analyst and patient; the result is superior wisdom and a transcendent calm when coping with life's struggles.

Applications

Jung developed several techniques aimed at uncovering material hidden in the unconscious. Like Freud, Jung believed that the content of dreams is indicative of unconscious attitudes. He believed that dreams have a compensatory function; that is, they are reflections of the side of personality that is not displayed during one's conscious, everyday state. The sophisticated librarian may have dreams of being an exotic dancer, according to Jung, as a way of expressing the ignored aspects of personality.

Jung gives an example of the compensatory aspects of dreams when describing the recollections of a dutiful son. The son dreamed that he and his father were leaving home and his father was driving a new automobile. The father began to drive in an erratic fashion. He swerved the car all over the road until he finally succeeded in crashing the car and damaging it very badly. The son was frightened, then became angry and chastised his father for his behavior. Rather than respond, however, his father began to laugh until it became apparent that he was very intoxicated, a condition the son had not previously noticed. Jung interpreted the dream in the context of the son's relationship with his father. The son overly idealized the father while refusing to recognize apparent faults. The dream represented the son's latent anger at his father and his attempt to reduce him in status. Jung indicated to the young man that the dream was a cue from his unconscious that he should evaluate his relationship with his father with a more balanced outlook.

Jung employed the method of amplification for interpreting dreams. This technique involved focusing repeatedly on the contents of the dream and giving multiple associations to them. Jung believed that the dream often is basically what it appears to be. This differs dramatically from Freudian interpretation, which requires the patient to associate dream elements with childhood conflicts.

The amplification method can be applied to a dream reported by a graduate student in clinical psychology. While preparing to defend his dissertation, the final and most anxiety-provoking aspect of receiving the doctorate, the student had a dream about his oral defense. Before presenting the project to his dissertation committee that was to evaluate its worth (and seemingly his own), the student dreamed that he was in the bathroom gathering his resources. He noticed he was wearing a three-piece brown suit; however, none of the pieces matched. They were different shades of brown. Fortunately, the pieces were reversible, so the student attempted to change them so they would all be the same shade. After repeated attempts he was unable to get all three pieces of the suit to be the same shade of brown. He finally gave up in despair and did not appear for his defense. With a little knowledge about the student, an analytical therapist would have an easy time with the meaning of this dream. This was obviously a stressful time in the young man's life, and the dream reflected his denied anxiety. In addition, the student did not like brown suits; one that does not match is even more hideous. It is apparent that he was unhappy and, despite his best attempts to portray confidence, the budding clinician was afraid that he was going to "look stupid." Jung would have encouraged him to face these fears of failure that were hidden in his unconscious.

A final application of analytical psychotherapy stems from Jung's method of active imagination. Jung believed that unconscious messages could come not only from dreams but also from one's artistic productions. He encouraged his patients to produce spontaneous, artistic material. Some patients sketched, while others painted, wrote poetry, or sang songs. He was interested in the symbols that were given during these periods, and he asked his clients to comment on them. Jung believed that considerable material in the unconscious could be discovered during these encounters. He also talked with his patients about the universal meanings of these symbols (as in his idea of the collective unconscious), and they would attempt to relate this material to the patients' cultural pasts.

Many modern therapies, such as art, music, and dance therapy, draw heavily from this idea that one can become aware of unconscious and emotional material through association involving one's artistic productions. These therapists believe, as did Jung, that patients are less defensive during these times of spontaneous work and, therefore, are more likely to discover unconscious material.

Context

Jung's analytical psychotherapy was a pioneering approach during the very early era of psychological treatment. He conformed to the beliefs of other psychodynamic therapists, such as Sigmund Freud and Alfred Adler, in the importance of discovering unconscious material. The psychoanalysts would be followed by the behavioral school's emphasis on environmental events and the cognitive school's focus on thoughts and perceptions. Psychoanalysis brought a prominence to psychology it had not known previously.

Jung expanded on Freud's beliefs about the unconscious. Rather than focus on instinctual forces, Jung chose to focus on the human being's spiritual side through his idea of the collective unconscious. His mystical beliefs about humankind's spirituality were new to the growing field of psychotherapy and have not been equalled since. Jung also took into account a person's cultural past. He proposed the idea of a universal human relatedness with his idea of common cultural symbols; however, it would be many years before this idea was fully developed.

Analytical psychotherapy is not considered a mainstream approach to psychotherapy, but it does have a small group of devoted followers. Some of Jung's techniques have been adapted into other, more common approaches. Many therapists agree with Jung's de-emphasis on specific techniques in favor of a focus on the establishment of a supportive therapy relationship. Jung moved away from the stereotypical analyst's couch in favor of face-to-face communication between doctor and patient. Many psychotherapists endorse Jung's belief that the analyst and patient should have relatively equal status and input. Jung also reduced the frequency of meeting with his patients to weekly, which is the norm today.

Jung's analytical approach changed the focus of psychotherapy from symptom relief to self-discovery. He was interested not only in patients with major problems but also in those who were dissatisfied with their mundane existences. These people were usually bright, articulate, and occupationally successful.

Jung's most lasting contributions probably have been his insights into the polarity of personality traits. The Myers-Briggs Type Indicator, based on Jungian personality descriptions, is one of the most widely used personality tests in business and industry. Jung also believed that personality changes throughout one's life, and he encouraged a continual evaluation of oneself. The idea of a "midlife crisis," a period when one reevaluates personal and occupational goals, is a product of Jung's theory. He believed that individuals continually should strive to achieve a balance in their personality and behavior.

Bibliography

Campbell, Joseph. *The Hero with a Thousand Faces*. New York: Pantheon Books, 1949. Campbell was a contemporary theorist who developed Jung's ideas of universal symbols and the power of myth. This book discusses Jung's idea of the hero, and Campbell relates this idea to spiritual leaders such as Moses, Jesus, and Muhammad.

Engler, Barbara. *Personality Theories: An Introduction*. 3d ed. Boston: Houghton Mifflin, 1991. Engler's chapter on Jung and his psychotherapy is easy to read and contains a good balance between theory and practical application.

Hall, Calvin Springer, and Gardner Lindzey. *Theories of Personality*. 3d ed. New York: John Wiley & Sons, 1978. This is a classic text in personality theory and application, and it gives a detailed description of Jung's theory. Recommended for the serious student of Jung.

Hall, Calvin Springer, and Vernon J. Nordby. *A Primer of Jungian Psychology*. New York: New American Library, 1973. This paperback attempts to provide a comprehensive treatment of Jung's ideas. It is intended for the beginning student of Jung.

Hannah, Barbara. *Jung: His Life and Work*. New York: Putnam, 1976. This is an interesting biographical account of Jung by a psychoanalyst who was his friend for more than thirty years. Gives an insight into how his personal beliefs and experiences shaped his theory.

Homans, Peter. *Jung in Context: Modernity and the Making of a Psychology*. 2d ed. Chicago: University of Chicago Press, 1995.

Stein, Murray. *Practicing Wholeness: Analytical Psychology and Jungian Thought*. New York: Continuum, 1996.

Wehr, Gerhard. *Portrait of Jung: An Illustrated Biography*. New York: Herder and Herder, 1971. This is an interesting biography of Jung as well as a good introduction to his theory and therapy. Contains numerous fascinating pictures that give insight to the man and his ideas.

Brett L. Beck

See also:

Analytical Psychology: Carl G. Jung, 49; Cognitive Behavior Therapy, 128; Cognitive Therapy, 153; Dream Analysis, 206; Person-Centered Therapy, 439; Psychoanalysis: Classical Versus Modern, 465.

ANIMAL EXPERIMENTATION

Type of psychology: Psychological methodologies
Fields of study: Experimental methodologies; methodological issues

Psychologists study animals and animal behavior as well as humans; sometimes the goal is to understand the animal itself, and sometimes it is to try to learn more about humans. Since there are many biological and psychological similarities between humans and other animals, the use of animal models can be extremely valuable, although it is sometimes controversial.

Principal terms

ANALOGY: behavioral similarity between two species based on similarity of their environments and lifestyles; often used in contrast to "homology"

APPLIED RESEARCH: research intended to solve existing problems, as opposed to "basic research," which seeks knowledge for its own sake

HOMOLOGY: behavioral similarity between two species based on genetic relatedness; often used in contrast to "analogy"

INSTITUTIONAL ANIMAL CARE AND USE COMMITTEES: local committees which, by federal law, are mandated to oversee animal research to ensure humane treatment

INVASIVE PROCEDURES: experimental techniques that involve direct bodily intervention, such as surgery, force-feeding, or the administration of drugs

Overview

Research psychologists are the fourth-largest group of scientists in the United States to use animals as experimental subjects, accounting for approximately 10 percent of the 25 to 35 million animals used per year. Psychologists who study animals can be roughly categorized into three groups. Biopsychologists, or physiological psychologists, study the genetic, neural, and hormonal controls of behavior, for example, eating behavior, sleep, sexual behavior, perception, emotion, memory, and the effects of drugs. Learning theorists study the learned and environmental controls of behavior, for example, stress, stimulus-response patterns, motivation, and the effects of reward and punishment. Ethologists and sociobiologists concentrate on animal behavior in nature, for example, predator-prey interactions, mating and parenting, migration, communication, aggression, and territoriality.

Psychologists study animals for a variety of reasons. Sometimes they study the behavior of a particular animal in order to solve a specific problem. They may study dogs, for example, to learn how best to train them as watchdogs, chickens to learn how to prevent them from fighting one another in hen houses; or wildlife to learn how to regulate populations in parks, refuges, or urban areas. These are all examples of what is called "applied research."

Most psychologists, though, are more interested in human behavior but study animals for practical reasons. A developmental psychologist, for example, may study an animal that has a much shorter life span than humans so that each study takes a much shorter time and more studies can be done. Animals may also be studied when an experiment requires strict controls; researchers can control the food, housing, and even social environment of laboratory animals but cannot control such variables in the lives of human subjects. Experimenters can even control the genetics of animals by breeding them in the laboratory; rats and mice have been bred for so many generations that researchers can special order from hundreds of strains and breeds and can even get animals that are as genetically identical as identical twins.

Another reason psychologists sometimes study animals is that there are fewer ethical considerations as compared to research with human subjects. Physiological psychologists and neuropsychologists, in particular, may utilize invasive procedures (such as brain surgery or hormone manipulation) that would be unethical to perform on humans. Without animal experimentation, these scientists would have to do all their research on human victims of accident or disease, a situation which would reduce the number of research subjects dramatically as well as raise additional ethical considerations.

There are drawbacks to using animals as experimental subjects. Most important are the clear biological and psychological differences between humans and nonhuman animals; results one gets in a study using nonhuman animals simply may not apply to humans. In addition, animal subjects cannot communicate directly with the researchers; they are unable to express their feelings, motivations, thoughts, and reasons for their behavior. If a psychologist must use an animal instead of a human subject for ethical or practical reasons, the scientist will want to choose an animal that is similar to humans in the particular behavior being studied. Three factors can create similarity between animal and human behavior; each of these three must be considered.

The first factor is homology. Animals that are closely related to humans are likely to have similar physiology and behavior because they share the same genetic blueprint. Monkeys and chimpanzees are the animals most closely related to humans and thus are homologically most similar. Monkeys and chimpanzees make the best subjects for psychological studies of complex behaviors and emotions, but because they are expensive and difficult to keep, and because there are serious ethical considerations when using them, they are not used when another animal would be equally suitable.

The second factor is analogy. Animals that have a similar lifestyle to humans are likely to have some of the same behaviors. Rats, for example, are social animals, as are humans; cats are not. Rats also show similarity to humans in their eating behavior (which is one reason rats commonly live around human habitation and garbage dumps); thus, they can be a good model for studies of hunger, food preference, and obesity. Rats, however, do not have a similar stress response to that of humans; for studies of exercise and stress, the pig is a better animal to study.

The third factor is situational similarity. Some animals, particularly domesticated animals such as dogs, cats, domestic rabbits, and some birds, adapt easily to experimental situations such as living in a cage and being handled by humans. Wild animals, even if reared from infancy, may not behave normally in experimental situations. The behavior of a chimpanzee that has been kept alone in a cage, for example, may tell something about the behavior of a human kept in solitary confinement, but it will not necessarily be relevant to understanding the behavior of most people in typical situations.

By far the most common laboratory animal used in psychology is *Rattus norvegicus*, the Norway rat. Originally, the choice of the rat was something of a historical accident. Since the rat has been studied so thoroughly over the past century, it is now often the animal of choice so that comparisons can be made from study to study. Fortunately, the rat shares many analogous features with humans. Other animals frequently used in psychological research include pigeons, mice, hamsters, gerbils, cats, monkeys, and chimpanzees.

Applications

One of the most important topics for which psychologists use animal experimentation is the study of interactive effects of genes and the environment on the development of the brain and subsequent behavior. These studies can only be done using animals as subjects because they require individuals with a relatively short life span that develop quickly, invasive procedures to measure cell and brain activity, or the manipulation of major social and environmental variables in the life of the subject.

In the 1920's, E. C. Tolman and Robert Tryon began a study of the inheritance of intelligence using rats. They trained rats to run a complex maze and then, over many generations, bred the fastest learners with one another and the slowest learners with one another. From the beginning, offspring of the "bright" rats were substantially faster than offspring of the "dull" rats. After only seven generations, there was no overlap between the two sets, showing that "intelligence" is at least partly genetic and can be bred into or out of animals just as size, coat color, or milk yield can be.

Subsequent work with selectively bred bright versus dull rats, however, found that the bright rats would only outperform the dull rats when tested on the original maze used with their parents and grandparents; if given a different task to measure their intelligence, the bright rats were no brighter than the dull rats. These studies were the first to suggest that intelligence may not be a single attribute that one either has much or little of; there may instead be many kinds of intelligence.

Traditionally, intelligence (IQ) tests measure two kinds of intelligence: one related to verbal skills and one related to spatial skills. Newer theories and tests, however, attempt to address the possibility that there are dozens of different kinds of intelligence. The newer tests may help to identify special talents that may otherwise go unrecognized, undeveloped, and unrewarded in people who are not especially good at tasks measured by the more traditional tests. The new theories of multiple intelligences are also being used in the field of artificial intelligence to develop computer and robotic systems which utilize less sequential processing and more parallel systems or netlike processing, more like the human brain.

Another series of experiments that illustrate the role of animal models in the study of brain and behavior is that developed by David Hubel and Torsten Wiesel, who study visual perception (mostly using cats). Hubel and Wiesel were able to study the activity of individual cells in the living brain. By inserting a microelectrode into a brain cell of an immobilized animal and flashing visual stimuli in the animal's visual field, they could record when the cell responded to a stimulus and when it did not.

Over the years, scientists have used this method to map the activities of cells in several layers of the visual cortex, the part of the brain that processes visual information. They have also studied the development of cells and the cell connections, showing how early experience can have a permanent effect on the development of the visual cortex. Subsequent research has demonstrated that the environment has major effects on the development of other areas of the brain as well. The phrase "use it or lose it" has some accuracy when it comes to development and maintenance of brain connections and mental abilities.

Perhaps the most famous psychological experiments on animals were those by Harry Harlow in the 1950's. Harlow was studying rhesus monkeys and breeding them in his own laboratory. Initially, he would separate infant monkeys from their mothers. Later, however, he discovered that, in spite of receiving adequate medical care and nutrition, these infants exhibited severe behavioral symptoms: They would sit in a corner and rock, mutilate themselves, and scream in fright at the approach of an experimenter, a mechanical toy, or another monkey. As adolescents, they were antisocial. As adults, they were psychologically ill-equipped to deal with social interactions: Male monkeys were sexually aggressive, and females appeared to have no emotional attachment to their own babies. Harlow decided to study this phenomenon (labeled "maternal deprivation syndrome") because he thought it might help to explain the stunted growth, low life expectancy, and behavioral symptoms of institutionalized infants which had been documented earlier by René Spitz.

Results of the Harlow experiments profoundly changed the way psychologists think about love, parenting, and mental health. Harlow and his colleagues found that the so-called mothering instinct is not very instinctive at all but rather is learned through social interactions during infancy and adolescence. They also found that an infant's attachment to its mother is based not on its dependency for food but rather on its need for "contact comfort." Babies raised with both a mechanical "mother" that provided milk and a soft, cloth "mother" that gave no milk preferred the cloth mother for clinging and comfort in times of stress.

Through these experiments, psychologists came to learn how important social stimulation is, even for infants, and how profoundly lack of such stimulation can affect mental health development. These findings played an important role in the development of staffing and activity requirements for foundling homes, foster care, day care, and institutions for the aged, disabled, mentally ill, and mentally retarded. They have also influenced social policies which promote parent education and early intervention for children at risk.

Context

Prior to the general acceptance of Charles Darwin's evolutionary theory in the late nineteenth century, animals were considered to be soulless machines with no thoughts or emotions. Humans, on the other hand, were assumed to be qualitatively different from other animals because of their abilities to speak, reason, and exercise free will. This assumption made it unreasonable to try to learn about the mind by studying animals.

After Darwin, however, people began to see that, even though each species is unique, the chain of life is continuous, and there are similarities as well as differences between species. Since animal brains and human brains are made of the same kinds of cells and have similar structures and connections, it was reasoned, the mental processes of animals must be similar to the mental processes of humans. This new insight led to the introduction of animals as psychological research subjects around the year 1900. Since then, animal experimentation has taught much about the brain and the mind, especially in the fields of learning, memory, motivation, and sensation.

For the same reasons that animals are useful in studying psychological processes, however, people have questioned the moral justification for such use. Since it is now realized that vertebrate animals can feel physical pain, and that many of them have thoughts and emotions as well, animal experimentation has become politically controversial.

In response to such concerns, the U.S. Congress amended the Animal Welfare Act in 1985 so that it would cover laboratory animals as well as pets. (Rats, mice, birds, and farm animals are specifically excluded.) Although the new regulations do not state specifically what experimental procedures may or may not be done on laboratory animals, they do set standards for humane housing, feeding, and transportation, and they require that all research on warm-blooded animals (except those listed above) be approved by a committee before it can be carried out. Each committee (they are called Institutional Animal Care and Use Committees, or IACUCs) is composed of at least five members that must include an animal researcher; a veterinarian; someone with an area of expertise in a nonresearch area, such as a teacher, lawyer, or clergyman; and someone who is unaffiliated with the institution where the experimentation is being done who can speak for the local community. In this way, those scientists who do animal experiments are held accountable for justifying the appropriateness of their use of animals as research subjects.

Alternatives to animal experimentation are becoming more widespread as technology progresses. Computer modeling and bioassays (tests using biological materials such as cell cultures) will never replace animal experimentation in the field of psychology, however, because computers and cell cultures will never exhibit all the properties of mind that psychologists want to study. At the same time, the use of animals as psychological research subjects cannot end the need for study of human subjects. While other animals may age, mate, fight, and learn much as humans do, they will never speak, compose symphonies, or run for office. Animal experimentation will always have an important, though limited, role in psychological research.

Bibliography

Blum, Deborah. *The Monkey Wars*. New York: Oxford University Press, 1994.

Committee on the Use of Animals in Research Staff of the National Academy of Sciences and the Institute of Medicine Staff. *Science, Medicine, and Animals*. Washington, D.C.: National Academy Press, 1991. This thirty-page pamphlet answers commonly asked questions about the use of animals in biomedical research. Although not focusing specifically on psychology, it does address research in psychomedical areas such as brain research and drug addiction.

Fox, Michael Allen. *The Case for Animal Experimentation*. Berkeley: University of California Press, 1986. Although the author is philosophically in favor of most animal experimentation, he gives a clear and thorough discussion of the entire context of animal experimentation from both sides. Includes sections on animal rights, similarities and differences between human and nonhuman subjects, the role of methodological considerations and replicability in scientific progress, and alternatives to animal testing. The author specifically addresses some of the uglier behavioral studies on animals, including some by Harry Harlow.

Gross, Charles G., and H. Philip Zeigler, eds. *Motivation*. Vol. 2 in *Readings in Physiological Psychology*. New York: Harper & Row, 1969. Although there are dozens of newer collections of articles in the area of physiological psychology, this one does a particularly good job of covering the broad diversity of topics in the field. In addition, all the work represented in this particular collection came from animal studies. This or a similar collection can be consulted for illustration of many specific methodologies utilized in research with animals.

Kimmel, Allan J. *Ethical Issues in Behavioral Research: A Survey.* Cambridge, Mass.: Blackwell, 1996.

Miller, Neal E. "The Value of Behavioral Research on Animals." *American Psychologist* 40 (April, 1985): 423-440. Good discussion of advances in the behavioral sciences that came from animal studies, including studies on effects of early experience on the brain and behavior, drug effects, eating disorders, and diseases of aging. Also includes some discussion of applied studies which benefit nonhuman species.

Rowan, Andrew N. *Of Mice, Models, and Men: A Critical Evaluation of Animal Research.* Albany, N.Y.: State University of New York Press, 1984. The author is in fact a supporter of the use of animals in scientific research; he addresses the history of animal research and the controversies surrounding it. In addition to psychological research, he covers the use of animals in medical and industrial testing.

U.S. Congress Office of Technology Assessment. *Alternatives to Animal Use in Research, Testing, and Education.* Washington, D.C.: Author, 1986. This 441-page document provides much more than its title indicates. In addition to alternative methodologies, the report discusses government use of animals, economic and ethical considerations, statistics and patterns of animal use, and federal policy.

Linda Mealey

See also:

Avoidance Learning, 93; Imprinting and Learning, 290; Instrumental Conditioning: Acquisition and Extinction, 309; Learned Helplessness, 359; Learning: Generalization and Discrimination, 370; Memory: Animal Research, 389; Pavlovian Conditioning, 433; Psychological Experimentation: Variables, 484.

ANXIETY DISORDERS

Type of psychology: Psychopathology
Fields of study: Anxiety disorders; behavioral and cognitive models; psychodynamic and neoanalytic models

Anxiety is a central concept in many different schools of psychology, and there are many widely varying theories concerning it; theories of anxiety often have spawned approaches to treating anxiety disorders.

Principal terms

EGO: in psychoanalytic theory, the mostly conscious part of the mind that deals with reality
LIBIDO: in psychoanalytic theory, the psychological aspect of sexual energy or drive
OPERANT CONDITIONING: learning in which a behavior increases or decreases depending on whether the behavior is followed by reward or punishment
PAVLOVIAN CONDITIONING: learning in which two stimuli are presented one after the other, and the response to the first changes because of the response automatically elicited by the second stimulus
PHOBIA: an anxiety disorder involving an intense fear of a particular thing (such as horses) or situation (such as heights)
PREPAREDNESS: the theory that animals and human beings are prepared by evolution to learn certain things—for example, that snakes are dangerous
REPRESSION: in psychoanalytic theory, a defense mechanism that keeps unacceptable thoughts and impulses from becoming conscious
THREE-SYSTEMS APPROACH: an important concept in behavioral formulations of anxiety, stating that anxiety has behavioral, physiological, and verbal components and that they do not necessarily provide the same information
TWO-FACTOR THEORY: a behavioral theory of anxiety that states that fear is caused by Pavlovian conditioning and that avoidance of the feared object is maintained by operant conditioning
VICARIOUS LEARNING: learning (for example, learning to fear something) without direct experience, either by observing or by receiving verbal information

Overview

Anxiety is an important concept in many schools of psychology; thus, there are many different theories about the nature and origin of anxiety disorders. The two most important and influential viewpoints on anxiety are the Freudian and the behavioral viewpoints. Although these theories attempt to explain many anxiety disorders, an examination of how they apply to phobias presents a good indication of how they work.

Sigmund Freud, who said that understanding anxiety "would be bound to throw a flood of light on our whole mental existence," had two theories of anxiety, an early (1917) and a later (1926) theory. In the early theory, libido (mental energy, often equated with sexual drive) builds up until it is discharged by some pleasurable activity. Sometimes the energy cannot be discharged, for example, when the sexual object is not attainable or is morally unacceptable. This undischarged energy is anxiety, and remains even when its original, unacceptable object is repressed, or eliminated from conscious awareness. This anxiety may attach itself to an otherwise harmless object, resulting in a phobia. This theory is best illustrated in one of Freud's most famous cases, that of "Little Hans," a five-year-old who developed a phobia of horses. Freud believed that Hans had a sexual desire for his mother and wanted his father dead so that he could have his mother to himself. This desire for his mother and hatred of his father were unacceptable impulses, and so were repressed from consciousness, resulting in anxiety. This anxiety attached itself to horses, Freud thought, because the black blinders and muzzle of the horse symbolized his father's glasses and mustache.

In Freud's first theory, repression causes anxiety. In the later theory, the relationship between them has changed: Anxiety causes repression. In this theory, anxiety acts as a signal to the ego (in Freud's theory, the rational, conscious part of the mind) that a forbidden impulse (such as Little Hans's desire for his mother) is trying to force its way into consciousness. This signal alerts the ego to try to repress the unwanted impulse. If the ego cannot successfully repress the forbidden impulse, it may try to transfer the forbidden impulse to an irrelevant object (horses, in Little Hans's case). This object can arouse all the emotions associated with the forbidden impulse, including the signal anxiety. In this way, it becomes a phobic object.

One influential behavioral approach to anxiety is O. Hobart Mowrer's two-factor theory. It uses the principles of Pavlovian and operant conditioning to explain fear and phobic avoidance, respectively. Fear is acquired through Pavlovian conditioning when a neutral object or situation is paired with something painful or punishing. For example, having an automobile accident can result in a fear of driving. At this point, operant learning principles take over to explain phobic avoidance. In operant learning, any action that leads to a reward is likely to be repeated. The person who is anxious about driving might avoid driving. Because this avoidance is rewarded by reduced anxiety, the person is more likely to avoid driving in the future. Continued avoidance makes it harder to get back behind the wheel again.

Many problems were found with two-factor theory, and many modifications have been made to it. Two problems will be discussed here to illustrate these changes. First, the theory predicts that people will be likely to fear things that are most often associated with pain. There are very few people in modern society, however, who are phobic of electrical sockets and end tables, even though almost everyone has received a shock from the former and stubbed a toe on the latter. On the other hand, many people are afraid of snakes and spiders, even if they have never been bitten by one. This has been explained through the concept of preparedness: Our evolutionary history has prepared us to learn that some things—such as reptiles, insects, heights, darkness, and closed spaces—are dangerous. These things are "easy" to learn to fear, and they account for a large proportion of phobias. On the other hand, our evolutionary ancestors had no experience with electric sockets or guns, so we are not prepared to become phobic of these objects even though they cause much more pain in modern society than do snakes or spiders.

Two-factor theory states that in order for something to cause fear, it must be paired with a painful or punishing experience. Yet people sometimes become phobic of objects or situations with which they have never had a bad experience. Indeed, many people who have never seen a live snake are afraid of them. Thus, there must be other ways in which fear is acquired. One of these is through vicarious transmission: Seeing someone act afraid of something can lead to acquiring that fear. For example, whether an infant becomes afraid of being in a high place depends on whether its mother is smiling or has an expression of fear on her face. In an ingenious set of experiments, Susan Mineka and her colleagues showed that vicarious transmission of fear is influenced by preparedness. She showed that rhesus monkeys that watched a videotape of other monkeys acting afraid of a snake became afraid of snakes themselves. Monkeys that watched other monkeys act afraid of rabbits, however, did not become afraid of rabbits because they were not evolutionarily prepared to fear rabbits. Human beings also can acquire fear by being told that something is dangerous. A child can come to avoid running in front of oncoming cars by being told not to do this by his or her parents; luckily, he or she does not have to be hit by a car or watch someone get hit in order to acquire this information.

Applications

All theories of anxiety disorders attempt to explain and organize what is known about fear and anxiety. Some of the theories, including the ones described here, also have been applied in developing treatments for anxiety disorders. As might be expected, clinical psychologists with very different ideas about the cause of anxiety will recommend very different treatments to eliminate it.

In the case of Little Hans, Freud thought that his anxiety about horses was caused by repressed sexual impulses toward his mother and hatred of his father. From this, it follows that these repressed impulses would need to be brought out into the open and resolved before his anxiety about horses would diminish. This was the basic goal of the psychoanalytic therapy Freud recommended for Hans.

On the other hand, if Little Hans's parents had taken him to a behaviorally oriented therapist, the therapist would have assumed that the child's fear stemmed from a fright he suffered in the presence of a horse. In fact, Freud stated that the phobia began when Hans saw a horse fall while pulling a bus. Further, the therapist would assume that now Hans was rewarded for avoiding horses by anxiety reduction and by getting extra attention from his parents. Treatment would involve having the boy gradually think about, look at, and even pet horses, and it would include being rewarded for approaching (rather than avoiding) horses.

Presented with these vastly different theories and treatments, the question arises, Which is right? The theoretical issues are still debated, but it is clear that treatments based on a behavioral model of anxiety are much more successful in reducing fear than are treatments based on the theories of Freud or his followers.

Cognitive theories of anxiety also illustrate how theory is applied to develop a treatment. There are many different cognitive models of anxiety, but all are similar in that they assume that there is a cognitive cause of the fear state. This cognitive step is sometimes called an irrational belief. A cognitive theorist might explain Little Hans's fear in the following way: Hans is afraid of horses because he has some irrational belief that horses are dangerous. The specific belief might be "The horse will bite me" or "The horse might get spooked and run into me" or even "Horses have germs, and if I go near one, I'll catch its germs and get sick." The theory assumes that anxiety will stop when the irrational belief is eliminated. Thus, a cognitive therapist would first carefully question Hans to find out the specific irrational belief causing his fear. Once that is determined, the therapist would use persuasion, logical reasoning, and evidence to try to change the belief. (Little Hans was used here only to continue with the same example. A therapist probably would not try to reason with a five-year-old, and a different treatment would be used. Cognitive therapies are more commonly used with adults.)

Physiological theories of anxiety are increasing in importance. As with behavioral, psychodynamic, and cognitive theories, there are many physiological theories. They differ with respect to the brain areas, pathways, or chemicals implicated in anxiety. It is likely that many physiological theories contain an element of truth. Anxiety is a complex state, involving multiple interacting parts of the nervous system, and it will take much additional research to develop a complete model of the brain's role in anxiety.

One physiological variable that has been integrated into many theories of anxiety is the panic attack. This is a sudden and usually short-lived attack that includes trouble with breathing, heart palpitations, dizziness, sweating, and fear of dying or going crazy. These attacks appear purely physiological in that they seem to come "out of the blue" at first; however, psychological factors determine whether they progress into a full-blown disorder. People can become anxious about having panic attacks, and this added anxiety leads to more attacks, producing panic disorder. Some people become afraid of having an attack in a place where they will be unable to cope or receive help. These people may progressively avoid more and more places. This is known as agoraphobia, which at its worst can result in people who are afraid to leave their homes.

The development of physiological theories also illustrates an important point in the relationship between theory and therapy. Thus far, it has been stressed that theories of anxiety help determine treatment. This relationship also works in reverse: Success or failure of treatments adds information used in theory development. This is most clear in physiological theories. For example, the physiological mechanisms of different types of anxiety-reducing tranquilizers have been investigated to provide clues as to how the brain is involved in anxiety.

Context

The concept of anxiety is one of the most often-used and loosely defined concepts in psychology. It can be used to describe a temporary state ("You seem anxious today") or an enduring personality trait ("He is an anxious person"). It is used to assign cause ("He stumbled over the words in his speech because he was anxious") and to describe an effect ("Having to give a speech sure makes me anxious"). It is seen as the result of discrete objects or situations such as snakes or heights, or as evolving from basic existential problems such as the trauma of birth or the fear of death. All major theories in psychology in some way confront anxiety.

Just as most theories in psychology have a view of anxiety, anxiety is an important concept in many areas of psychology. Obviously, anxiety is very important in the fields of psychopathology and psychotherapy. It also has been very important in learning theory; experiments with conditioned fear have advanced knowledge about Pavlovian and operant conditioning. Anxiety is also an important trait in theories of personality, and it figures in theories of motivation. It might be said that anxiety is everywhere in psychology.

Theoretical developments in anxiety have also been incorporated into other areas of psychology. For example, in the early 1960's, Peter Lang described fear and anxiety as being composed of three systems—that is, there are three systems in which fear is expressed: verbal (saying "I'm anxious"), behavioral (avoiding or running away from a feared object), and physiological (experiencing an increase in heart rate or sweating). An important point in understanding the three systems of fear is that the systems do not always run along parallel tracks. A person may speak of being anxious about the condition of the world environment without any physiological arousal. Alternatively, a boy's heart might pound at the sight of a snake in the woods, but he reports no fear and does not run away in the presence of his friends. Describing fear in a three-systems framework presents an important challenge to any theory of anxiety. An adequate theory must explain why the three systems sometimes give the same information and sometimes do not. The three-systems approach not only has been very influential in anxiety theory and research, but also has been applied to many other areas of psychology, such as studying emotion, stress, and pain.

Another major challenge for theories of anxiety is to begin to integrate different positions. The present theories are not all mutually exclusive. The fact that a behavioral theory of anxiety has some validity does not mean that cognitive approaches are wrong. Also, psychological theories need to be integrated with physiological theories that describe brain activity during anxiety. Although theory and research in anxiety has a long and fruitful history, there is much work to be done, and many important developments lie ahead.

Bibliography

Barlow, David H. *Anxiety and Its Disorders*. New York: Guilford Press, 1988. The author, one of the leaders in the field of anxiety research, presents his integrative theory of anxiety. The book also describes assessment and treatment of anxiety and includes a separate chapter on each recognized anxiety disorder. The book's intended audience is graduate students and professionals in psychology, but it is very well written and worth the effort for anyone interested in an up-to-date and comprehensive presentation of anxiety disorders.

Bellenir, Karen, ed. *Mental Health Disorders Sourcebook*. Detroit, Mich.: Omnigraphics, 1996.

Delprato, D. J., and F. D. McGlynn. "Behavioral Theories of Anxiety Disorders." In *Behavioral Theories and Treatment of Anxiety*, edited by Samuel M. Turner. New York: Plenum Press, 1984. Behaviorally oriented psychologists have been extremely active in testing and revising theories of anxiety. This chapter of nearly fifty pages describes the obvious and the subtle differences between various behavioral theories. It also compares behavioral to cognitive theories of anxiety.

Freud, Sigmund. "Analysis of a Phobia in a Five-Year-Old Boy." In *The Standard Edition of the Complete Psychological Works of Sigmund Freud*, edited by James Strachey. Vol. 10. London: Hogarth Press, 1955. Originally published in 1909, this is Freud's description of the case of Little Hans, the most famous patient in the history of anxiety disorders. Freud is an excellent writer, and he presents many vivid details in this case history, making it interesting to read. One could also look up Joseph Wolpe and Stanley Rachman's behavioral interpretation of Little Hans's phobia, "Psychoanalytic 'Evidence': A Critique Based on Freud's Little Hans," in *Journal of Nervous and Mental Disease* 131, no. 2 (1960): 135-148.

_____. "Inhibition, Symptoms, and Anxiety." In *The Standard Edition of the Complete Psychological Works of Sigmund Freud*, edited by James Strachey. Vol. 20. London: Hogarth Press, 1959. In this paper, originally published in German in 1926, Freud describes his revised theory of anxiety. The paper covers a wide range of topics (including a redescription of Little Hans) and is not as readable as the initial presentation of the case. It is, however, an interesting illustration of the change in Freud's thinking about anxiety.

Marks, Isaac Meyer. *Living with Fear: Understanding and Coping with Anxiety*. New York: McGraw-Hill, 1978. This is a work written for the general public by Britain's foremost authority on fear and anxiety. It is accessible and provides a good introduction to theory and treatment of anxiety.

Tuma, A. Hussain, and Jack D. Maser, eds. *Anxiety and the Anxiety Disorders*. New York: Lawrence Erlbaum, 1985. This thousand-page book contains forty-three chapters of high quality, with most of the leaders in the field of anxiety represented. Every important theoretical approach to anxiety is covered. There are two hundred pages of references, an author index, and a subject index, making it easy to find information on specific topics.

Scott R. Vrana

See also:

ATTACHMENT AND BONDING IN INFANCY AND CHILDHOOD

Type of psychology: Developmental psychology
Fields of study: Infancy and childhood; interpersonal relations

Bonding and attachment are two theoretical constructs that psychologists have used to describe and explain the intense emotional tie that develops between a caregiver and child. Research has helped psychologists to explain the development of several common social behaviors in infancy and to use individual differences in infant behavior to predict aspects of later development.

Principal terms

APPROACH BEHAVIORS: infant behaviors that bring the infant closer to the mother, such as clinging, non-nutritional sucking, and following

ATTACHMENT BEHAVIORS: a general term used to describe any infant behavior that serves to bring the caregiver and infant into closer contact

AVOIDANCE: an infant response to the return of a caregiver following a brief period of separation; involves ignoring the mother and showing no sign of positive or negative affect

FELT SECURITY: an infant's sense of security in the availability and predictability of the caregiver; the ultimate goal of the infant's developing attachment to the caregiver

RESISTANCE: an infant response to the return of a caregiver following a brief period of separation; includes signs of ambivalence about seeking and maintaining contact with the caregiver and evidence of anger

SEPARATION PROTEST: an infant's negative response to the departure of a caregiver, most often evidenced in fussing, crying, and clinging

SIGNALLING BEHAVIORS: infant behaviors that bring the mother closer to the child, such as crying, babbling, and clinging

"STRANGE SITUATION": an experimental technique designed to measure the quality of the mother-infant attachment relationship

STRANGER ANXIETY: the negative reaction of an infant to an approaching stranger, most often expressed as fussing or crying

Overview

Bonding refers to the development of an emotional tie of the mother to the infant. This biologically based process is believed to occur in mothers shortly after the birth of an infant, a time period during which the mother's intense emotional response is triggered by contact with her newborn. The existence of such a bond is then evidenced in the mother's behavior. Attachment, on the other hand, refers to a relationship between the caregiver and infant that develops over the infant's first year of life; the quality of the attachment is apparent in the behavior of the infant.

Evidence for the biologically based bonding process has been inconsistent. In contrast, there exists considerable scientific evidence to support the notion of attachment. Thus, the remainder of this discussion will focus on the development of the attachment relationship.

The work of British psychiatrist John Bowlby played an important role in the acceptance and understanding of the notion of mother-infant attachment. Bowlby argued that the behaviors of infants are not random and that, in fact, some of the behaviors exhibited most commonly by infants actually serve a single goal. Specifically, he argued that the infant behaviors of crying, babbling, smiling, clinging, non-nutritional sucking, and following all play an important role in bringing the infant into close contact with the caregiver. He believed that, for the infant, seeking and maintaining proximity to the caregiver are essential for survival because the infant is dependent upon the caregiver for food, shelter, and protection. Thus, the infant's behavior is organized and goal-directed. During early infancy, however, this goal is neither understood nor learned by the infant. Rather, humans are born with a biological predisposition to engage in certain behaviors that aid in the maintenance of proximity to the caregiver. Thus, the goal of maintaining proximity is built into the human infant, as are some initial behaviors that serve the function of achieving that goal. With further development, the infant becomes more aware of the goal, and therefore his or her behaviors become more intentional.

The infant's emotional state is also believed to play an important role in attempts to seek and maintain proximity to the caregiver. That is, the infant's behavior is dependent upon his or her sense of emotional security. For example, as long as a child is in the immediate presence of the attachment figure, or within easy reach, the child feels secure and may then attend to important developmental tasks such as exploration of the environment, using the mother as a secure base from which to explore. Upon the threat of loss of the attachment figure, however, the infant may lose that sense of security and may exhibit attachment behaviors designed to increase the proximity of the attachment figure. Thus, the infant's attempts to seek or maintain proximity to the caregiver are determined by how secure he or she feels with the caregiver in a specific environment.

The attachment relationship and the infant's sense of security develop over the period of infancy. Bowlby has described four phases in the development of the attachment to the caregiver. In phase one, the newborn shows limited discrimination of people and therefore exhibits no preferential or differential behaviors, thus behaving in a friendly manner toward all people. In phase two, the eight- to twelve-week-old infant shows the ability to discriminate the caregiver from others but exhibits no preferential behavior toward the caregiver. In phase three, which generally appears at approximately seven or eight months of age, the infant clearly discriminates the caregiver from other people and begins to show preferential treatment toward him or her. For example, the infant begins to follow a departing mother, greets mother upon her return, and uses her as a base from which to explore an unfamiliar environment. Furthermore, during phase three, the infant begins to treat strangers with caution and may withdraw from a stranger. In phase four, the child maintains a "goal-directed partnership" with the caregiver, a more complex relationship in which the child is acquiring some insight into the caregiver's own feelings and motives, and thus interacts with the caregiver as a partner. This final phase is not apparent in most children until after age two.

Applications

During the second half of the first year of life (after about eight months of age), infants begin to show very clear attempts at exploration when their mothers are present. In fact, research reported by Mary Ainsworth in the mid-1970's suggests that once an infant is able to crawl, he or she does not always remain close to the mother. Instead, the child begins to move away from the mother, more carefully exploring objects and people. From time to time he or she returns to her, as if to check her whereabouts or to check in with her. If the mother moves away, however, or if the infant is frightened by some event, he or she will either approach the mother or will signal to bring the mother in closer proximity. For example, the infant often fusses, cries, and clings to the caregiver at the first sign of the caregiver's possible departure, a response known as separation protest. At about the same time, infants begin to express stranger anxiety or stranger wariness by fussing and crying when an unfamiliar person enters the room or approaches.

Ainsworth designed a special laboratory technique, known as the "strange situation," that allows direct observation of the interactions between the behaviors associated with exploration, attachment, separation protest, and stranger anxiety. This situation places an infant in an unfamiliar setting with a stranger, both in the presence and in the absence of the mother. The procedure consists of a series of three-minute episodes (the process lasts a total of about twenty minutes) in which the child is exposed to an unfamiliar playroom containing a set of age-appropriate toys. During the initial episodes, the mother remains in the playroom with the infant. Mother and infant are then joined in the playroom by a female stranger, who first talks to the mother, then approaches the baby. Next, the mother leaves the room, and the baby and stranger are left alone together. Mother then returns and the stranger leaves, so that the baby is reunited with the mother. Following this episode, the baby is left alone in the room, then joined by the stranger; finally, the mother again returns and the stranger leaves.

This strange situation, therefore, exposes a child to three potentially upsetting experiences: separation from the caregiver, contact with a stranger, and unfamiliar surroundings. The episodes are arranged in such a way that they present a series of stressful experiences to the infant and thus present an opportunity to observe not only the infant's immediate response to a stranger and to separation from the mother, but also his or her ability to derive comfort from the mother and to use her as a secure base for exploration.

Ainsworth has reported that, while there are many similarities in infant responses to this strange situation, there are also important individual differences. In her initial study of twelve-month-old infants and their mothers, Ainsworth reported three distinct patterns of responding to the events of the strange situation, and the validity of these behavior patterns has been demonstrated by much additional research.

A majority of the infants exhibited active exploration of the new environment and the available toys when their mothers were present. Some of these infants showed distress during the first separation from mother, and by the second separation, the majority of these infants expressed distress. Upon reunion with their mother, they actively sought contact with her and were easily comforted by her, showing considerable signs of positive emotion but very little, if any, signs of negative emotion. Furthermore, these infants frequently returned to play and exploration after a period of contact with their mother. In general, then, these infants used their mothers as a secure base from which to explore the novel environment, exhibited appropriate attachment behaviors following her departure, and were easily comforted by the mother upon her return. Ainsworth suggested that this pattern of behavior reflects a secure attachment relationship.

A second group of infants showed a very different pattern of behavior. This minority group showed no evidence of distress during separation. They did sometimes show distress when left alone in the playroom but were easily comforted by the returning stranger. Furthermore, this group actually avoided or ignored their mothers when they returned. In essence, the mothers were treated very much as were the strangers. These infants showed virtually no signs of separation protest or stranger anxiety and exhibited very few attachment behaviors. Ainsworth suggested that this pattern of behavior reflects an insecure, avoidant attachment relationship.

Finally, a third group of children were extremely distressed upon separation yet, despite their obvious separation and stranger anxiety, resisted comfort from their mothers. Their behavior suggested an angry ambivalence—they objected to being left alone, but they refused to be consoled when reunited with their mothers. This group of infants often exhibited distress upon first entering the unfamiliar room with their mothers, and they rarely left her side to explore the toys or the environment, either before or after separation, suggesting a lack of a sense of security. Ainsworth suggested that this behavior pattern reflects an insecure, resistant, or ambivalent attachment relationship.

The development of these distinct patterns of attachment is believed to be the result of the history of interaction between the caregiver and infant. Specifically, attachment theory suggests that responsive and consistent caregiving results in a secure mother-infant attachment, unresponsive caregiving results in an avoidant attachment, and inconsistent caregiving results in a resistant/ambivalent attachment. The "avoidant" mother has been described as cold and disliking physical contact with the infant, who responds by acting aloof and avoiding social interaction. The "resistant" mother, on the other hand, has been described as unpredictable, sometimes responding but sometimes not, and the infant often responds with anger and ambivalence.

As the infant matures, the specific behaviors that indicate the existence of the attachment relationship may change. The research evidence strongly suggests, however, that such individual differences in the quality of the mother-infant attachment relationship are predictive of later behavior. For example, infants who exhibit secure attachment patterns at one year of age have been found to be more cooperative with adults, to show greater enthusiasm for learning, to be more independent, and to be more popular with their peers during the preschool years. Thus, the quality of the mother-infant attachment relationship may have long-range effects. This does not mean that the child's future is determined solely by the quality of the attachment relationship. The evidence indicates that certain negative consequences of an insecure attachment relationship may be overcome by changes in the nature of the child's important relationships.

Context

The existence of a mother-infant attachment relationship has been recognized for many years. For most of those years, however, psychologists explained the development of this attachment by way of traditional learning theory. That is, behaviorists argued that the infant-mother attachment develops because mothers are associated with the powerful, reinforcing event of being fed. In this way, the mother becomes a conditioned reinforcer.

This reinforcement theory of attachment, however, came into question as a result of the work of Harry and Margaret Harlow in the early 1960's.

The Harlows' work was not with human infants but with infant rhesus monkeys. They removed newborn monkeys from their mothers at birth and raised them in the laboratory with two types of artificial or surrogate mothers. One surrogate mother was made of terrycloth and could provide "contact comfort." The other surrogate mother was made of wire. A feeding bottle was attached to one of the substitute mothers for each of the monkeys. Half of the monkeys were fed by the wire mother; the other half were fed by the cloth mother. This allowed the Harlows to compare the importance of feeding to the importance of contact comfort for the monkeys.

In order to elicit attachment behaviors, the Harlows introduced some frightening event, such as a strange toy, into the cages of the young monkeys. They expected that if feeding were the key to attachment, then the frightened monkeys should have run to the surrogate mother that fed them. This was not the case, however: All the young monkeys ran to their cloth mothers and clung to them, even if they were not fed by them. Only the cloth mothers were able to provide security for the frightened monkeys. The Harlows concluded that a simple reinforcement explanation of attachment was inaccurate and that the contact comfort, not the food, provided by a mother plays a critical role in the development of attachment.

This research provided the impetus for the development of Bowlby's ethological account of attachment. Since that time, research by Mary Ainsworth and Alan Sroufe, as well as many others, has provided important information for the continuing development of understanding of the complex relationship between caregivers and infants.

Bibliography

Ainsworth, Mary D. Salter, Mary C. Blehar, Everett Waters, and S. Wall. *Patterns of Attachment*. Hillsdale, N.J.: Lawrence Erlbaum, 1978. Outlines, in general terms, the development of Bowlby's attachment theory. Describes in detail the procedures and scoring techniques for the strange situation and describes the patterns of behavior associated with the secure, avoidant, and resistant attachments. Discusses the research that addresses the antecedents of individual differences in the attachment relationship.

Bowlby, John. *Attachment and Loss*. 2d ed. New York: Basic Books, 1982. Examines the theoretical foundation of the attachment construct and discusses attachment behavior. Outlines the development, maintenance, and function of attachment in both humans and animals.

Crockenberg, S. B. "Infant Irritability, Mother Responsiveness, and Social Support Influences on the Security of Infant-Mother Attachment." In *Contemporary Readings in Child Psychology*. 3d ed., compiled by E. Mavis Hetherington and Ross D. Parke. New York: McGraw-Hill, 1988. Describes a research project that shows that infant characteristics, such as infant temperament, as well as maternal responsiveness, can influence the development of the mother-infant attachment relationship. Also shows that the availability of social support to the mother can influence the development of attachment.

Damon, William. *Social and Personality Development*. New York: W. W. Norton, 1983. This textbook is an introduction to the social development of the child. Contains an excellent discussion of attachment theory and presents many clear, concise examples of infant and child attachment behaviors. Relates the development of attachment behavior to other important developments in infancy and early childhood.

Dunn, Judy. *Distress and Comfort*. Cambridge, Mass.: Harvard University Press, 1977. Addresses questions commonly asked by parents about infant and child distress. Outlines the development of separation protest and stranger anxiety and discusses the importance of parental behavior in the continuing emotional development of the child.

Klaus, Marshall H., John H. Kennell, and Phyllis H. Klaus. *Bonding: Building the Foundations of Secure Attachment and Independence*. Reading, Mass.: Addison-Wesley, 1995.

Lamb, Michael E., and Joseph J. Campos. *Development in Infancy*. New York: Random House, 1982. A comprehensive textbook on infant development that presents a variety of theories of infant emotional development.

Newsweek. "Your Child from Birth to Three." (Spring/Summer, 1997). Special child development issue.

Loretta A. Reiser-Danner

See also:

Cognitive Development Theory: Jean Piaget, 135; Emotion, Development of, 229; Gender-Identity Formation, 254; Imprinting and Learning, 290; Moral Development, 399; Motor Development, 410; Psychoanalytic Psychology and Personality: Sigmund Freud, 478.

ATTRACTION THEORIES

Type of psychology: Social psychology
Field of study: Interpersonal relations

Theories of interpersonal attraction attempt to specify the conditions that lead people to like, and in some cases love, each other. Attraction is a two-way process, involving not only the person who is attracted but also the attractor.

Principal terms

EQUITY THEORY: a theory suggesting that attraction tends to occur when two people both believe that their relationship is fair

MATCHING PHENOMENON: the tendency for people to choose romantic partners whose level of attractiveness is close to their own

MERE EXPOSURE: a psychological phenomenon in which liking tends to increase as a person sees more of something or someone

PHYSICAL ATTRACTIVENESS STEREOTYPE: the tendency to attribute other positive characteristics to a physically attractive person

PROXIMITY: physical closeness; a determinant of attraction

RECIPROCITY: a principle of attraction that suggests that people tend to like others who like them back

REINFORCEMENT MODEL: a general model of interpersonal attraction that suggests that attraction is determined by the rewards provided by the relationship

SOCIAL EXCHANGE THEORY: a theory that suggests that attraction is determined by weighing the benefits of a relationship against the costs involved

Overview

Relationships are central to human social existence. Personal accounts by people who have been forced to endure long periods of isolation serve as reminders of people's dependence on others, and research suggests that close relationships are the most vital ingredient in a happy and meaningful life. In short, questions dealing with attraction are among the most fundamental in social psychology.

The major theories addressing interpersonal attraction have a common theme: reinforcement. The principle of reinforcement is one of the most basic notions in all of psychology. Put simply, it states that behaviors that are followed by desirable consequences (often these take the form of rewards) tend to be repeated. Applied to interpersonal relations, this principle suggests that when one person finds something rewarding in an interaction with another person (or if that person anticipates some reward in a relationship that has not yet been established), then the person should desire further interaction with that other individual. In behavioral terms, this is what is meant by the term "interpersonal attraction," which emerges in everyday language in such terms as "liking" or, in the case of deep romantic involvement, "loving." Appropriately, these theories based on the notion that individuals are drawn to relationships that are rewarding and avoid those that are not are known as reinforcement or reward models of interpersonal attraction.

The first and most basic theory of this type was proposed in the early 1970's by Donn Byrne and Gerald Clore. Known as the reinforcement-affect model of attraction ("affect" means "feeling" or "emotion"), this theory proposes that people will be attracted not only to other people who reward them but also to those people whom they associate with rewards. In other words, a person can learn to like others through their connections to experiences that are positive for that individual. It is important to recognize that a major implication here is that it is possible to like someone not so much because of that person himself or herself, but rather as a consequence of that person's merely being part of a rewarding situation; positive feelings toward the experience itself get transferred to that other person. (It also follows that a person associated with something unpleasant will tend to be disliked.)

For example, in one experiment done during the summer, people who evaluated new acquaintances in a cool and comfortable room liked them better than when in a hot and uncomfortable room. In another, similar, study subjects rating photographs of strangers gave more favorable evaluations when in a nicely furnished room than when they were in a dirty room with shabby furniture. These findings provide some insight into why married couples may find that their relationship benefits from a weekend trip away from the children or a romantic dinner at a favorite restaurant; the pleasant event enhances their feelings for each other.

There are other models of interpersonal attraction that involve the notion of rewards but consider the degree to which they are offset by the costs associated with a relationship. Social exchange theory suggests that people tend to evaluate social situations; in the context of a relationship, a person will compare the costs and benefits of beginning or continuing that relationship. Imagine, for example, that Karen is considering a date with Dave, who is kind, attractive, and financially stable but fifteen years older. Karen may decide that this relationship is not worth pursuing because of the disapproval of her mother and father, who believe strongly that their daughter should be dating a man her own age. Karen's decision will be influenced by how much she values the approval of her parents and by whether she has other dating alternatives available.

A third model of attraction, equity theory, extends social exchange theory. This approach suggests that it is essential to take into account how both parties involved in a relationship assess the costs and benefits. When each person believes that his or her own ratio of costs to benefits is fair (or equitable), then attraction between the two tends to be promoted. On the other hand, a relationship may be placed in jeopardy if one person thinks that the time, effort, and other resources being invested are justified, while the other person does not feel that way.

Considering the rewards involved in the process of interpersonal attraction provides a useful model, but one that is rather general. To understand attraction fully, one must look more specifically at what people find rewarding in relationships. Social psychological research has established some definite principles governing attraction that can be applied nicely within the reward framework.

Applications

The first determinant of attraction, reciprocity, is probably fairly obvious, since it most directly reflects the reinforcement process; nevertheless, it is a powerful force: People tend to like others who like them back. There are few things more rewarding than genuine affection, support, concern, and other indicators that one is liked by another person.

The second principle, proximity, suggests that simple physical closeness tends to promote attraction. Research has confirmed what many people probably already know: People are most likely to become friends (or romantic partners) with others with whom they have worked, grown up, or gone to school. Other studies have shown that people living in dormitories or apartments tend to become friends with the neighbors who live closest to them. Simply being around people gives an individual a chance to interact with them, which in turn provides the opportunity to learn who is capable of providing the rewards sought in a relationship.

It seems, however, that there is yet another force at work, a very basic psychological process known as the mere exposure phenomenon. Research has demonstrated consistently that repeated exposure to something new tends to increase one's liking for it, and examples of the process are quite common in everyday life. It is not uncommon, for example, for a person to buy a new tape or compact disc by a favorite musical artist without actually having heard the new material, only to be disappointed upon listening to it. The listener soon discovers, however, that the album "grows" on him or her and finds himself or herself liking it quite a bit after hearing it a few times. Such occurrences probably involve the mere exposure phenomenon. In short, familiarity breeds liking, and physical closeness makes it possible for that familiarity to develop.

Generally speaking, the same factors that promote the development of friendships also foster romantic attraction. The third principle of attraction, physical attractiveness, is somewhat of an exception, however, since it is more powerful in the romantic context.

In a classic study published by Elaine (Hatfield) Walster and her associates in 1966, University of Minnesota freshmen males and females were randomly paired for dates to a dance. Prior to the date, these students had provided considerable information about themselves, some of it through personality tests. During the evening, each person individually completed a questionnaire that focused primarily on how much the person liked his or her date, and the participants were contacted for follow-up six months later. Despite the opportunity to discover complex facts about attraction, such as what kinds of personality traits link up within a couple to promote it, the only important factor in this study was physical appearance. For both sexes, the better-looking the partner, the more the person liked his or her date, the stronger was the desire to date the person again, and the more likely the individual was actually to do so during the next six months.

The potent effect of physical attractiveness in this study sparked much interest in this variable on the part of researchers over the next decade or so. The earliest studies determined rather quickly that both men and women, given the opportunity to select a date from a group of several members of the opposite sex representing a range of attractiveness levels, almost invariably would select the most attractive one. Dating in real life, however, is seldom without the chance that the person asking another out might be turned down. When later experiments began building the possibility of rejection into their procedures, an interesting effect emerged, one that has been termed the "matching phenomenon." People tend to select romantic partners whose degree of attractiveness is very similar to their own.

Other research revealed that physically attractive people are often judged favorably on qualities other than their appearance. Even when nothing is known but what the person looks like, the physically attractive individual is thought to be happier, more intelligent, and more successful than someone who is less attractive. This finding is referred to as the "physical attractiveness stereotype," and it has implications that extend the role of appearance well beyond the matter of dating. Studies have shown, for example, that work (such as a writing sample) will be assessed more favorably when produced by an attractive person than when by someone less attractive, and that a cute child who misbehaves will be treated more leniently than a homely one. What is beautiful is also good, so to speak. Finally, one may note that physical attractiveness fits well with the reward model: It is pleasant and reinforcing both to look at an attractive person and to be seen with him or her, particularly if that person is one's date.

The last principle of attraction, similarity, is the most important one in long-term relationships, regardless of whether they are friendships or romances. An extremely large body of research has demonstrated consistently that the more similar two people are, especially attitudinally, the more they will like each other. It turns out that the old adage, "opposites attract," is simply false. (Note that the matching phenomenon also reflects similarity.) A friend or spouse who holds attitudes similar to one's own will provide rewards by confirming that one's own feelings and beliefs are correct; it is indeed reinforcing when someone else agrees.

Context

Much of the work on the social psychology of interpersonal attraction represents at least relatively recent developments in the field. Proximity was really the first factor to be investigated; its role in promoting attraction was established by the late 1950's. Much of the research on similarity was conducted in the 1960's, and its importance was well understood by the end of that decade. Still, it seems that interest in the psychology of attraction did not fully blossom until physical attractiveness emerged as a major research topic.

Curiously, although it would seem to be of obvious importance, physical appearance as a determinant of romantic attraction was simply neglected by researchers until the mid-1960's. Perhaps they mistakenly assumed the widespread existence of an old ideal that one should judge someone on the basis of his or her intrinsic worth, not on the basis of a superficial characteristic. Nevertheless, when the Minnesota study discussed earlier produced a physical attractiveness effect so strong as to eliminate or at least obscure any other factors related to attraction in the context of dating, social psychologists took notice. In any science, surprising or otherwise remarkable findings usually tend to stimulate additional research, and such a pattern definitely describes the course of events in this area of inquiry.

By around 1980, social psychology had achieved a rather solid understanding of the determinants of attraction to strangers, and the field began turning more of its attention to the nature of continuing relationships. Social psychologist Zick Rubin had first proposed a theory of love in 1970, and research on that topic flourished in the 1980's as investigators examined such topics as the components of love, different types of love, the nature of love in different kinds of relationships, and the characteristics of interaction in successful long-term relationships. Still other lines of research explored how people end relationships or attempt to repair those that are in trouble.

People view relationships with family, friends, and lovers as central to their happiness—a research finding that is totally consistent with common experience. One need only look at the content of motion pictures, television programs, musical lyrics, novels, and poetry—where relationships, particularly romantic ones, are so commonly a theme—to find evidence for that point. Yet nearly half of all marriages end in divorce, and the lack of love in the relationship is usually a precipitating factor. Whatever social psychology can teach people about what determines and maintains attraction can help improve the human condition.

Bibliography

Berscheid, Ellen, and Elaine Hatfield Walster. *Interpersonal Attraction*. 2d ed. Reading, Mass.: Addison-Wesley, 1978. Presents a solid overview of the psychology of attraction. Directed toward the reader with no background in social psychology, the book is quite readable; nevertheless, it is highly regarded and frequently cited within the field. Clever illustrations feature many cartoons.

_____. "Physical Attractiveness." In *Advances in Experimental Social Psychology*, edited by Leonard Berkowitz. New York: Academic Press, 1974. A very thorough review of the research examining the role of physical attractiveness in interpersonal attraction. This is a frequently cited and extensively documented chapter that includes interesting discussions of how people judge attractiveness and how attractiveness affects the individual.

Duck, Steve. *Relating to Others*. Chicago: Dorsey Press, 1988. Duck deals briefly with the traditional work on interpersonal attraction, but this book is most notable for being devoted primarily to reviewing the research on personal relationships, which became important in the 1980's. It covers thoroughly such topics as developing and maintaining relationships, exclusivity in relationships, and repairing and ending them. A good reference for taking the reader beyond the principal focus of the present article.

Hatfield, Elaine, and Susan Sprecher. *Mirror, Mirror: The Importance of Looks in Everyday Life*. Albany: State University of New York Press, 1986. An extremely thorough and very readable review of all the different affects of personal appearance—not only on the attraction process but also on the person himself or herself. Explores how judgments of attractiveness are made and addresses the effects of beauty across the entire life span. Nicely supported with effective photographs and illustrations.

Myers, David G. *Social Psychology*. 3d ed. New York: McGraw-Hill, 1990. This very popular social psychology textbook features an unusually good chapter on interpersonal attraction. Offers a solid survey of the research relating to the principles of attraction and provides particularly good coverage of work on love. The author's engaging writing style makes this an excellent starting point for further exploration of the topic.

Steve A. Nida

See also:

THE AUDITORY SYSTEM

Type of psychology: Sensation and perception
Field of study: Auditory, chemical, cutaneous, and body senses

The auditory system is the sensory system that enables people to hear sounds and to learn spoken language well. Malfunction or lack of function of the auditory system makes it difficult to understand spoken language, and the resultant sensory deprivation can lead to psychological problems.

Principal terms

ADVENTITIOUS DEAFNESS: deafness acquired after birth, through accident or disease

CARTILAGE: a tough white fibrous tissue, attached to articular surfaces of bones

LABYRINTH: an intricate biological structure composed of interconnecting anatomical cavities

MUCOUS MEMBRANE: the membrane lining body cavities that are in contact with the air (such as the respiratory and digestive systems), the glands of which secrete mucus

MUCUS: a thick mixture of cells, carbohydrate, water, and other chemicals that serves as a protective lubricant coating for mucous membranes

NEUROSIS: any functional disorder of the mind or the emotions, occurring without obvious brain damage and involving anxiety, phobic responses, or other abnormal behavior symptoms

OSCILLOSCOPE: an electronic instrument that produces a visual display of electron motion on the screen of a cathode ray tube

PSYCHOSIS: a severe mental disorder, with or without brain damage, characterized by deterioration of normal intellectual and social functioning and withdrawal from reality

TEMPORAL BONE: either of two complex bones that form the sides and base of the skull

Overview

Communicating and understanding the world are essential to humans. One very important aspect of both these processes is the utilization of sounds, perceived by the auditory system. These include spoken language and the sounds produced by inanimate objects (such as wind, thunder, or music). The auditory system is composed of the ear and the auditory nerve (the eighth cranial nerve), which carries all perceived sounds to the brain for interpretation.

The ear is usually divided into three parts, for purposes of description: an outer ear, a middle ear, and an inner ear. The outer ear contains two important portions. First, a fleshy auricle (which people see and think of as the ear) is attached to the side of the head. The auricle—composed of cartilage, skin, and fat—catches sounds and conveys them into a short tube that enters the head.

This skin-covered, 3-centimeter-long tube, the external auditory canal (auditory meatus), is the second important part of the outer ear. The first third of the canal is lined with fine hairs and with tiny glands that produce ear wax. The hairs and wax keep dust and other foreign particles from injuring the rest of the canal. When too much wax forms in an ear canal, it should be removed by a physician, because the wax can shut off the canal and press against the eardrum, producing pain and/or decreasing the ability to hear.

The end of the external auditory canal, the eardrum, lies against one end of the middle ear (the tympanic cavity), a small space in the temporal bone of the skull. When a sound enters the ear, it passes through the external ear canal and causes the eardrum to vibrate. Then, three small, attached bones—the hammer (malleus), anvil (incus) and stirrup (stapes)—in the middle ear also vibrate. These bones span the middle ear and transmit sounds across it. The transmission begins when the malleus, attached to the eardrum, vibrates. The vibration is next transmitted to the incus, and finally to the stapes. The stapes fits into an interior opening of the cavity, the so-called oval window, and when sound waves cause it to vibrate, the vibrations ultimately stimulate the auditory nerve.

Some hearing is retained even when a large hole is made in the eardrum or when one bone of the inner ear is missing. This residual hearing is attributable to several things. First, a secondary eardrum that can vibrate and carry sound is located in a hole—the round window—just below the oval window, and its vibration can also stimulate the auditory nerve. Second, sound can be carried through the bones of the skull—bone conduction—to the auditory nerve. Bone conduction and secondary eardrum action are not nearly as effective as sound transmission via an intact eardrum and functional malleus, incus, and stapes bones.

The air-filled tympanic cavity is connected to the throat by the eustachian tube, which equalizes the air pressure on both sides of the eardrum, preventing unequal pressure from bursting the eardrum. Pressure equalization occurs when yawns or swallowing open the tube, which is usually closed; such opening can spread throat infections to the mucous membrane of the middle ear.

The 2-centimeter-long inner ear, or bony labyrinth, connects the middle ear to the auditory nerve. This labyrinth begins with a chamber, or vestibule, that leads into three semicircular canals involved in balance and a bony cochlea, involved in hearing; the cochlea looks somewhat like a snail shell. The soft, interior contents of the bony labyrinth are the vehicle for connection to the auditory nerve. This tissue is surrounded by a fluid called perilymph and filled with a fluid called endolymph. The outermost portion of the membranous labyrinth contains the connections to the auditory nerve.

Within the vestibule, a saclike portion of the membranous labyrinth (the saccule) is connected to the middle ear and to the cochlea. The cochlea itself is divided by membranes into vestibular, tympanic, and cochlear canals, which run its entire length. Vestibular and tympanic canals, filled with perilymph, receive vibrations (sound waves) from the stapes (stirrup bone) and the secondary eardrum, respectively.

The cochlear canal contains the organ of Corti, filled with thousands of fibers (or hairs) of differing lengths. These fibers are relatively short at the beginning of the cochlea but increase in length as they approach its end. When sound waves move through the perilymph of the inner ear, they make the fibers vibrate. Low-pitched sounds make long fibers vibrate, and high-pitched sounds make short fibers vibrate. Because of the variation of lengths of the fibers, the average human ear can distinguish sounds that exhibit nearly sixteen hundred differences in pitch. The cochlea is only 0.5 centimeter long.

Sounds arise from sound waves, which range from low-pitched ones that vibrate fifteen times a second to very high-pitched ones that vibrate twenty thousand times a second. The vibration of the organ of Corti fibers stimulates the auditory nerve and carries a complex sound message to the brain, where it is translated. Loud sounds are loud because they stimulate the vibration of many more fibers than soft sounds do.

The ear is easily damaged by disease and by accidents. For example, it is easily reached by mouth and throat infections, which produce ear infections. Inadequate treatment can damage the ear and lessen the ability to hear, causing partial hearing loss or deafness, the complete inability to hear. Sounds that are excessively loud can also damage the ear and hearing.

Furthermore, some careless actions meant in fun, or done in ignorance, can produce ear and hearing damage. Two common occurrences of this kind are "boxing" a person's ear and attempting to remove ear wax from one's own ear. The first action, a blow to the ear with an open palm that completely covers the ear, can push air into the ear forcefully enough to rupture an eardrum and cause deafness. Attempts to clear ear wax from an ear with cotton swabs or sharp objects are also potentially dangerous because they can rupture the eardrum and may push the wax further into the ear, where it can cause damage that will decrease hearing. For these reasons, physicians often advise people to keep all objects "smaller than an elbow" out of their ears.

Applications

An understanding of the anatomy and mechanistics of the auditory system allows examination of the basis for hearing. It can be shown with electrodes inserted into the ear, for example, that the cochlea transduces all audible sounds into electrical impulses, acting much like a microphone. The action of this auditory microphone can be amplified and recorded on an oscilliscope and can be converted into sounds by use of a loudspeaker. In addition, when the different areas of the cochlea are tested in this way, it can be shown that low tones are picked up by fibers at its apex and high tones are picked up by those at its base. It is believed that the auditory microphone then stimulates the auditory nerve and carries the sound to the brain for interpretation.

Three classical theories of the mechanism of hearing are a resonance theory, which bases differentiation of sounds on the place at which stimulation of the cochlear system occurs; a frequency (telephone) theory, supposing that the frequency of individual sound waves is translated directly to nerve impulses; and a combined theory, which is more current. The telephone theory was proposed in 1886. Its main shortcoming is the fact that nerve fibers cannot transmit impulses at high enough rates to allow detection of all the sounds that humans can hear.

The resonance theory was proposed by Hermann von Helmholtz in the middle of the nineteenth century. It views the cochlear apparatus as a vibrational analyzer that responds, at specific places, to individual sound frequencies, activating specific nerve sites. Helmholtz viewed such nerve activation as causing subsequent activation of the brain at a specific point—depending on the original sound—to produce the perception of a particular pitch. Among the observations that led researchers to question the complete validity of this theory is the fact that cochlear nerve fibers are not organized appropriately to allow resonance recognition to happen precisely.

More recently, a "resonance-volley" theory has become accepted as a compromise that explains the observations of contemporary research. The theory proposes that within certain limits, several nerve fibers can act together—in a volley—to allow the perception of sounds that exceed the upper limit of a single fiber. Above a permissible range, it is presumed that a frequency mechanism takes over. Therefore, the perception of low-pitched sounds is believed to depend on the telephone theory, while that of higher-pitched ones is presumed to depend upon the position of nerve stimulation.

Although many deaf people are born lacking hearing (congenital deafness), adventitious deafness can develop at almost any time in life. Both congenital and adventitious deafness can be divided into conductive, sensorineural, and central types. These problems arise, respectively, from impaired sound conduction to the inner ear, abnormalities of the inner ear or the auditory nerve, or dysfunction of the central nervous system.

Deafness can result from a wide variety of causes; already mentioned are buildup of ear wax, accidents such as breaking an eardrum by boxing an ear, and ear infection. Middle ear infection—otitis media—is a common cause of conductive deafness. Such infections often begin when upper respiratory infection or allergy causes nasal secretions to back up the eustachean tube, block the middle ear, and cause pressure inequalities. These inequalities can restrict eardrum action or even rupture the eardrum.

Many genetic problems cause deafness, including oterosclerosis, in which decalcification of the bone is followed by the production of abnormal bone that prevents the movement of the stirrup bone (stapes) and greatly decreases the amount of sound that reaches the inner ear. Certain chemicals, loud noises, loss of sensory cells in old age, and central nervous system damage are only a few of the other causes of deafness.

Deafness at birth is a serious disability, because the acquisition of spoken language through hearing pervades all aspects of life. People with congenital deafness have diminished communication capacities. Their educational achievement, intellectual function, personality and vocational development, and overall quality of life can all be affected. The presumption that other senses "sharpen" to compensate for a lack of hearing is not true, according to experts such as Brian Bolton. Studies have shown deaf people to be more introverted than individuals with unimpaired hearing; depression has also been linked to deafness.

Context

The primary problem associated with the auditory system is deafness. Handling deafness in the young is particularly important. Better understanding of the auditory system has led to more effective methods for the prevention, the diagnosis, and the treatment of some of the problems related to deafness. For example, it is presently realized that immunization against viral disease, careful attention to upper respiratory bacterial infections (accompanied by quick antibiotic therapy), and removal of the tonsils and/or adenoids helps to prevent many potential hearing problems that lead to deafness. Successful use of such methodologies have somewhat decreased the incidence of deafness.

As to diagnostic techniques, the use of professional audiologists has become more common, which both allows early identification of the symptoms that indicate developing hearing impairment and shows how best to treat the problem. Such diagnosis and treatment are currently available in hospitals, in schools, and in hearing clinics.

Once hearing impairment or deafness is identified, treatment methods available include antibiotic therapy and various types of surgery. One example of surgical treatment is stapedectomy, where the oterosclerotic patient can be rescued by repairing the junction between the oval window of the inner ear and the stapes (stirrup) bone. The immobile stapes and oval window are removed and replaced by a tissue graft coupled to an artificial stapes that is connected appropriately with the incus (anvil) bone of the middle ear. Other surgical techniques available include repair of perforated eardrums (myringoplasty) and cochlear implants that can help to restore hearing by allowing direct electrical stimulation of the auditory nerve.

Nonmedical treatments of hearing impairments include use of electroacoustic hearing aids and special education techniques that teach deaf people to communicate by nonaural methods, including sign language. In addition, social counseling and the efforts of psychologists and psychiatrists have become quite useful for treatment of neuroses and psychoses that may stem from sensory deprivation and other problems that accompany deafness.

The best approaches to deafness are still cautious conservation of hearing by avoiding loud noise and other environmental occurrences that can produce deafness; obtaining quick, effective treatment for diseases that can cause hearing impairment; and early identification of impairment, followed by its cure before deafness results. It is hoped that continuing research will increase the avenues for prevention of deafness by surgical, medical, and psychological methods and will identify methods for preventing congenital deafness.

Bibliography

Ballantyne, John Chalmers, and J. A. M. Martin. *Deafness*. 4th ed. Edinburgh: Churchill Livingstone, 1984. This expert book attempts "a general account couched in simple terms, of the disability of deafness and its relief." Coverage includes description of the auditory system, diagnosis of deafness and explanation of its causes, description of hearing aids, exploration aspects, and rehabilitation of the deaf.

Bess, Fred H., and Larry E. Humes. *Audiology: The Fundamentals*. Baltimore: Williams & Wilkins, 1990. This introductory book is designed for students of audiology. Its clear, simple language, abundant vignettes, and many literature references make it useful. Topics of interest include the nature of sound, auditory system structure and function, assessment of auditory function, and management strategies for the hearing impaired.

Bolton, Brian, ed. *Psychology of Deafness for Rehabilitation Counselors*. Baltimore: University Park Press, 1976. Provides useful information on problems associated with deafness and their treatment. A good counterpoint to the aspects of the normal auditory system. Included are aspects of intellectual and vocational development, academic achievement, psychiatry of deafness, and intervention and rehabilitation programs.

Daniloff, Raymond, Gordon Schuckers, and Lawrence Feth. *The Physiology of Speech and Hearing: An Introduction*. Englewood Cliffs, N.J.: Prentice-Hall, 1980. This introductory book does a thorough job, using clear, simple language. The chapter entitled "Audition: The Sense of Hearing" is important. In addition, chapters providing overviews of speech and hearing, basic neuroscience, and acoustics are quite useful.

Durrant, John D., and Jean H. Lovrinic. *Bases of Hearing Sciences*. 3d ed. Baltimore: Williams & Wilkins, 1995.

Keidel, Wolf Dieter, S. Kallert, and M. Korth. *The Physiological Basis of Hearing*. New York: Thieme-Stratton, 1983. This expert, technical text comprehensively reviews the physiology and operation of the auditory system. Well worth examining, it includes excellent descriptions of the anatomy, physiology, and operation of the auditory system, as well as theories of its operation, with experimental and theoretical explanations. Almost thirteen hundred references are included.

Matlin, Margaret W., and Hugh J. Foley. *Sensation and Perception*. 4th ed. Boston: Allyn &
    Bacon, 1996.
Moore, Brian C., ed. *Hearing*. 2d ed. New York: Academic Press, 1995.

Sanford S. Singer

See also:

THE AUTONOMIC NERVOUS SYSTEM

Type of psychology: Biological bases of behavior
Field of study: Nervous system

The sympathetic and parasympathetic divisions of the nervous system are responsible for the maintenance of homeostasis in vertebrates. These two systems make constant physiological adjustments to compensate for changes that are occurring in the internal and external environment of the animal. In doing so, they influence the behavior of animals in many ways.

Principal terms

ADRENAL GLAND: one of the endocrine glands associated with the autonomic nervous system

AUTONOMIC NERVOUS SYSTEM: the portion of the peripheral nervous system responsible for the maintenance of homeostasis

EPINEPHRINE: the neurotransmitter released from the adrenal gland as a result of innervation of the autonomic nervous system

HOMEOSTASIS: the maintenance of the internal environment of living organisms within narrow parameters that provide the optimum chance for survival

INNERVATION: the nervous stimulation of a muscle cell or another nerve

NEUROTRANSMITTERS: chemical messengers released from neurons that can conduct nerve impulses to other neurons or can stimulate the contraction of muscle cells

NOREPINEPHRINE: the neurotransmitter released from neurons and the adrenal gland when the autonomic nervous system is stimulated

Overview

The nervous system of humans is categorized according to function into two discrete units, the somatic and the autonomic nervous systems. These systems not only have different functions but also operate through different parts of the brain and different nerves. The somatic system deals with those activities of the brain and spinal cord which stimulate the contraction of the skeletal muscle and thus control posture and movement. All these activities are under voluntary control, which means that the maintenance of posture and movements are dependent upon the will of the animal.

The autonomic nervous system is responsible for the maintenance of homeostasis, often referred to as the internal environment of the animal. The internal environment includes such things as heart rate, rate of respiration, and blood pressure. The activities of the autonomic nervous system are called the visceral responses and are generally considered to be involuntary. The animal is unaware of most of these activities, even though they are essential to life. The autonomic nervous system operates by stimulating smooth muscle, cardiac muscle, or glands.

The autonomic nervous system is further divided into two divisions, the sympathetic and the parasympathetic. Just as the somatic and autonomic systems use different nerves and have different functions, so the sympathetic and parasympathetic divisions of the nervous system are independent of each other and have different functions.

The sympathetic branch is responsive when a person is very active physically or is placed in a stressful situation. It not only involves the nervous system but also stimulates the medullary portion of the adrenal gland. During the sympathetic activity, epinephrine or norepinephrine (also called adrenaline and noradrenaline) are released by the nervous system, which in turn stimulates release of more neurotransmitter from the adrenal medulla. This has often been called the fight-or-flight reaction. The term is derived from the sympathetic responses of animals who are often subject to attack by predators. The fight-or-flight reaction suggests that the animal has been frightened or attacked by a predator and must either attempt an escape or prepare to remain and fight the predator. During this reaction there is an increase in heart rate and in the strength of contraction of the heart; there is also an elevation of blood pressure. Blood flow is directed to the skeletal muscle and to the brain, the pupils of the eyes are dilated, and the airways to the lungs are opened to allow more air to enter. Sweating becomes more common and, particularly in some animals, the hair stands on end. The body must also be concerned with supplying food to the muscles. In order to accomplish this, the liver breaks glycogen down to glucose, the adipose tissue of the body releases fatty acids into the bloodstream as a secondary source of food, and metabolic rate increases. All these responses are consistent with an increase in mental alertness and strenuous physical activity.

The parasympathetic system stimulates many of the same organs or glands as the sympathetic system; however, the response is not the same. The parasympathetic system directs the body's activities to a more vegetative state. When the parasympathetic system is active, the person is more relaxed and sedate. During the parasympathetic response, there is a decreased heart rate and blood pressure, respiration is slowed, and blood flow is directed to the digestive system for the absorption of food. The liver stores excess glucose as glycogen, and fatty acids in circulation are sequestered and stored in the adipose tissue. In addition, both the sympathetic and parasympathetic systems play an important role in reproduction. The parasympathetic system is responsible for erection in the penis of the male, and the sympathetic system is responsible for ejaculation.

During much of the day, a person is in a condition in which the state of the autonomic nervous system is a balance between the sympathetic and parasympathetic systems. The person is neither preparing for a stressful situation nor involved in digestion of food. The body can quickly switch from one state to another, and the response, though very rapid, may last for several minutes or even hours. This is possible because the response is directed by both the autonomic nervous system and the endocrine system. The nervous system generally has a very rapid response, which is local and is relatively short-lived because of the rapid metabolism or uptake of the neurotransmitters. The endocrine system is slower to respond but has a much more general response, involving tissues in all parts of the body. The endocrine hormones remain in circulation far longer than the neurotransmitters, because they are much more slowly metabolized.

Applications
The parasympathetic system is designed to ensure that, after eating, the body has the time,

energy, and resources to metabolize food. All of its activities contribute to this activity. The classic example, often used, of a person whose body is being innervated by the parasympathetic system is the post-Thanksgiving dinner repose. The feeling is one of complete relaxation, associated with a sense of heavy limbs. It seems to be difficult to move, let alone to accomplish any chores.

Internally, the blood flow would be directed to the digestive system, where it would be absorbing nutrients to be distributed to the various parts of the body. The salivary glands would be producing large quantities of saliva, and other accessory glands of the digestive system would be producing their respective products that aid in digestion. Also in the digestive system, the muscles of the stomach and small intestine would be very active in an effort to move the food through the stomach at the appropriate rate.

In a parasympathetic mode, the heart rate would be slowed and, as a result, little blood would be circulated to the brain. Because of the decreased blood supply to the brain, it is difficult to concentrate and most persons would have little difficulty falling asleep. Since the brain is not very alert, there is little need for light to enter the eye; the pupils are constricted. For most people, this is not the best time to study or to do any work that is mentally or physically demanding. The body is not at its peak for this type of activity during the parasympathetic response.

Innervation of the sympathetic system leads to physiological responses that are compatible with physical activity. During the sympathetic response, the body is prepared for action. Blood flow is directed away from the digestive system to the skeletal muscle and the brain. Increased blood flow increases the mental alertness and physiological activity of the brain. In addition, the eyes respond by dilating, allowing more light to penetrate, thereby improving visual acuity. A person who is experiencing a sympathetic response is prepared for enhanced concentration: These are ideal times to study and to perform challenging mental tasks. In public speakers, performers, or athletes, the sympathetic response may enhance performance and sharpen skills. In some cases, however, when the response is more extreme, the effect may interfere with performance. For example, when the parasympathetic response is turned off in favor of the sympathetic response, one of the effects is a decrease in saliva, which results in a very dry mouth—so dry as to make speaking difficult.

In humans, the sympathetic response can also be caused by a variety of other factors, such as job-related stress. In lower animals, the sympathetic response is relatively short-lived. The animal encounters the predator, then flees the site or fights the predator. In either case, the experience lasts only a short time; if it is lucky, the animal is free to go about the daily activities that ensure its survival. In humans who encounter job stress, the response may last for the entire day or, in some cases, continue even after leaving the workplace. The consequences are strain on the heart, elevated blood pressure, and the agitation induced by epinephrine or norepinephrine.

The sympathetic response in humans can also be experienced with strenuous physical activity such as jogging, weight training, or swimming. In this case, however, the duration of the response continues only as long as the exercise and is followed physiologically by a period of relaxation. All parts of the human body need to be used to be efficient. Regular exercise accomplishes this goal, and the activity of the heart and the circulatory response to the exercise followed by relaxation is beneficial to a healthy body.

In some cases, the body is suddenly changed from one state (sympathetic) to another (parasympathetic). The result may be discomfort or more serious consequences. One such example is the person who performs strenuous activity too quickly after having eaten a large meal. The parasympathetic system should be digesting food, but because of the strenuous activity, the blood is directed to skeletal muscle. This is likely to leave the person with nausea or stomach cramps.

The sympathetic system is also helpful in regulation of body temperature. Many of the activities of the system, such as muscular contraction and increased metabolism, increase body temperature. If the body experiences a decrease in body temperature of any consequence, there is likely to be a rapid sympathetic response. It is usually adequate to reverse slight changes in temperature. Temperature decreases that are long-term generally will be corrected by release of other hormones.

Context

It was recognized in the seventeenth and eighteenth centuries that the body is equipped with an involuntary nervous system. Ganglia scattered throughout the body were presumed to be little brains, each with its own portion of the body to control. They were all believed to be working in concert to coordinate the body.

Claude Bernard was the first to propose the concept of the internal environment and regulatory mechanisms that keep it constant. It was during the nineteenth century that scientists came to understand the structure and function of the autonomic nervous system. J. N. Langley was the first to describe how the system operates and note the importance of the autonomic nervous system to the healthy body. He demonstrated the sympathetic and parasympathetic systems as antagonistic and coined the term "autonomic."

The autonomic nervous system is well understood, compared to some other aspects of the nervous system. The anatomy has been described, and it releases only three neurotransmitters: acetylcholine, epinephrine, and norepinephrine. Only recently have scientists begun to realize that the system is not as clear-cut and simple as once believed.

Since its discovery, it has been described as the involuntary nervous system. Now, however, investigators have come to realize that people do have voluntary control of some of the organs controlled by the autonomic nervous system. For example, adult humans can consciously control the emptying of the urinary bladder even though the brain receives a signal that it is full and that it is time for the parasympathetic system to empty the bladder. This skill must be learned.

It is also obvious that, with training, certain other parameters of the body once thought to be involuntary can be controlled by the will. This is the basis of biofeedback. In biofeedback, individuals can be taught to control their heart rate, blood pressure, distribution of blood, respiration rate, and other physiologic conditions. Some persons become very adept at controlling these functions. It does, however, take a long time to develop the skills necessary to achieve control of involuntary physiologic activities.

The extent to which a person can successfully achieve control of these functions is not yet clear; much work is being done in this area. This research, and the potential to control human behavior and disease through the use of biofeedback, has revitalized interest in the autonomic nervous system.

Bibliography

Amenta, Francesco, ed. *Aging of the Autonomic Nervous System*. Boca Raton, Fla.: CRC Press, 1993.

Campbell, Neil A. *Biology*. Menlo Park, Calif.: Benjamin/Cummings, 1987. A biology textbook written for college students that is easily understood even by those with less scientific background. Background information describes the general concepts of the nervous system, chemical messengers, and the autonomic nervous system.

Durham, Ross M. *Human Physiology: Functions of the Human Body*. Dubuque, Iowa: Wm. C. Brown, 1989. An easily read textbook of general physiology that is illustrated with clear diagrams and colorful pictures. Understandable even by the novice with little background information.

Gordon, Malcolm S., George A. Bartholomew, et al. *Animal Physiology: Principles and Adaptations*. 4th ed. New York: Macmillan, 1982. The physiology of various types of animals is examined. The role of the endocrine system in lower vertebrates is included in this easily readable text. This book is well written and covers a broader scope than most books.

The Nervous System: Circuits of Communication. New York: Torstar Books, 1985. An informative and well-illustrated book for the layperson. It clearly describes the autonomic nervous system and its role in behavior. Anyone should be able to read it and understand the information. Includes a history of the subject and supportive information relevant to the topic.

Robertson, David, Phillip A. Low, and Ronald J. Polinsky, eds. *Primer on the Autonomic Nervous System*. San Diego, Calif.: Academic Press, 1996.

Vander, Arthur J., James H. Sherman, and Dorothy S. Luciano. *Human Physiology: The Mechanisms of Body Function*. 5th ed. New York: McGraw-Hill, 1990. This general physiology text for the college student can be easily read by the high school student. The chapter on homeostatic mechanisms, which includes a section on receptors, will shed much light on the study of the autonomic nervous system. Well illustrated and contains a wealth of knowledge in an easy-to-understand format. References are provided for further reading.

Annette O'Connor

See also:

AVOIDANCE LEARNING

Type of psychology: Learning
Fields of study: Aversive conditioning; instrumental conditioning; Pavlovian conditioning

Studies of avoidance learning have provided important information about the ways in which organisms respond to aversive stimuli. Although much of the work has been done in animal laboratories, the findings have resulted in broad application to the clinical treatment of anxiety disorders in humans.

Principal terms

ACTIVE AVOIDANCE: an avoidance task that requires some specific response to avert the presentation of an aversive stimulus

AVOIDANCE RESPONSE: a response occurring during a signal that averts the presentation of an aversive stimulus

CONDITIONED STIMULUS (CS): a neutral stimulus that predicts the occurrence of a biologically important stimulus

ESCAPE RESPONSE: a response that terminates an aversive stimulus

FREE OPERANT AVOIDANCE: an avoidance task in which the unconditioned response is predicted by the passage of time rather than by an explicit conditioned response

PASSIVE AVOIDANCE: an avoidance task in which the aversive stimulus can be avoided by simply not performing some response

SHUTTLE BOX: a two-compartment chamber that is used in the study of avoidance learning

TWO-FACTOR THEORY: a theory which holds that avoidance learning involves both Pavlovian and instrumental conditioning

UNCONDITIONED STIMULUS (US): a biologically important stimulus

Overview

Avoidance learning is behavior that reduces or prevents exposure to aversive situations. In a typical laboratory experiment, a rat is placed into one end of a rectangular box that has a metal bar floor. A bell begins to ring; after five seconds, the grid floor is electrified, and the rat experiences an electrical shock. During the next few seconds, the rat tries various behaviors until, finally, it jumps over a small barrier to safety in the other end of the box. The rat is returned to the first chamber, and the process is repeated. After a few such trials, the rat quickly moves to safety when the shock begins. Later, the rat moves to safety as soon as the bell rings, avoiding the shock altogether.

The terminology used to describe avoidance learning is as follows: The aversive event is called the unconditioned stimulus (US). The event that signals the forthcoming US is called the conditioned stimulus (CS). The period of CS presentation before the US begins is the CS-US interval. Once the US begins, the response that leads to safety is the escape response. A response that occurs during the CS-US interval and negates exposure to the aversive event is an avoidance response. There are several categories of avoidance learning.

In passive avoidance, the US can be avoided by passively not engaging in some behavior. For example, if a child touches a hot radiator, future exposures can be avoided simply by not going into that corner of the room.

Shuttle-box avoidance is one of the most common forms of avoidance learning. The apparatus is a two-compartment chamber in which the subject avoids the US by "shuttling" from one side to the other, as described above. In one-way avoidance, each trial begins by placing the rat into the same side of the apparatus, with avoidance (or escape) responses all being in the same direction. In two-way avoidance, the shuttle box is symmetrical, such that the CS and US can be presented in either chamber. After the first presentation of the CS followed by the US, the subject has reached safety by shuttling in one direction into the other chamber. After an appropriate period of time, the next trial begins by presenting the CS and US in the "safe" chamber, and the rat shuttles back in the opposite direction, and so on.

On the surface, these two procedures appear to be essentially identical. In practice, one-way avoidance tends to be easily mastered, whereas two-way avoidance learning is extremely difficult. These differences offer insights into the nature of avoidance learning. The subject does not learn a surgically precise response to the CS. In one-way avoidance, the subject also learns that one location is dangerous and another is safe. Most subjects will perform the response after a few trials even if the CS is not presented. In two-way avoidance, however, there is no safe location. On each trial, the CS is presented and the subject is being asked to return to the same (dangerous) location from which it just escaped. In other words, this task involves a passive avoidance component that interferes with the active avoidance by creating a conflict.

Free operant avoidance (sometimes called Sidman avoidance) does not use an explicit CS; the passage of time is the CS. In a typical setting, the subject is placed into an operant chamber that has a lever. After a few seconds, brief pulses of electric shock are delivered through the grid floor at specified intervals (typically about five seconds apart). These shocks will continue until the lever is pressed, which delays the occurrence of the next shock for some longer period of time (typically about twenty seconds). The free operant procedure is defined by the S-S interval (time between shocks) and the R-S interval (time between a response and the next shock). Subjects can avoid the US by pressing the lever at least once each twenty seconds, but typical subjects respond two to three times faster than the rate required by the R-S interval.

Avoidance learning seems straightforward enough but presents the question of how subjects, especially simple organisms such as rats or earthworms, can base their behavior on some event that is going to take place in the future. Learning theorists solved the problem of ongoing motivation by developing the two-factor theory of avoidance learning. The two factors are classical conditioning of fear and instrumental learning of responses that reduce the fear. Initially, the subject has no way of knowing the requirements of the task. The CS is followed by the US, and the subject responds in various ways until it successfully escapes. Buried within this experience, however, are the elements of classical conditioning. Each pairing of the CS and US gives the CS the ability to elicit fear. After a few pairings, the subject does not have to look into the future for some reason to behave: The CS is itself aversive. Responses that terminate the CS are rewarding because they reduce fear, in the same way that responses the terminate the US are rewarding because they reduce discomfort. According to this theory, avoidance learning is, in some sense, learning to perform escape responses to reduce a learned fear.

Applications

Avoidance learning is interesting in its own right, but it also contributes to a better understanding of the human condition. Aversive situations—hot stoves, small places, big places, big dogs, elevators, reprimands, snakes, failing grades, and unrequited love, to name a few—are a fact of life. As a result, much of human behavior is directed toward the escape from or avoidance of aversive consequences. Normally, this is an efficient process. In some cases, however, the individual dedicates more and more energy to avoidance behavior, and it begins to interfere with other activities.

Phobias are irrational fears of everyday objects or situations (for example, elevators or examinations). Phobic individuals avoid contact with the feared object, sometimes so successfully that the problem goes unrecognized by other people, or even by the affected individual. Some everyday situations, however, are impossible to avoid, and the individual suffers intense distress from both actual exposure and fear of exposure. The initial cause of the fear may remain a mystery. Some aversive consequence (perhaps a loud noise or a menacing individual) may have occurred in the presence of an everyday object, which then become a CS that predicts aversive consequences. The seed of fear has been planted, and avoidance behavior conserves that fear while imagined consequences nurture it.

Fortunately, it is not necessary for one to know the initial cause of the phobia to treat it. The most successful treatment, called systematic desensitization, uses the laws of classical conditioning to reverse the fear. Consider, for example, a person who fears elevators. The therapist first trains the individual to relax in a quiet setting. Then, the subject is asked to think about some remote example of the feared object, perhaps looking down the street at a tall building. If relaxation continues, the subject is asked to imagine standing in front of the building. The therapist works carefully and progressively to guide the subject through imagery that is closer and closer to the feared object, all the while maintaining relaxation. After a few sessions, the individual may be able to stand in the hallway by an elevator while maintaining relaxation. After a few more sessions, the individual may be able to ride the elevator, and the irrational fear dissolves.

The most common problem involving learned fear is termed vague anxiety. The individual cannot identify a specific fear, but a disturbing sense of foreboding permeates the day's activities. The cause of this vague anxiety may be some specific fear of an aversive consequence in the workplace or the home that has not been fully recognized by the individual. While it may seem odd that a source of debilitating fear might not be recognized, it must be kept in mind that one effective avoidance response is to avoid thinking about the disturbing problem. Vague anxieties may also involve the misinterpretation of bodily symptoms of fear. For example, muscle tension caused by poor posture at a work station may be misinterpreted as anxiety. In treating these cases, the therapist trains the individual to recognize the early stages of anxiety and to engage in relaxation techniques to counter these feelings.

A particularly debilitating form of vague anxiety is agoraphobia, which literally means "fear of the marketplace." This condition may begin as a specific phobia (for example, fear of elevators). This fear generalizes to buildings that may contain elevators, streets that may go near these buildings, neighborhoods that these streets lie within, and so on. This gradually restricts the range of activities until the individual may be too fearful even to leave the home. This disorder is more difficult to treat than simple phobias but still responds to many of the same treatment strategies. Unfortunately, the nature of the disorder makes it unlikely that the individual will seek help, because therapists are more likely to be found in the "market-place" than in one's home.

To summarize, avoidance learning can be viewed in the much larger context of the response of humans to adversity. In the normal course of events, a person comes into contact with a wide range of aversive stimuli, ranging from the purely physical to complex social interactions. An individual learns to fear these stimuli and to fear the stimuli with which they are associated. In some cases, these associated stimuli are everyday objects or situations, and the fear is deemed by others to be irrational.

The all-too-common response to irrational fears is to treat them as inappropriate behaviors. Children may taunt individuals who have such fears, employers may suspect them, casual acquaintances may evade them, and family members may punish them. All these approaches heighten the fears and anxieties to make a bad situation worse.

The study of avoidance learning has provided a deeper understanding of the nature of these disorders. Most fears are established through classical conditioning. Specific responses that reduce these fears are acquired and strengthened as avoidance responses; however, the fears may be reduced in ways that do nothing to alleviate the actual problem. Furthermore, successful avoidance responses may interfere with other behaviors.

The foundation for the successful treatment of these disorders is the application of the laws of avoidance learning. Therapists use counter-conditioning techniques to replace fears with more positive feelings. They replace ineffective avoidance responses that conserve fear with responses that actually reduce the aversive situation. In most cases, the application of this knowledge can eliminate the fears and return the individual to more comfortable and productive activities.

Context

Psychologists began to study avoidance learning in the early 1900's as part of a more general effort to define the laws of learning. Ivan Pavlov, a Russian physiologist, had already described many of the laws of association that are now known as Pavlovian, or classical, conditioning. The important distinction of classical conditioning is that the subject has no ability to control the stimuli, but simply learns the association between the stimuli. American psychologists, under the guidance of Edward L. Thorndike, took a more interactive approach and concentrated most of their efforts on Thorndikian, or instrumental, conditioning. In instrumental conditioning, the subject can learn to manipulate and control certain aspects of the environment. Studies of the aversive control of behavior progressed naturally from escape learning to avoidance learning.

Some learning theorists had difficulty with avoidance behavior, especially in simple organisms, because there was an implication that the behavior was based on purely cognitive events such as expectancies. This dilemma was solved by O. Hobart Mowrer, who introduced the two-factor theory of avoidance learning in 1939. According to this theory, avoidance responses were reinforced directly by the reduction of classically conditioned fear. In the 1960's, Richard Solomon and his students provided direct support for this theory by showing that classically conditioned stimuli could directly influence an instrumental avoidance response. In particular, a stimulus that had been used as a Pavlovian CS to predict shock increased the rate of a free operant avoidance response. By contrast, a stimulus that had been explicitly unpaired with shock—a safety signal—reduced the rate of avoidance responding. Neither of these stimuli had ever been experienced during the free operant task, so the clear interpretation was that the changes in behavior were the result of conditioned fear and conditioned safety, respectively.

Studies of avoidance learning and, especially, the two-factor theory caused a tremendous increase in the interest of American psychologists in Pavlovian conditioning. The notion that fears can be learned through direct association of stimuli in the environment and that these fears can then influence a person's interactions with the environment has become the cornerstone for understanding many forms of clinical disorders. As experimental psychologists described the laws that apply to aversively controlled behavior, clinicians began to find that the application of these principles improved their ability to treat patients suffering from phobias, anxiety disorders, and even depression.

Bibliography

Ferrari, Joseph R., et al. *Procrastination and Task Avoidance: Theory, Research, and Treatment.* New York: Plenum Press, 1995.

Flaherty, Charles F. *Animal Learning and Cognition.* New York: Alfred A. Knopf, 1985. Provides a thorough, clearly written review of the experimental and theoretical foundations of learning theory. Contains references to and discussions of all major contributions to the study of avoidance learning.

Hamilton, Leonard W., and C. Robin Timmons. *Principles of Behavioral Pharmacology.* Englewood Cliffs, N.J.: Prentice-Hall, 1990. Although the emphasis of this textbook is on pharmacology, three chapters are devoted to the effects of aversive control of behavior. Topics include anxiety, fear, pain, and depression.

Pavlov, Ivan P. *Conditioned Reflexes.* London: Oxford University Press, 1927. This translation of Pavlov's work has become a classic in psychology. Early chapters clearly outline the principles of classical conditioning; later chapters go into considerable detail.

Seligman, Martin E. P. *Helplessness: On Depression, Development, and Death.* San Francisco: W. H. Freeman, 1975. An easy-to-read account of the role of aversive conditioning in the cause and treatment of clinical disorders in humans.

Solomon, Richard L. "The Opponent-Process Theory of Acquired Motivation: The Costs of Pleasure and the Benefits of Pain." *American Psychologist* 35 (1980): 691-712. Provides an excellent summary of opponent-process theory, which is a modern extension of the two-process theory of avoidance learning. Includes speculation on a variety of disorders, including addictive behaviors.

Leonard W. Hamilton

See also:

BEHAVIORISM

Type of psychology: Origin and definition of psychology
Fields of study: Experimental methodologies; instrumental conditioning

Behaviorism rejects the idea that psychology should be the study of conscious experience or mental processes, proposing instead that its proper subject matter is the objective and observable behavior of human and animal life. Behaviorists believe that the behavior of an organism is determined by its interactions with observable forces in its environment.

Principal terms

BEHAVIOROLOGY: the science that treats the study of behavior from a strict selectionist philosophy, or what is called radical behaviorism

CONTINGENCY: a relationship between a response and its consequence or between two stimuli; sometimes considered a dependency

ENVIRONMENT: the context or conditions in which behaviors take place

OPERANT: a behavior whose frequency can be altered by changing its consequences; usually, a striated-muscle response controlled by the "voluntary" nervous system

PSYCHOLOGICAL SYSTEM: a particular approach that states what psychology should be and how it should explain psychological issues

PUNISHMENT: a procedure that leads to a reduction in the frequency of a behavior

REINFORCER: a stimulus or event that, when delivered contingently upon a response, will increase the probability of the recurrence of that response

RESPONDENT: a behavior that is elicited by an antecedent stimulus; usually, a smooth-muscle or glandular response controlled by the "involuntary" nervous system

Overview

Behaviorism is a philosophical point of view concerning the scientific study of human and other animal behavior. It is not the science of behavior but the philosophical underpinnings of that science. Behaviorism arose as a purely American system in reaction to other, primarily German, approaches to the study of psychological phenomena. Behaviorism begins with the assumption that the objective and observable behavior of all animal life is the proper subject matter of psychology. Behaviorists resist the idea that psychology should be the study of conscious experience or mental processes. They argue that the factors that establish and control behavior are found in the environment, not inside the organism. Thus, behavior is considered a product of the biological organism's interaction with events in the environment that literally select and "shape" individual behavior.

According to behaviorists, the way to study behavior is to manipulate objects and events in the environment and systematically observe changes in behavior in order to establish functional relationships. The explanation, or understanding, of observed behavior is simply a statement of those functional relations that exist between behavior and the manipulated environmental factors. That is, behavior is not regarded as caused by some unseen forces that allegedly exist in the mind but, rather, is viewed as a result of environment-behavior interaction. At its inception, this concept was a dramatic reconsideration of what psychologists should study. The philosophy of behaviorism has changed from the days of its origin, and it can no longer be treated as a single system. This essay broadly defines behaviorism with a bias toward the discipline known as the experimental analysis of behavior. This particular behavioral approach has had the most influence on psychology in general.

Behaviorists say that day-to-day behavior depends on its consequences, meaning that the consequences of an occurrence of a behavior will have profound effects on the subsequent probability of that behavior. For example, if a person touches a hot stove, the painful consequences of that action will reduce that person's "stove-touching behavior" in the future. The probability of the person's future stove-touching behavior has been influenced by the consequences of his or her experience. Conversely, a person who receives a perfect score on a test after studying is more likely to study before a test in the future. This may appear to be common sense. Good things following a behavior increase the future likelihood of that behavior, and bad things following a behavior reduce the future likelihood of that behavior.

Behaviorism is only one discipline within psychology; psychologists treat the source and control of behavior by means of many different systems and schools of thought. For example, the branch of psychology known as cognitive psychology is characterized not by a particular philosophy or set of principles but by a willingness to attempt to explain behavior by reference to unobserved mental processes. Behaviorism, in contrast, considers such an approach simply an appeal to "explanatory fiction" and rejects the entire idea. Behaviorists assume that behavior is lawful, determined, predictable, and objectively analyzable. Further, they believe that objective—not interpretive or speculative—behavior analysis will eventually explain behavior in terms of the functional relationships that exist between behavior and the environment. No intervening hypothetical variables such as a mind, a will, expectations, thoughts, or personalities are considered necessary. Behavior, for behaviorists, can be predicted and controlled, and therefore explained, by manipulation of and reference to environmental events. Explanations at other levels of analysis or speculation are considered unnecessary, diversionary, and wrong.

It does not really help a teacher or a parent, for example, to be told that a child has a poor "self-concept" or a "bad attitude." Behaviorists consider these terms as mere labels for certain observed behaviors, not explanations for those behaviors. The teacher and parent need to know which events (variables) in the environment can be manipulated so that the child becomes skillful and competent and obtains many positive consequences for behaving appropriately. Teachers and parents cannot read "minds" or deal with internal "attitudes," but they can attend to overt behaviors and the consequences that follow those behaviors. A behaviorist attributes inappropriate behavior to the individual's being reinforced for the wrong kinds of activities and not sufficiently reinforced for the right kinds. For example, a child may "act out" in school not because of a bad attitude but because other students praise or in some other way positively reinforce the acting out. In addition, the teacher may not positively reinforce good behavior often enough. The point is that the explanation for the behavior, according to the behaviorist, does not lie inside the child but in events in the environment.

Behaviorists advocate an experimental approach to behavior in the sense that objective data are carefully gathered, manipulations of response consequences are made, and subsequent changes in the behavior are again carefully observed. When such a series of events actually takes place, the behavior is said to be caused by, and under the control of, the contingencies in the environment that were manipulated, rather than by some hypothetical inner process or imagined internal thing such as an attitude. For example, a child asking for water does not ask because of thirst and an expectation that water will follow, but because asking has been followed by water on earlier occasions. Thus, it is the history of reinforcement that actually controls the asking response, not something unseen and only supposed to exist inside the child's mind—not even thirst.

A behavioral procedure is replicable in that if the conditions are stable it will result in the same behavioral outcome every time. Such controlled repeatability does not happen when interpretations or intuitions are made regarding the basic causes of behavior. A behavioral approach is based upon the fact that behavior is adaptive as a product of altering the consequences of the behavior.

Very few behaviors of much interest to behaviorists are "hard-wired" into the organism to such an extent that they cannot be altered by changing their consequences. Most physiological activity and behaviors called instincts are left for others (physiologists and ethologists) to understand. It is the systematic study of the relationship between antecedent and consequent environmental events *and* behavior that is the professional activity of interest to behaviorists. The genetics and neurochemistry of the organism are for other disciplines to study. Behaviorists consider behavior, by itself, an adequate problem for focused research. Nonbehavioral psychologists may observe behavior, but they are prone to attribute what they see to something they cannot see, such as cognition; behaviorists attribute what they see to things they can see—events in the environment.

Applications

Behaviorism, as a systematic and coherent approach to studying and modifying behavior, is not very old. The manipulation of consequences to alter human behavior, however, is probably as old as humankind. Certainly any grandmother knows that when she gives a child a cookie for saying "please," the child is much more likely to say "please" the next time. She also knows that a child who was harmed by some action avoids that behavior in the future. Her grandparents knew it as well. The use of rewards, or reinforcers, to increase the probability of the behavior's occurrence is well known. Dogs that become more obedient after being petted for coming when called have been reinforced by the petting. Children who are praised for doing good are more likely to do good in the future. Employees who receive fair pay and appreciation for a job well done will probably remain at that job and continue to do it well. If, however, a person is cursed, fined, spanked, or shocked for doing something, that person will probably do that thing much less often. Behavior is therefore a function of its consequences.

The behavioral consequence of an action cannot be accurately labeled as a reinforcer or a punisher until the behavioral effects of the consequating event are observed. One might think that some action is aversive or pleasant and will be suitable punishment or reinforcement, but that does not mean that everyone else will agree. Only after the change in behavior frequency is observed can the consequence be correctly labeled. A cow that receives a strong electric shock upon touching a wire with her nose does not often do that again. Such treatment is called punishment because of its effects on behavior, not because of the use of the electric shock. Punishment is the procedure of reducing the probability of a behavior by using contingent consequences. One cannot always predict beforehand what will be a reinforcer and what will be a punisher. For example, if an electric shock of a certain type and intensity is delivered directly to a particular area of the brain in humans, and many other animals as well, the individual human reports a pleasant sensation, and the animals will work to receive further shocks. The point is that the behavior-changing effects are what is important, not the stimulus. Thus, electric shock can either decrease behaviors and act as punishment or increase behaviors and act as reinforcement.

The principles of behavior analysis developed by behaviorists have been applied in almost all areas of human activity. Such applications have included individual therapy, training in business and industry, educational programming, experimental psychopharmacology, parenting, developmental disabilities, behavioral medicine, and pain management, to name only a few. Every activity involving the behavior of organisms can be approached by behavioral means. This is one of the features of behaviorism that sets it apart from most other schools of psychology. It is a practical and useful approach that has generated an extremely helpful technology of behavior management. Even such private events as thinking, feeling, perceiving, and reasoning have been, when these activities have been behaviorally defined, subjected to behavioral analysis and manipulation. They are not considered causes of behavior but instead are treated as, and considered to be, concomitants to operant and respondent behavior and are therefore subject to analysis.

Certain fundamental laws of learning that govern behavior are common to many different species of animals. In particular, the principles of reinforcement and punishment, stimulus control, and shaping, as well as many others, apply to human beings, rats, dogs, fish, birds, and many other creatures. These laws, having been worked out primarily by behaviorists in laboratories, apply to the prediction and control of behavior regardless of the species of the behaving organism. Some animals, such as humans, exhibit much more complicated behavior than others. All animals, however, share many basic mechanisms of selective adaptation.

Behavioral principles are often worked out in the laboratory with nonhuman species as subjects and then tested and used with humans in "real-world" situations. This approach of simplifying things in the laboratory first and then making applications to complex situations is a characteristic of the scientific method. Because behavior is the subject matter of behavioral investigation, the behaving animal species is not critical. A comparable situation is employed in other sciences, in which models or simple devices are used in controlled tests of predictions or theories.

Context

Behaviorism as a way of considering psychological problems began as an alternative to the prominent German schools of structuralism and Gestalt psychology and to Sigmund Freud's psychoanalysis. It was developed as a school of psychology in the early years of this century by John B. Watson. In 1903, Watson received the first doctorate in psychology, awarded by the University of Chicago. In 1913, he wrote the behaviorists' manifesto, "Psychology as the Behaviorist Views It." It appeared to Watson that, if psychology were ever to become a "real" science, there needed to be some systematic application of the scientific method to behavior. Watson set out to develop an appropriate basic philosophy and an appropriate methodology. He began by saying that overt, objectively defined behavior was the subject matter of psychological inquiry and that the method of psychological analysis was to be objective observation. In other words, a behavioral scientist should report only what was actually observed and should not make inferences, or guesses, about the possibility of other events occurring at other levels. For example, most psychologists were (and many still are) interested in behavior only as evidence of some underlying process, often called the "mind." Such mentalism was to play no part in Watson's behaviorism.

Watson's behaviorism was of the stimulus-response type originally developed in Russia by Ivan Pavlov. Watson believed that the concept of the reflex (a stimulus eliciting a response) was the basis of all psychological phenomena; the reflex was his behavioral unit. Subsequent behaviorists, especially B. F. Skinner, viewed action on a larger scale, not merely the reflex, as the correct subject matter of psychology. Skinner separated behavior into two categories: operants, defined as skeletal muscle actions that operate upon the environment; and respondents, which are smooth-muscle or glandular responses elicited by some prior stimulus. Operants, which are controlled by the consequences they generate, are measured in terms of instances per unit time—that is, rate. Respondents, or reflexes, as Pavlov showed with salivating dogs, are elicited by a stimulus and measured in terms of latency and magnitude. Each of these two categories of behavior has its own set of experimental procedures and findings.

From the 1930's through the 1950's, behaviorism was the prevailing system of psychology. Among the major proponents of the behavioral approach, after Watson, were Edward Tolman, Edwin Guthrie, Clark Hull, and Skinner. Skinner became the most creative, active, and eloquent spokesperson for a behavioristic psychology that he called the experimental analysis of behavior. His philosophical position, known as radical behaviorism, held that the best way to study and understand behavior is to stop making inferences about possible inner causes (the mind) and to concentrate on the environment as the source of behavioral selection. For example, instead of attributing an instance of behavior to something called a "self-concept," Skinner argues that it is infinitely better to investigate which environmental variables could be involved in the production and management of such behavior. If "self-concept" behavior can be modified by environmental events, the supposition of an internal self-concept as a driving force is unnecessary. The behavior is the self-concept; it is not the manifestation of an internal nonbehavioral thing. The label for a behavior that anyone could observe is not to be taken as the cause of the behavior. Psychologists, it has been argued, will give a name to a behavior and then try to explain the behavior simply by referring to the name. (They say that a person exhibits autistic behavior and then say that the person acts that way because he has autism.)

As an objective orientation toward psychology and psychological issues, behaviorism has lost much of its standing in professional psychology. The division (number 25) of the American Psychological Association (APA) devoted to a behavioristic approach is a minority of the membership. It sometimes seems that psychology and behaviorology are two different disciplines and that they are not compatible in their philosophies, objectives, or methods. Nevertheless, the application of behavioral principles, research from a behavioral standpoint, commitment to a behavioral philosophy, and the promotion of behavioral organizations outside the APA are growing.

Psychology as an important field of study evolved from many sources, including theology, biology, and philosophy. The different orientations of these fields have affected, even confused, the development and maturation of psychology as a science. As a result, there are fads and cycles, and there has always been disagreement among psychologists regarding what the subject matter and methodology of psychology should be. Psychology has the complicated task of understanding behavior and devising ways of predicting, explaining, and controlling it. As a result of this complex assignment and psychology's divergent roots, there have been many suggestions about what psychology should do and how it should do it. Behaviorism is one of those suggestions.

Bibliography

Boakes, Robert A. *From Darwin to Behaviorism.* New York: Cambridge University Press, 1984. The evolution of the scientific consideration of the minds of animals, including man, is described, along with a look at the people involved.

Chance, Paul. *Learning and Behavior.* 2d ed. Belmont, Calif.: Wadsworth, 1988. Chance defines and explains the basic principles of an experimental analysis of behavior in a very understandable way.

Ishaq, Waris, ed. *Human Behavior in Today's World.* New York: Praeger, 1991. Chapters written by different behaviorists indicate how a behavioral analysis is generated, what some basic principles are, and how they can be applied to cultural and social, as well as individual, actions.

Lee, Vicki L. *Beyond Behaviorism.* Hillsdale, N.J.: Lawrence Erlbaum, 1988. This book describes the differences between the positions of Watson and other "behaviorists," as well as the radical behaviorism of B. F. Skinner.

Rachlin, Howard. *Introduction to Modern Behaviorism.* 2d ed. San Francisco: W. H. Freeman, 1976. This dated but excellent text reviews the development of behavioral thinking and reviews how behaviorism is translated into action.

Skinner, B. F. *About Behaviorism.* New York: Alfred A. Knopf, 1974. This book is Skinner's attempt to explain his philosophy of behaviorism in terms of questions and behavioral answers.

_____. *Science and Human Behavior.* New York: Macmillan, 1953. This early work sets forth the basics of radical behaviorism and discusses its application to many kinds of behavioral questions.

Staddon, John. *Behaviorism: Mind, Mechanism, and Society.* London: Duckworth, 1993.

Todd, James T., and Edward K. Morris, eds. *Modern Perspectives on B. F. Skinner and Contemporary Behaviorism.* Foreword by Ernest R. Hilgard. Westport, Conn.: Greenwood Press, 1995.

Watson, John Broadus. *Behaviorism.* New York: W. W. Norton, 1925. This is the ultimate statement of behaviorism as intended and presented by the father of this approach to psychology.

Carl D. Cheney

See also:

Animal Experimentation, 59; Cognitive Behavior Therapy, 128; Instrumental Conditioning: Acquisition and Extinction, 309; Learning, 364; Learning: Generalization and Discrimination, 370; Pavlovian Conditioning, 433; Radical Behaviorism: B. F. Skinner, 501; Social Learning: Albert Bandura, 559.

Bipolar Disorder

Type of psychology: Psychopathology
Field of study: Depression

Knowledge about bipolar disorder, a cyclical mood disorder that includes shifts from mania to depression and back to normal mood, has grown extensively. Advanced neurobiological research and assessment techniques have shown the biochemical origins and the genetic element of this disorder; stress also may play a role in precipitating recurrence of episodes. The main treatment interventions include lithium and psychotherapy.

Principal terms

BREAKTHROUGH EPISODE: a relapse of either hypomania, mania, or depression in a client with bipolar disorder who has been relatively symptom-free

CYCLOTHYMIA: a milder version of a cyclical mood disorder in which mood swings can occur but are not as intense as in bipolar disorder

DEXAMETHASONE SUPPRESSION TEST (DST): a test of cortisol hypersecretion that diagnoses depression in many individuals

GENETIC MARKER: a particular gene or set of genes that investigators are attempting to locate which might account for the inheritance of a predisposition to bipolar illness

LITHIUM CARBONATE: an alkaline compound that modulates the intensity of mood swings and is particularly effective in the dampening of symptoms of manic excitability

MANIA: a phase of bipolar disorder in which the mood is one of elation, euphoria, or irritability; a disorder in which manic symptoms occur and then are followed by a return to normal mood state

MELATONIN: a hormone produced in the brain that increases in the dark winter months; people with this condition are diagnosed as having seasonal affective disorder (SAD), a form of cyclical depression

SEASONAL AFFECTIVE DISORDER (SAD): a form of bipolar illness that is associated with darkness and melatonin excess

TOXICITY: potential poisonous effects of medication, such as lithium on the kidneys, necessitating the monitoring of medication levels in the blood

Overview

Bipolar affective disorder, or bipolar disorder (also called manic-depressive disorder), has been identified as a major psychiatric disorder that is characterized by dramatic mood and behavior changes. These changes, ranging from episodes of high euphoric moods to deep depressions, with accompanying behavioral and personality changes, are devastating to the victims of the disorder and perplexing to the loved ones of those affected. Clinical psychiatry has been effective in providing biochemical intervention in the form of lithium carbonate to stabilize or modulate the ups and downs of this illness; however, lithium treatment has only been effective for approximately 70 percent of those administered the compound. One medication, Depocate, is showing promise in helping some people with the disorder who were formerly referred to as lithium nonresponders. Psychotherapy, either for the individual or in the form of support groups such as the Manic Depressive Association, is seen by most practitioners as a necessary adjunct or in some cases a primary part of treatment.

Bipolar disorder has four subcategories. They are "bipolar, depressed," in which the moods cycle from normal to depressed; "bipolar, manic," in which moods cycle from normal to manic but there has been at least one episode of depression; "bipolar, mixed," in which the mood fluctuations cover all three phases (depressed, normal, and manic); and "seasonal affective disorder" (SAD), in which mood changes are thought to be triggered by a lack of sunlight and an increase in the hormone melatonin. Two associated categories are related to bipolar disorder. The first one is "cyclothymia," in which the mood swings and characteristic symptoms are less intense than in the full bipolar condition. In addition, there is a category called "bipolar disorder, not otherwise specified," which means that the symptom presentation differs from any of the other described categories but the cyclical nature of the mood changes is present. Bipolar disorder usually first manifests itself in early adulthood and is more common in single and divorced people. Bipolar disorder is also believed to be more prevalent in the homeless population than in the general population. The factor of increased stress in the environment of the homeless is no doubt a critical component in the reported higher rates.

The initial episode of bipolar disorder is typically one of mania or elation, although in some people a depressive episode may signal the beginning of the disorder. Episodes of bipolar disorder can recur rapidly—within hours or days—or may have a much slower recurrence rate, even of years. The duration of each episode, whether it is depression or mania, varies widely across individuals but normally remains fairly consistent for each individual. Manic episodes often have a shorter duration than the depressive episodes. Bipolar disorder must be differentiated from depressive disorders, which include major depression (unipolar depression) and dysthymia, a milder but chronic form of depression. It is also differentiated from mania, a mood disorder in which manic episodes are interspersed between normal mood functioning.

Biological scientists have attempted to locate genetic markers for the disorder. Their effort has been based on the observation that the disorder often affects several members of a given family. This was the goal when Janice Egeland published the findings of her study of the Old Order Amish sect of Lancaster County, Pennsylvania, in 1983. The Old Order Amish provided a relatively intact bloodline and were considered an ideal homogeneous population for the investigation of the potential genetic key to bipolar disorder. The Amish, a simple people, do not use electricity, do not use drugs or alcohol, and do not condone war or crime. Therefore, the generations of the original forebears had been largely preserved. The Amish were familiar with mood disorder (and with suicide associated with it) that appeared to affect only certain families and their offspring. As a result, they were eager to have Egeland help them find out about the disease they said "is in the blood."

Although Egeland had thought she could eventually locate a gene for bipolar disorder on the short arm of chromosome 11, subsequent analyses of the data indicated that the answer may be more complex. Some molecular biologists believe that more than one gene is responsible for transmission of the illness, and others believe the answer to be far more complicated. A diathesis-stress model has been proposed for some psychosomatic disorders such as hypertension and ulcers; this interactive model may also explain why some people develop bipolar disorder in early adulthood and others do not. In this model, a genetic or biochemical predisposition toward the disorder (the bipolar diathesis) may lie dormant until stress from puberty, adulthood, or physical or psychological trauma triggers the emergence of the illness.

A number of mediating factors, such as social support, coping skills, and regular sleep, exercise, and nutritional habits, may serve as buffers to protect a person against development of the disorder. Much more work is needed to prove or disprove these theories, although they offer clues for treatment. Prevalence rates of bipolar disorder run at about 1 percent (0.4 to 1.2) of the American population. The disorder is divided fairly equally along the gender dimension. As many as 15 percent of those with the illness have committed suicide. This frightening reality makes early intervention, relapse prevention, and treatment of the disorder necessary to prevent such a tragic outcome.

Many brilliant and successful people have reportedly suffered from bipolar disorder and have been able to function successfully with competent and responsible treatment. The book *The Key to Genius: Manic-Depression and the Creative Life* (1988), written by D. J. Hershman and Julian Lieb, provides an overview of the creativity and productivity of some people with the disorder. Some people who have taken lithium for bipolar disorder, in fact, have complained that it robs them of their energy and creativity and said that they actually miss the energy associated with manic phases of the illness. This perceived loss, some of it realistic, can be a factor in relapse associated with lithium noncompliance.

Local mental health associations are able to recommend psychiatric treatment by board-certified psychiatrists and licensed psychologists who specialize in the treatment of mood disorders. Often, temporary hospitalization is necessary for complete diagnostic assessment, initial mood stabilization and intensive treatment, medication adjustment, or monitoring an individual who feels suicidal.

Applications

The heritability of the cyclical mood disorders has led to the search for biochemical or genetic markers. Modern brain imaging techniques such as the positron emission tomography (PET) scan have been utilized to help solve the biochemical underpinnings of the disorder. Electroencephalograms (EEGs), used to study brain-wave functioning, have been instrumental in tracking the sleep disturbance and insomnia that often precede an episode of the disorder. John Hanley, in 1989, wrote that the EEG has been grossly underutilized as a potential tool for solving some of the mysteries of major psychiatric disorders, including bipolar disorder and schizophrenia.

Medications and diagnostic techniques have been developed to aid in correcting the biochemical imbalance thought to be part of the illness. Lithium carbonate is usually effective for about 70 percent of those who take it. Depocate, a newer medication, is under trial to help those whom lithium is unable to help. A diagnostic test called the dexamethasone suppression test (DST) was developed to determine which individuals suffer from "biological" depression in both unipolar depression and bipolar depression. The DST is a diagnostic test measuring cortisol hypersecretion that is thought to be diagnostic of depression in many individuals. Authors Frederick Goodwin and Kay Jamison wrote extensively about the DST and its pattern of results in individuals with bipolar disorder in their 1990 book *Manic-Depressive Illness*. They report that results of this test have been studied extensively in individuals with bipolar mood disorder.

There is apparently a wide range of abnormal DST results in clients with bipolar disorder during depressed phases; between 25 and 60 percent show abnormal DST results. Goodwin and Jamison summarize findings of those investigators who have found that the abnormal DST findings return to normal during manic or hypomanic episodes. They mention that several confounding variables can interfere with the results of the test.

One of the most intriguing treatments of a major mood disorder involves the use of "light therapy" for the treatment of one of the subcategories of bipolar disorder, seasonal affective disorder (SAD). Exposure to increased full-spectrum light, for two to three hours a day, is thought to aid the brain's metabolism of the hormone melatonin and thus prevent or alleviate episodes of depression associated with melatonin excess. SAD is thought to be more prevalent in females and in populations residing in high-latitude countries where there is a longer period of darkness in winter months.

Many individuals well known to the public have suffered from bipolar disorder; among them is actress Patty Duke, who wrote a book about her experiences with the illness in a book entitled *Call Me Anna: The Autobiography of Patty Duke* (1987). Political activist Abbie Hoffman, who died in 1989, also suffered from the disorder. Hoffman had been a "Yippie" and was one of the so-called Chicago Seven, a group of radical activists who attempted to disrupt the Democratic National Convention in 1968. He had been familiar with discrimination as a Jewish youth reared in a New York suburb; as a result, he made it his cause to fight against discrimination and racial oppression. This cause took him into the realm of political activism. Hoffman experienced legal problems associated with drug possession and use, however, and chose to go into hiding for an extended period of his life. He was eventually diagnosed with bipolar disorder, late in his life, and was treated with lithium. He reportedly wrote to his relatives of the exhaustion caused by the disorder shortly before he committed suicide from a Phenobarbital overdose. Although Hoffman had long been under stress from financial problems, his suicide was a shock to a public that had known him as a fighter. Even some of those people closest to him could not believe that he had chosen to take his own life. This example clearly shows the devastating toll the disorder can impose on those afflicted with it. Some believe that the illness puts people on an "emotional roller coaster" in which their ups and downs are so severe that resulting behavior can have its own disastrous consequences. For example, people suffering from episodes of mania sometimes use drugs, alcohol, money, or sex to excess, then later have to deal with an additional set of problems and trauma brought about by their behavioral excess and impulsivity.

Support groups such as the Manic Depressive Association have provided a way for people to share the pain as well as triumph over the illness. Many people have found comfort in knowing that there are others who have suffered from the mood shifts, and they can draw strength from one another. Family members and friends can be the strongest supporters and advocates for those who have bipolar disorder or other mood disorders. Many patients have credited their families' constant, uncritical support, in addition to competent treatment including psychotherapy and lithium, with pulling them through the devastating effects of the illness.

Context

The characteristic pattern of cyclical mood swings and resultant shifts in personality and behavior caused by bipolar disorder (manic-depressive disorder) have been written about for more than two thousand years. Emil Kraepelin is credited with providing the world with one of the first clinical descriptions of the disorder in a 1921 monograph that included "manic depressive insanity."

Goodwin and Jamison cover what they term the "evolution of the bipolar-unipolar concept" in a thorough chapter in their *Manic-Depressive Illness*. The focus of the early Greeks on the biological imbalance presumed to underlie bipolar disorder is remarkably in tune with theoretical models of today. French scientists are credited with recognizing that mania and depression can be two sides of the same disorder; the "circular disorder" was discussed by French scientists in the nineteenth century. The distinction between unipolar and bipolar disorder has become more convincing over time, especially when one reviews clinical case histories that differentiate the two disorders. Goodwin and Jamison summarize the importance of the classification of unipolar and bipolar disorder as separate illnesses. They argue that this classification, in the *Diagnostic and Statistical Manual of Mental Disorders* (rev. 3d ed., 1987, DSM-III-R, the diagnostic manual of the American Psychiatric Association), has led to important research that helped uncover key information regarding genetic, biochemical, clinical, and medical (pharmaceutical) components of the major mood disorders.

Various differences in incidence (or rate of occurrence) of bipolar disorder have been noted for some time. In the early 1900's, Kraepelin reported higher rates of manic and depressive illness in people from Java and Singapore when compared to people of European descent. In a study by B. E. Jones et al., published in 1983, the authors reported that poor Hispanics in the city of New York had a prevalence rate of bipolar disorder that was more than three times that of the overall United States population. An earlier (1981) study by the same authors that investigated the prevalence rate of the disorder in poor urban blacks included findings that their rate was 15 percent. Research is needed that can separate the potential influence of poverty, stress, substance abuse, and urban environment from racial factors related to predisposition for the disorder. Chinese researchers report a prevalance of 2 to 3 percent for mood disorders; 1.2 percent had been diagnosed as having bipolar disorder. This figure corresponds to the 0.4 to 1.2 percent prevalence rate for the illness in the United States cited in DSM-III-R.

Cross-cultural studies of bipolar disorder are relatively rare, however, as most research on the disorder has been carried out in modernized, Western countries. Therefore, it becomes difficult to understand clearly the impact of cultural variables as they interact with individual genetic or psychological predispositions to bipolar disorder. Clearly, more research into these variables and into the complex picture of genetic markers and predisposition for bipolar disorder is desperately needed if scientists are to understand the complexity of interactive forces associated with the illness.

Bibliography
Basco, Monica Ramirez, and A. John Rush. *Cognitive-Behavioral Therapy for Bipolar Disorder*. Foreword by Robert M. Post. New York: Guilford Press, 1996.

Bauer, Mark S., and Linda McBride. *Structured Group Psychotherapy for Bipolar Disorder: The Life Goals Program*. New York: Springer Publishing, 1996.

Fieve, Ronald R. *Moodswing: The Third Revolution in Psychiatry*. New York: William

Morrow, 1975. This popular book written for the general public offers helpful, informative insight into the many facets of bipolar disorder (manic depression). Accounts of famous people who had the disorder and yet were successful in their lives give hope to those afflicted.

Goodwin, Frederick K., and Kay Redfield Jamison. *Manic-Depressive Illness*. New York: Oxford University Press, 1990. A comprehensive book on bipolar disorder. Historical events, from diagnosis to treatment, are covered in depth. Issues of treatment and theory are also examined in great detail.

Hershman, D. Jablow, and Julian Lieb. *The Key to Genius: Manic-Depression and the Creative Life*. Buffalo, N.Y.: Prometheus Books, 1988. A publication for the general reader. This intriguing book covers some of the phenomena long written about, including facts of great men and women who may have suffered from bipolar illness.

Heston, Leonard L. *Mending Minds: A Guide to the New Psychiatry of Depression, Anxiety, and Other Serious Mental Disorders*. New York: W. H. Freeman, 1992. This leading-edge book, written for the layperson yet useful for the professional, covers many disorders—depression, bipolar disorder, and anxiety, to name a few. The types of treatments available, both biological and psychological, are explained from the viewpoint of the potential consumer of these specialized services. Includes a guide to support groups, more readings, and other resources.

Jefferson, James W., and John H. Greist. *Primer of Lithium Therapy*. Baltimore: Williams & Wilkins, 1977. Described as being for the layperson, but contains important information about the usefulness and special precautions of lithium therapy and prophylaxis.

Karen Wolford

See also:

Abnormality, 1; Amnesia, Fugue, and Multiple Personality, 43; Anxiety Disorders, 65; Depression, Clinical, 194; Depression: Theoretical Explanations, 200; Obsessions and Compulsions, 427; Schizophrenia: Theoretical Explanations, 517; Substance Abuse, 604; Suicide, 610.

CASE-STUDY METHODOLOGIES

Type of psychology: Psychological methodologies
Field of study: Descriptive methodologies

Case-study methodologies represent a number of techniques to study people, events, or other phenomena within their natural setting. Typically, case studies involve careful observations made over an extended period of time in situations where it is not possible to control the behaviors under observation. The results and interpretation of the data are recorded in narrative form.

Principal terms

EXTRANEOUS VARIABLE: a variable that has a detrimental effect on a research study, making it difficult to determine if the result is attributable to the variable under study or to some unknown variable not controlled for

INDEPENDENT VARIABLE: the variable in a study that is under the control of the experimenter

LABORATORY RESEARCH: a method in which phenomena are studied in an artificial setting with rigorous procedures in place to control for outside influences

NATURALISTIC OBSERVATION: a method in which, in contrast to laboratory research, subjects are studied in the environment in which they live, with little or no intervention on the part of the researcher

QUASI-EXPERIMENTS: experiments that do not allow subjects to be assigned randomly to treatment conditions

SYSTEMATIC INTERVIEWING TECHNIQUES: structured interviews that ask a series of questions that have been prepared in advance

Overview

According to social scientist Robert Yin, case-study research is one of the most frequently misunderstood methods used to study behaviors. Yin, in his book *Case Study Research: Design and Methods* (1984), points out that misconceptions have come about because of the limited coverage that case-study research receives in the average textbook on research methods. In addition, most texts typically confuse the case-study approach with either "qualitative" research methods or specific types of quasi-experimental designs.

Yin defines a case study as a method for studying contemporary phenomena within their natural setting, particularly when the behaviors under study cannot be manipulated or brought under the experimenter's control. Thus, unlike studies which are performed in the well-controlled—and sometimes rigidly sterile—confines of the laboratory, the case-study approach collects data where the behaviors occur in real-life contexts. Although behavior in natural settings can lead to a mother lode of data waiting to be mined, it also has its drawbacks. One who uses this approach needs to recognize that the lack of control over extraneous variables can compound the difficulty associated with trying to identify the underlying variables that are causing the behaviors. Despite this concern, case-study methods are seen as valuable research tools to help unlock the mysteries behind events and behaviors. The approach has been used by psychologists, sociologists, political scientists, anthropologists, historians, and economists, to name a few.

Yin suggests that case-study designs vary according to two distinct dimensions. One dimension accounts for the number of "cases" being studied: the presence of either single- or multiple-case designs. A second dimension allows for case studies to be either "holistic"—that is, studying the entire unit of analysis as a single global entity—or "embedded," which allows multiple units of analysis to be studied for the purpose of understanding their interworkings. According to Yin, this classification system leaves the researcher with a choice among four different design types: single-case (holistic) design, single-case (embedded) design, multiple-case (holistic) design, and multiple-case (embedded) design. Choosing among these designs involves the kinds of research questions the researcher is attempting to answer.

Case-study methods are initiated for a variety of reasons, one of which is to serve as a vehicle for exploratory research. As a new research area begins to develop, the initial uncharted territory is sometimes best studied (particularly when the research questions are ill-defined) using a case-study method to determine which direction should be first pursued. This method has therefore been commonly misperceived as being able to contribute only in a limited exploratory capacity; however, the case study can, and should, be used not only to help focus initial research questions but also to describe and explain behaviors. As Yin makes clear, both "how" and "why" questions can be answered by this approach.

A frequently asked question is "When should one choose to conduct a case study, rather than an experiment?" To answer this question, it is important to understand some basic differences between case-study methods and experimental designs. Experiments allow the researcher to manipulate the independent variables that are being studied. For example, in a study to determine the most effective treatment approach for severe depression, subjects could be randomly assigned to one of three different treatments. The "treatments" are under the control of the researcher in the sense that he or she determines who will get a particular treatment and exactly what it will be. On the other hand, case studies are used in situations where the variables cannot be manipulated. Experiments typically, although not exclusively, are performed in a laboratory setting; case studies, as previously described, occur in naturalistic settings. Experiments are characterized as having rigorous control over extraneous variables; case studies typically lack such control. Experiments place a heavy emphasis on data-analysis procedures that use numbers and statistical testing; case studies emphasize direct observation and systematic interviewing techniques, and they are communicated in a narrative form. Experiments are designed so that they can be repeated; case studies, by their very nature, can be quite difficult to repeat.

Applications

One of Yin's dimensions for classifying case studies involves single-case versus multiple-case studies. In some instances, only a single-case study is necessary or at times even possible; this is true when a unique "case" comes along that presents a valuable source of information. For example, a social scientist wanting to explore the emotional impact of a national tragedy on elementary school children might choose to study the *Challenger* space shuttle disaster, or perhaps the Chernobyl nuclear catastrophe, as a single-case study.

Eminent Russian psychologist Aleksandr Luria, in his book *The Mind of a Mnemonist: A Little Book About a Vast Memory* (1968), has, in a most engaging style, described a single-case (holistic) study. The case involved a man by the name of Shereshevskii (identified in the book as subject "S"), who possessed an extraordinary memory. Luria began to observe "S" systematically in the 1920's after "S" had asked him to test his memory. Luria was so astounded by the man's ability to study information for brief periods of time and then repeat it back to him without an error that he continued to observe and test "S" over the next thirty years. Luria was convinced that this man possessed one of the best memories ever studied.

Because of the nature of the phenomenon—an unusually vast memory—and the fact that this man was capable of performing memory feats never before witnessed, a single-case (holistic) study was begun. Studying rare phenomena, as in this instance, it is not possible to find the number of subjects typically required for an experiment; thus, the case-study approach presents the best alternative. Over the next thirty years, Luria carefully documented the results of literally hundreds of memory feats. In some instances, Luria presented "S" with a list of words to memorize and asked him to recall them immediately. At other times, without any forewarning, Luria asked "S" to recall words from lists given more than fifteen years before. In most of these instances, "S" recalled the list with only a few errors. Luria commented on much more than the results of these memory tests; he also carefully studied the personality of "S." Luria wanted to understand him as a whole person, not only as a person with a great memory. Closely involved with the subject, Luria personally gave the instructions and collected the data. Whereas the data from the memory tasks provided some degree of objectivity to the study, most of the information came from the subjective observations and judgments made by Luria himself. The study was reported in a book-length narrative.

A second example involves a case study that was part of a larger group of studies known as the Hawthorne studies, conducted at the Western Electric Company, near Chicago, in the 1920's. One particular study called the Bank Wiring Observation Room Study was initiated to study the informal social interactions that occur within a small group of employees in an industrial plant.

A group of fourteen men was moved to a self-contained work room which simulated the plant environment; a psychologist was assigned to observe the behavior of the group. No manipulation of any variables occurred; there was only passive observation of the employees' behavior. As might be expected, the presence of the observer discouraged many of the men from behaving as they normally would if someone was not present. The men were suspicious that the psychologist would "inform" their supervisor of any behaviors that were not allowed on the job. After a month passed, however, the men became accustomed to the observer and started to behave as they normally did inside the plant. (Notice the length of time needed to begin observing "normal" work behaviors; most experiments would have been terminated long before the natural behaviors surfaced.) The informal social interactions of this group were studied for a total of eight months.

This study was significant in that it exposed a number of interesting social phenomena that occur in a small division at work. One finding was that informal rules were inherent in the group and were strictly enforced by the group. For example, workers always reported that the same number of units were assembled for that day, regardless of how many were actually assembled. This unspoken rule came from a group that had considerable influence over the rate of production. Also, despite a company policy that forbade an employee to perform a job he was not trained to do, men frequently rotated job assignments to counteract the boredom that typically occurs in this kind of work.

This study was important because it systematically observed the naturally occurring relationships and informal social interactions that exist in an industrial setting. The case-study method proved to be very effective in bringing this information to light.

Context

Long before the scientific community began to formalize the procedures associated with conducting case studies, scientists, philosophers, and physicians were studying phenomena in their natural contexts by making direct observations and later systematically recording them. Although it is difficult to pinpoint how long this method has been used, there are a number of documented cases dating back to the second and third centuries. Galen, a leading physician in Rome in the second century, spent five years as a surgeon to the gladiators in the Roman Colosseum. During this time, Galen made painstaking observations correlating head injuries the gladiators received with the loss of intellectual abilities. In a sense, this was a prelude to the case study of today.

Psychology has been heavily influenced by the natural sciences. Since the natural sciences gave birth to the scientific method, with its emphasis on experiments, it is not surprising that psychology adopted a modified version of the scientific method that could be applied to the study of people and other organisms. It soon became apparent, however, that not all situations lend themselves to study by an experiment. Thus, it was important for alternative methodologies to be developed and used. The case study is an outgrowth of this quest to find alternative methods for studying complex phenomena.

Over the years, case-study methods have not received universal acceptance. This can even be seen in the limited exposure they receive in social science textbooks on methodology; it is not uncommon for a textbook to devote only a few paragraphs to this method. This is attributable in part to some of the criticisms raised about case-study designs. One criticism is that this technique lends itself to distortions or falsifications while the data are being collected. Since direct observation may rely on subjective criteria, in many instances based on general impressions, it is alleged that this data should not be trusted. A second criticism is that it is difficult to draw cause-and-effect conclusions because of the lack of control measures to rule out alternative rival hypotheses. Third, the issue of generalization is important after the data have been collected and interpreted. There will often be a question regarding the population to which the results can be applied.

During the second half of the twentieth century, there appears to have been a resurgence of the use of case-study methods. Part of the impetus for this change came from a reactionary movement against the more traditional methods that collect data in "artificial" settings. The case-study method plays a significant role in studying behavior in real-life situations, under a set of circumstances that would make it impossible to use any other alternative.

Bibliography

Baker, Therese L. *Doing Social Research*. New York: McGraw-Hill, 1988. Gives the reader a general introduction to field research, observational studies, data collection methods, survey research, and sampling techniques, as well as other topics which will help the reader evaluate "good" field experiments from those that are poorly constructed.

Berg, Bruce L. *Qualitative Research Methods for the Social Sciences.* Boston: Allyn & Bacon, 1989. Discusses a field strategy used by anthropologists and sociologists to study groups of people; in addition, discusses the ethical issues that arise while conducting research. Looks at the dangers of covert research and provides the guidelines established by the National Research Act.

Griffin, John H. *Black Like Me.* New York: American Library, 1962. This excellent book is a narrative of the author's experiences traveling around the United States observing how people react to him after he takes on the appearance of a black man. This monumental field study, which contributed to an understanding of social prejudice, provides the reader with an excellent example of the significance of and need for conducting field research.

Lawler, Robert W., and Kathleen M. Carley. *Case Study and Computing: Advanced Qualitative Methods in the Study of Human Behavior.* Norwood, N.J.: Ablex, 1996.

Luria, Aleksandr R. *The Mind of a Mnemonist: A Little Book About a Vast Memory.* Pickering, Ontario: Basic Books, 1968. A fascinating case study written by the "father of neuropsychology," who was one of the most significant Russian psychologists. Directed toward a general (nonspecialist) audience. The case study focuses on his subject Shereshevskii (subject "S") and the extraordinary memory he possessed.

McCall, G. J., and J. L. Simmons. *Issues in Participant Observation: A Text and Reader.* Reading, Mass.: Addison-Wesley, 1969. This text provides an in-depth discussion on how to get inside a group as a participant observer and conduct observational field research. Also provides a number of examples from the literature to help understand how this research is conducted.

Nation, Jack R. *Research Methods.* Upper Saddle River, N.J.: Prentice Hall, 1997.

Singleton, Royce, Jr., et al. *Approaches to Social Research.* New York: Oxford University Press, 1988. This well-written text discusses various aspects of field experimentation such as how to select a research setting and gather information, how to get into the field, and when a field study should be adopted. The chapter on "experimentation" can be used to contrast "true" experiments with field studies.

Yin, Robert K. *Case Study Research: Design and Methods.* Beverly Hills, Calif.: Sage Publications, 1984. This rare volume is perhaps the finest single source on case-study methods in print. Yin shows the reader exactly how to design, conduct, analyze, and even write up a case study. Approximately forty examples of case studies are cited with brief explanations. The book is written for an audience that is not highly technical.

Bryan C. Auday

See also:

Animal Experimentation, 59; Psychoanalytic Psychology and Personality: Sigmund Freud, 478; Psychological Experimentation, 484; Survey Research: Questionnaires and Interviews, 615.

The Central and Peripheral Nervous Systems

Type of psychology: Biological bases of behavior
Fields of study: Auditory, chemical, cutaneous, and body senses; nervous system; thought

The central nervous system (CNS) includes the brain and spinal cord; the peripheral nervous system (PNS) consists of nerve branches which connect the brain or spinal cord with other regions of the body, including fingers and toes. Signals from the PNS are processed within the brain, resulting in thought and senses.

Principal terms

ALZHEIMER'S DISEASE: a form of presenile dementia, characterized by disorientation, loss of memory, and speech disturbances

CEREBELLUM: the portion of the brain which controls voluntary muscle activity; located behind the brain stem

CEREBRUM: the largest and uppermost portion of the brain; the cerebrum performs sensory and motor functions and affects memory, speech, and emotional functions

GRAY MATTER: tissue within the brain or spinal cord; consists primarily of the cell bodies from neurons

MEDULLA OBLONGATA: the bulbous portion of the brain stem, which directly connects with the spinal cord; controls cardiac and respiratory activity

NEURON: the basic nerve cell of the nervous system, which consists of a cell body with one or more extensions called axons

PONS: the nerve connection between the cerebellum and the brain stem

WHITE MATTER: the tissue within the central nervous system, consisting primarily of nerve fibers

Overview

The nervous system in humans is anatomically divided into two sections: the central nervous system (CNS) and the peripheral nervous system (PNS). The CNS consists of the brain and spinal cord, while all nerve structures outside the CNS are considered part of the PNS. The peripheral nervous system, in turn, can be subdivided into a somatic division (monitoring senses and muscle movement) and an autonomic division (regulating involuntary functions, such as heart rate or blood pressure).

The dominant feature of the central nervous system is the brain. The average human brain weighs about 1.4 kilograms (or about 3 pounds) and consists primarily of two types of cells: neurons, or nerve cells, which carry out CNS activity, and glial cells, which provide support function.

The brain is generally divided into three regions: the forebrain, midbrain, and hindbrain. The midbrain and hindbrain are collectively called the brain stem. The forebrain is the largest and most obvious portion of the brain. It includes the cerebrum, with an outer layer of gray matter (nerve cells) and an underlying mass of nerve extensions (axons) called white matter. The cerebrum is divided into right and left hemispheres, each half consisting of gray and white matter. When one visualizes the brain, it is generally the cerebrum one pictures, with its convoluted and lobed regions. Lobes within the cerebrum perform so-called higher functions, such as processing senses (such as smell and touch and speech). The brain's electrical activity, which can be recorded on a machine called an electroencephalograph for identification of states of consciousness or for determination of brain dysfunction, originates within the cerebrum. Also found within the forebrain is the thalamus, an entry point of sensory nerves. It is this portion of the forebrain which integrates sensory information from various parts of the body, sending the signals to the appropriate regions of the cerebrum. For this reason, the thalamus has been called the brain's "relay station." The region below the thalamus is the hypothalamus; this is the portion of the brain which regulates metabolism in the body and influences human "drives" such as those for eating, thirst, and sex.

The midbrain connects the forebrain and hindbrain. Large numbers of nerve tracts pass through the midbrain into the forebrain, including those which receive stimuli from the eyes or ears. Response to sights or sounds is in part processed within this region, including the control of eye movements and dilation of the pupils in response to changes in light.

The hindbrain is found within the lowest portion of the brain, and it serves as the entry point for impulses from nerves in the spinal cord. This portion of the brain is divided into the cerebellum, the medulla oblongata, and the pons. The cerebellum is in the lower rear portion of the brain, in the back of the head. It has been described as having the shape and size of a walnut. Its function lies primarily in the coordination of movements, some of which are involuntary, reflexive types of motions. Sensory input from other parts of the body, including eyes and ears, is intricately involved in this function.

The medulla oblongata is the lowest portion of the brain and is the region through which spinal nerves enter the brain. It is within the medulla that breathing and heart rate are regulated. The pons is found just above the medulla, and it contains nerve tracts which link the cerebellum with the forebrain. The spinal cord exits the base of the brain and passes into the spine, extending as far as the lumbar region near the pelvis (approximately 0.5 meter, or 1.5 feet). It consists of nerve pathways which, like the brain, can be differentiated into white and gray matter. The cord is protected by the bones of the spine, or vertebrae. Emerging from spaces between individual vertebrae are spinal nerves, which eventually branch into the structure referred to as the peripheral nervous system.

The peripheral nervous system contains twelve pairs of cranial nerves, thirty-one pairs of spinal nerves, plus the branches from this system found in far reaches of the body. Sensory (called afferent) nerves transmit information from these regions of the body back to the central nervous system, while motor (or efferent) nerves transmit information from the CNS to organs or muscles. Both voluntary (somatic) movements and involuntary (autonomic) responses are controlled by elements of the PNS. For example, the rapid heartbeat which results from a sudden onset of fear (or from observing a person to whom one is attracted) is a function of the autonomic portion of the peripheral nervous system.

Though divided into specialized areas, the CNS and PNS clearly carry out closely related functions. The 160,000 or so kilometers of nerve fibers within the body provide an intricate system of interactions which reach and regulate activities throughout the organism, producing bodywide communication. All that one perceives and does—the essence of one's being—is a function of the nervous system.

Applications

A fuller understanding of the relationship of much of the central and peripheral nervous systems has come about through the study of pathologies in those systems. In fact, many of the so-called psychological disorders have their origins in nervous system disorders. These disorders can include dementias, "insanity," and even drug and alcohol addiction.

When most persons visualize the brain, they think of the region called the cerebrum. Certainly this area, with its large convoluted surface, is the most obvious portion of the central nervous system. The cerebrum is found in all vertebrate animals (those with backbones), but the development and function differ significantly when one compares one type of animal with another. For example, as Robert Wallace has pointed out, if the cerebrum is removed from a frog's brain, little change is seen in the animal's behavior. The frog is still capable of catching flies and still exhibits normal sexual behavior. A cat from which the cerebrum is removed can still meow and eat. Primates (humans, apes, and monkeys) which have suffered cerebral damage, however, become paralyzed and blind. As animals have become more highly evolved, more brain functions have become associated with the cerebrum, rather than occurring within other portions of the brain.

In humans, the cerebrum is divided into four lobes. In the frontal lobe, body movements and speech are regulated; in the occipital lobe, sight is regulated. The parietal lobe, containing sensory areas which respond to touching of the skin, also allows for the perception of spatial relationships of objects. The fourth lobe is the temporal lobe, in which the senses of hearing and smell are analyzed.

Though each of these cerebral areas is obviously of importance, the frontal lobe is arguably the region which makes humans most "human." (It should be pointed out, however, that the frontal lobes of chimpanzees and gorillas are equally well developed.) It is within the frontal lobe, for example, that sensory information is sorted out and is even integrated with emotional information derived from other regions.

Much of what is known of frontal lobe function has come about through two sources. In the mid-nineteenth century, a railway construction foreman was injured when, during an accidental explosion, a tamping iron was blown into his head. The damage to his frontal lobe resulted in significant behavioral changes. Literally overnight, he changed from a responsible, hardworking individual to a profane drifter unable to hold a job. Additional understanding of the role played by the frontal lobe has come through observation of individuals who have undergone frontal lobotomies—that is, the surgical removal of the frontal lobe—or through observations of persons suffering from frontal lobe tumors.

Certain changes in behavior seem to be common among these individuals. These persons frequently exhibit diminished levels of caring, even showing indifference to the outside world. In some tragic cases, the person assumes what is almost a vegetative state. In addition, the person's ability to plan or reason is often affected. He or she may exhibit a lack of ethics or show inappropriate behaviors, such as laughing or crying uncontrollably. On the other hand, damage to the frontal lobe generally has little effect on memory or intellect.

Within the central nervous system is a series of structures often called the limbic system. Though the system is at best ill-defined, it primarily includes the regions of the thalamus and hypothalamus, in addition to the hippocampus and amygdala (both regions being found within the temporal lobe). The limbic system is connected with other areas of the brain, linking the forebrain and midbrain, and is generally modulated by those regions. Regions of this system are associated with emotions or feelings, including anger, fear, sadness, and sexual arousal. If the amygdala, a group of cells within the temporal lobe, is electrically stimulated, fits of rage may result. Removal of the amygdala results in docility.

The hypothalamus has been described as the heart of the limbic system. Its primary function is to maintain homeostasis, a constancy of the internal environment. It consists primarily of densely packed neurons and secretory cells which respond to stimuli from the peripheral nervous system. In this manner, body temperature, appetite, and sleep are regulated. Tumors in the hypothalamus have been known to activate a "rage" center, causing the person to act uncontrollably.

The peripheral nervous system consists of nerve branches that connect the central nervous system to all regions of the body. As noted above, the PNS is divided into a somatic system, which regulates voluntary muscles, and an autonomic nervous system, which controls involuntary functions. The autonomic nervous system within the PNS primarily carries out a motor function. Nerve impulses are transmitted from the central nervous system for regulation of various organs. People are generally unaware of these functions, except in moments of stress. At these times, a reflex popularly known as the "fight-or-flight" response is activated. Many people can remember when, as children, they encountered a school bully. Suddenly one's heart rate accelerated, one began breathing more deeply, while one's mouth seemed to dry up. In an extreme case, bladder control might even be lost. If the bully then walked in the other direction, however, each of these responses was reversed. Both the induction of these activities and their later relaxation are under the control of the peripheral nervous system. It is critical to remember that neither the central nervous system nor the peripheral system functions in a vacuum. Each depends on the other, and each functions smoothly only in conjunction with the other.

Context

Modern knowledge of functions associated with the nervous system dates from the late nineteenth and early twentieth century work of Sir Charles Scott Sherrington. In 1884, in collaboration with John N. Langley, Sherrington demonstrated the localization of cerebral function through the experimental excision of the cerebral cortex of a dog. Over the following three decades, Sherrington published more than three hundred research papers in which he mapped areas of motor function in the cortex of the brain. Among those who were to advance this work was Edgar Douglas Adrian, a British neurophysiologist and major figure in the study of brain functions until the mid-twentieth century.

Langley was himself a pioneer in the study of the peripheral nervous system. In particular, he studied autonomic functions within that system. In fact, it was Langley who first applied, in 1898, the term "autonomic nervous system" to those portions of the PNS which innervate involuntary muscles and glands. His major work, *The Autonomic Nervous System,* was published in 1921.

It was clear from these works that the ability to monitor the outside world is a function of the nervous system. Input from the senses—taste, touch, smell, and so on—travels along the peripheral nerves to the spinal cord and brain, where it is processed, coordinated, and interpreted. Changes that result in the brain form the basis of thought and learning. Damage to those same areas results in loss of function and even loss of memory.

It is particularly in this area of loss of function that one may hope to see great advancements in the future. Since nerves, unlike most other cells in the body, do not regenerate, death or damage to regions of the nervous system often results in permanent loss of function. In the case of a stroke, damage is often extensive and catastrophic. The ability to replace or repair nervous tissue could significantly reverse this damage.

Tragically, the natural process of aging is often accompanied by dementia, the loss of cognitive function. The most common form of late-life dementia is Alzheimer's disease. First described by Alois Alzheimer in 1907, the disease is characterized by loss of memory, confusion, and speech disturbances. Often developing in the late middle years, Alzheimer's disease is associated with formation of fibrous plaques throughout much of the brain. In particular, cortical areas of the cerebral lobes are affected. This accounts for at least some of the symptoms typical of the disease. While no reversal of the disease is in sight, it is hoped that the course of the illness can at least be slowed.

The human nervous system is thus composed of two parts: a central nervous system, in which information is processed, and a peripheral system, which serves as a window to the world. All regions of the body are served, and in turn, each region has a part in the protection and function of the body.

Bibliography

Clarke, Edwin, and C. D. O'Malley. *The Human Brain and Spinal Cord: A Historical Study Illustrated by Writings from Antiquity to the Twentieth Century.* 2d ed. San Francisco: Norman, 1996.

Cotman, Carl W., and James L. McGaugh. *Behavioral Neuroscience: An Introduction.* New York: Academic Press, 1980. An excellent introduction to the area. Descriptions of nervous system function are basic and easily understood by nonexperts. Sections of the book cover material in great depth. Summaries and definitions are provided at the end of each topic.

McEwen, Bruce S., and Harold M. Schmeck, Jr. *The Hostage Brain.* New York: Rockefeller University Press, 1994.

Scientific American 241 (September, 1979). This entire issue of the journal deals with the topic of the brain. Articles are somewhat technical, but they are well written and nicely illustrated.

Selkoe, Dennis J. "Amyloid Protein and Alzheimer's Disease." *Scientific American* 265 (November, 1991): 68-78. A summary of the pathology and possible cause of the most common form of aging dementia. Written for the person with at least college-level knowledge of science, but well illustrated. Diagrams are at a basic level.

Stevens, Leonard A. *Explorers of the Brain.* New York: Alfred A. Knopf, 1971. A history of the explanation of brain function. Chapters are devoted to those researchers who mapped out the areas of the brain. A good overview to how research in the past was carried out, written at the level of the nonexpert.

Wallace, Robert A., Gerald P. Sanders, and Robert J. Ferl. *Biology: The Science of Life.* 3d ed. New York: HarperCollins, 1991. Though a college text, the book contains several excellent chapters on the functions of the nervous system which should be easily understood by persons not in the field. Illustrations are plentiful and clear. Definitions and a summary are provided at the end of each chapter.

Richard Adler

See also:

The Autonomic Nervous System, 88; The Cerebral Cortex, 121; The Endocrine System, 248; Neuropsychology, 422; Reflexes, 507.

THE CEREBRAL CORTEX

Type of psychology: Biological bases of behavior
Fields of study: Nervous system; thought; vision

The outer gray matter of the cerebrum, the cortex, contains sensory and motor regions and areas that integrate these functions. Intelligence, memory, language, personality, and other behavioral characteristics are controlled there.

Principal terms

BRAIN WAVES: electrical activity produced by the neurons of the cerebral cortex and recorded using an electroencephalograph; these produce distinct patterns related to healthy and diseased brain functions

CEREBRAL CORTEX: the outer covering of the cerebrum, consisting of gray matter that conducts most of the integrative aspects of higher brain functions

CEREBRAL HEMISPHERES: the right and left halves of the cerebrum, separated incompletely by the longitudinal fissure

FRONTAL LOBE: the anterior portion of each cerebral hemisphere, containing control of motor areas and most of the higher intellectual functions of the brain, including speech

GRAY MATTER: unmyelinated neurons that make up the cerebral cortex, so called because they lack the fatty covering (myelin) found on neurons of the white matter

INTEGRATION: the function of most of the neurons of the cerebral cortex, summarizing the incoming sensory information and producing a consensus as to what the nervous system will do next

OCCIPITAL LOBE: the posterior portion of each cerebral hemisphere, where visual stimuli are received and integrated

PARIETAL LOBE: the side and upper middle part of each cerebral hemisphere, site of sensory reception from skin, muscles, and other areas, and containing part of the general interpretive area

TEMPORAL LOBE: the lower side portion of each cerebral hemisphere, containing the sites of sensory interpretation, memory of visual and auditory patterns, and part of the general interpretive area

Overview

The cerebrum is the largest portion of the brain in higher vertebrates. In lower vertebrates, it develops from the front end of the embryonic nerve cord as the forebrain or prosencephalon and is specialized for smell and taste. This development progresses in higher vertebrates to a highly convoluted structure called the telencephalon, most of which becomes the cerebrum—the location of the highest levels of behavioral control. In humans, deep convolutions of the cerebrum produce a greatly increased surface area, the cerebral cortex, also called the neocortex because it is the newest development in the evolution of vertebrate brains. The cortex is the site of the integration of sensory nerve impulses and of the intellectual processes, such as memory and learning. It is also the site of the initiation of voluntary motor impulses to the skeletal muscles. One theory for the massive enlargement of the cerebral cortex in humans as compared to other mammals is that such growth resulted from the development of language in early social groups. This is thought to have increased the integrative or associative functions, producing the rise in intelligence and cortical surface that accompanied language development.

The cerebral cortex is the largest portion of the cerebrum by volume and generally consists of four to six layers of the cell bodies of neurons. This is called gray matter because the cells are not covered with a white fatty myelin coating, and they look darker than cells that are myelinated. The cortex overlies a region of white matter made of the myelinated axons that extend from the cell bodies of cortical neurons. The tissue of the cortex composes about 80 percent of the brain in a human; it varies in thickness from about 1.5 to 3 millimeters. The wrinkling of the convoluted tissue greatly increases the cortex area that can be contained within the small volume of the cranial cavity, with a surface area of about 2,500 square centimeters. The clefts and ridges of the convolutions are called sulci and gyri respectively (singular, sulcus and gyrus). A deeper cleft, called a fissure, is usually recognized as the boundary between different lobes of the cerebrum.

The cerebrum is divided into nearly symmetrical right and left halves, called the cerebral hemispheres, by the medial longitudinal fissure. Each hemisphere is further divided into four sections called the frontal, parietal, temporal, and occipital lobes. The gyri and sulci within each lobe may differ slightly between the two hemispheres of a single individual, and they can vary widely among different individual brains. The frontal lobes are the largest, extending backward in each hemisphere from the front of the brain to the central sulcus, and downward to the lateral fissure. Each parietal lobe begins just behind the central sulcus and extends downward to the lateral fissure. Below the lateral fissure of each hemisphere is the temporal lobe, under the frontal and parietal lobes on each side of the head, and separated from the occipital lobe by the parieto-occipital sulcus. The back portion of each hemisphere is occupied by the occipital lobe. Each of these lobes does not have a single recognizable function, but they are useful as anatomical markers for the location of many different activities that occur in each lobe. These activities may vary in their placement from one individual to another, so localizations are not exact.

Different regions of the cortex are connected by three kinds of projections of axons from neurons. Many short linkages connect neurons in adjacent gyri; longer connections join together one lobe and another from the same hemisphere; and commissures link the same points in opposite hemispheres. In addition to pathways from one part of the cortex to another, there are also links between cortical neurons and cells of other areas of the brain, such as the thalamus. This further complicates the task of determining the functions of parts of the brain, since a pathway may lead from an area of the cortex to the thalamus and then to another cortical area. Damage to such a linkage may produce the same kind of behavioral response as damage to the cortical area that actually controls the behavior.

Crossed pathways from one hemisphere to the other are of great importance in the perception of sensations and the origination of movements. Each hemisphere of the brain controls the activities of the contralateral (opposite) side of the body, so that an itchy sensation on the right arm will send the great majority of its sensory impulses to the cortex of the left side of the brain. Similarly, a motor impulse to the left hand to scratch the itch will originate from the cortex of the right side of the brain. A variation of this rule is seen in the visual system, where incoming sensory impulses from the two eyes are sent to both sides of the brain. Half the fibers of the optic nerve from each eye cross before reaching the visual cortex, and the information that arrives as an upside-down image is interpreted as if it were right-side up. This allows the production of a continuous image, which would not be possible if each eye sent its impulses to only one side of the brain, either the contralateral or ipsilateral (same) side.

Applications

Neuroanatomists and psychologists construct different kinds of topographical maps based on the various functions of the cerebral cortex that are being examined. Projection maps of the sensory and motor functions are built by tracing the pathways of sensory neurons from different areas of the body to the different parts of the brain, or the pathways of motor neurons from the brain to different action sites in the body. Functional maps are made from studies of the brain itself, either by directly stimulating different brain regions electrically and observing the resultant behavior, or by recording brain waves produced by particular areas of the brain during certain behaviors. Histological study of the kinds of neurons and accessory cells in different areas of the cortex is used in the development of cytoarchitecture maps.

Using a primary sensory projection map, one can link the visual system to the posterior occipital lobe, the auditory system to the temporal lobe, and the somatosensory system (carrying sensation from most of the body) to the postcentral gyrus of the parietal lobe. Most primary motor projections come from the precentral gyrus of the frontal lobe, immediately in front of the central sulcus that separates the frontal and parietal lobes. Nearby areas that receive information from primary sensory areas or that send information to primary motor areas of the cortex are called secondary projection areas. These regions in turn contain pathways leading to or from tertiary projection areas. The secondary and tertiary areas are parts of the association cortex, where integration of impulses takes place to interpret the various kinds of information. It is a major oversimplification, however, to consider the different lobes to have only the one function mentioned, since sensory, motor, and integrative activities occur in all parts of the cerebral cortex. The listed functions are simply most concentrated in the given areas.

The best-known functional map of the human cerebral cortex was described by W. G. Penfield and his associates in the 1950's. It was developed through research done during brain surgery on conscious individuals. Patients were asked what sensations were perceived when certain specific regions of the postcentral gyrus (somatic sensory area) were electrically stimulated. The precentral gyrus (motor area) was also stimulated, and observations were made of what muscles responded by contracting. As a result of such work in numerous subjects, Penfield was able to draw a sensory homunculus and a motor homunculus—strangely distorted humans with enormous lips, tongues, and hands, and tiny bodies. The homunculi extend along the precentral and postcentral gyri, with each part drawn to correspond to its functional representation on the sensory or motor cortex. The lips and hands are large on the sensory homunculus because of the large number of sensory receptors located there. The hands are large on the motor homunculus because there are many nerves supplying the fine muscular control of the fingers. The bodies are small because of the relative lack of sensory reception and motor control there. The homunculi do not represent all the functions of the cerebral cortex, only those of the motor and sensory areas on either side of the dividing central fissure between the frontal and parietal lobes.

Early in the 1900's, histological studies produced a cytoarchitecture map that highlights the different kinds of cell combinations occurring in the six or so layers of neurons in the cerebral cortex. Later, similar maps have increased the level of detail and complexity. Brodmann's map and his regional numbering system are still widely used to differentiate anatomical regions of the cortex. The relationship between anatomical structure and function is quite striking, with distinct boundaries between cellular regions being reproduced in the limits of functional regions. Areas with indistinct cytoarchitectural boundaries seem to be most concerned with associative or integrative functions that are not strongly delineated.

Context

Studies of the location of neurological and behavioral functions have been undertaken for more than 150 years. As early as the 1830's, it was recognized that aphasia, a loss of speech capability, was associated with brain lesions in an area of the left frontal lobe. Many subsequent studies involving damaged areas of the brain and electrical stimulation during surgery have shown the locations of numerous functions in different areas of the cerebral cortex. The ability to understand speech has been localized to a part of the temporal lobe, near the auditory cortex. Impulses from the retinas are known to stimulate the visual cortex in the posterior part of the occipital lobes, with associative visual areas located nearby. Sensory impulses from the skin and body surface are processed by the somatosensory regions of the parietal lobes. These sensory regions seem to be organized into columnar structures within the six layers of neurons in the cortex. Studies of these columns have been most thorough in the visual cortex, where it is known that adjacent columns of cells are stimulated by the opposite eyes. Association areas located near the sensory regions are usually involved in the integration of information brought to the brain through the sensory neurons.

Knowledge of the functions of various areas of the cerebral cortex is important in psychology and related disciplines because of the need to know where to look for a lesion or for damage that might cause a neurological or behavioral disorder. One way of looking for brain damage in a behaviorally disordered patient is through production of an electroencephalogram, or EEG. This noninvasive procedure involves the use of electrodes attached to the head in particular locations over the cortical areas to be examined for electrical current production. Very tiny currents are recognized from each area, with cycles of wavelengths that vary according to the level of activity and normality of function of the targeted area. Records are made of the brain waves produced from each hemisphere or lobe during periods of different kinds of activity. Alpha waves show a rhythm of about 8 to 13 cycles per second and moderate amplitude, and indicate resting or reduced use of a brain area. Reduced height and increased frequency of the waves (14 to 30 cycles per second) are characteristic of beta waves. Production of these from an area is indicative that the area is being more active than when waves of high amplitude are produced. Delta waves are much less frequent (1 to 5 cycles per second); in an awake adult, they indicate brain damage.

Studies of these electrical aspects of the working brain are still rather crude, but they can be used to show the relative use of the two hemispheres during different kinds of tasks. Information from these observations supports the concept that the right side of the brain is more involved with spatial, artistic, and musical processing, while the left side is concerned with logical, mathematical, and verbal activities. This lateralization of brain function is further supported by observations made on patients following the complete surgical separation of the two hemispheres of the brain. The hemispheres are normally connected by the corpus callosum, a set of fibers containing millions of cells that link the two sides of the brain. Split-brain procedures undertaken to relieve epilepsy, as well as accidental separation of the two hemispheres, produce individuals who literally fit the expression "the right hand doesn't know what the left hand is doing." In such individuals the right brain, controlling the left hand, can reproduce a drawing that the right hand (controlled by the left brain) is unable to copy. An unseen object placed in the left hand can be recognized by the right brain, but the left brain is unable to describe it verbally because the connection between the sides is lost. It is a mystery why such separation of function should occur, but the lateralization exists in normal individuals as well as in those with lesions. It is stronger in men than in women, one of several anatomical and functional differences in brain development between the sexes. If an injury occurs to one side of the brain, as in a stroke, often the other side can be trained to take over the functions of the damaged region, especially in children and younger individuals.

Higher associative functions such as personality, memory, and learning are also associated with the cerebral cortex, as well as with other parts of the brain. Memories are stored in certain specific areas of the cerebral cortex. Some neurons code for simple features of visual memory, for example, such as edges and the orientation of objects that are seen. Other neurons code for shape and color of objects, especially in the secondary visual areas of the occipital lobe. Information is sent from these neurons to the visual area of the temporal lobe, where they seem to be interpreted and remembered. Interpretation of sensory information and storage of the information in memory areas have been further localized to different areas for different kinds of information, such as faces, places, names, shapes, language, and motor functions. Further studies in humans, monkeys, and even rats will lead to greater understanding of the newest and most human portion of the brain, the cerebral cortex. The study of the cerebral cortex has been called the greatest frontier of research in neuroscience, and it is likely to remain so for a long time to come.

Bibliography

Chadwick, David, Niall Cartlidge, and David Bates. *Medical Neurology*. Edinburgh: Churchill Livingstone, 1989. This medical resource discusses disorders of the nervous system and problems associated with them. Chapter 6 includes disorders of awareness and mental function, often caused by damage to areas of the cerebral cortex. Chapter 19 covers functional and psychiatric disorders. Clinical features and the causes of these disorders, diagrams of affected brain areas, and numerous tables are included. References.

Gutnick, Michael J., and Istvan Mody, eds. *The Cortical Neuron*. New York: Oxford University Press, 1995.

Kirshner, Howard S. *Behavioral Neurology: A Practical Approach*. New York: Churchill Livingstone, 1986. Discusses various disorders of behavior that have their source in dysfunction of the brain, particularly the cerebral cortex. Areas covered include language, reading and writing, learned movement, recognition, memory, dementias, and epilepsy. Specific disorders of the right cerebral hemisphere and the frontal lobes are also considered. References accompany each chapter.

Kolb, Bryan, and Ian Q. Whishaw. *Fundamentals of Human Neuropsychology*. 2d ed. New York: W. H. Freeman, 1985. Much of this undergraduate textbook addresses the functions and disorders of the cerebral cortex. Part 3 includes chapters on neocortical organization and the sensory and motor systems. Part 4 contains chapters on cerebral asymmetry and the individual cerebral lobes. Higher functions, development, and recovery are discussed in parts 5 and 6. An excellent resource with many references.

McCrone, John. *The Ape That Spoke: Language and the Evolution of the Human Mind*. New York: William Morrow, 1991. While not addressing the cerebral cortex directly, this book for general readers discusses the increased size of the cortex as being associated with the development of language. It gives an interesting outlook on how the mind functions by capturing and holding each thought for a short time only. Bibliographical notes include numerous references.

Montgomery, Geoffrey. "The Mind's Eye." *Discover* 12 (May, 1991): 50-56. This article is written for the nontechnical reader. Presents an excellent discussion of the formation of visual maps in the function of the visual cortex. Comparison is made among reptiles, primitive mammals, and primates in how they perceive visual stimuli.

Ornstein, Robert Evan, and Richard F. Thompson. *The Amazing Brain*. Boston: Houghton Mifflin, 1984. This is a clearly written and well-illustrated book for the nonscientist, presented as a tour of the brain. It discusses the architecture of the brain and how it receives sensory impulses, with emphasis on those for vision. Memory and the effects of separating the two cerebral hemispheres are also covered.

Romero-Sierra, C. *Neuroanatomy: A Conceptual Approach*. New York: Churchill Livingstone, 1986. Addresses the simple concepts of the nervous system components first, then their integration as a functioning whole. Several chapters cover material on the cerebral hemispheres and the functions of the cerebral cortex. A brain atlas is useful in finding structures, and a wide bibliography is included.

Springer, Sally P., and Georg Deutsch. *Left Brain, Right Brain*. 3d ed. New York: W. H. Freeman, 1989. Provides a thorough discussion of the differences between the right and left hemispheres. Techniques of measurement are considered, along with the physiological correlates of asymmetry. Normal brain and split-brain studies show variation between individuals and between the sexes. Numerous references.

Tortora, Gerard J., and Nicholas P. Anagnostakos. *Principles of Anatomy and Physiology*. 6th ed. New York: Harper & Row, 1990. Chapter 14 of this undergraduate college text covers the brain, and chapter 15 is about the sensory, motor, and integrative systems that are contained within the cerebral cortex. Numerous photographs and diagrams help the reader visualize the area under discussion. Excellent as introductory coverage of this material. Selected readings at the end of each chapter refer to easily accessible material.

Van De Graaff, Kent Marshall, and Stuart Ira Fox. *Concepts of Human Anatomy and Physiology*. 2d ed. Dubuque, Iowa: Wm. C. Brown, 1989. An undergraduate text that covers introductory information on the brain clearly and succinctly. The cerebrum is discussed in chapter 15, accompanied by numerous diagrams and tables. References are given at the end of the book.

Jean S. Helgeson

See also:

The Autonomic Nervous System, 88; The Central and Peripheral Nervous Systems, 115; The Endocrine System, 248; Neuropsychology, 422; Reflexes, 507.

COGNITIVE BEHAVIOR THERAPY

Type of psychology: Psychotherapy
Field of Study: Behavioral therapies

A number of approaches to therapy fall within the scope of cognitive behavior therapy. These approaches all share a theoretical perspective that assumes that internal cognitive processes, called thinking or cognition, affect behavior; that this cognitive activity may be monitored; and that desired behavior change may be effected through cognitive change.

Principal terms

BEHAVIOR THERAPY: a branch of psychotherapy narrowly conceived as the application of classical and operant conditioning to the alteration of clinical problems, but more broadly conceived as applied experimental psychology in a clinical context

COGNITION: private or internal processes such as imagery, symbolic representation of external events, and the verbal coding of experience

COGNITIVE RESTRUCTURING: any behavior therapy procedure that attempts to alter the manner in which clients think about life so that they change their overt behavior and emotions

COGNITIVE THERAPY: a therapeutic approach developed by Aaron T. Beck, the goal of which is for patients to discover for themselves the irrationality of their thoughts

DEPRESSION: strong feelings of sadness, dejection, and often apathy that last more than two weeks and pervade a person's thoughts

Overview

The cognitive behavior therapies are not a single therapeutic approach, but rather a loosely organized collection of therapeutic approaches that share a similar set of assumptions. At their core, cognitive behavior therapies share three fundamental propositions: Cognitive activity affects behavior; cognitive activity may be monitored and altered; and desired behavior change may be effected through cognitive change.

The first of the three fundamental propositions of cognitive behavior therapy suggests that it is not the external situation which determines feelings and behavior, but rather the person's view or perception of that external situation that determines feelings and behavior. For example, if one has failed the first examination of a course, one could appraise it as a temporary setback to be overcome or as a horrible loss. While the situation remains the same, the thinking about that situation is radically different in the two examples cited. Each of these views will lead to significantly different emotions and behaviors.

The third cognitive behavioral assumption suggests that desired behavior change may be effected through cognitive change. Thus, while cognitive behavior theorists do not reject the notion that rewards and punishment (reinforcement contingencies) can alter behavior, they are likely to emphasize that there are alternative methods for behavior change, one in particular being cognitive change. Many approaches to therapy fall within the scope of cognitive behavior therapy as it is defined above. While these approaches share the theoretical assumptions described above, a review of the major therapeutic procedures subsumed under the heading of cognitive behavior therapy reveals a diverse amalgam of principles and procedures, representing a variety of theoretical and philosophical perspectives.

Rational-emotive therapy, developed by psychologist Albert Ellis, is regarded by many as one of the premier examples of the cognitive behavioral approach; it was introduced in the early 1960's. Ellis proposed that many people are made unhappy by their faulty, irrational beliefs, which influence the way they interpret events. The therapist will interact with the patient or client, attempting to direct the patient to more positive and realistic views. Cognitive therapy, pioneered by Aaron T. Beck, has been applied to such problems as depression and stress. For stress reduction, ideas and thoughts that are producing stress in the patient will be questioned; the therapist will get the patient to examine the validity of these thoughts; thought processes can then be restructured so the situations seem less stressful. Cognitive therapy has been found to be quite effective in treating depression, as compared to other therapeutic methods. Beck held that depression is caused by certain types of negative thoughts, such as devaluing the self or viewing the future in a consistently pessimistic way.

Rational behavior therapy, developed by psychiatrist Maxie Maultsby, is a close relative of Ellis' rational-emotive therapy. In this approach, Maultsby combines several approaches to include rational-emotive therapy, neuropsychology, classical and operant conditioning, and psychosomatic research; however, Maultsby was primarily influenced by his association with Albert Ellis. In this approach, Maultsby attempts to couch his theory of emotional disturbance in terms of neuropsychophysiology and learning theory. Rational behavior therapy assumes that repeated pairings of a perception with evaluative thoughts lead to rational or irrational emotive and behavioral reactions. Maultsby suggests that self-talk, which originates in the left hemisphere of the brain, triggers corresponding right-hemisphere emotional equivalents. Thus, in order to maintain a state of psychological health, individuals must practice rational self-talk that will, in turn, cause the right brain to convert left-brain language into appropriate emotional and behavioral reactions.

Rational behavior therapy techniques are quite similar to those of rational-emotive therapy. Both therapies stress the importance of monitoring one's thoughts in order to become aware of the elements of the emotional disturbance. In addition, Maultsby advocates the use of rational-emotive imagery, behavioral practice, and relaxation methods in order to minimize emotional distress.

Self-instructional training was developed by psychologist Donald Meichenbaum in the early 1970's. In contrast to Ellis and Beck, whose prior training was in psychoanalysis, Meichenbaum's roots are in behaviorism and the behavioral therapies. Thus Meichenbaum's approach is heavily couched in behavioral terminology and procedures. Meichenbaum's work stems from his earlier research in training schizophrenic patients to emit "healthy speech." By chance, Meichenbaum observed that patients who engaged in spontaneous self-instruction were less distracted and demonstrated superior task performance on a variety of tasks. As a result, Meichenbaum emphasizes the critical role of "self-instructions"—simple instructions such as, "Relax. . . . Just attend to the task"—and their noticeable effect on subsequent behavior.

Meichenbaum developed self-instructional training to treat the deficits in self-instructions manifested in impulsive children. The ultimate goal of this program was to decrease impulsive behavior. The way to accomplish this goal, as hypothesized by Meichenbaum, was to train impulsive children to generate verbal self-commands, to respond to their verbal self-commands, and to encourage the children to self-reinforce their behavior appropriately.

The specific procedures employed in self-instructional training involve having the child observe a model performing a task. While the model is performing the task, he or she is talking aloud. The child then performs the same task while the model gives verbal instructions. Subsequently, the child performs the task while instructing himself or herself aloud, then while whispering the instructions. Finally, the child performs the task covertly. The self-instructions employed in the program included questions about the nature and demands of the task, answers to these questions in the form of cognitive rehearsal, self-instructions in the form of self-guidance while performing the task, and self-reinforcement. Meichenbaum and his associates have found that this self-instructional training program significantly improves the task performance of impulsive children across a number of measures.

Systematic rational restructuring is a cognitive behavioral procedure developed by psychologist Marvin Goldfried in the mid-1970's. This procedure is a variation on Ellis' rational-emotive therapy; however, it is more clearly structured than Ellis' method. In systematic rational restructuring, Goldfried suggests that early social learning experiences teach individuals to label situations in different ways. Further, Goldfried suggests that emotional reactions may be understood as responses to the way individuals label situations, as opposed to responses to the situations themselves. The goal of systematic rational restructuring is to train clients to perceive situational cues more accurately.

The process of systematic rational restructuring is similar to systematic desensitization, in which a subject is to imagine fearful scenes in a graduated order from the least fear-provoking to the more fear-provoking scenes. In systematic rational restructuring, the client is asked to imagine a hierarchy of anxiety-eliciting situations. At each step, the client is instructed to identify irrational thoughts associated with the specific situation, to dispute them, and to reevaluate the situation more rationally. In addition, clients are instructed to practice rational restructuring in specific real-life situations.

Stress inoculation training incorporates several of the specific therapies already described in this section. This procedure was developed by psychologist Donald Meichenbaum. Stress inoculation training is analogous to being inoculated against disease. That is, it prepares clients to deal with stress-inducing events by teaching them to use coping skills at low levels of the stressful situation, and then gradually to cope with more and more stressful situations. Stress inoculation training involves three phases: conceptualization, skill acquisition and rehearsal, and application and follow-through.

In the conceptualization phase of stress inoculation training, clients are given an adaptive way of viewing and understanding their negative reactions to stressful events. In the skills-acquisition and rehearsal phase, clients learn coping skills appropriate to the type of stress they are experiencing. With interpersonal anxiety, the client might develop skills that would make the feared situation less threatening (for example, learning to initiate and maintain conversations). The client might also learn deep muscle relaxation to lessen tension. In the case of anger, clients learn to view potential provocations as problems that require a solution rather than as threats that require an attack. Clients are also taught to rehearse alternative strategies for solving the problem at hand.

The application and follow-through phase of stress inoculation training involves the clients practicing and applying the coping skills. Initially, clients are exposed to low levels of stressful situations in imagery. They practice applying their coping skills to handle the stressful events, and they overtly role-play dealing with stressful events. Next, the client is given homework assignments that involve gradual exposure to actual stressful events in his or her everyday life. Stress inoculation training has been effectively applied to many types of problems. It has been used to help people cope with anger, anxiety, fear, pain, and health-related problems (for example, cancer and hypertension). It appears to be suitable for all age levels.

Problem-solving therapy, as developed by psychologists Thomas D'Zurilla and Marvin Goldfried, is also considered one of the cognitive behavioral approaches. In essence, problem-solving therapy is the application of problem-solving theory and research to the domain of personal and emotional problems. Indeed, the authors see the ability to solve problems as the necessary and sufficient condition for emotional and behavioral stability. Problem solving is, in one way or another, a part of all psychotherapies.

Applications

Cognitive behavior therapists have taught general problem-solving skills to clients with two specific aims: to alleviate the particular personal problems for which clients have sought therapy, and to provide clients with a general coping strategy for personal problems.

The actual steps of problem solving that a client is taught to carry out systematically are as follows. First, it is necessary to define the dilemma as a problem to be solved. Next, a goal must be selected which reflects the ultimate outcome the client desires. The client then generates a list of many different possible solutions, without evaluating their potential merit (a kind of brainstorming). Now the client evaluates the pros and cons of each alternative in terms of the probability that it will meet the goal selected and its practicality, which involves considering the potential consequences to oneself and to others of each solution. The alternative solutions are ranked in terms of desirability and practicality, and the highest one is selected. Next, the client tries to implement the solution chosen. Finally, the client evaluates the therapy, assessing whether the solution alleviated the problem and met the goal, and, if not, what went wrong—in other words, which of the steps in problem solving needs to be redone.

Problem-solving therapies have been used to treat a variety of target behaviors with a wide range of clients. Examples include peer relationship difficulties among children and adolescents, examination and interpersonal anxiety among college students, relapse following a program to reduce smoking, harmony among family members, and the ability of chronic psychiatric patients to cope with interpersonal problems.

Self-control therapy for depression, developed by psychologist Lynn Rehm, is an approach to treating depression which combines the self-regulatory notions of behavior therapy and the cognitive focus of the cognitive behavioral approaches. Essentially, Rehm believes that depressed people show deficits in one or some combination of the following areas: monitoring (selectively attending to negative events), self-evaluation (setting unrealistically high goals), and self-reinforcement (emitting high rates of self-punishment and low rates of self-reward). These three components are further broken down into a total of six functional areas.

According to Rehm, the varied symptom picture in clinically depressed clients is a function of different subsets of these deficits. Over the course of therapy with a client, each of the six self-control deficits is described, with emphasis on how a particular deficit is causally related to depression, and on what can be done to remedy the deficit. A variety of clinical strategies are employed to teach clients self-control skills, including group discussion, overt and covert reinforcement, behavioral assignments, self-monitoring, and modeling.

Structural psychotherapy is a cognitive behavioral approach that derives from the work of two Italian mental health professionals, psychiatrist Vittorio Guidano and psychologist Gianni Liotti. These authors are strongly persuaded by cognitive psychology, social learning theory, evolutionary epistemology, psychodynamic theory, and cognitive therapy. Guidano and Liotti suggest that for an understanding of the full complexity of an emotional disorder and subsequent development of an adequate model of psychotherapy, an appreciation of the development and the active role of an individual's knowledge of self and the world is critical. In short, in order to understand a patient, one must understand the structure of that person's world.

Guidano and Liotti's therapeutic process utilizes the empirical problem-solving approach of the scientist. Indeed, the authors suggest that therapists should assist clients in disengaging themselves from certain ingrained beliefs and judgments, and in considering them as hypotheses and theories subject to disproof, confirmation, and logical challenge. A variety of behavioral experiments and cognitive techniques are utilized to assist the patient in assessing and critically evaluating his or her beliefs.

As can be seen, the area of cognitive behavior therapy involves a wide collection of therapeutic approaches and techniques. The approaches described here are but a representative sample of possible cognitive behavioral approaches. Also included within this domain are anxiety management training, which comes from the work of psychologist Richard Suinn, and personal science, from the work of psychologist Michael Mahoney.

The cognitive behavioral approaches are derived from a variety of perspectives, including cognitive theory, classical and operant conditioning approaches, problem-solving theory, and developmental theory. All these approaches share the perspective that internal cognitive processes, called thinking or cognition, affect behavior, and that behavior change may be effected through cognitive change.

These approaches have several other similarities. One is that all the approaches see therapy as time-limited. This is in sharp distinction to the traditional psychoanalytic therapies, which are generally open-ended. The cognitive behavior therapies attempt to effect change rapidly, often with specific, preset lengths of therapeutic contact. Another similarity among the cognitive behavior therapies is that their target of change is also limited. For example, in the treatment of depression, the target of change is the symptoms of depression. Thus, in the cognitive behavioral approaches to treatment, one sees a time-limited focus and a limited target of change.

Context

Cognitive behavior therapy evolved from two lines of clinical and research activity: First, it derives from the work of the early cognitive therapists (Albert Ellis and Aaron Beck); second, it was strongly influenced by the careful empirical work of the early behaviorists.

Within the domain of behaviorism, cognitive processes were not always seen as a legitimate focus of attention. That is, in behavior therapy, there has always been a strong commitment to an applied science of clinical treatment. In the behavior therapy of the 1950's and 1960's, this emphasis on scientific methods and procedures meant that behavior therapists focused on events that were directly observable and measurable. Within this framework, behavior was seen as a function of external stimuli which determined or were reliably associated with observable responses. Also during this period, there was a deliberate avoidance of such "nebulous" concepts as thoughts, cognitions, or images. It was believed that these processes were by their very nature vague, and one could never be confident that one was reliably observing or measuring these processes.

It is important to note that by following scientific principles, researchers developed major new treatment approaches which in many ways revolutionized clinical practice (among them are systematic desensitization and the use of a token economy). Yet during the 1960's, several developments within behavior therapy had emphasized the limitations of a strict conditioning model to understanding human behavior.

In 1969, psychologist Albert Bandura published his influential volume *Principles of Behavior Modification*. In this volume, Bandura emphasized the role of internal or cognitive factors in the causation and maintenance of behavior. Following from the dissatisfaction of the radical behavioral approaches to understanding complex human behavior and the publication of Bandura's 1969 volume, behavior therapists began actively to seek and study the role of cognitive processes in human behavior.

Bibliography

Basco, Monica Ramirez, and A. John Rush. *Cognitive-Behavioral Therapy for Bipolar Disorder*. Foreword by Robert M. Post. New York: Guilford Press, 1996.

D'Zurilla, Thomas J., and Arthur M. Nezu. "Social Problem-Solving in Adults." In *Advances in Cognitive-Behavioral Research and Therapy*, edited by Philip C. Kendall. Vol. 1. New York: Academic Press, 1982. An excellent summary of problem-solving therapy. As indicated by its title, the Kendall book in which this article appears also contains other informative articles dealing with cognitive behavior therapy.

Goldfried, Marvin R. "The Use of Relaxation and Cognitive Relabeling as Coping Skills." In *Behavioral Self-Management: Strategies, Techniques, and Outcomes*, edited by Richard B. Stuart. New York: Brunner/Mazel, 1977. A description of systematic rational restructuring by Marvin Goldfried, who developed the technique; reveals its similarities to and differences from rational-emotive therapy.

Maultsby, Maxie C., Jr. *Rational Behavior Therapy*. Englewood Cliffs, N.J.: Prentice-Hall, 1984. An excellent summary of rational behavior therapy, as developed by Maultsby; discusses self-talk and its emotional and behavioral consequences.

Meichenbaum, Donald. *Cognitive Behavior Modification*. New York: Plenum Press, 1977. A well-written introduction to Meichenbaum's approaches, with clear examples of the applications of self-instructional training to impulsive children and schizophrenic patients.

_____. *Stress Inoculation Training*. New York: Pergamon Press, 1985. This short training manual presents a clear, useful overview of stress inoculation training, along with a detailed account of the empirical research completed in testing the approach.

Donald G. Beal

See also:

Analytical Psychotherapy, 54; Behaviorism, 98; Cognitive Therapy, 153; Person-Centered Therapy, 439; Psychoanalysis: Classical Versus Modern, 465; Radical Behaviorism: B. F. Skinner, 501.

COGNITIVE DEVELOPMENT THEORY
Jean Piaget

Type of psychology: Development psychology
Field of study: Cognitive development

Jean Piaget, in one of the twentieth century's most influential development theories, proposed a sequence of maturational changes in thinking. From the sensorimotor responses of infancy, the child acquires symbols. Later, the child begins relating these symbols in such logical operations as categorizing and quantifying. In adolescence, abstract and hypothetical mental manipulations become possible.

Principal terms

ACCOMMODATION: adjusting the interpretation (schema) of an object or event when the old interpretation does not fit a new instance

ASSIMILATION: the interpretation of a new instance of an object or event in terms of one's preexisting schema (or understanding); the fit, never perfect, is close enough

CONCRETE OPERATIONS STAGE: a cognitive stage characterized by a mental capacity to manipulate relationships of equivalence (quantitative rearrangements, categorization) that can be visualized

CONSERVATION: the comprehension of the essential equivalence when a given quantity (number, length, mass, volume) is rearranged; a basic concrete-operational skill

EGOCENTRIC THOUGHT: the assumption that everyone shares one's own perspective and the cognitive inability to understand the different perspective of another

FORMAL OPERATIONS STAGE: a cognitive stage in which reasoning can be speculative and include abstract ideals, hypothetical cases, and unobserved logical possibilities

OPERATIONS: mental transformations that can be reversed; for example, the concept that one gallon put into four quart bottles could also be put back into the gallon container

PREOPERATIONAL STAGE: a transitional stage of the preschool child, after mental representations (symbols) are acquired but before these can be logically manipulated

SCHEMA (*pl.* schemata): any process of interpreting an object or event, including habitual responses, symbols, or mental manipulations

SENSORIMOTOR STAGE: the stage (infancy) in which objects become familiar and are interpreted by appropriate habitual reactions

Overview

Jean Piaget (1896-1980), a Swiss psychologist, generated the twentieth century's most influential and comprehensive theory of cognitive development. Piaget's theory describes how the maturing child's interactions with the environment result in predictable sequences of changes in certain crucial understandings of the world about him or her. Such changes occur in the child's comprehension of time and space, quantitative relationships, cause and effect, and even right and wrong. The child is always treated as an actor in his or her own development. Advances result from the active desire to develop concepts or schemata which are sufficiently similar to the real world that this real world can be fitted or assimilated into these schemata. When a schema ("Cats smell nice") is sufficiently discrepant from reality ("That cat stinks"), the schema itself must be accommodated or altered ("That catlike creature is a skunk"). For children everywhere, neurologically based advances in mental capacity introduce new perceptions that make the old ways of construing reality unsatisfactory and compel a fundamentally new construction of reality—a new stage of development. Piaget conceptualizes four such stages: sensorimotor (in infancy), preoperational (the preschool child), concrete operational (the school-age child), and formal operational (adolescence and adulthood).

In the sensorimotor stage, the infant orients himself or herself to objects in the world by consistent physical (motor) movements to those sensory stimuli that represent the same object (for example, the sight of a face, the sound of footsteps, or a voice all represent "mother"). The relationship between motor responses and reappearing objects becomes progressively more complex and varied in the normal course of development. First, reflexes such as sucking become more efficient; then sequences of learned actions that bring pleasure are repeated (circular reactions). These learned reactions are directed first toward the infant's own body (thumb sucking), then toward objects in the environment (the infant's stuffed toy).

The baby seems to lack an awareness that objects continue to exist when they are outside the range of his or her senses. When the familiar toy of an infant is hidden, he or she does not search for it; it is as if it has disappeared from reality. As the sensorimotor infant matures, the infant becomes convinced of the continuing existence of objects that disappear in less obvious ways for longer intervals of time. By eighteen months of age, most toddlers have achieved such a conviction of continuing existence, or object permanence.

In the preoperational stage, the preschool child begins to represent these permanent objects by internal processes or mental representations. Now the development of mental representations of useful objects proceeds at an astounding pace. In symbolic play, blocks may represent cars and trains. Capable of deferred imitation, the child may pretend to be a cowboy according to his memory image of a motion-picture cowboy. The most important of all representations are the hundreds of new words the child learns to speak.

As one might infer from the word "preoperational," this period, lasting from about age two through ages six or seven, is transitional. The preschool child still lacks the attention, memory capacity, and mental flexibility to employ his or her increasing supply of symbolic representations in logical reasoning (operations). It is as if the child remains so focused upon the individual frames of a motion picture that he or she fails to comprehend the underlying plot. Piaget calls this narrow focusing on a single object or salient dimension "centration." The child may say, for example, that a quart of milk he or she has just seen transferred into two pint containers is now "less milk" because the child focuses upon the smaller size of the new containers. Fido is seen as a dog, not as an animal or a mammal. The child uncritically assumes that other people, regardless of their situation, share his or her own tastes and perspectives. A two-year-old closes his eyes and says, "Now you don't see me, Daddy." Piaget calls this egocentrism.

The concrete operations stage begins at age six or seven, when the school-age child becomes capable of keeping in mind and logically manipulating several concrete objects at the same time. The child is no longer the prisoner of the momentary appearance of things. In no case is the change more evident than in the sort of problem in which a number of objects (such as twelve black checkers) are spread out into four groups of three. While the four-year-old, preoperational child would be likely to say that now there are more checkers because they take up a larger area, to the eight-year-old, it is obvious that this transformation could easily be reversed by regrouping the checkers. Piaget describes the capacity to visualize the reversibility of such transformations as "conservation." This understanding is fundamental to the comprehension of simple arithmetical manipulations. It is also funda-mental to a second operational skill: categorization. To the concrete-operational child, it seems obvious that while Rover the dog can for other purposes be classified as a household pet, an animal, or a living organism, he will still be a "dog" and still be "Rover." A related skill is seriation: keeping in mind that an entire series of objects can be arranged along a single dimension, such as size (from smallest to largest). The child now is also capable of role-taking, of understanding the different perspective of a parent or teacher. No longer egocentric, the child becomes able to see himself as others see him and to temper the harshness of absolute rules with a comprehension of the viewpoints of others.

The formal operations stage begins in early adolescence. In childhood, logical operations are concrete ones, limited to objects that can be visualized, touched, or directly experienced. The advance of the early adolescent into formal operational thinking involves the capacity to deal with possibilities that are purely speculative. This permits coping with new classes of problems: those involving relationships that are purely abstract or hypothetical, or that involve the higher-level analysis of a problem by the systematic consideration of every logical (sometimes fanciful) possibility. The logical adequacy of an argument can be examined apart from the truth or falsity of its conclusions.

Concepts such as "forces," "infinity," or "justice," nowhere directly experienced, can now be comprehended. Formal operational thought permits the midadolescent or adult to hold abstract ideals and to initiate scientific investigations.

Applications

Piaget was particularly clever in the invention of problems which illustrate the underlying premises of the child's thought. The crucial capability that signals the end of the sensorimo-tor period is object permanence, the child's conviction of the continuing existence of objects that are outside the range of his or her senses. Piaget established the gradual emergence of object permanence by hiding from the child familiar toys for longer periods of time, with the act of hiding progressively less obvious to the child. Full object permanence is not considered achieved until the child will search for a familiar missing object even when he or she could not have observed its being hidden.

The fundamental test of concrete operational thought is conservation. In a typical conservation task, the child is shown two identical balls of putty. The child generally affirms their obvious equivalence. Then one of the balls of putty is reworked into an elongated, wormlike shape while the child watches. The child is again asked about their relative size. Younger children are likely to say that the wormlike shape is smaller, but the child who has attained conservation of mass will state that the size must still be the same. Inquiries concerning whether the weights of the differently shaped material (conservation of weight) are the same, and whether they would displace the same amount of water (conservation of volume) are more difficult questions, generally answerable at older ages.

Since Piaget's original demonstrations, further progress has necessitated the standardization of these problems with materials, questions, procedures, and scoring so clearly specified that examiners can replicate one another's results. Such standardization permits the explanation of the general applicability of Piaget's concepts. Standardized tests have been developed for measuring object permanence, egocentricity, and role-taking skills. The "Concept Assessment Kit: Conservation," for example, provides six standard conservation tasks for which comparison data (norms) are available for children in several widely diverse cultures. The relative conceptual attainments of an individual child (or culture) can be measured. It is encouraging that those who attain such basic skills as conservation early have been shown to be advanced in many other educational and cognitive achievements.

Piaget's views of cognitive development have broad implications for educational institutions charged with fostering such development. The child is viewed as an active seeker of knowledge. This pursuit is advanced by his or her experimental engagement with problems which are slightly more complex than those problems successfully worked through in the past. The teacher is a facilitator of the opportunities for such cognitive growth, not a lecturer or a drillmaster. The teacher provides physical materials that can be experimentally manipulated. Such materials can be simple: Blocks, stones, bottle caps, and plastic containers all can be classified, immersed in water, thrown into fire, dropped, thrown, or balanced. Facilitating peer relationships and cooperation in playing games is also helpful in encouraging social role-taking and moral development.

Since each student pursues knowledge at his or her own pace, and in his or her own idiom, great freedom and variety may be permitted in an essentially open classroom. The teacher may nudge the student toward cognitive advancement by presenting a problem slightly more complex than that already comprehended by the student. A student who understands conservation of number may be ready for problems involving the conservation of length, for example. Yet the teacher does not reinforce correct answers or criticize incorrect ones. Sequencing is crucial. The presentation of knowledge or skill before the child is ready can result in superficial, uncomprehended verbalisms. Piaget does not totally reject the necessity of the inculcation of social and cultural niceties (social-arbitrary knowledge), the focus of traditional education. He would maintain, however, that an experimentally based understanding of physical and social relationships is crucial for a creative, thoughtful society.

Context

Piaget hypothesized sequences of age-related changes in ways of dealing with reality. His conclusions were based on the careful observation of a few selected cases. The voluminous research since Piaget's time overwhelmingly supports the sequence he outlined. The process almost never reverses. Once a child understands the conservation of substance, for example, his or her former conclusion that "Now there is more" seems to the child not simply wrong but absurd. Even within a stage, there is a sequence. Conservation of mass, for example, precedes conservation of volume.

Post-Piagetian research has nevertheless led to a fine-tuning of some of his conclusions and a modification of others. Piaget believed that transitions to more advanced cognitive levels awaited neurological maturation and the child's spontaneous discoveries. Several researchers have found that specific training in simplified and graded conservation and categorization tasks can lead to an early ripening of these skills. Other research has called into question Piaget's timetable. The fact that, within a few months of birth, infants show subtle differences in their reaction to familiar versus unfamiliar objects suggests that recognition memory for objects may begin earlier than Piaget's age for object permanence. If conservation tasks are simplified—if all distraction is avoided, and simple language and familiar materials are used—it can be shown that concrete operations also may begin earlier than Piaget thought. Formal operations, on the other hand, may not begin as early or be applied as universally in adult problem solving as suggested by Piaget's thesis. A significant percentage of older adolescents and adults fail tests for formal operations, particularly in new problem areas.

More basic than readjustments of his developmental scheduling is the reinterpretation of Piaget's stages. The stage concept implies not only an invariant sequence of age-related changes but also developmental discontinuities involving global and fairly abrupt shifts in an entire pattern or structure. Yet the prolonged development and domain-specific nature of many operational skills, cited above, suggest a process that is neither abrupt nor global. An alternative view is that Piaget's sequences can also be understood as the results of continuous improvements in attention, concentration, and memory. Stages represent only transition points on this continuous dimension. They are more like the points of a scale on a thermometer than the stages of the metamorphosis of a caterpillar into a moth.

Even with the caveat that his stages may reflect, at a more fundamental level, an underlying continuum, Piaget's contributions can be seen as a great leap forward in approximate answers to one of humankind's oldest questions: how human beings know their world. The eighteenth century philosopher Immanuel Kant described certain core assumptions, such as quantity, quality, and cause and effect, which he called "categories of the understanding." Human beings make these assumptions when they relate specific objects and events to one another—when they reason. Piaget's work became known to a 1960's-era American psychology that was dominated by B. F. Skinner's behavioral view of a passive child whose plastic nature was simply molded by the rewards and punishments of parents and culture. The impact of Piaget's work shifted psychology's focus back to a Kantian perspective of the child as an active reasoner who selectively responds to aspects of culture he or she finds relevant. Piaget himself outlined the sequence, the pace, and some of the dynamics of the maturing child's development of major Kantian categories. Such subsequent contributions as Lawrence Kohlberg's work on moral development and Robert Selman's work on role-taking can be viewed as an elaboration and extension of Piaget's unfinished work. Piaget, like Sigmund Freud, was one of psychology's pivotal thinkers. Without him, the entire field of developmental psychology would be radically different.

Bibliography

Ault, Ruth L. *Children's Cognitive Development: Piaget's Theory and the Process Approach.* New York: Oxford University Press, 1977. This short work both describes and illustrates Piaget's concepts and illuminates the implications of the theory by contrasting them with the non-Piagetian approach of experimental child psychology. Lucid, non-technical, but thought-provoking.

Burman, Erica. "Continuities and Discontinuities in Interpretive and Textual Approaches in Developmental Psychology." *Human Development* 39 (Nov./Dec., 1996): 330-346.

Gelman, Rochel, and R. Baillargeon. "A Review of Some Piagetian Concepts." In *Handbook of Child Psychology*, edited by Paul H. Mussen. 4th ed. Vol. 3. New York: John Wiley & Sons, 1983. A thorough review, concept by concept, of the developmental research on the various types of conservation and classification problems. These authors conclude that the hypothesis of domain-specific changes fits the experimental research better than the idea of global stages does.

Phillips, John L. *The Origins of Intellect: Piaget's Theory*. 2d ed. San Francisco: W. H. Freeman, 1975. This thorough, clearly written text explains Piaget's concepts by providing many examples. An excellent source for the introductory-level student who seeks a comprehensive understanding of Piaget's ideas. Available in paperback.

Piaget, Jean. *The Essential Piaget*. Edited by Howard E. Gruber and J. Jacques Vonèche. New York: Basic Books, 1977. Contains English translations of most of Piaget's writings, from his earliest work (1909), which was heavily biological. Many of these earlier writings were unknown to Americans until translated from the French in the 1950's. Since reading Piaget himself is more difficult than most general works about his theory, the student might consult Piaget's papers selectively on topics of particular interest.

Schumaker, Richard. "A Foundational Thinker." *UNESCO Courier*, November, 1996, 48-51.

Sigel, Irving E., and Rodney R. Cocking. *Cognitive Development from Childhood to Adolescence: A Constructivist Perspective*. New York: Holt, Rinehart and Winston, 1977. A readable, condensed version of Piaget's theory. Can be used as an alternative to the Phillips summary if the reader finds this book easier to obtain. A good place for the introductory-level reader to begin.

Thomas E. DeWolfe

See also:

Adolescence: Cognitive Skills, 13; Aging: Cognitive Changes, 37; Attachment and Bonding in Infancy and Childhood, 71; Gender-Identity Formation, 254; Moral Development, 399; Motor Development, 410.

Cognitive Dissonance Theory

Type of psychology: Social psychology
Field of study: Attitudes and behavior

Cognitive dissonance theory examines the effects of inconsistencies between attitudes and behaviors. It has evolved into an important theory of attitude change and has offered insights into diverse topics such as the effects of rewards, punishment, and choice on attitudes.

Principal terms

ATTITUDE: positive or negative evaluations of a person, place, or thing
COGNITION: knowledge one has about one's attitudes, beliefs, and behaviors
CONSONANCE: the psychological state in which cognitions are not in conflict
DISSONANCE: an unpleasant psychological and physiological state caused by an inconsistency between cognitions
EXTERNAL JUSTIFICATION: an environmental factor that can account for an inconsistency between cognitions

Overview

Cognitive dissonance theory, developed by social psychologist Leon Festinger, suggests that there is a basic human tendency to strive for consistency between and among cognitions. Cognitions are defined as what people know about their attitudes and behaviors. If an inconsistency does arise—for example, if an individual does something that is discrepant with his or her attitudes—cognitive dissonance is said to occur. Dissonance is an uncomfortable state of physiological and psychological tension. It is so uncomfortable, in fact, that when individuals are in such a state, they become motivated to rid themselves of the feeling. This can be done by restoring consistency to the cognitions in some way.

What does dissonance feel like? Although it is difficult to describe any kind of internal state, the reactions one has when one hurts the feelings of a loved one or when one breaks something belonging to someone else are probably what Festinger meant by dissonance.

When in a state of dissonance, there are three ways a person can restore consistency or (in the language of the theory) consonance. One is to reduce the importance of the conflicting cognitions. The theory states that the amount of dissonance experienced is a direct function of the importance of the conflicting cognitions. Consider, for example, a man who actively pursues a suntan. The potential for dissonance exists with such behavior, because the cognition "I am doing something that is increasing my chances for skin cancer" may be in conflict with the cognition "I would like to remain healthy and live a long life." To reduce dissonance, this person may convince himself that he would rather live a shorter life filled with doing enjoyable and exciting things than live a longer, but perhaps not so exciting, life. The inconsistency still exists, but the importance of the inconsistency has been reduced.

A second way to reduce dissonance is to add numerous consonant cognitions, thus making the discrepancy seem less great. The suntanner may begin to believe he needs to be tan to be socially accepted because all of his friends have tans. The tanner may also begin to believe that suntanning makes him look more attractive and healthier and, indeed, may come to believe that suntanning does promote health.

The last way that Festinger proposed that people could reduce dissonance is the simplest, but it is the one that caught the attention of many social psychologists. It is simply to change one of the discrepant cognitions. The suntanner could either stop suntanning or convince himself that suntanning is not associated with an increased risk of skin cancer. In either case, the inconsistency would be eliminated.

This latter possibility intrigued social psychologists because it offered the possibility that people's behaviors could influence their attitudes. In particular, it suggested that if someone does something that is inconsistent with his or her attitudes, those attitudes may change to become more consistent with the behavior. For example, imagine that a woman wanted a friend to favor a particular candidate in an upcoming election, and the friend favored the opposing candidate. What would happen if this woman convinced the friend to accompany her to a rally for the candidate the friend did not support? According to the theory, the friend should experience some degree of dissonance, as the behavior of attending a rally for candidate X is inconsistent with the attitude "I do not favor candidate X." To resolve the inconsistency, the friend may very well begin to convince herself that candidate X is not so bad and actually has some good points. Thus, in an effort to restore consonance, the friend's attitudes have changed to be more consistent with behavior.

Changes in behavior cannot always be expected to lead to changes in attitudes. Dissonance-induced attitude change—that is, attitudes that change in an effort to be consistent with a behavior—is likely to happen only under certain conditions. For one, there must not be any external justification for the behavior. An external justification is an environmental cause that might explain the inconsistency. If the friend was paid a hundred dollars to attend the rally for the candidate or was promised a dinner at a fancy restaurant, she most likely would not have experienced dissonance, because she had a sufficient external justification. Dissonance is most likely to occur when no external justification is present for a behavior.

Second, dissonance is most likely to occur when individuals believe that the behavior was done of their own free will—that is, when they feel some sort of personal responsibility for the behavior. If the friend had been simply told that she was being taken out for an exciting evening and was not told that she was going to this candidate's rally until she got there, she most likely would not have experienced dissonance.

Third, dissonance is more likely to occur when the behavior has some sort of foreseeable negative consequences. If the friend knew that when attending the rally, each person was required to pay a donation or was required to hand out pamphlets for the candidate, and she still elected to go, she would probably have experienced considerable dissonance; now she is not only attending a rally for a candidate she opposes but also actively campaigning against her preferred candidate.

Applications

Perhaps the most-researched application of dissonance theory concerns the effects on attitudes of rewarding people for doing things in which they do not believe. In one study,

Festinger and J. M. Carlsmith had students perform a boring screwturning task for one hour. They then asked the students to tell another student waiting to do the same task that the task was very interesting. In other words, they asked the students to lie. Half the students were offered twenty dollars to do this; the other half were offered one dollar. After the students told the waiting student that the task was enjoyable, the researchers asked them what they really thought about the screwturning task. The students who were paid twenty dollars said they thought the screwturning task was quite boring. The students who were paid only one dollar, however, said that they thought the task was interesting and enjoyable.

Although surprising, these findings are precisely what dissonance theory predicts. When a student informed a waiting student that the task was enjoyable, the possibility for dissonance arose. The cognition "This task was really boring" is inconsistent with the cognition "I just told someone that this task was quite enjoyable." The students paid twenty dollars, however, had a sufficient external justification for the inconsistency. Hence, there was no dissonance and no need to resolve any inconsistency. The students paid one dollar, however, did not have the same external justification; most people would not consider a dollar to be sufficient justification for telling a lie, so these students were in a real state of dissonance. To resolve the inconsistency, they changed their attitudes about the task and convinced themselves that the task was indeed enjoyable, thereby achieving consonance between attitudes and behavior. Thus, the *less* people are rewarded for doing things they might not like, the more likely it is that they will begin to like them.

Dissonance theory makes equally interesting predictions about the effects of punishment. In a study by Elliot Aronson and Carlsmith, a researcher asked preschool children to rate the attractiveness of toys. The researcher then left the room, but, before leaving, he instructed the children not to play with one of the toys they had rated highly attractive. This became the "forbidden" toy. The researcher varied the severity of the punishment with which he threatened the children if they played with the forbidden toy. For some children, the threat was relatively mild. The researcher said he would be upset. For others, the threat was more severe. The researcher said that he would be angry, would pack up the toys and leave, and would consider the child a baby.

Both threats of punishment seemed to work, as no children played with the forbidden toy. When the researcher asked the children later to rerate the attractiveness of the toys, however, it was apparent that the severity of the threat did make a difference. For children who were severely threatened, the forbidden toy was still rated as quite attractive. For the mildly threatened children, however, the forbidden toy was rated as much less attractive.

By not playing with the forbidden toy, children were potentially in a state of dissonance. The cognition "I think this is an attractive toy" is inconsistent with the cognition "I am not playing with the toy." Those in the severe threat condition had a sufficient external justification for the discrepancy. Hence, there was no dissonance and no motivation to resolve the inconsistency. Those in the mild threat condition had no such external justification for the inconsistency, so they most likely felt dissonance, and they resolved it by convincing themselves that the toy was not so attractive. Thus, perhaps surprisingly, the more mild the threats used to get children not to do something, the more likely it is that they will come to believe that it is not something they even want to do.

A last type of everyday behavior for which dissonance theory has implications is decision making. According to the theory, many times when one makes a decision, particularly between attractive alternatives, dissonance is likely to occur. Before making a decision, there are probably some features of each alternative that are attractive and some that are not so attractive. When the decision is made, two sets of dissonant cognitions result: "I chose something that has unattractive qualities" and "I did not choose something that has attractive qualities." To resolve this dissonance, people tend to convince themselves that the chosen alternative is clearly superior to the unchosen alternative. So, although before the decision was made, each alternative was seen as equally attractive, after the decision, the chosen alternative is seen as much more attractive. For example, Robert Knox and James Inkster went to a racetrack and asked a sample of people who were waiting in line to place their bets how confident they were that their horse was going to win. They then asked a sample of people who were leaving the betting window the same question.

As might have been predicted by now, bettors were much more confident about their horse's chances after having placed the bet. Before placing a bet, there is no dissonance. After actually placing money on the horse, the potential for dissonance ("I placed money on a horse that might lose and I didn't bet on a horse that might win") arises. To avoid or resolve this dissonance, bettors become much more confident that their horse will win and, by default, more confident that other horses will not.

Context

Cognitive dissonance theory was introduced in 1957, at a time when interest in the motives underlying people's attitudes and behaviors was at a peak in social psychology. Although dissonance theory has emerged as perhaps the best-known and most-researched theory in social psychology, when it was first developed it was one of a handful of theories, now collectively known as cognitive consistency theories, that proposed that people are motivated to seek consistency among and between thoughts, feelings, and behaviors.

There are numerous explanations as to why cognitive dissonance theory has become as important as it has, but two seem particularly intriguing. One concerns the intellectual climate in psychology during the time the theory was introduced. At the time, research in most fields of psychology, including social psychological research on attitude change, was influenced by learning theory. Learning theory suggests that behavior is a function of its consequences: People do those things for which they are rewarded and do not do those things for which they are not rewarded or for which they are punished. Therefore, according to this perspective, to change significantly any form of behavior, from overt actions to attitudes and beliefs, some kind of reward or incentive needs to be offered. The bigger the incentive, the more change can be expected (similarly, the stronger the punishment, the more change can be expected). Research on attitude change, therefore, also focused on the role of rewards and punishment. What made dissonance theory stand out was its prediction that sometimes *less* reward or incentive will lead to more change. This counterintuitive prediction, standing in stark contrast to the generally accepted ideas about the roles of rewards and punishment, brought immediate attention to dissonance theory not only from the social psychological community but also from the psychological community in general; it quickly vaulted the theory to a position of prominence.

A second reason dissonance has become such an important theory was its particular influence on the field of social psychology. Before the theory was introduced, social psychology was identified with the study of groups and intergroup relations. Dissonance theory was one of the first social psychological theories to emphasize the cognitive processes occurring within the individual as an important area of inquiry. As a result, interest in the individual waxed in social psychology, and interest in groups waned. Indeed, the study of groups and intergroup relations began, in part, to be considered the province of sociologists, and the study of the individual in social settings began to define social psychology. Thus, dissonance theory can be credited with significantly changing the focus of research and theory in social psychology.

Bibliography

Aronson, Elliot. "The Theory of Cognitive Dissonance." In *Advances in Experimental Social Psychology*. Vol. 4, edited by Leonard Berkowitz. New York: Academic Press, 1969. This chapter by one of the leading dissonance researchers critically examines the original theory and offers a revised version of the theory based on empirical findings. Clearly written and easily accessible to nonpsychologists.

Beauvois, Jean-Leon, and Robert-Vincent Joule. *A Radical Dissonance Theory*. Bristol, Pa.: Taylor & Francis, 1996.

Brehm, Jack Williams, and Arthur R. Cohen. *Explorations in Cognitive Dissonance*. New York: John Wiley & Sons, 1962. The sixteen chapters in this volume examine, among other things, the implications of dissonance for decision making, the role of personality factors in the experience of dissonance, and possible physiological factors underlying dissonance. In addition, practical applications of the theory are discussed.

Devine, Patricia G., David L. Hamilton, and Thomas M. Ostrom, eds. *Social Cognition: Impact on Social Psychology*. San Diego, Calif.: Academic Press, 1994.

Festinger, Leon. *A Theory of Cognitive Dissonance*. Stanford, Calif.: Stanford University Press, 1957. Festinger's seminal work represents the formal introduction of the theory. Theory and data on decision making, attitude change, and exposure to attitude-discrepant information are addressed. It is interesting to compare this original work with later versions of the theory, such as Aronson's chapter.

Kiesler, Charles A., Barry E. Collins, and Norman Miller. *Attitude Change*. New York: John Wiley & Sons, 1969. Offers a critical analysis of dissonance theory. Also compares and contrasts dissonance theory with other prominent theories of attitude change and persuasion. An excellent general introduction to theory and research on attitude change.

Wicklund, Robert A., and Jack Williams Brehm. *Perspectives on Cognitive Dissonance*. Hillsdale, N.J.: Lawrence Erlbaum, 1976. Contains seventeen chapters that not only review the evidence for the basic tenets of the theory but also explore implications of the theory for areas such as politics, marketing, and clinical psychology. In addition, alternative explanations for dissonance phenomena are entertained.

Kenneth G. DeBono

See also:

COGNITIVE PSYCHOLOGY

Type of psychology: Cognition
Fields of study: Cognitive processes; thought

Cognitive psychology is concerned with the scientific study of human mental activities involved in the acquisition, storage, retrieval, and utilization of information. Among its wide concerns are perception, memory, reasoning, problem solving, intelligence, language, and creativity; research in these areas has widespread practical applications.

Principal terms

ARTIFICIAL INTELLIGENCE: a branch of computer science whose goal is to create a computer capable of mimicking human intelligence

AVAILABILITY HEURISTIC: a decision-making heuristic whereby a person estimates the probability of some occurrence or event depending on how easily examples of that event can be remembered

COGNITIVE SCIENCE: a multidisciplinary approach to the study of cognition from the perspectives of psychology, computer science, neuroscience, philosophy, and linguistics

EXPERT SYSTEMS: computer programs built to simulate human expertise in particular domains

HEURISTIC: a shortcut or rule of thumb used for decision making or problem solving that often leads to, but does not guarantee, a correct response

INFORMATION-PROCESSING MODEL: the approach of most modern cognitive psychologists; it interprets cognition as the flow of information through interrelated stages, in much the same way that information is processed by a computer

INTROSPECTION: the self-report of one's own sensations, experiences, and thoughts

Overview

Cognitive psychology is that branch of psychology concerned with human mental activities. A staggering array of topics fit under such a general heading. In fact, it sometimes seems that there is no clear place to end the catalog of cognitive topics, as mental operations intrude into virtually all human endeavors. As a general guideline, one might consider the subject matter of cognitive psychology as those mental processes involved in the acquisition, storage, retrieval, and utilization of information.

Among the more specific concerns of cognitive psychologists are perception, attention, memory, and imagery. Studies of perception and attention might be concerned with how much of people's vast sensory experience they can further process and make sense of, and how they recognize incoming information as forming familiar patterns. Questions regarding the quality of memory include how much information can be maintained, for how long, and under what conditions; how information is organized in memory and how is it retrieved or lost; and how accurate the memory is, as well as what can be done to facilitate a person's recall skills. Cognitive researchers concerned with imagery are interested in people's ability to "see" in their minds a picture or image of an object, person, or scene that is not physically present; cognitive researchers are interested in the properties of such images and how they can be manipulated.

In addition to these concerns, there is great interest in the higher-order processes of planning, reasoning, problem solving, intelligence, language, and creativity. Cognitive psychologists want to know, for example, what steps are involved in planning a route to a destination or a solution to a problem, and what factors influence people's more abstract ability to reason. They seek to understand the importance of prior knowledge or experience, to discover which strategies are effective, and to see what obstacles typically impede a person's thinking. They are interested in the relationships between language and thought, and between creativity and intelligence.

The following exchange is useful in illustrating some of the topics important to cognitive psychologists. Imagine that "Jacob" and "Janet" are two children on a busy playground:

JACOB: Do you want to play some football?

JANET: Sure! Tell me where the ball is and I'll go get it.

JACOB: The football's in my locker in the equipment room. Go back in the building. Go past our classroom, turn right at the water fountain, and it's the second door on your left. My locker is number 12, and the combination is 6-21-13.

JANET: Okay, it'll just take me a couple of minutes. [As she runs to get the ball, Janet repeats over and over to herself, "12; 6, 21, 13."]

JACOB: [*shouting*] The football field's being watered; meet me in the gym.

Even such a simple encounter involves and depends upon a rich assortment of cognitive skills. At a basic level, Jacob and Janet have to be aware of each other. Their sensory systems allow the detection of each other, and their brains work on the raw data (information) from the senses in order to perceive or interpret the incoming information. In this case, the data are recognized as the familiar patterns labeled "Jacob" and "Janet." During the course of the brief conversation, the children must also attend to (concentrate on) each other, and in doing so they may be less attentive to other detectable sights and sounds of their environment.

This scenario illustrates the use of more than one type of memory. Janet stores the locker number and combination in short-term memory (STM), and she maintains the information by rehearsing it. After Janet retrieves the ball and redirects her attention to choosing teams for the football game, she will probably quickly forget this information. Long-term memory (LTM) is also being displayed by the children. Jacob does not need to rehearse his combination continually to maintain it; rather, his frequent use of his combination and the meaningfulness of this information have helped him to store it in LTM. The language comprehension of the children also illustrates LTM. When Janet hears the words "football," "water fountain," and "locker," she effortlessly retrieves their meanings from LTM. Furthermore, metamemory, an understanding of the attributes of one's own memories, is demonstrated. Janet knows to rehearse the combination to prevent forgetting it.

Jacob probably employed mental imagery and relied on a cognitive map in order to direct Janet to the equipment room. From his substantial mental representation of the school environment, Jacob retrieved a specific route, guided by a particular sequence of meaningful landmarks. Seemingly without thought, both children communicate through the highly abstract symbol system of language. Not only do they have ample vocabularies, but also they know the relationships between words and how to arrange the words meaningfully; they have sophisticated knowledge of syntax and grammar.

In addition to their language capabilities and their abilities to form and follow routes, a number of other higher-level mental processes suggest something of the intelligence of these children. They appear to be following a plan that will result in a football game. Simple problem solving is demonstrated by Janet's calculation of how long it will take to retrieve the football and in Jacob's decision to use the gym floor as a substitute for the football field.

To understand cognitive psychology, one must be familiar not only with the relevant questions—the topic matter of the discipline—but also with the approach taken to answer these questions. Cognitive psychologists typically employ an information-processing model to help them better understand mental events. An assumption of this model is that mental activities (the processing of information) can be broken down into a series of interrelated stages and scientifically studied. A general comparison can be made between the information processing of a human and a computer. For example, both have data input into the system, humans through their sense organs and computers via the keyboard. Both systems then translate and encode (store) the data. The computer translates the keyboard input into electromagnetic signals for storage on a disk. People oftentimes translate the raw data from their senses to a linguistic code which is retained in some unique human storage device (for example, a piercing, rising-and-falling pitch may be stored in memory as "baby's cry"). Both humans and computers can manipulate the stored information in virtually limitless ways, and both can later retrieve information from storage for output. Although there are many dissimilarities between how computers and humans function, this comparison accurately imparts the flavor of the information-processing model.

Finally, it should be emphasized that cognitive psychologists employ a scientific approach. While the workings of the mind cannot be directly seen, one can objectively record the data input into the system and the ensuing response. One can also objectively measure the accuracy of, and the time required for, the response. Based upon this information, one can draw logical inferences as to the mental steps involved in generating that response. One of the continuing challenges of cognitive psychology is the construction of experiments in which observable behaviors accurately reveal mental processes.

Applications

For many psychologists, the desire to "know about knowing" is sufficient reason to study human cognition; however, there are more tangible benefits. Examples of these widespread practical applications may be found in the fields of artificial intelligence and law, and in the everyday world of decision making.

Artificial intelligence (AI) is a branch of computer science that strives to create a computer capable of reasoning, processing language, and, in short, mimicking human intelligence. While this goal has yet to be obtained in full, research in this area has made important contributions. The search for AI has improved the understanding of human cognition; it has also produced applied benefits such as expert systems. Expert systems are computer programs that simulate human expertise in specific domains. Such programs have been painstakingly developed by computer scientists who have essentially extracted knowledge in a subject area from a human expert and built it into a computer system designed to apply that knowledge. Expert systems do not qualify as true artificial intelligence, because, while they can think, they can only do so very narrowly, on one particular topic.

A familiar expert system is the "chess computer." A computerized chess game is driven by a program that has a vast storehouse of chess knowledge and the capability of interacting with a human player, "thinking" about each game in which it is involved. Expert systems are also employed to solve problems in law, computer programming, and various facets of industry. A medical expert system has even been developed to consult interactively with patients and to diagnose and recommend a course of treatment for infectious diseases.

There are legal implications for the cognitive research of Elizabeth Loftus and her colleagues at the University of Washington. Some of their experiments demonstrate the shortcomings of human long-term memory, research relevant to the interpretation of eyewitness testimony in the courtroom. In one study, Loftus and John Palmer showed their subjects films of automobile accidents and asked them to estimate the speeds of the cars involved. The critical variable was the verb used in the question to the subjects. That is, they were asked how fast the cars were going when they "smashed," "collided," "bumped," "hit," or "contacted" each other. Interestingly, the stronger the verb, the greater was the speed estimated. One interpretation of these findings is that the nature of the "leading question" biased the answers of subjects who were not really positive of the cars' speeds. Hence, if the question employed the verb "smashed," the subject was led to estimate that the cars were going fast. Any astute attorney would have no trouble capitalizing on this phenomenon when questioning witnesses to a crime or accident.

In a second experiment, Loftus and Palmer considered a different explanation for their findings. Again, subjects saw filmed car accidents and were questioned as to the speeds of the cars, with the key verb being varied as previously described. As before, those exposed to the verb "smashed" estimated the fastest speeds. In the second part of the experiment, conducted a week later, the subjects were asked additional questions about the accident, including, "Did you see any broken glass?" Twenty percent of the subjects reported seeing broken glass, though none was in the film. Of particular interest was that the majority of those who made this error were in the group which had been exposed to the strongest verb, "smashed."

Loftus and Palmer reasoned that the subjects were melding actual information that they had witnessed with information from another source encountered after the fact (the verb "smashed" presented by the questioner). The result was a mental representation of an event that was partly truth and partly fiction. This interpretation also has implications for the evaluation of eyewitness testimony. Before testifying in court, a witness will likely have been questioned numerous times (and received many suggestions as to what may have taken place) and may even have "compared notes" with other witnesses. This process is likely to distort the originally experienced information.

Consider next the topic of decision making, an area of research in cognitive psychology loaded with practical implications. Everyone makes scores of decisions on a daily basis, from choosing clothing to match the weather, to selecting a college or a career objective. Psychologists Amos Tversky and Daniel Kahneman are well known for their research on decision making and, in particular, on the use of heuristics. Heuristics are shortcuts or rules of thumb that are likely, but not guaranteed, to produce a correct decision. It would seem beneficial for everyone to appreciate the limitations of such strategies. For example, the availability heuristic oftentimes leads people astray when their decisions involve the estimating of probabilities, as when faced with questions such as, Which produces more fatalities, breast cancer or diabetes? Which are more numerous in the English language, words that begin with k or words that have k as the third letter? Experimental subjects typically, and incorrectly, choose the first alternative in the above questions. Kahneman and Tversky's research indicates that people rely heavily on examples that come most easily to mind—that is, the information most available in memory. Hence, people overestimate the incidence of breast-cancer fatalities because such tragedies get more media attention relative to diabetes, a more prolific but less exotic killer. In a similar vein, words that begin with *k* come to mind more easily (probably because people are more likely to organize their vocabularies by the initial sounds of the words) than words with *k* as the third letter, although the latter in fact outnumber the former. One's decision making will doubtless be improved if one is aware of the potential drawbacks associated with the availability heuristic and if one is able to resist the tendency to estimate probabilities based upon the most easily imagined examples.

Context

The workings of the human mind have been pondered throughout recorded history. The science of psychology, however, only dates back to 1879, when Wilhelm Wundt established the first laboratory for the study of psychology in Leipzig, Germany. Although the term was not yet popular, Wundt's primary interest was clearly in cognition. His students laboriously practiced the technique of introspection (the careful attention to, and the objective report of, one's own sensations, experiences, and thoughts), as Wundt hoped to identify through this method the basic elements of human thought. Wundt's interests remained fairly popular until around 1920. At that time, John B. Watson, a noted American psychologist and behaviorist, spearheaded a campaign to redefine the agenda of psychology. Watson was convinced that the workings of the mind could not be objectively studied through introspection and hence mandated that the proper subject matter for psychologists should be overt, observable behaviors exclusively. In this way, dissatisfaction with a method of research (introspection) led to the abandonment of an important psychological topic (mental activity).

In the 1950's, a number of forces came into play that led to the reemergence of cognitive psychology in America. First, during World War II, considerable research had been devoted to human-factors issues such as human skills and performance within, for example, the confines of a tank or cockpit. After the war, researchers showed continued interest in human attention, perception, decision making, and so on, and they were influenced by a branch of communication science, known as information theory, that dealt abstractly with questions of information processing. The integration of these two topics resulted eventually in the modern information-processing model, mentioned above.

Second, explosive gains were made in the field of computer science. Of particular interest to psychology were advances in the area of artificial intelligence. It was a natural progression for psychologists to begin comparing computer and brain processes, and this analogy served to facilitate cognitive research.

Third, there was growing dissatisfaction with behavioral psychology as defined by Watson and with its seeming inability to explain complex psychological phenomena. In particular, Noam Chomsky, a well-known linguist, proposed that the structure of language was too complicated to be acquired via the principles of behaviorism. It became apparent to many psychologists that to understand truly the diversity of human behavior, internal mental processes would have to be accepted and scientifically studied.

Cognitive psychology is now a vibrant subdiscipline that has attracted some of the finest scientific minds. It is a standard component in most undergraduate and graduate psychology programs. More than half a dozen academic journals are devoted to its research, and it continues to pursue answers to questions that are important to psychology and other disciplines as well. The cognitive perspective has heavily influenced other subfields of psychology. For example, many social psychologists are interested in social cognition, the reasoning underlying such phenomena as prejudice, altruism, and persuasion. Some clinical psychologists are interested in understanding the abnormal thought processes underlying problems such as depression and anorexia nervosa, and cognitive developmentalists research the way people's thought processes change across the life span.

The burgeoning field of cognitive science represents a contemporary union of cognitive psychology, neuroscience, computer science, linguistics, and philosophy. Cognitive scientists are concerned with mental processes but are particularly interested in establishing general, fundamental principles of information processing as they may be applied by humans or machines. Their research is often heavily dependent on complex computer models rather than experimentation with humans. With fast-paced advances in computer technology, and the exciting potential of expertise shared in an interdisciplinary fashion, the field of cognitive science holds considerable promise for answering questions about human cognition.

Bibliography

Ashcraft, Mark H. *Human Memory and Cognition.* Glenview, Ill.: Scott, Foresman, 1989. A fine textbook, geared for college students who have had some background in psychology but accessible to the inquisitive layperson. Ashcraft writes informally and provides chapter outlines and summaries, a glossary of key terms, and suggested supplemental readings. Perception and attention, memory, language, reasoning, decision making, and problem solving are all well covered.

Baddeley, Alan D. "The Cognitive Psychology of Everyday Life." *British Journal of Psychology* 72, no. 2 (1981): 257-269. An interesting journal article in which Baddeley describes his research conducted outside the laboratory environment. Considers such practical topics as absentmindedness, alcohol effects, and the effectiveness of saturation advertising. A must for those who question the ecological validity (the real-life applicability) of cognitive research.

Berger, Dale E., Kathy Pezdek, and William P. Banks, eds. *Applications of Cognitive Psychology.* Hillsdale, N.J.: Lawrence Erlbaum, 1987. Five chapters each on three topics: educational applications, teaching of thinking and problem solving, and human-computer interactions. The chapters range in sophistication and accessibility, so this book should appeal to readers of diverse backgrounds. There are helpful name and subject indexes.

French, Christopher C., and Andrew M. Colman, eds. *Cognitive Psychology.* New York: Longman, 1995.

Kahneman, Daniel, Paul Slovic, and Amos Tversky, eds. *Judgment Under Uncertainty: Heuristics and Biases.* Cambridge, England: Cambridge University Press, 1982. A comprehensive source on heuristics and decision making with an easy-to-understand introductory chapter by the editors. A four-chapter section is devoted to the availability heuristic, and there is an interesting chapter on probabilistic reasoning in clinical medicine.

Kendler, Howard H. *Historical Foundations of Modern Psychology*. Chicago: Dorsey Press, 1987. A well-written account of the emergence of cognitive psychology and the contributions of other disciplines such as linguistics, engineering, and computer science. Approachable for the layperson; provides a fine historical backdrop. It is of limited use, beyond review, for the upper-level college student.

Komatsu, Lloyd K., ed. *Experimenting with the Mind: Readings in Cognitive Psychology*. Pacific Grove, Calif.: Brooks/Cole, 1994.

Wells, Gary L., and Elizabeth F. Loftus, eds. *Eyewitness Testimony: Psychological Perspectives*. Cambridge, England: Cambridge University Press, 1984. A fourteen-chapter source with heavy consideration of laboratory research, but with references to courtroom cases as well. There is nice coverage of research on children as witnesses, as well as on "earwitness" testimony and the use of hypnosis as a memory aid.

Mark B. Alcorn

See also:

Behaviorism, 98; The Cerebral Cortex, 121; Cognitive Development Theory: Jean Piaget, 135; Cognitive Therapy, 153; Neural Anatomy and Cognition, 415; Neuropsychology, 422; Psychoanalytic Psychology, 471.

COGNITIVE THERAPY

Type of psychology: Psychotherapy
Field of study: Cognitive therapies

Cognitive therapy holds that emotional disorders are largely determined by cognition or thinking, that cognitive activity can take the form of language or images, and that emotional disorders can be treated by helping patients modify their cognitive distortions. Treatment programs based on this model have been highly successful with depression, panic disorder, generalized anxiety disorder, and other emotional problems.

Principal terms

ARBITRARY INFERENCE: the process of drawing a conclusion from an experience where there is no evidence to support such a conclusion

AUTOMATIC THOUGHTS: thoughts experienced by individuals of which they are dimly aware and that seem believable, but that can be highly unrealistic and maladaptive

COGNITIVE SPECIFICITY HYPOTHESIS: the idea that each of the emotional disorders is characterized by its own patterns of thinking or cognitive distortions

COGNITIVE TRIAD: seen as the core of depression; consists of a negative view of the self, one's experiences, and the future

SCHEMATA: fundamental beliefs people hold about themselves or the world; these beliefs appear to be the rules by which one lives

SELECTIVE ABSTRACTION: focusing on something taken out of context and conceptualizing the experience on the basis of this particular element

Overview

Cognitive therapy, originally developed by Aaron T. Beck, is based on the view that cognition (the process of acquiring knowledge and forming beliefs) is a primary determinant of mood and behavior. Beck developed his theory while treating depressed patients. He noticed that these patients tended to distort whatever happened to them in the direction of self-blame and catastrophes. Thus, an event interpreted by a normal person as irritating and inconvenient (for example, the malfunctioning of an automobile) would be interpreted by the depressed patient as another example of the utter hopelessness of life. Beck's central point is that depressives draw illogical conclusions and come to evaluate negatively themselves, their immediate world, and their future. They see only personal failings, present misfortunes, and overwhelming difficulties ahead. It is from these cognitions that all the other symptoms of depression derive.

It was from Beck's early work with depressed patients that cognitive therapy was developed. Shortly thereafter, the concepts and procedures were applied to other psychological problems, with notable success.

Two concepts of particular relevance to cognitive therapy are the concepts of automatic thoughts and schemata (schemata is the plural of schema). Automatic thoughts are thoughts that appear to be going on all the time. These thoughts are quite brief—only the essential words in a sentence seem to occur, as in a telegraphic style. Further, they seem to be autonomous, in that the person made no effort to initiate them, and they seem plausible or reasonable to the person (although they may seem farfetched to somebody else). Thus, as a depressed person is giving a talk to a group of business colleagues, he or she will have a variety of thoughts. There will be thoughts about the content of the material. There is also a second stream of thoughts occurring. In this second channel, the person may experience such thoughts as: "This is a waste of time," or "They think I'm dumb." These are automatic thoughts.

Beck has suggested that although automatic thoughts are occurring all the time, the person is likely to overlook these thoughts when asked what he or she is thinking. Thus, it is necessary to train the person to attend to these automatic thoughts. Beck pointed out that when people are depressed, these automatic thoughts are filled with negative thoughts of the self, the world, and the future. Further, these automatic thoughts are quite distorted, and finally, when these thoughts are carefully examined and modified to be more in keeping with reality, the depression subsides.

The concept of schemata, or core beliefs, becomes critical in understanding why some people are prone to having emotional difficulties and others are not. The schema appears to be the root from which the automatic thoughts derive. Beck suggests that people develop a propensity to think crookedly as a result of early life experiences. He theorizes that in early life, an individual forms concepts—realistic as well as unrealistic—from experiences. Of particular importance are individuals' attitudes toward themselves, their environment, and their future. These deeply held core beliefs about oneself are seen by Beck as critical in the causation of emotional disorders. According to cognitive theory, the reason these early beliefs are so critical is that once they are formed, the person has a tendency to distort or view subsequent experiences to be consistent with these core beliefs. Thus, an individual who, as a child, was subjected to severe, unprovoked punishment from a disturbed parent may conclude "I am weak" or "I am inferior." Once this conclusion has been formulated, it would appear to be strongly reinforced over years and years of experiences at the hands of the parent. Thus, when this individual becomes an adult, he or she tends to interpret even normal frustrations as more proof of the original belief: "See, I really am inferior." Examples of these negative schemata or core beliefs are: "I am weak," "I am inferior," "I am unlovable," and "I cannot do anything right." People holding such core beliefs about themselves would differ strongly in their views of a frustrating experience from those people who hold a core belief such as "I am capable."

Another major contribution of cognitive therapy is Beck's cognitive specificity hypothesis. Specifically, Beck has suggested that each of the emotional disorders is characterized by its own patterns of thinking. In the case of depression, the thought content is concerned with ideas of personal deficiency, impossible environmental demands and obstacles, and nihilistic expectations. For example, a depressed patient might interpret a frustrating situation, such as a malfunctioning automobile, as evidence of his or her own inadequacy: "If I were really competent, I would have anticipated this problem and been able to avoid it." Additionally, the depressed patient might react to the malfunctioning automobile with: "This is too much, I cannot take it anymore." To the depressed patient, this would simply be another example of the utter hopelessness of life.

While the cognitive content of depression emphasizes the negative view of the self, the world, and the future, anxiety disorders are characterized by fears of physical and psychological danger. The anxious patient's thoughts are filled with themes of danger. These people anticipate detrimental occurrences to themselves, their family, their property, their status, and other intangibles that they value.

In phobias, as in anxiety, there is the cognitive theme of danger; however, the "danger" is confined to definable situations. As long as phobic sufferers are able to avoid these situations, then they do not feel threatened and may be relatively calm. The cognitive content of panic disorder is characterized by a catastrophic interpretation of bodily or mental experiences. Thus, patients with panic disorder are prone to regard any unexplained symptom or sensation as a sign of some impending catastrophe. As a result, their cognitive processing system focuses their attention on bodily or psychological experience. For example, one patient saw discomfort in the chest as evidence of an impending heart attack.

The cognitive feature of the paranoid reaction is the misinterpretation of experience in terms of mistreatment, abuse, or persecution. The cognitive theme of the conversion disorder (a disorder characterized by physical complaints such as paralysis or blindness, where no underlying physical basis can be determined) is the conviction that one has a physical disorder. As a result of this belief, the patient experiences sensory and/or motor abnormalities that are consistent with the patient's faulty conception of organic pathology.

Applications

The goal of cognitive therapy is to assist the patient to evaluate his or her thought processes carefully, to identify cognitive errors, and to substitute more adaptive, realistic cognitions. This goal is accomplished by therapists helping patients to see their thinking about themselves (or their situation) as similar to the activity of a scientist—that they are engaged in the activity of developing hypotheses (or theories) about their world. Like a scientist, the patient needs to "test" his or her theory carefully. Thus, patients who have concluded that they are "worthless" people would be encouraged to test their "theories" rigorously to determine if this is indeed accurate. Further, in the event that the theories are not accurate, patients would be encouraged to change their theories to make them more consistent with reality (what they find in their experience).

A slightly different intervention developed by Beck and his colleagues is to help the patient identify common cognitive distortions. Beck originally identified four cognitive distortions frequently found in emotional disorders: arbitrary inference, selective abstraction, overgeneralization, and magnification or minimization. These were later expanded to ten or more by Beck's colleagues and students.

Arbitrary inference is defined as the process of drawing a conclusion from a situation, event, or experience when there is no evidence to support the conclusion or when the conclusion is contrary to the evidence. For example, a depressed patient on a shopping trip had the thought, "The salesclerk thinks I am a nobody." The patient then felt sad. On being questioned by the psychologist, the patient realized that there was no factual basis for this thought. Selective abstraction refers to the process of focusing on a detail taken out of context, ignoring other, more salient features of the situation, and conceptualizing the whole experience on the basis of this element. For example, a patient was praised by friends about the patient's child-care activities. Through an oversight, however, the patient failed to have her child vaccinated during the appropriate week. Her immediate thought was, "I am a failure as a mother." This idea became paramount despite all the other evidence of her competence.

Overgeneralization refers to patients' patterns of drawing a general conclusion about their ability, their performance, or their worth on the basis of a single incident. For example, a student regards his poor performance on the first examination of the semester as final proof that he "will never make it in college." Magnification and minimization refer to gross errors in evaluation. For example, a person, believing that he has completely ruined his car (magnification) when he sees that there is a slight scratch on the rear fender, regards himself as "good for nothing." In contrast, minimization refers to minimizing one's achievements, protesting that these achievements do not mean anything. For example, a highly successful businesswoman who was depressed concluded that her many prior successes "were nothing . . . simply luck." Using the cognitive distortions, people are taught to examine their thoughts, to identify any distortions, and then to modify their thoughts in order to eliminate the distortions.

In terms of the therapeutic process, the focus is initially on the automatic thoughts of patients. Once patients are relatively adept at identifying and modifying their maladaptive automatic thoughts, the therapy begins to focus on the maladaptive underlying beliefs or schemata. As previously noted, these beliefs are fundamental beliefs that people hold about themselves. These beliefs are not as easy to identify as the automatic thoughts. Rather, they are identified in an inferential process. Common patterns are observed; for example, the person may seem to be operating by the rule: "If I am not the best _____, then I am a failure," or "If I am not loved by my spouse or mate, then I am worthless." As in the case of the earlier cognitive work with automatic thoughts, these beliefs are carefully evaluated for their adaptability or rationality. Maladaptive beliefs are then modified to more adaptive, realistic beliefs.

A variety of techniques have been developed by cognitive therapists for modifying maladaptive cognitions. One example of these techniques is self-monitoring. This involves the patient's keeping a careful hour-by-hour record of his or her activities, associated moods, or other pertinent phenomena. One useful variant is to have the patient record his or her mood on a simple zero-to-one-hundred scale, where zero represents the worst he or she has ever felt and one hundred represents the best. In addition, the patient can record the degree of mastery or pleasure associated with each recorded activity.

A number of hypotheses can be tested using self-monitoring, such as: "It does not do any good for me to get out of bed," "I am always miserable; it never lets up," and "My schedule is too full for me to accomplish what I must." By simply checking the self-monitoring log, one can easily determine if one's miserable mood ever ceases. A careful examination of the completed record is a far better basis for judging such hypotheses than is the patient's memory of recent events, because his or her recollections are almost always tainted by the depression.

As therapy progresses and patients begin to experience more elevated moods, the focus of treatment becomes more cognitive. Patients are instructed to observe and record automatic thoughts, perhaps at a specific time each evening, as well as recording when they become aware of increased dysphoria. Typically, the thoughts are negative self-referents ("I am worthless"; "I will never amount to anything"), and initially, the therapist points out their unreasonable and self-defeating nature. With practice, patients learn "distancing," that is, dealing with such thoughts objectively and evaluating them rather than blindly accepting them. Homework assignments can facilitate distancing: The patient records an automatic thought, and next to it he or she writes down a thought that counters the automatic thought, as the therapist might have done. According to Beck, certain basic themes soon emerge, such as being abandoned, as well as stylistic patterns of thinking, such as overgeneralization. The themes reflect the aforementioned rules, and the ultimate goal of therapy is to assist the patient to modify them.

Finally, cognitive therapy has been applied to a variety of psychological disorders with striking success. For example, studies from seven independent centers have compared the efficacy of cognitive therapy to antidepressant medication, a treatment of established efficacy. Comparisons of cognitive therapy to drugs have found cognitive therapy to be superior or equal to antidepressant medication. Further, follow-up studies indicate that cognitive therapy has greater long-term effects than drug therapy. Of special significance is the evidence of greater sustained improvement over time with cognitive therapy.

Cognitive therapy has been successfully applied to panic disorder, resulting in practically complete reduction of panic attacks after twelve to sixteen weeks of treatment. Additionally, cognitive therapy has been successfully applied to generalized anxiety disorder, eating disorders, and inpatient depression.

Context

Cognitive theory and cognitive therapy originated in Aaron T. Beck's observation and treatment of depressed patients. Originally trained in psychoanalysis, Beck observed that his patients experienced specific types of thoughts, of which they were only dimly aware, that they did not report during their free associations. Beck noticed that these thoughts were frequently followed by an unpleasant effect. Further, he noted that as the patients examined and modified their thoughts, their mood began to improve.

At the time of the emergence of the cognitive model, the treatment world was dominated primarily by the psychoanalytic model (with its heavy emphasis on the unconscious processes) and to a lesser extent by the behavioral model (with its emphasis on the behavioral processes, to the exclusion of thought). The psychoanalytic model was under attack, primarily because of a lack of careful empirical support. In contrast, behavior therapists were actively demonstrating the efficacy of their approaches in carefully designed studies. Beck and his students began to develop and test cognitive procedures systematically, and they have developed an impressive body of research support for the approach.

Bibliography

Beck, Aaron T. *Cognitive Therapy and the Emotional Disorders*. New York: International Universities Press, 1976. An easy-to-read book that presents a general overview of the cognitive model and illustrates the cognitive model of different psychological disorders.

Beck, Aaron T., and Gary Emery. *Anxiety Disorders and Phobias: A Cognitive Perspective*. New York: Basic Books, 1985. Presents the cognitive theory and model of anxiety disorders, as well as the clinical techniques used with anxious patients.

Beck, Aaron T., A. J. Rush, B. F. Shaw, and Gary Emery. *Cognitive Therapy of Depression*. New York: Guilford Press, 1979. Presents the cognitive theory of depression and actual techniques used with depressed patients. Both makes a theoretical contribution and serves as a clinical handbook on depression.

Bieber, Irving. *Cognitive Psychoanalysis: Cognitive Processes in Psychopathology.* Northvale, N.J.: Jason Aronson, 1996.

Bucci, Wilma. *Psychoanalysis and Cognitive Science: A Multiple Code Theory.* New York: Guilford Press, 1997.

Burns, David D. *Feeling Good: The New Mood Therapy.* New York: William Morrow, 1980. Readable introduction to the major concepts and techniques of cognitive therapy; written by one of Beck's students.

Emery, Gary, Steven D. Hollom, and Richard C. Bedrosian, eds. *New Directions in Cognitive Therapy: A Casebook.* New York: Guilford Press, 1981. Contains cases presented by major cognitive therapists. Focuses on the application of cognitive therapy to a wide range of presenting problems (such as loneliness and agoraphobia), as well as diverse populations (such as adolescents, the elderly, and the psychologically naïve).

Donald G. Beal

See also:

Analytical Psychotherapy, 54; Cognitive Behavior Therapy, 128; Cognitive Psychology, 146; Person-Centered Therapy, 439; Psychoanalysis: Classical Versus Modern, 465.

FUNCTIONS OF CONSCIOUSNESS

Type of psychology: Consciousness
Field of study: Cognitive processes

Although the functions of consciousness are debated by psychologists, most believe that consciousness serves to help people adapt to novel situations. Consciousness occurs as aspects of the environment are selected, attended to, and interpreted.

Principal terms

BEHAVIORISM: the theoretical approach which argues that the proper subject matter of psychology is observable behavior, not internal mental processes

CONSCIOUSNESS: a stream of awareness forming the subjective character of experience, including awareness of the external world and of one's own mental states

EPIPHENOMENON: a secondary by-product of a phenomenon, not essential for an understanding of the phenomenon

FUNCTIONALISM: the early school of psychology that emphasized the means by which organisms adapt to their environments

MINDLESSNESS: interacting with the world in an automatic fashion, following habitual scripts

SCRIPT: a temporally organized frame of knowledge; an internal representation of a sequence of events

STRUCTURALISM: a school of psychology which emphasized the studying of the mind by conscious introspection in an attempt to find the elementary units of conscious experience

Overview

The nature, origin, and functions of consciousness are some of the great mysteries of human existence. Although the nature of consciousness was explored by the first psychologists, contemporary psychology has been relatively silent about normal, everyday consciousness. Psychologists have studied altered states of consciousness such as those produced by drugs, dreams, and hypnosis. The importance of everyday consciousness is attested by the study of altered states of consciousness, in that one must have at least an intuitive sense of normal consciousness in order to identify a deviation from that normal state. The importance of normal, everyday consciousness is also attested when psychologists use people's reports of their own intentions, observations, attitudes, and evaluations as research evidence.

Some psychologists equate consciousness with the totality of mental life, whereas others equate it with all of adaptive behavior; however, each of these classifications seems too broad. A better definition equates consciousness with awareness, acknowledging that many aspects of mental life and adaptive behavior occur without conscious awareness. For example, when one drives one's car on a familiar route, one can execute very complex behaviors, adapting to a variety of environmental conditions such as traffic and weather, yet do so without conscious awareness of driving. Similarly, one may be consciously aware of the answer to an arithmetic problem—for example, know that two plus three equals five—but have no awareness of the cognitive processes that actually do the addition.

Clearly, people are not aware of everything, so their consciousness is the result of selection and construction. The mind selects stimuli to which to attend and places meaning on those stimuli. In this way, consciousness forms the subjective, personal character of human experience. Awareness of the world and awareness of one's own self are two components of consciousness. Human consciousness might be defined, then, as a stream of awareness, including the perception of the external world and an awareness of one's own mental state. Given that consciousness is not always present when one solves problems or engages in complex behaviors, the functions of consciousness have been debated. Some have argued that consciousness serves no function at all. From this point of view, it is an epiphenomenon—simply a by-product of brain activity, as exhaust is a by-product of a car engine. From this point of view, consciousness does not *do* anything; it does not cause thoughts or actions.

The epiphenomenalist position has been criticized on several grounds. First, it contradicts everyday experiences. People feel that they have conscious intentions or plans which they follow through in behavior, and conscious attention does seem to aid learning and problem solving in many cases; however, intuitions and common sense are sometimes wrong. A stronger argument against epiphenomenalism can be made by considering an evolutionary perspective. From an evolutionary perspective, characteristics are continued in a species because they give the species a reproductive advantage. That is, members who have the characteristic are more likely to reproduce, or to have more offspring, than others. From this point of view, consciousness must have arisen because it functions, in some way, to sustain life.

Most psychologists adopt the functionalist position described above. From this position, consciousness is viewed as functioning to facilitate humans' adaptations to novel situations. Conscious awareness requires cognitive effort; it seems to accompany the allocation of a certain amount of cognitive capacity or energy. As such, consciousness may be viewed as an aspect of mental activity rather than a mechanism per se. According to psychologist Robert Ornstein, the readiness to respond to novel stimuli *is* consciousness. Incoming stimuli are selected for one's conscious awareness when they are perceived as dissimilar to previous stimuli—when a well-learned automatic behavior may not be appropriate to the situation. An interpretation of the situation may then be sought with conscious awareness, and a response decided upon. For example, while automaticity may be the rule when one drives a car on a familiar route, consciousness generally intervenes when the road situation becomes hazardous. Consciousness, then, functions as a control mechanism, selecting stimuli and constructing interpretations and responses to those stimuli. This aids human survival, and those who survive longer have more opportunities to have offspring.

A related, but radical, analysis of consciousness has been suggested by Julian Jaynes. According to Jaynes, consciousness involves the left hemisphere of the brain, the part of the brain that in most people is responsible for language. Jaynes suggests that, prehistorically, people were not conscious, but rather experienced their mental "voices" as the voices of the gods. As societies became complex, experienced stress, and encountered other societies with different organizations and beliefs, the voices became internalized and people became conscious. Jaynes's theorizing is controversial, but his argument concerning the functions of consciousness is compatible with the evolutionary perspective mentioned above. Instead of addressing the functional adaptation of individuals, however, Jaynes argues that consciousness arose in order to help societies adapt to novel situations.

Applications

Although references to consciousness are not widely found in psychological research, the topic has fascinated some individuals from a variety of subdisciplines in psychology. Ellen Langer, a social psychologist interested in interpersonal interactions, began studying conscious awareness in the 1970's in her research on "mindlessness." Some physiological psychologists have also pondered the implications for consciousness of their research on the structure of the brain.

Langer argues that much of human adult social interaction is "mindless." That is, she says that people follow social scripts that they have learned over their lifetimes and thus do not consciously attend to their social world. In one study, Langer, Arthur Blank, and Benzion Chanowitz had individuals approach a person who was using a copying machine and make one of three requests: "May I use the copy machine?"; "May I use the copy machine because I have to make copies?"; or "May I use the copy machine because I'm in a rush?" Subjects were more likely to respond positively to the request when it was phrased in either of the latter two ways than when the requester simply asked to use the machine. Although addition of the comment "because I have to make copies" adds no information to the simple request to use the machine, it is responded to as if a meaningful reason for the request were being given.

Langer argues that the subjects in this study were using a script which says that when a request, in addition to a reason, is given, one should comply; they were not really paying conscious attention to what was said. Many interactions may have this scripted quality. While the use of scripts may free cognitive energy for conscious attention to more important tasks, Langer argues that all too often people simply fall into mindless habits. If people can be taught to be mindful, to attend consciously to their world, they will, in Langer's view, be more likely to think creatively, consider alternative solutions for problems, and live more rational and productive lives. In one particular study, Langer, Chanowitz, and Richard Bashner trained people to be mindful. The subjects were shown slides of individuals with physical handicaps and were told to attend to the unique characteristics of these people. The researchers found that when people were thus trained to be mindful, they were less likely than untrained, "mindless" people to think stereotypically about others who have handicaps. Thus, consciousness may help people think more clearly about other people.

In another area of psychology, physiological psychologists have pondered the implications for consciousness of their theories about the structure of the mind. Although people experience their conscious mental lives as a unified whole, some psychologists argue that in fact there may be subcomponents to the mind; the mind may have a modular structure. If so, might consciousness itself have several discrete components?

This question is of particular interest when individuals who have undergone split-brain operations are considered. In split-brain operations, the corpus callosum, the fibers connecting the right and left hemispheres of the brain, are severed. The operation is done in order to improve severe conditions of epilepsy that have not responded to less extreme treatments. When the two hemispheres of the brain cannot communicate, do two separate consciousnesses arise? Does one become twice as intelligent; does one's ability to adapt to the environment double?

People who have undergone split-brain operations do not double their intelligence quotient (IQ) scores, and, over time, no obvious differences from normal people can be seen in their behavior. It can be argued, however, that the split-brain operation produces two different spheres of awareness. In controlled research, information can be directed to one hemisphere of the brain of the split-brain patient or the other. Information that is directed to the left hemisphere (the one where specialized language centers are usually located) can be responded to verbally. Thus it seems that the left hemisphere possesses conscious awareness. The right hemisphere is mute, and at first it may not seem to have consciousness. Yet when stimuli are directed to the right hemisphere, it too can respond—not verbally, but by pointing to a correct answer. For example, if a picture of a cat were presented to the left hemisphere of a person who had undergone a split-brain operation, the person could say "I saw a cat," thus demonstrating conscious awareness. If the same picture were shown to only the right hemisphere, the person would not be able to say what was seen. The person would, however, be able to point to the picture if it were presented along with several alternatives. Thus, the right hemisphere also seems to have a type of consciousness. Such research raises the interesting possibility that consciousness may be multifaceted in all people. Verbal consciousness may simply function as an interpreter for the brain's various subcomponents of awareness.

Context

Consciousness played an important role in the early history of psychology. The earliest experimental psychologists believed that conscious experience was the proper subject matter of psychology. The school of psychology called structuralism, which flourished in the late 1800's, used introspection in order to identify the basic units of consciousness. Their approach was criticized both because it reduced complex experience to elemental units and because introspection is inherently subjective.

The functions of consciousness were emphasized by the American school of psychology termed functionalism, which also flourished in the late 1800's. Functionalists such as William James were influenced by the evolutionary theory of Charles Darwin, and they thus explained consciousness in terms of its adaptive significance. James's writings on consciousness are particularly significant and continue to be meaningful to contemporary psychology.

In the United States, with the advent of behaviorism in the twentieth century, interest in consciousness waned. Behaviorists such as John B. Watson argued that observable behaviors, not inferred characteristics of the mind such as consciousness, are the proper subject matter of psychology. Until the 1950's, the behaviorist approach dominated psychology, particularly in the United States. Consciousness itself was not a common topic of psychology, although unconscious processes were studied by Freudian theorists and altered states of consciousness were a topic of some investigations.

With the cognitive revolution of the 1950's, and with the advancement of research in physiological psychology, normal, everyday consciousness again became a topic of study for at least a few psychologists. The computer revolution of the 1950's gave psychologists a new model of how the mind might work, the information-processing model. With this development, the mind in general, and consciousness in particular, again found a place in psychology. The information-processing approach often equates consciousness with attention or short-term memory, perhaps neglecting its broader implications. The focus on cognition has, however, opened the door for consciousness to be studied by a wide range of psychologists interested in personality, social interaction, and development.

Physiological research has also inspired some discussion of consciousness. With the study of the separate functions of the two hemispheres of the brain, researchers have speculated about the localization, function, and essence of consciousness. Some equate consciousness with the left hemisphere's ability to use language, but it is clear that the right hemisphere, too, possesses awareness. It is this research which in part inspired the speculative theorizing of Julian Jaynes, who argues that the consciousness which people experience is a relatively new development of the human mind. On the whole, consciousness remains a mystery, but contemporary psychology has found it to be a topic worthy of study. There is reason to hope that parts of the mystery will be solved as psychologists focus more energy on this topic.

Bibliography

Anderson, William. *The Face of Glory: Creativity, Consciousness, and Civilization.* London: Bloomsbury, 1996.

Flanagan, Owen J., Jr. "Naturalizing the Mind: The Philosophical Psychology of William James." In *The Science of the Mind.* Cambridge, Mass.: MIT Press, 1984. A readable introduction, written by a philosopher, to the central philosophical and psychological issues of consciousness. Discusses criteria and functions for conscious mental life. A good introduction to reading William James. Further information relevant to consciousness may be found in the chapter in the same volume entitled "Cognitive Psychology and Artificial Intelligence: Philosophical Assumptions and Implications."

Gazzaniga, Michael S. *The Social Brain.* New York: Basic Books, 1985. A readable, interesting account of Gazzaniga's development as a physiological psychologist. Written for a general audience. Describes research on the brain, including research with split-brain patients. Discusses Gazzaniga's own speculative theory about the modular organization of the mind, which argues for the central role of language in consciousness.

Hunt, Harry T. *On the Nature of Consciousness: Cognitive, Phenomenological, and Transpersonal Perspectives.* New Haven, Conn.: Yale University Press, 1995.

James, William. "Consciousness." In *Psychology: The Briefer Course.* 1892. Reprint. New York: Harper & Row, 1961. Describes the nature and functions of consciousness from the perspective of the historically important functionalist school of psychology. Significant historically, but also relevant to contemporary psychology. Delightfully written for a relatively sophisticated audience. A fuller treatment of the topic of consciousness may be found in James's *The Principles of Psychology* (1890).

Jaynes, Julian. *The Origins of Consciousness in the Breakdown of the Bicameral Mind.* Harmondsworth, Middlesex, England: Pelican Books, 1976. A fascinating but highly speculative account of the origins of consciousness; not widely accepted by psychologists. Initial chapters provide a good review of the nature and functions of consciousness. Later chapters synthesize information from anthropology, history, and physiological and abnormal psychology into Jaynes's own unique theory.

Klein, David B. "The Functions of Consciousness." In *The Concept of Consciousness: A Survey*. Lincoln: University of Nebraska Press, 1884. A thorough and readable account of consciousness, excellent for getting an overview on the topic. The cited chapter provides an overview of the functions of consciousness, as considered historically in psychology, and discusses contemporary biological and psychological evidence. Written for a college audience.

Langer, Ellen J. *Mindfulness*. Reading, Mass.: Addison-Wesley, 1990. Reviews research showing the lack of consciousness, termed "mindlessness," in everyday life and argues for the importance of becoming more conscious ("mindful") for a healthy and adaptive life. Offers suggestions on how to increase mindfulness. Written for a general audience. A somewhat speculative presentation of the implications of Langer's social psychological research.

Ornstein, Robert E. *The Psychology of Consciousness*. 2d rev. ed. New York: Penguin Books, 1986. A readable account of consciousness by one of the first contemporary psychologists to address the issue. Contrasts the everyday consciousness of the Western world with the states of consciousness induced by meditation that are more common in the philosophies of the Eastern world. Argues for a unification of these two forms of consciousness.

Shevrin, Howard, et al. *Conscious and Unconscious Processes: Psychodynamic, Cognitive, and Neurophysiological Convergences*. New York: Guilford Press, 1996.

Susan E. Beers

See also:

LEVELS OF CONSCIOUSNESS

Type of psychology: Consciousness
Fields of study: Cognitive processes; personality theory

Consciousness or awareness can be divided into three levels: unconscious, preconscious, and conscious. Given that one cannot be aware of everything that is going on around one all the time, the kind of processes that occur at each of these levels has profound implications for thought, behavior, and personality.

Principal terms

CONSCIOUSNESS: a level of experience that includes those things of which individuals are aware at any given moment, such as current ideas, thoughts, accessed memories, and feelings

EGO: the conscious aspect of personality postulated by Sigmund Freud that serves as a watchdog and helps to satisfy the desires of the id safely

ID: one of the unconscious aspects of personality postulated by Freud, the sole purpose of which is to satisfy animalistic urges and desires

PRECONSCIOUS: the transition level from those things occurring in one's mind of which one is unaware (unconscious) and those of which one is aware (conscious)

SUPEREGO: the third aspect of personality, according to Freud, which incorporates the moral values of parents and society, helping one to know right from wrong

UNCONSCIOUS: the deep-rooted aspects of the mind; Freud claimed that it includes negative instincts and urges that are too disturbing for people to become aware of consciously

Overview

Theories concerning levels of consciousness have painted elaborate pictures of the human mind and psyche. It is easy to take for granted the myriad complicated processes that must occur automatically every day in order for one to make sense of the world, make the hundreds of decisions that each day demands, and still have time and mental energy left over to concentrate on work, study, or play. Theories about levels of consciousness attempt to explain how it is that one can perform so many demanding tasks simultaneously and still do most of them well.

It is obvious that many bodily functions occur at a level that is below awareness. For example, if a man had to concentrate on breathing, regulating heart rate, and worrying about digesting the tacos he ate at lunch, there would be little attention left to give to the tasks required by a job or school. Human bodies are perfectly capable of performing many of these functions automatically without having constantly to get permission from a higher authority. The mind is divided in much the same way. If the individual had to concentrate on keeping each eye in focus, turning the ears on and off, keeping memories stored, and so on, trying to study for an examination or solve a crossword puzzle would be extremely difficult at best.

Contemporary psychologists tend to agree that the functions of the mind can be studied at three levels. These levels correspond roughly to the degree to which one is aware of what resides in, or is going on at, each level. The common analogy for this division of consciousness is an iceberg. Sigmund Freud was the first to use this analogy, and it easily demonstrates the varying levels of conscious awareness. Imagine an iceberg floating in the ocean. A person looks out of a ship and sees the tip. The part of the iceberg that floats above the surface of the water corresponds to "consciousness." Consciousness includes all those things of which a person is aware at any given moment. A woman may be aware of the words she is reading and of their meaning; she may also be aware of her stomach growling or of music playing in the background. Like the tip of the iceberg that can be seen above the water level, consciousness includes everything about people that they can "see," if their attention is focused on the self.

There is much more to an iceberg, however, than what meets the eye. As the passengers and crew of the *Titanic* quickly came to realize, the real power of the iceberg lies hidden below the surface. It is the same with levels of consciousness. Below the surface of consciousness lies a transition level, known as the "preconscious." The preconscious represents everything that is accessible to a person at any given time but is currently out of consciousness. This can include one's reservoir of memories and habits. Things can be drawn from the preconscious into consciousness. A person may not be aware at this moment of the name of his or her first-grade teacher, but this information can be pulled from the preconscious into consciousness with a bit of mental effort. Once something is no longer needed mentally or is no longer being given conscious attention, it will drop back into the preconscious, where it will reside until it is needed and pulled temporarily back into consciousness.

The largest piece of the iceberg lies deep below the surface of the water. This buried, "unconscious" aspect of the mind is a reservoir of things that are beyond awareness but that nevertheless exert a constant and powerful effect on behavior. This level of consciousness may include the tendency to be aggressive, needs or drives, and personality traits that may influence behavior without one being aware. People are not aware of what goes on at the unconscious level, but the level is very important in helping people handle day-to-day life. Unconscious processes include the filtering of incoming stimuli—organizing information as it is taken in from the environment and sending important bits of information to consciousness for further attention and processing. Without this level of consciousness, it would be impossible to process more than a few pieces of information at any time. Thus, one's mental capacity is greatly enhanced by this three-part division of consciousness. The unconscious contains those processes that can occur automatically to free conscious awareness for the moment-to-moment changes in one's environment. The preconscious allows a person to keep things in a sort of permanent file, where they can be called forth and refiled as many times as necessary. Consciousness provides a person with the unique powers of higher reasoning (for example, problem solving, self-contemplation, and free choice), which many consider to be the main thing separating humans from other animals.

Applications

Ideas concerning levels of consciousness have had a profound impact on psychological theory and methods since the early 1900's. At that time, Sigmund Freud developed a comprehensive theory of human personality in order to understand how and why humans behave the way they do. In this theory, which came to be called psychoanalytic theory, Freud proposed a tripartite division of personality that is intricately linked with levels of consciousness. Each of the three levels of consciousness is responsible for different mental functions and aspects of personality. Though Freud's theory was created to help explain the abnormal behavior of many of his patients, he believed that the theory worked to explain the normal everyday functioning of the mind as well. Freud argued that various aspects of personality reside at different levels of consciousness and that, in order to understand human behavior (because it is driven by personality), one must understand how personality and levels of consciousness tie together.

According to Freud, people are born with only one aspect of consciousness or personality, called the id. The id is a reservoir of psychic energy, which Freud called libido. The id is primarily driven by the need to be satisfied, and it will constantly push for libido energy to be used to carry out its wishes. For the most part, the id seeks gratification of sexual and aggressive urges that are buried deep in the unconscious, away from one's awareness. The problem with the id is that it seeks immediate gratification of its desires without any thought given to potential consequences of actions. According to Freud, this quickly leads to conflict in which the reality of the world clashes with the id's impulsive wishes.

To help the id deal with these conflicts, the second aspect of personality develops. This aspect of personality resides at the conscious level and is called the ego. The ego's function is to help the id by finding safe ways for the id's urges to be satisfied. Rather than walking into a bank during broad daylight and demanding all the money, for example, the ego may scheme and design a method by which the money can be stolen without the fear and danger of being caught. It must be remembered that the ego does not pass judgment on the id's desires. The ego's goal is to help the id get what it wants safely, regardless of how society and others feel about those actions.

Freud believed that human beings would quickly destroy one another in their rapid desire to satisfy urges if only the id and ego were at work. For this reason, Freud postulated a third aspect of personality that resides at the preconscious level. This is called the superego, and its job is to keep both the id and ego in check by making a person feel guilty for bad deeds and moral for good deeds; this can also be called the conscience.

The most widespread use of the levels of consciousness has been the application of Freud's psychoanalytic theory. Psychologists and psychiatrists alike have used this theory of the connection between levels of consciousness and aspects of personality to understand and explain both normal and abnormal behaviors. There have been increasing uses of the concept of levels of consciousness to help understand self-concept development and information processing. If a patient has been experiencing terrible dreams that keep him or her awake nights and cause general anxiety during the day, the psychiatrist's ability to help the patient may depend on the patient's ability to find the unconscious conflict that is serving as the energizing force for the dream.

Psychoanalytic theory claims that human behavior is driven by these unconscious forces and conflicts. If an abnormal behavior is to be eliminated, the therapist must help the client dig into the unconscious and expose the hidden cause. When the cause is uncovered, the problem often will disappear. In this way, levels of consciousness have been used comprehensively in the treatment of behavioral disorders.

Behaviorists have made many attempts to use the principles of reinforcement and punishment to eliminate unwanted behaviors and increase desired behaviors. Although most behaviorists would disagree with the terminology, the real goal is to alter behavior at an unconscious level. By consistently rewarding desired behaviors, it is possible for children to incorporate such behavior into their normal behavioral pattern. In this way, children can learn new, more acceptable behaviors without ever being consciously aware of the fact that it was external reward that caused them to engage in the behavior in the first place. Regardless of what motivated the behavior, once it is internalized, it becomes a significant influence on future behavior. In this way, unconscious ideas and feelings can alter the outward behavior.

Context

Though Sigmund Freud created the most comprehensive theory of levels of consciousness and their effects on human behavior, he was not the first to argue that there are different levels of consciousness. In ancient Greece, Plato argued for a three-part theory of the soul. He believed that the soul had three components: reason, feeling, and appetite. (Although Plato discussed these in terms of the concept of "soul," it is important to note that the meaning of "soul" in ancient times differed considerably from what the term means today.) These terms seem very similar to the functions of id, ego, and superego discussed by Freud. This historical precedent is critical because of the influence of philosophy on the birth of psychology as a science. Plato is often cited as a founding father in the science of psychology, and his historical influence on the unborn science deserves mention.

In the late 1600's, more than two hundred years before the writings of Freud, Gottfried Wilhelm Leibniz suggested that there can be varying levels of consciousness. This was a very early suggestion that processes which are below the threshold of conscious awareness can influence human behavior. The historical importance of levels of consciousness continues to grow as psychoanalytic theory is further refined. As already mentioned, the idea of levels of consciousness has gained importance in areas besides psychotherapy and the explanation and treatment of abnormal behavior. The field of psychology has become so dependent on these constructs and the belief in this three-part division in awareness and consciousness that it is often taken for granted. When a person says, "I did it without thinking," other people have no trouble understanding what this person means. This kind of understanding would be impossible if people did not have some intuitive understanding that they are not always aware of everything they do or the reasons they have for doing these things.

As society becomes more complicated and the demands on one's time become more urgent, certain tasks must be relegated to the unconscious. Driving a car, for example, would be impossible if every aspect of the task had to be consciously processed. There are too many small tasks to complete, too many instantaneous decisions to be made, and too many cars on the road for a driver to function if he or she had to concentrate to remember each time what a red light means or to recall which pedal is the brake. Psychology has been shaped so strongly by this three-part view of consciousness that it is difficult to imagine what the science of psychology would be like without it.

Bibliography

Eccles, John Carew, and Daniel N. Robinson. *The Wonder of Being Human*. New York: Free
    Press, 1984. An interesting short book that explains the connection between language,

thought, and the brain. Discusses processes that range from unconscious to conscious levels. Although the book is somewhat technical, introductory psychology students will find it interesting and helpful.

McIntosh, Donald. *Self, Person, World: The Interplay of Conscious and Unconscious in Human Life*. Evanston, Ill.: Northwestern University Press, 1995.

Ornstein, Robert Evan, ed. *The Nature of Human Consciousness*. New York: Viking Press, 1973. A scholarly and useful book that presents original writings by some of the pioneer thinkers in levels of consciousness. Covers a wide range of topics from understanding humans to altered states of consciousness. The writing is technical and geared for a fairly advanced college audience.

_____. *The Psychology of Consciousness*. San Francisco: W. H. Freeman, 1972. Designed to help the general audience gain an understanding of consciousness and how to put consciousness to work effectively. Includes scientific research as well as self-help suggestions.

Pelletier, Kenneth R. *Toward a Science of Consciousness*. New York: Delacorte, 1978. Covers theories of consciousness from metaphysical, scientific, and self-help perspectives. Appropriate for high school or college students, or a general audience. Although some of the chapters are not quite mainstream, the overall effect is successful.

Shevrin, Howard, et al. *Conscious and Unconscious Processes: Psychodynamic, Cognitive, and Neurophysiological Convergences*. New York: Guilford Press, 1996.

Smith, Barry D., and Harold J. Vetter. *Theories of Personality*. 2d ed. Englewood Cliffs, N.J.: Prentice-Hall, 1990. Although this is a college-level textbook, the writing is straightforward and easy to understand. Presents perhaps the best explanation of Sigmund Freud's iceberg analogy and his views of the connection between personality structures and levels of consciousness. High school and college students will find the book interesting.

Strawson, Galen. *Mental Reality*. Cambridge, Mass.: MIT Press, 1994.

Randall E. Osborne

See also:

Analytical Psychology: Carl G. Jung, 19; Consciousness, Functions of, 159; Dream Analysis, 206; Dreams, 212; Psychoanalytic Psychology and Personality: Sigmund Freud, 478; Sleep: Stages and Functions, 546.

The Contact Hypothesis

Type of psychology: Social psychology
Fields of study: Interpersonal relations; prejudice and discrimination; social perception and cognition

According to the contact hypothesis, intergroup bias (prejudice, stereotypes, and discrimination) arises, in part, from ignorance and misinformation; favorable face-to-face contact between members of different groups will foster more accurate perceptions, greater intergroup attraction, and less bias directed at one another.

Principal terms

DISCRIMINATION: behavior (usually unfavorable) toward persons that is based on their group membership rather than on their individual personalities

IN-GROUP: a social group to which a person belongs or with which a person identifies, thereby forming part of the self-concept

INTERGROUP BIAS: unfavorable reactions to members of another group that can occur as any combination of discrimination, prejudice, or stereotypes

OUT-GROUP: a social group to which a person does not belong and with which he or she does not identify

PREJUDICE: liking or disliking of persons based on their category or group membership rather than on their individual personalities

STEREOTYPE: a belief about members of a social group that applies to all or most members of that category

SUPERORDINATE GOAL: an outcome desired by members of different groups that can be attained only through cooperation between the groups

Overview

Intergroup bias manifests itself in three interrelated yet distinctive manners: feelings and attitudes (prejudice), generalized beliefs (stereotypes), and behaviors that favor one group over another (discrimination). In general, persons who are biased against members of another social group dislike those persons (prejudice), believe that they possess unpleasant or negative characteristics (stereotypes), and actively avoid or denigrate them (discrimination). Social psychologists have studied how intergroup bias arises and what tactics may be employed to ameliorate bias. They have observed that persons generally feel a sense of self-investment and identification with groups to which they belong (in-groups) rather than with groups to which they do not belong (out-groups). Consequently, they may associate with fellow in-group members more so than with out-group members and obtain a more accurate and complete knowledge of the in-group than of the out-group.

Ignorance of the out-group may contribute to intergroup bias, as persons are motivated to maintain a positive view of themselves by assuming the best about their in-groups and the worst about out-groups. Accurate information about an out-group that disconfirms negative expectations (prejudice and stereotypes) should improve intergroup relations, and accurate information may be obtained through face-to-face contact with members of the out-group.

The contact hypothesis refers to the proposition that bias between groups can be reduced by bringing members of different groups together for face-to-face interaction. The contact hypothesis rests on two assumptions. First, intergroup bias is frequently based on ignorance or misinformation. Contact between group members provides the opportunity to disconfirm their erroneous beliefs and feelings about the groups. Second, the contact experience(s) will be sufficiently positive or pleasant to preclude exacerbation of existing bias.

Gordon Allport, in *The Nature of Prejudice* (1954), most clearly articulated the contact hypothesis when he argued that bringing members of disliked groups together can have a beneficial impact on intergroup relations, provided that the contact occurred under what have been termed favorable conditions. These include cooperative interaction, common goals, support from authorities or institutions outside the groups, and some degree of personal (as opposed to formal or superficial) contact. Research has generally supported these criteria as important in fostering contact that reduces bias between groups. Cooperation between groups produces more pleasant intergroup experiences than competition in which one group's gain comes at the expense of the other. Pursuit of a common goal, in particular a superordinate goal, encourages cooperation. Support for the contact from authorities and institutions helps to maintain it. Personal contact between members of the different groups can foster interpersonal attachments and reveal similarities and common interests between members of the different groups. Following Allport, the most influential voices in the area of the contact hypothesis have been Stuart Cook, Thomas Pettigrew, and Yehudi Amir.

Much of Stuart Cook's influential research has focused on the benefits of intimate contact with out-group members. Using laboratory groups engaged in cooperative tasks, Cook has found that contact is most effective in disconfirming stereotypes when it has "acquaintance potential." In other words, contact is most helpful when the different groups interact individually and get to know one another as unique persons, rather than as representatives of their groups. Unfortunately, Cook's research also indicates that while intergroup contact can improve relations among those involved in the contact experience, generalization of the positive experience to the out-group as a whole or to specific out-group members not present during the contact experience is often problematic.

Thomas Pettigrew has argued that to be successful, favorable contact with an out-group member must be interpreted positively by the parties. The attributions that group members make about the contact experience will determine the success of the experience. Thus, favorable contact with an out-group member may be ineffective if that experience is discounted as an atypical event, one that does not reflect the true intentions or dispositions of the out-group members. For the experience to be most effective, out-group members who behave positively in a contact setting must be seen as having behaved voluntarily (not forced to act pleasantly) and as being typical of others in their group (not exceptions to the rule). Laboratory research has found support for this conclusion. For example, in an experiment reported by David Wilder, subjects had a favorable contact experience with a member of a disliked out-group. The contact person was presented as either a typical or atypical member of the out-group. Results showed that the contact experience was effective in reducing intergroup bias when the contact person was seen as typical or representative of the out-group.

Proponents of social identity theory have raised some criticisms of the contact hypothesis. Factors that maximize the success of intergroup contact in promoting positive relations among persons in the contact setting may yield the least generalization to the out-group as a whole. As already mentioned, contact that involves positive, intimate experiences with out-group members is likely to create friendship bonds and reveal interindividual similarities that cut across the different group memberships, thereby diminishing the importance of the group categories for one's self-identity in that setting. Yet the contact person(s) may be perceived to be less representative of others in their group, with the result that generalization of the favorable contact experience to the out-group as a whole should suffer. For contact to be most effective, therefore, the contact persons must be judged to be very typical of their respective groups while behaving in an unexpectedly positive manner.

A related difficulty with the contact hypothesis is the assumption that contact will be effective to the extent that it reduces assumed differences between the groups. Yet reducing differences between groups may threaten each group's sense of uniqueness and identity. Social identity researchers argue that contact will be most successful if it focuses on diminishing negative beliefs and feelings between the groups, yet still perpetuates some distinctive differences between the groups. Ideally, then, the contact experience should not strive to eliminate all differences between the groups, but rather should reduce unfavorable and inaccurate beliefs while preserving those differences that cast both groups in a positive light.

Finally, the success of contact depends in part on the measurements used to assess its impact. While contact may foster a change in beliefs or feelings about an out-group, it may not always yield a change in behavior. For example, one may feel more positively toward a group following a favorable contact experience but may be reluctant to act differently toward members of that group because of social pressure from prejudiced members of one's own group. On the other hand, one may feel obligated to behave positively toward members of an out-group who have treated one well but may still harbor prejudice and unfavorable stereotypes of the out-group as a whole. For contact to be effective in producing the broadest change in intergroup bias, it not only must be favorable (involve cooperation in pursuit of common goals) but also should occur frequently across many situations and with many members of the out-group.

The contact hypothesis is best considered as a working hypothesis based largely on consistency and reward theories of social interaction. People prefer rewarding experiences and strive to maintain consistency among their beliefs and behaviors. To the extent that biased beliefs and attitudes are based on misconceptions or ignorance, favorable contact with members of the disliked out-group will generate positive feelings and will disconfirm negative stereotypes. The inconsistency between the favorable contact experience and prior beliefs about the out-groups should weaken those beliefs, provided that the contact experience cannot be dismissed as an "exception to the rule."

Applications

Several good examples of the contact hypothesis can be found in a variety of settings, ranging from small-scale experiments conducted by social psychologists to social policies implemented at the national level. Two examples will be discussed in some detail, because they reflect the strengths and weaknesses of the contact hypothesis in both research and naturalistic settings.

In a classic set of field experiments, Muzafer Sherif and his colleagues created hostility between groups of boys at summer camps and then employed intergroup contact as a means of reducing the hostility. In their experiments, the boys were divided into groups at the beginning of the camp session. The boys mainly associated with their fellow in-group members (they ate, played, and slept with one another). Initially, intergroup contact was designed to encourage intergroup hostility. For example, groups played against one another in competitive games. The researchers added fuel to the fire by staging pranks and other inconveniences for which each group blamed the others. After the groups had developed a severe dislike of one another, the experimenters, posing as camp counselors, attempted to reduce the intergroup hostility. They found that merely bringing the groups together to engage in pleasant activities, such as a party, was insufficient, as the group members hurled insults at one another upon sight. Sherif and his colleagues reported that intergroup contact was effective only when the groups interacted in pursuit of a "superordinate goal"—an objective desired by all groups but unattainable without mutual cooperation. After a series of cooperative encounters in pursuit of superordinate goals, they reported that intergroup barriers weakened and the boys were as likely to choose members of other groups as friends as members of their own group. The contact experiences were effective because they served both to create pleasant events (attainment of shared goals) and to dispel unpleasant assumptions about out-group members.

On a larger scale, the contact hypothesis has served as an argument for school and residential racial desegregation within the United States. The argument has been that part of the prejudice between blacks and whites can be attributed to the ignorance and misinformation that is the legacy of segregation. In American society, interracial contact experiences have usually been characterized by unequal status, with whites occupying a superior role (employer or landowner). Consequently, much of the contact has not met the equal-status, cooperative, and intimate conditions that maximize the probability that contact will dispel negative stereotypes and modify prejudice. Following the 1954 United States Supreme Court ruling that outlawed racial segregation in public schools, researchers have looked at the schools as a testing ground for the contact hypothesis.

Evidence indicates that contact is effective only under the limited conditions already discussed. Merely throwing black and white students together in classrooms is not sufficient to reduce intergroup bias. Indeed, forced contact can exacerbate bias when community and institutional support is absent. Moreover, contact situations may fail because persons feel uncomfortable in the unfamiliar position of interacting with the out-group, preferring to seek out fellow in-group members. At many integrated American colleges, a visitor can see how blacks mainly interact with blacks and whites with whites.

Interracial contact in the classroom appears to work best when it is patterned after the techniques advocated by Allport and used by Sherif in his summer-camp studies. Elliot Aronson has created a "jigsaw" procedure for classroom contact that consists of forming black and white children into integrated work groups. In these groups, all members are peers with equal status. The groups are given tasks to solve as a team so that cooperation is reinforced, rather than the interpersonal competition that characterizes many traditional classrooms. Under these circumstances, where contact is of equal status, is cooperative in pursuit of a common goal, and is sanctioned by authorities (a teacher), the contact experience produces a marked improvement in interracial relations.

Context

In social psychology, the contact hypothesis most clearly dates from the writings of Gordon Allport. Along with other social psychologists who had conducted research during World War II, he was struck both by the extent to which prejudice was based on ignorance and misinformation and by the lack of direct contact between social groups. Combining these observations, it seemed reasonable to infer that intergroup bias might be reduced by encouraging face-to-face contact between members of the groups. Intellectually, then, the contact hypothesis has grown from the assumption that ignorance and secondhand information encourage erroneous inferences, while direct experience with objects (in this case, members of an out-group) generates more accurate beliefs and attitudes about them. Furthermore, it has been implicitly assumed that the contact experiences will generate more positive than negative experiences and reveal more similarities and common values than dissimilarities. A large body of social psychological research has shown that similarity promotes attraction. People like those who share their beliefs and values, unless they are in a competitive, winner-take-all relationship with them.

In addition, the contact hypothesis can be related to another fundamental psychological principle, that of affective association or conditioning. Pleasant experiences with out-group members should generate positive affect, which becomes associated with those out-group members. After multiple favorable interactions, the presence of out-group members should elicit a favorable response to them. By stimulus generalization, that positive response should spread to other members of the out-group as well.

The prediction that favorable contact with members of an out-group will generalize to the out-group as a whole can also be derived from work on the principle of cognitive consistency among cognitions. The argument goes as follows: If one likes X, and X is associated with Y, then one should like Y as well. Balance or consistency among one's cognitions (thoughts, beliefs, and attitudes) is satisfying inasmuch as it provides greater certainty in one's dealings with the world. When one detects inconsistency, one strives to restore consistency either by changing one or more of the inconsistent cognitions or by generating an explanation that resolves the contradiction. Therefore, if contact with members of an out-group causes one to like them, then one should also feel more positively toward others with whom those persons are associated, including other members of that out-group.

Bibliography

Allport, Gordon Willard. *The Nature of Prejudice.* Cambridge, Mass.: Addison-Wesley, 1954. The classic social psychological study of prejudice. While the examples and terminology are dated, the theoretical insights and engaging writing are as fresh as ever. Reviews early conceptualization and research on the contact hypothesis as well as theories of how prejudice develops and what techniques can be used to reduce it. Accessible to the novice and expert alike.

Amir, Yehudi. "The Role of Intergroup Contact in Change of Prejudice and Ethnic Relations." In *Towards the Elimination of Racism,* edited by Phyllis A. Katz. New York: Pergamon Press, 1976. Comprehensive review of empirical studies examining the contact hypothesis along with a complete bibliography. Covers research from the 1940's through the early 1970's.

Aronson, Elliot, et al. *The Jigsaw Classroom.* Beverly Hills, Calif.: Sage Publications, 1978.

Presents the rationale of and reviews the findings from a research program designed to create favorable interethnic contact in classroom settings. Students are assigned to equal-status mixed racial groups to work cooperatively on projects.

Hewstone, Miles, and Rupert Brown, eds. *Contact and Conflict in Intergroup Encounters.* Oxford, England: Basil Blackwell, 1986. A collection of chapters by leading researchers in the field of intergroup relations. Several chapters examine the success of the contact hypothesis with the following conflicts: Arabs/Jews, blacks/whites in U.S. schools, Catholics/Protestants in Northern Ireland, English speakers/French speakers in Quebec, and blacks/whites in South Africa. Other chapters evaluate the success of the contact hypothesis as well as its limitations.

Leyens, Jacques Philippe, Vincent Yzerbyt, and Georges Schadron. *Stereotypes and Social Cognition.* Thousand Oaks, Calif.: Sage Publications, 1994.

Miller, Norman, and Marilynn B. Brewer, eds. *Groups in Contact: The Psychology of Desegregation.* Orlando, Fla.: Academic Press, 1984. Chapters assess the consequences of intergroup contact in a variety of settings. Several chapters look at issues of multiethnic relations in the United States such as the impact of school desegregation as a means of fostering favorable interracial contact. Like the Hewstone and Brown book, this consists of contributions by active researchers discussing their areas of expertise.

Sherif, Muzafer. *Group Conflict and Cooperation.* London: Routledge & Kegan Paul, 1967. Well-written analysis of how intergroup conflict arises and the role of cooperation in reducing conflict. Includes a good description of his classic field experiments using children at summer camps in which intergroup conflict is created and resolved through contact in pursuit of superordinate goals.

Spears, Russell, et al., eds. *The Social Psychology of Stereotyping and Group Life.* Cambridge, Mass.: Blackwell, 1997.

David A. Wilder

See also:

Affiliation and Friendship, 25; Aggression, 31; Attraction Theories, 77; Cognitive Dissonance Theory, 141; Self: Definition and Assessment, 524.

CREATIVITY AND INTELLIGENCE

Type of psychology: Intelligence and intelligence testing
Field of study: General issues in intelligence

Creativity and intelligence are two aspects of cognitive performance in humans. Creativity refers to having inventive, productive, and imaginative qualities; intelligence refers to having mental acuteness, the ability to understand, and the ability to act effectively to solve problems within one's environment. The areas of creativity and intelligence have provided insights into what it means to be gifted and talented.

Principal terms

ANALOGICAL PROBLEM SOLVING: a process in which a person attempts to determine relationships between two terms, concepts, or situations and to correlate the relationship to two other terms, concepts, or situations

ANALOGY: a statement of a relationship between words, concepts, or situations

COGNITIVE ABILITIES: the effectiveness of a person's thinking processes

CREATIVITY: a person's cognitive abilities in areas such as fluency, flexibility, originality, elaboration, visualization, metaphorical thinking, problem definition, and evaluation

EMINENCE: recognition and ranking of one's talents by others who are experienced in appreciating and judging particular performance and results

GIFTEDNESS: consistent cognitive performance, usually based on a score on a standardized intelligence test, beyond the level normally expected for a given age; this may refer to people who are talented and creative

INTELLIGENCE: the ability to perform various mental tasks which include reasoning, knowledge, comprehension, memory, applying concepts, and manipulating figures

PROBLEM SOLVING: the way people seek to answer or respond to a situation that is unknown to them

Overview

Creativity and intelligence are two areas of cognitive functioning and performance which have been examined by researchers, educators, and others. Creativity refers to the process of being imaginative and innovative. A creative person is able to link existing information with new information in productive ways. Students who are creative may often be referred to as being gifted and/or talented. Charles F. Wetherall has listed many characteristics of gifted, talented, and/or creative students. Creative students, for example, have a keen sense of observation and a desire to improve their abilities, produce a variety of possible solutions to problems, are curious, are original, have the characteristic of persistence, are comfortable with ambiguity, are able to work independently, are able to analyze and synthesize information, demonstrate compulsivity and an urgency to complete a task or execute an idea, and have multiple latent abilities. Thus, when one's existing knowledge and information combine in a unique way, a creative product or idea is formed.

Many others have also sought to describe creativity. Characteristics of creative persons and creativity according to Gary A. Davis and Sylvia Rimm include valuing creative thinking, appreciating novel and far-fetched ideas, being open-minded and receptive to zany ideas, and being mentally set to produce creative ideas. Robert Sternberg describes creative people as those who have the ability and willingness to go beyond the ordinary limitations of themselves and their environment and think and act in unconventional and perhaps dreamlike ways. Further, he states that creative people go beyond the unwritten canons of society, have aesthetic taste, and are inquisitive and intuitive. Contributions of a major nature have been made to many fields of endeavor as a result of creative enterprise.

Creativity has been studied by research that sought to examine personality and family issues related to creativity, the ecology of creativity, musical creativity, and creative ability in women. Research by Robert Albert which examined relationships between creativity, identity formation, and career choice caused him to make six suggestions for parents and teachers to help students achieve maximally. This information would be beneficial both to students who are gifted and to those who are not. His suggestions include helping students experience emotions such as anger, joy, fear, and passion; teaching involvement rather than techniques to students; seeking to discover what people can do; allowing students to experience some novelty and flexibility; encouraging the students to ask the questions What do I think? How do I think? What can I do? and How do I feel about it now that I have tried?; and enhancing learning by being actively engaged with and taking chances with one another.

Intelligence, according to Paul Kline, refers to a person's ability to learn, understand, and deal with novel situations. The intelligent person may be viewed as quickwitted, acute, keen, sharp, canny, astute, bright, and brilliant. Robert Sternberg, in *Intelligence Applied: Understanding and Increasing Your Intellectual Skills* (1986), described intelligence as comprising a very wide array of cognitive and other skills; he does not see intelligence as a single ability.

After examining many theories of intelligence, Sternberg developed the triarchic (three-part) theory of intelligence. In the componential subtheory, the first part of the theory, intelligence is related to the external world of the individual. For example, a person who is intelligent in this area obtains high scores on standardized tests and is excellent in analytical thinking. The second part of the theory, the experiential subtheory, specifies intelligence in situations. A person who is intelligent in handling novel tasks with creativity, but who may not have the best standardized test scores, is demonstrating intelligence in this area. In the third part of the theory, the contextual subtheory, intelligence is related to the external world of the individual. For example, a person who is able to achieve success when interacting on the job or when influencing other people is demonstrating contextual intelligence.

Characteristics of intelligent persons include greater preference for, more attention to, and highly developed abilities for dealing with novelty; an ability to process information rapidly; an ability to ignore irrelevant information; and an ability to solve problems accurately. Problem-solving ability in intelligence may be observed in a person's ability to complete many tasks successfully. Among these tasks would be a person's ability to solve analogies.

Analogies are statements of a relationship between words, concepts, or situations. Problem solving by analogy occurs when students attempt to use the conditions and solution to one problem to assist them in understanding the conditions and solutions of another problem. Put another way, students use the relationships they see in one context or situation to assist them in understanding relationships in another context or situation. Many educators believe that solving analogies helps students to concretize their thinking, gauge how they understand information, tap and develop a facility for visual thinking, exercise and nurture creative and critical thinking, clarify and organize unfamiliar subject matter, and synthesize instructional material. Past research has pointed to an ability to solve analogies as one of the best predictors of intellectual ability. Intelligence has also been studied by examining the way that students who have been identified as gifted (based on high intelligence test scores) solve problems. It was found that highly intelligent people are better able to separate relevant and irrelevant information.

Applications

Both creativity and intelligence can be assessed by specialized tests designed for that purpose. E. Paul Torrance developed the Torrance Tests of Creative Thinking; these tests seek to assess creativity as it relates to fluency, flexibility, originality, and elaboration. Each of these areas can be understood in the context of examples. Fluency in creativity is the ability one has to produce numerous original ideas that solve problems. For example, persons may demonstrate fluency when they can give multiple uses for a ballpoint pen. Flexibility in creativity is the ability to produce ideas that show a variety of approaches that may be used. Originality is the ability to create uncommon or unusual responses; for example, a unique or unconventional use of the ballpoint pen would be classified as original. Elaboration refers to a person's ability to add details to a basic idea. For example, if a common item such as a ballpoint pen is discussed in extreme and minute details that do not focus on obvious aspects of the pen, elaboration is being demonstrated.

Intelligence tests consist of standardized questions and tasks which seek to determine the mental age of a person or the person's relative capacity to solve problems and absorb new information. Intelligence tests try to measure students' capacity to learn separate from their actual academic achievement.

Intelligence tests are either group administered or individually administered; in group testings, large numbers of students can be assessed at the same time. According to Miles Storfer, individual intelligence tests such as the Stanford-Binet and the Wechsler series provide a good approximation of most people's abilities in the cognitive skills that the tests are designed to measure. These cognitive skills include being able to solve problems well, reasoning clearly, thinking logically, having a good vocabulary, and knowing an abundance of information in many areas.

Creative discovery has led to many technological breakthroughs and innovations in science and industry. Technological breakthroughs and success in science and industry have been evident in the extensive research into creative activity conducted by W. J. Gordon. He provides some source material that points to the relationship between invention, discovery, and learning. There are a wide variety of technological fields wherein creativity and analogies have led to breakthroughs.

One example of the many technological breakthroughs and innovations in science and industry presented by Gordon occurred in 1865. A man named Dunlop was trying to think of a way to help his son be more comfortable when riding his bicycle over cobblestone streets. While watering his garden, he noticed how the hose resisted his fingers when he pressed his hand more firmly around it. He made the connections between the elastic resistance of the hose and how this type of elasticity would make his son more comfortable when biking. His first successful tire was made from a piece of garden hose.

Context

One of the first people to examine the concept of intelligence in the United States was James McKeen Cattell (1860-1944). He is credited with the introduction of the use of the phrase "mental tests." After studying in Europe, Cattell developed and sought to refine tests which focused on the cognitive skills that he believed indicated intellectual ability: strength, reaction time, and sensory discrimination.

The first test to examine individual differences in intelligence was devised and published in France by Alfred Binet and Theodore Simon in 1905; it was called the Binet-Simon test. The Binet-Simon test was translated into English and went through a series of revisions by various people. The version of the Binet-Simon test most used in the United States was the Stanford-Binet, which was first published in 1916.

Certain issues related to creativity and intelligence have evolved from discrepancies that have been found in obtaining relationships between creativity and intelligence. It is a mistake to lump creative and intelligent people together: Creative ability is not synonymous with intellectual ability. Many students who are very high in intelligence, as measured by a test, are not high in other intellectual functions, such as creativity. Many students who are high in creativity are not also high in intelligence.

The study of creativity and intelligence has developed based on studies in cognitive, developmental, and educational psychology. Given that psychology as a discipline may be defined as "the systematic study of the mind and behavior," when one studies creativity and intelligence, one learns how to improve performance and lead those persons who are creative, gifted, and talented to new heights. Specifically, when one studies creativity, one gains information about students' abilities in imagination, discovery, and ability to invent. When one studies intelligence, one gains information about students' abilities in logic, memory, and organization.

Creativity and intelligence have played a significant role in the history of psychology and an even greater role in the history of humankind. Progress in education is evident by at least three occurrences. First, interest in measuring individual differences led to the development of tests to quantify creative and intellectual abilities. Second, attention to persons who have been identified as creative, gifted, talented, or highly intelligent has led to the development of special programs, learning experiences, and scholarships for these students. Third, the needs of these students have led to research on the students themselves. The results of numerous empirical students have been published to aid parents, educators, and even the gifted or creative individual in understanding the needs of those with special abilities.

The study of creativity and intelligence will continue to play a role in the study of psychology. The need to assess individual differences will continue, as will the need to gain information about how people solve problems. The development of more refined tests will lead to more efficient testing and to more accurate and informative results. They will provide better information to parents, educators, and psychologists about how to encourage and understand creative, gifted, talented, and intelligent students and will help identify persons with special needs. As technology continues to advance, there is a growing need for persons with a high capacity for understanding information as well as persons with the ability to approach old problems with new solutions to be placed in key positions that involve problem solving. Such persons may help address issues related to space exploration as well as maintaining and preserving natural resources.

Bibliography

Albert, Robert S. "Identity, Experiences, and Career Choice Among the Exceptionally Gifted and Eminent." In *Theories of Creativity*, edited by Mark A. Runco and Robert S. Albert. Newbury Park, Calif.: Sage, 1990. This twelve-chapter book on creativity is a compilation of the expertise of persons who have studied creativity in areas such as anthropology, behavior, cognition, development, and ecology. Topics are varied and include creativity in adolescents, creativity in women, relationships between emotional difficulties and creativity, and social factors that influence creativity.

Anderson, William. *The Face of Glory: Creativity, Consciousness, and Civilization*. London: Bloomsbury, 1996.

Davis, Gary A., and Sylvia B. Rimm. *Education of the Gifted and Talented*. Englewood Cliffs, N.J.: Prentice-Hall, 1985. Presents various skills, behaviors, and characteristics of students who are gifted, talented, and/or creative. The abilities and skills involved in creative problem solving are explained in clear language. An excellent source to gain information on the educational needs of gifted, talented, or creative students.

Epstein, Robert. *Cognition, Creativity, and Behavior: Selected Essays*. Westport, Conn.: Praeger, 1996.

Gordon, W. J. "Some Source Material in Discovery-by-Analogy." *Journal of Creative Behavior* 8, no. 4 (1974): 239-257. Focusing on an associative view of invention, discovery, and learning, Gordon cites thirty-eight examples of associative analogical connections which have triggered famous innovations and breakthroughs. A wide variety of technological fields are included. Interesting reading; gives the foundations of many items used in everyday life.

Kline, Paul. *Intelligence: The Psychometric View*. New York: Routledge, 1991. Provides a summary of studies focusing on the nature of intelligence and other human abilities. Topics include the history of the concept of intelligence, and ways to measure intelligence. The definitions of statistical and technical terms are presented in a clear and readable fashion.

Sternberg, Robert J. *Intelligence Applied: Understanding and Increasing Your Intellectual Skills*. Orlando, Fla.: Harcourt Brace Jovanovich, 1986. A training program based on the triarchic theory of intelligence that Sternberg has developed. Details effective strategies for solving various types of problems, including science insight problems and analogies. Exercises for practice are included.

_____. *Successful Intelligence: How Practical and Creative Intelligence Determine Success in Life*. New York: Simon & Schuster, 1996.

Storfer, Miles D. *Intelligence and Giftedness: The Contributions of Heredity and Early Environment*. San Francisco: Jossey-Bass, 1990. Storfer presents information on the effects of nurture on intelligence, focusing on the nature and development of intellectual giftedness and the characteristics of intellectually gifted people. The concept of intelligence in different socioeconomic conditions, in enrichment programs, and in its varying types are highlighted in separate chapters. The factors that influence intelligence and giftedness are examined in detail.

Torrance, Ellis Paul. *Education and the Creative Potential.* Minneapolis: University of Minnesota Press, 1963. A compilation of seven papers and six experimental studies conducted by Torrance, who developed a test to measure creative thinking and conducted longitudinal studies on creativity. Information on topics such as developing creative potential in schoolchildren and factors that facilitate or inhibit creativity in children.

Weisberg, Robert W. *Creativity: Genius and Other Myths.* New York: W. H. Freeman, 1986. Weisberg discusses the behaviors, activities, and finished products of individuals who have been described as creative. Defines creativity by giving real-life examples and discusses the role that intense knowledge or expertise plays in creative problem solving.

Debra A. King-Johnson

See also:

Intelligence: Definition and Theoretical Models, 321; Intelligence: Giftedness and Retardation, 327; Intelligence Tests, 333; Race and Intelligence, 495.

CROWD BEHAVIOR

Type of psychology: Social psychology
Field of study: Group processes

Crowd behavior is a form of group behavior that is characterized by a heightened sense of personal and/or physical anonymity. It results from the reciprocal influence of a temporary, often organized collective of individuals. Studies of the dynamics of crowd behavior have been valuable in understanding the nature of collective behavior, both prosocial (for example, heroic interventions) and antisocial (for example, rioting) in nature.

Principal terms

COACTOR: a person who interacts, even on a temporary basis, with a crowd
CROWD: a temporary collection of anonymous coactors that interact with and influence one another
DEINDIVIDUATION: the loss of self-awareness and evaluation apprehension that accompanies situations that foster personal and physical anonymity
DIFFUSION OF RESPONSIBILITY: the reduction of one's personal responsibility commonly experienced in group situations; diffusion of responsibility increases as the size of the crowd increases
EVALUATION APPREHENSION: the awareness that others are observing and evaluating one's behavior; it is associated with a concern for following situational norms and maintaining others' approval
MERE EXPOSURE EFFECT: the heightening of physiological arousal and an amplification of emotional responses as a result of one's spatial proximity to others
SOCIAL FACILITATION: the enhancement of a person's most dominant response as a result of the presence of others; for some tasks, such as simple ones, performance is enhanced, while for others, such as novel tasks, performance is impaired
SOCIAL LOAFING: the tendency to expend less effort while in the presence of others; this phenomenon is most likely to occur on additive tasks in which one's individual effort is obscured as a result of the collective efforts of the group

Overview

One of the first observations made by early psychologists involved the differences between individual and group behavior. A crowd is a collective of individuals who are temporarily engaged in social interaction that may involve a collective task (for example, participating in a demonstration march) or a common focus of attention (for example, listening to a speaker's address). Typically, members of a crowd are interacting in close spatial proximity, and people become influenced by their interactions with their immediate neighbors. Crowd behavior is a particular form of group behavior that is characterized by a heightened sense of personal and/or physical anonymity. Individual members of large crowds, in particular, are unlikely to be personally identifiable. Hence, people in a crowd respond as a collective rather than an aggregate of independent agents.

Crowd behavior is characterized by coactors' decreased sense of self-awareness and an increased sensitivity to situational cues. In particular, three psychological phenomena play important roles in the genesis and maintenance of crowd behavior. Individuals who become members of a crowd experience heightened levels of physiological arousal, diffusion of personal responsibility, and deindividuation.

One of the first systematic observations of the effect of the crowd on individual behavior was the influence of the crowd on physiological arousal. Norman Triplett noticed that cyclists who were pitted against other cyclists raced faster than when they were racing alone against the clock. He tested his notion about the energizing effect of the crowd in 1898 by conducting a laboratory study in which children were timed as they wound fishing reels, both in groups and alone. He found that children worked harder and reeled in their lines faster when they were in the presence of others. The results of this classic study were repeated by other investigators, who reported similar findings. A number of studies support the general rule that the presence of others is associated with enhanced performance in both human samples (for example, people perform simple problem-solving tasks more quickly in a group) and animal samples (for example, chickens eat more feed in a group). The evidence from these early studies suggests that individual levels of physiological arousal are heightened by the presence of coactors. In turn, heightened levels of physiological arousal facilitate the performance of well-learned tasks (that is, a person's dominant response). This phenomenon, the social facilitation effect, has been used to explain the energizing influence of the crowd on individual behavior.

The energizing nature of the crowd on people's levels of physiological arousal also is manifested in other ways. Robert Zajonc has argued that close proximity to others is reliably associated with elevations in subjects' blood pressure and heart rate. This phenomenon, the mere exposure effect, can help to explain the often extremely emotional reactions of crowds. Physiological arousal plays an important role in the experience of emotion. Thus, individual experiences of various emotional states can be intensified by increases in physiological arousal. Hence, in addition to its influence on task performance, the presence of a crowd can heighten the emotional reactions experienced by coactors.

The second phenomenon experienced by members of a crowd is diffusion of responsibility. Diffusion of responsibility refers to the reduction of a coactor's perception of individual responsibility for the consequences of the crowd's behavior. When a person acts alone, for example, he or she is fully responsible for the consequences of his or her behavior. Thus, if a person commits an antisocial act, such as throwing a brick through a windowpane, that person alone is responsible for that action. On the other hand, individual responsibility is diffused as the number of coactors increases. For example, a woman might be one of many members of a large crowd that is "baiting" a police officer. Alone, she may never scream obscenities at police officers. As a member of a crowd, however, she is not the only person responsible for the officer's harassment. She shares responsibility for the incident with other members of the crowd, thus lowering her sense of personal responsibility for the incident. In most people's perceptions, the crowd itself, rather than individual members, is responsible for its behavior.

Diffusion of responsibility is related to another psychological change in addition to decreased perceptions of personal responsibility. As members of a crowd, coactors are often relieved of any evaluation apprehension they might ordinarily experience. Evaluation apprehension involves the awareness that others are observing and evaluating one's behavior. People who experience evaluation apprehension are concerned with maintaining a positive impression and conforming to social norms. In a crowd, the focus of coactors is often away from the individual; thus, the individual may not be as concerned with maintaining a positive appearance for others' sake. Further, if a crowd is involved in a common task that involves a pooling of effort, studies show that diffusion of responsibility has been associated not only with reduced evaluation apprehension, but also with reduced effort. Coactors expend less effort in a common group task, such as a tug-of-war game, than when they are acting alone. The resultant behavior, social loafing, has been proposed as an explanation for the tendency of coactors to expend less effort in situations that encourage the diffusion of responsibility among the members of a crowd.

The final phenomenon, deindividuation, results from both the heightened levels of physiological arousal and the diffusion of responsibility experienced by members of a crowd. Deindividuation is a psychological state of reduced self-awareness that is particularly acute when crowd conditions foster physical and personal anonymity. Anonymity is heightened in very large crowds, crowds that form at night, and crowds that engage in ritualistic, rhythmic behaviors such as chanting, singing, or clapping. The individual experience of deindividuation involves a complete loss of evaluation apprehension, diminished attention to oneself and one's behavior, and a loss of self-restraint. When individuals experience deindividuation as a result of being part of a crowd, they become particularly responsive to the social cues of the situation. Hence, participants in a large religious ceremony may become extremely emotional, cry out, and become carried away by the ecstasy of their communal religious experience. Conversely, members of an angry mob may become increasingly angry, restless, and hostile, and ultimately cause a riot.

Applications

Over the last hundred years, a number of laboratory and field studies concerning the influence of others on the individual have been conducted by social psychologists. These studies are designed to identify and describe the situational factors that are critical in the elicitation and maintenance of crowd behavior.

One important finding is that the energizing effect of the crowd increases with the number of coactors and, thus, the density of the crowd. Jonathan Freedman and his colleagues investigated the effects of density on an audience's reactions to two films. In the low-density condition, subjects were instructed to spread out in a theater in order to ensure that they were comfortable. In the high-density condition, subjects were instructed to sit in the center of a theater. In each condition, a confederate of the experimenter was instructed to applaud loudly at the conclusion of only the second film. The results of this study suggested that the positive emotional response generated by the confederate was enhanced in the high-density condition. The experimenters' ratings of the audience responses to the second film indicated that there was much more applause in the high-density than in the low-density condition.

The proximity of others can explain the social facilitation effort observed in this study. Two factors are particularly important in explaining the response of the audience to the confederate's cued applause. First, high density is associated with increased arousal in both animals and humans. Second, coactors' responses are a valuable source of information when individuals assess a social situation. Subjects in this study reported how much they enjoyed each film, and although the audience as a whole responded more positively to the second film than the first, individual ratings of enjoyment did not differ between films. On the other hand, subjects reported that others in the audience had enjoyed the second film much more than the first. Thus, the social feedback one gathers from the responses of others in a crowd may play an important role in assessing and responding to the situation.

The presence of others, however, does not always produce a positive social facilitation effect. Psychologist Alan Ingham and his colleagues investigated the influence of the diffusion of responsibility on coactors' performance. In particular, these researchers were interested in identifying the factors that produce social loafing in a group that is charged with completing a task for which everyone is responsible but no one is individually accountable. An apparatus was designed for this experiment that simulated a tug-of-war game. Subjects were led, blindfolded, to an apparatus that had positions for six participants. They were then told to pull on a rope with all their strength.

In the alone condition, subjects were told that they were pulling on the rope by themselves. In the diffusion-of-responsibility conditions, subjects were told that they were pulling with two to five other persons. The results of the study indicated that subjects pulled 18 percent harder when they knew they were alone than when they believed they were working as a member of a group. As predicted, since subjects' individual performances could not be evaluated by others, the social-loafing effect was observed. Further, it is possible that the blindfolds eliminated any evaluation apprehension that subjects might have felt in this experiment.

These studies were concerned with fairly innocuous social behaviors performed in the safety of the laboratory. Other studies of crowd behavior are concerned with the antisocial nature of crowds. Social psychologist Brian Mullen was interested in studying the influence of crowd density on a particularly antisocial and virulent form of crowd behavior, the lynch mob. He collected sixty newspaper accounts of lynchings and analyzed them to determine the degree of violence and atrocity expressed by the mobs. Mullen assessed the density of the mob by comparing the number of victims with the total number of participants in each situation. He also recorded the occurrence of five acts of violence (hanging, shooting, burning, stabbing, and mutilation of the victim) and evaluated the duration of the lynching (relatively quick, moderate, or torturous).

First, Mullen predicted that the lynchers would exhibit decreased self-awareness and increased deindividuation as the size of the mob increased relative to the number of victims. Then he predicted that the savagery of the attack directed toward the victim would increase as deindividuation increased. These predictions were upheld. As the size of the mob increased, behavioral self-restraint declined. The larger mobs were found to have committed the most savage acts of atrocity against the victims.

Context

Many historical events appear to have resulted from the collective behavior of the crowd. As such, the crowd has long been the focus of study in the humanities and social sciences. The psychology of crowd behavior began as a European phenomenon. Gustave Le Bon published the first systematic study, *Psychologie de foules* (1895; *The Crowd: A Study of the Popular Mind*, 1896). In Le Bon's view, individual logic and rationality are lost in the emotional contagion generated by the crowd. The group mind is presumed to take over, and the crowd becomes a homogeneous social organism, a spontaneous and violent entity that eschews rationality and responds to primeval, unconscious motivation. While Sigmund Freud agreed with Le Bon concerning inherent antisocial crowd behavior, he did not accept the concept of a group mind. Freud posited that membership in a crowd allowed the ego to relax its repression of the id impulse. As a result, when a person becomes a member of a crowd, he or she regresses and exhibits the free expression of the primitive libidinal energy of the id.

Le Bon's seminal work was further elaborated upon by his contemporary Gabriel Tarde, who described various types of crowds and crowd behaviors. In particular, his description of organized crowds, or masses, provided a means of analyzing the social effects of institutions such as the military and the church. His work described the process of suggestibility and imitation that characterizes crowds that have been mobilized by a charismatic leader. Tarde also provided early insights into the interactive roles of the media, public-opinion leaders, and mass communication.

These early theoretical formulations provided an important cornerstone for the European and American social psychological studies of crowd behavior that emerged after World War II. The orientation of social psychology moved the study of crowds away from the group mind and suggestibility to the identification of situational factors that encourage the expression of crowd behavior. Experimental and field studies of crowd behavior flourished within the context of the political unrest of the 1960's and public concerns over the dehumanizing consequences of urbanization. It is important to note that not all social psychological research has addressed the antisocial nature of the crowd. Perhaps as a result of cultural events such as the surprisingly peaceful Woodstock music festival of 1969, which had a crowd of 300,000 people, and the encounter movement of the late 1960's, a number of studies have investigated the prosocial consequences of crowd behavior.

Bibliography

Brown, Hedy. *People, Groups, and Society.* Philadelphia: Open University Press, 1985. An extremely accessible introduction to group influence and crowd behavior that includes an introduction to general principles of social influence and intergroup relations. The similarities and differences between crowds and other social groups are also discussed.

Galanter, Marc. *Cults: Faith, Healing, and Coercion.* New York: Oxford University Press, 1989. A fascinating study of charismatic groups that is particularly appropriate for the general reader. Discusses the unique social factors that characterize such groups and provides three famous case histories (Jonestown, the Unification Church, and Alcoholics Anonymous). A detailed explanation of the social forces that are experienced by members of cults and other extremely cohesive social groups.

Gaskell, George, and Robert Benewick, eds. *The Crowd in Contemporary Britain.* London: Sage, 1987. This edited volume is an excellent collection of studies and observations of crowd behavior. Theories of crowd behavior are introduced, then historical and contemporary examples of crowd behavior are presented. The chapters in this volume are concerned with a range of crowd behaviors, from peaceful to violent actions.

Hogg, Michael A., and Dominic Abrams. *Social Identifications: A Social Psychology of Intergroup Relations and Group Processes.* London: Routledge, 1988. This volume adopts a social-identity perspective on group influence. Two chapters are particularly relevant to the effects of crowd membership on personal identity and behavior. The authors present an excellent summary of the effects of the presence of others on social performance. Another excellent chapter addresses the nature of collective behavior and deindividuation. An accessible review of complex issues.

Kelly, Caroline, and Sara Breinlinger. *The Social Psychology of Collective Action: Identity, Injustice, and Gender*. London: Taylor & Francis, 1996.

Milgram, Stanley. *The Individual in a Social World: Essays and Experiments*. Reading, Mass.: Addison-Wesley, 1977. An excellent introduction to group influence and crowd behavior. Milgram, a prominent researcher in the field, describes a number of classic experiments on social influence and crowd behavior. The articles in part 1 ("The Individual in the City") and part 2 ("The Individual and the Group") of this work are particularly relevant to crowd behavior.

Paulus, Paul B., ed. *Psychology of Group Influence*. 2d ed. Hillsdale, N.J.: Lawrence Erlbaum, 1989. This edited volume contains a selection of articles on many aspects of crowd behavior. Specific topics include the social facilitation effect, deindividuation, and environmental influences on crowds. An excellent source of theoretical perspectives and empirical data relevant to crowd behavior for the college-level reader.

Perry, Joseph B., Jr., and Meredith David Pugh. *Collective Behavior: Response to Social Stress*. St. Paul, Minn.: West, 1978. A general discussion of the crowd and its social influence. The authors first present a theoretical discussion of the crowd, rumor, contagion, and deindividuation, then provide many examples of crowd violence, control, mobilization, and social movements. A very accessible introduction to the topic with specific focus on collective behavior.

Zimbardo, Philip G. "The Human Choice: Individuation, Reason, and Order Versus Deindividuation, Impulse, and Chaos." In *Nebraska Symposium on Motivation: 1969*, edited by William J. Arnold and D. Levine. Lincoln: University of Nebraska Press, 1970. An accessible and authoritative discussion of the factors that elicit deindividuation. Presents a number of experiments, anecdotes, and everyday examples of the prosocial and antisocial behavioral effects of increased urbanization and other sociocultural factors that increase anonymity and reduce individual self-awareness and behavioral inhibitions.

Cheryl A. Rickabaugh

See also:

Affiliation and Friendship, 25; Aggression, 31; The Contact Hypothesis, 170; Helping: Bystander Intervention, 272; Self: Definition and Assessment, 524.

Dementia, Alzheimer's Disease, and Parkinson's Disease

Type of psychology: Psychopathology
Field of study: Organic disorders

Dementia is the loss of memory. Alzheimer's disease is one of the most common causes of premature memory loss (presenile dementia); its effects on the patient, and often on the patient's family, are devastating. Parkinson's disease, another disorder of the central nervous system, can also cause memory loss.

Principal terms

CEREBELLUM: a part of the hindbrain; it is involved with controlling posture and body movement

EXTRAPYRAMIDAL MOTOR SYSTEM: one of the two parts of the nervous system involved in performing voluntary movement (the other is the pyramidal system); the cerebellum directs its functioning

NEURON: an individual nerve cell, the basic unit of the nervous system

NEUROTRANSMITTER: a chemical substance that enables a neuron to "communicate" with another neuron or a muscle cell

PATHOGENIC: relating to the causing of a disease; capable of causing a disease

PYRAMIDAL MOTOR SYSTEM: one of the two parts of the nervous system involved in performing voluntary movement (the other is the extrapyramidal system)

Overview

Aging has traditionally been blamed for a loss of intellectual abilities and is widely accepted to be the cause of memory failure. The word "senility" has therefore come to be equated with forgetfulness and loss of intellect; correctly, however, senility simply means old age, not those other characteristics that have come to be associated with it. Many studies have shown that cognitive abilities decrease only slightly with age and have suggested strongly that environmental and situational factors have greater impact on memory or cognitive loss than physiological factors do.

The accurate term for age-associated forgetfulness is "dementia." If dementia occurs in old age, it is called senile dementia; if its onset occurs prior to the conventional age of sixty-five or so, it is referred to as presenile dementia. Dementia as a clinical syndrome is a progressive cognitive deterioration that eventually causes functional impairment. It develops over time and causes deficits in intelligence, memory, affect (emotion), judgment, orientation, and visual-spatial skills. Dementia may be caused or affected by many variables. Injury to the brain, as from an automobile accident, is one example. The most frequently noted cause is Alzheimer's disease.

The cause of Alzheimer's disease is not known. Therefore, neither preventive nor demonstrably effective curative treatments are available. It is estimated that there are more than 4 million people in the United States suffering from Alzheimer's disease. Even though age per se does not cause the disease, it is among the variables involved. For example, nearly 10 percent of the elderly between the ages of sixty-five and seventy-five suffer from Alzheimer's disease, whereas 35 to 45 percent of the elderly eighty years of age and older suffer from the disease.

Alzheimer's disease is the primary cause of dementia. Its symptoms, progressing from the earliest to the final stages, may involve the loss of recent memory, disorientation, drastic changes in judgment and personality, and loss of long-term memory, including the names of close relatives. It is considered primarily a cognitive disorder, but it also influences one's social behavior, increases agitation and anger, and disrupts patterns of family relationships.

There are many theories of the cause of Alzheimer's disease, all of which have mustered some degree of support from experimental evidence. Neuronal losses, changes in neurotransmitters, aluminum toxicity, and genetic factors are among the most probable causes being researched. Alois Alzheimer originally indicated that there is a loss of cortical neurons associated with the disease; quantitative documentation of his hypothesis was provided later. In general, at autopsy, a clear loss of brain tissues in comparison with the same age group without Alzheimer's disease can be seen. Perhaps of equal importance is the dramatic cognitive dysfunction that is caused by the disruption in the flow of neurotransmitters because of the loss of tissue.

Studies of neurotransmitters, their receptors, and the enzymes responsible for their synthesis and degeneration have demonstrated a vast amount of alteration. The major changes are observed to occur in a specialized group of neurons that are known as the cholinergic system. The cholinergic system is involved in the functioning of the cerebral cortex as well as other vital parts of the brain. Changes in neurotransmitters such as acetylcholine and somatostatin lead to interruptions of the cortical function of the brain, researcher Paul Newhouse has noted. It has been established that there is a correlation between the loss of cholinergic markers in the brain and the degree of cognitive dysfunction that occurs in the latter stages of Alzheimer's disease.

Evidence of genetic factors in Alzheimer's disease has also been found. In investigating large groups of patients with both presenile and senile dementia, 5 to 15 percent of the affected individuals have shown familial patterns; in most instances, the disease follows a dominant pattern of inheritance. In a study of a family of Alzheimer's disease patients in the northeastern New York area, Taher Zandi and Linda Morreale found a dominant pattern of familial Alzheimer's disease that can be traced up to four generations. Among the group of individuals with familial type Alzheimer's disease, it is common to find other disorders that may have been transferred genetically. For example, leukemia is reported to be a frequently observed disorder in correlation with both Alzheimer's disease and Down syndrome. All patients who live beyond the age of thirty-five with Down syndrome (Trisomy 21) develop pathological changes in the brain that are the same as the changes used to diagnose Alzheimer's disease (Karen Bick, 1987). Scientists are searching for a connection between chromosome number 21 and Alzheimer's disease.

Investigators of patients who are on renal (kidney) dialysis have shown that a small number of patients develop a progressive dementia that seems to be associated with an accumulation of aluminum in the brain. Animal studies have found that rabbits that were injected with an aluminum solution showed damage within the neurons that is similar to that of Alzheimer's disease. This possible connection to aluminum deposits is among the most controversial of the suggested causes of the disease.

The effects of Parkinson's disease, or parkinsonism, consist of an expressionless face, slowness (and minimization) of voluntary movement, tremors (mainly when at rest), a stooped posture, rigidity, and a festinating gait (that is, a gait that is abnormally affected by "chasing" the person's center of gravity). The onset of parkinsonism usually occurs between the ages of forty and seventy. It affects both sexes equally; past age fifty, the rate of incidence is 1 percent.

Parkinson's disease has been tied to a degeneration of certain neurons (dopaminergic neurons) in the midbrain. These neurons are crucial in the regulation of the parts of the nervous system that control voluntary movements—the pyramidal and extrapyramidal motor systems. In the pyramidal system, the motor cortex of the brain transmits commands from the cortex via the pyramidal tracts; the motor cortex of the right side of the brain stimulates the left side of the body, and vice versa. Technically, the remainder of the motor nervous system is called the extrapyramidal system, but the term most frequently is applied to the area of the basal ganglia and the cerebellum. It modulates the activities of the pyramidal motor system. Disease in this system causes rigidity, tremor, and lack of coordination (especially if the cerebellum itself is diseased). Furthermore, cranial motor neurons and spinal-cord motor neurons are also affected.

The extrapyramidal motor system sets the timing and pattern of action of the skeletal muscles in any projected action. Disease of the system may cause paresis (weakness of the muscle, but with some function remaining) or paralysis (complete loss of a muscle's function). Any of these conditions may be incapacitating. Fine tuning of the pyramidal and extrapyramidal networks requires a proper balance of certain neurotransmitters, specifically acetylcholine (the excitatory neurotransmitter) and dopamine (the inhibitor). In Alzheimer's disease, too little acetylcholine (ACh) occurs in certain localities of the brain. In Parkinson's disease, there is too little dopamine. Too little acetylcholine in the body results in myasthenia, a muscle weakness disease; too much acetylcholine in the body causes convulsions. As people age, the cells in the substantia nigra area of the brain's motor cortex become fewer, decreasing from some 425,000 cells in young adults to 200,000 cells at the age of eighty. In most cases of parkinsonism, there are fewer than 100,000 cells left. The enzyme for forming dopamine also decreases with age. These changes make elderly people more vulnerable to parkinsonism.

Applications

Although there are many theories seeking to explain the causes of Alzheimer's and Parkinson's diseases, none is yet exclusive or completely convincing. The major problem for those investigating the diseases has to do with the difficulty in distinguishing among the primary symptoms of the disorders, their manifestations, and the secondary reaction of individuals toward these symptoms.

Alzheimer's disease is defined by certain pathologies that are found in the nervous systems (specifically, in the brains) of people with the condition. These pathologies are found in the frontal, parietal, and temporal cortex areas of the brain as well as in the hippocampus, a primary memory storage area. They consist of what are called "neurofibrillary tangles" and "neuritic plaques." The neurofibrillary tangles have been found to be protein filaments. Neuritic plaques are accumulated dead neurons. The number of these looplike neurofibrillary tangles observed has been linked to the degree of dementia that existed in the patient. (The actual diagnosis based on these brain abnormalities can only practically be made in postmortem examination during an autopsy.) Another significant finding has been that both the neurotransmitter acetylcholine and the enzyme choline acetyltransferase are found in smaller amounts in the brains of patients with Alzheimer's disease. Again, there is a correlation with the severity of the disease's symptoms; the smaller the amounts of both chemicals, the worse the symptoms of the disease.

Unlike some other neurological disorders, there has been an absence of animal models for Alzheimer's disease, which has contributed to the mysteriousness of the disease. The characteristic neurofibrillary tangles have never been seen in old animals. In some very limited circumstances Alzheimer's disease has been induced in animals, but the induction procedure is based on a theory that may explain the disease partially at best, according to A. M. Clarfield.

Parkinson's disease is commonly treated through administration of L-dopa. L-dopa is a form of dopamine (the "levorotatory" form, essentially a chemical mirror-image of dopamine) that has been found most effective. It acts by binding to the dopamine receptors and producing almost the same effects as dopamine itself does. Side effects include nausea, hypertension, depression (which can be severe enough to result in suicide), and a heightening of the sex drive. Elevated mood and activity can result in fractures or even in heart attacks (myocardial infarctions). Amantadine, an antiviral drug also used in treating influenza, acts by releasing dopamine from striatal neurons.

Important in the attempt to understand the causes of these disorders—and thus to develop curative treatments for them—is their early recognition. Diagnosing Alzheimer's disease is complicated by the fact that the definitive indications of the disease can be found only upon autopsy. Since true cures do not yet exist, the efficient management of primary and secondary symptoms of the illnesses is of great importance. For example, memory loss, a primary behavioral symptom of Alzheimer's disease, results in communication difficulty between patient and caregiver, which often increases the patient's frustration and the care provider's stress. Behavioral management strategies can provide the caregiver with the proper skills, thus reducing the unneeded tension that is created in family life. Another important type of management strategy is medication management, which may improve the patient's sleeping pattern and therefore make life more manageable for the family members as well as for the patient.

Context

Alzheimer's disease is named for Alois Alzheimer, the German neurologist who first identified the disease in 1907. For most of the twentieth century, the disease remained extremely mysterious. It was not frequently recognized or diagnosed, and older people with severe memory and disorientation problems were considered to be suffering from extreme cases of the "normal" problems of growing old. Since the 1970's, however, investigations into both Alzeimer's and Parkinson's diseases have increased considerably, and much has been learned about the fundamental aspects of the diseases. Many advances have been related to technological improvements, such as the development and refinement of microchips for neurological imaging, as well as the availability of other instruments. It remains for scholars and researchers entering the fields of geriatrics, neurology, psychiatry, psychology, and other relevant disciplines to continue the search for cures for these diseases until preventive measures can become a reality.

Alzheimer's disease has a profound and disturbing impact on the spouse and family of the person affected by the disease. Emotionally, they must watch a person they know and love gradually lose memory and the ability to function and care for himself or herself. In the earlier stages of the disease, the patient is usually disturbed by the losses. Ironically, as the disease progresses and worsens, the patient is less aware of the problems, but the burden on the family increases as family members must care for the patient or decide to put the person in a nursing home or other care facility. The financial burden becomes immense, and it is unfortunately not uncommon for Alzheimer's patients and their spouses to lose all their savings as well as their homes in the frustrating attempt to pay the bills for a condition that can only get worse. Health insurance frequently is designed to cover hospital expenses but not long-term care in a nursing home. Medicaid, a federal program, will pay for "custodial" care, but only for people who cannot pay themselves—in other words, a person must first lose everything he or she has.

There is hope that research will develop ways to prevent, cure, or at least delay such degenerative diseases. New techniques for imaging the brain in detail are aiding research efforts. Positron emission tomography (PET scanning) and magnetic resonance imaging (MRI) technologies, for example, show promise in researching and diagnosing neurological disease. MRI is based on the unique magnetic properties of certain atoms within the body, and it applies a powerful magnetic field to the body, then, with computers, evaluates the results.

Bibliography

Bradley, W. "Alzheimer's Disease: Theories of Causation." In *New Directions in Understanding Dementia and Alzheimer's Disease*, edited by Taher Zandi and Richard J. Ham. New York: Plenum Press, 1990. Bradley has investigated the role of genetics in the development of Alzheimer's disease. In this article he discusses the role of chromosome 21 and its possible linkage to Alzheimer's disease.

Clarfield, A. M. "The Reversible Dementias: Do They Reverse?" *Annals of Internal Medicine* 109 (1988): 476-486. Clarfield reviews a very important question of dementia. His analysis of more than twenty investigations of dementia suggests that the number of reversible dementias may be less than 2 percent.

Cutler, Neal R., and John J. Sramek. *Understanding Alzheimer's Disease*. Jackson: University Press of Mississippi, 1996.

Hodgson, Harriet W. *Alzheimer's: Finding the Words*. Minneapolis, Minn.: Chronimed Publishing, 1995.

Miner, Gary D., et al., eds. *Caring for Alzheimer's Patients: A Guide for Family and Healthcare Providers*. New York: Plenum Press, 1989. Presents a considerable amount of useful information in its 292 pages. Includes sections on the biology of the disease and on dealing with the disease (including legal information, caring for the patient, and public policy issues). Good references and helpful appendices.

Oliver, Rose, and Frances A. Bock. *Coping with Alzheimer's: A Caregiver's Emotional*

Survival Guide. New York: Dodd, Mead, 1987. The emphasis is on advice for those taking care of a patient with Alzheimer's disease on how to handle the stresses they themselves will experience. Covers common emotional responses such as denial, anger, shame, and self-pity.

Zandi, Taher, and Richard J. Ham, eds. *New Directions in Understanding Dementia and Alzheimer's Disease*. New York: Plenum Press, 1990. Zandi and Ham provide a multidisciplinary look at this disorder. Discusses the fact that Alzheimer's disease, even though a neuropsychiatric disorder, has profound social and political implications that affect family members.

Taher Zandi

See also:

Aging: Cognitive Changes, 37; The Central and Peripheral Nervous Systems, 115; Depression, Clinical, 194; Neuropsychology, 422.

CLINICAL DEPRESSION

Type of psychology: Psychopathology
Field of study: Depression

Clinical depression is an emotional disorder characterized by extreme sadness and a loss of ability to experience pleasure. Its clinical features also include cognitive (for example, low self-worth), behavioral (for example, decreased activity level), and physical (for example, fatigue) symptoms. Depression is a frequently diagnosed disorder in both inpatient and outpatient mental health settings.

Principal terms

ANHEDONIA: a symptom of clinical depression; a loss of the capacity to experience pleasure

BECK DEPRESSION INVENTORY (BDI): a brief questionnaire used to measure the severity of depression; developed by Aaron Beck

CHILDREN'S DEPRESSION INVENTORY (CDI): a modified version of the BDI that was developed to measure the severity of depression in children; developed by Maria Kovacs

COGNITIVE THERAPY FOR DEPRESSION: a treatment that helps depressed clients think more accurately and effectively about their experiences; largely based on Aaron Beck's cognitive theory of depression

DYSPHORIA: a symptom of clinical depression; extreme sadness

DYSTHYMIC DISORDER: a form of depression in which mild to moderate levels of depressive symptoms persist chronically

HELPLESSNESS: the belief that one has little or no control over the events in one's life; viewed by Martin Seligman as an important cause of depression

MONOAMINE OXIDASE (MAO) INHIBITORS: a class of antidepressant drugs

TRICYCLICS: a class of antidepressant drugs

Overview

Clinical depression is a severe emotional disorder that is characterized by four classes of symptoms: emotional, cognitive, behavioral, and physical. The major emotional symptoms, at least one of which is necessary for the diagnosis of depression, are dysphoria (extreme sadness or depressed mood) and anhedonia (lack of capacity to experience pleasure). Other emotional symptoms, which may but do not necessarily occur in depression, are anxiety and anger. Depressed individuals also experience cognitive symptoms. They have negative or pessimistic thoughts about themselves, the world around them, and the future. They misinterpret their experiences so as to support these negative views. In some cases, the negative views of self and future are so extreme that the individual contemplates suicide. Behavioral symptoms of depression include decreased activity level and slowed rate of activity. Depressed individuals also experience several physical symptoms. They become easily fatigued, lose their appetites, and experience sleep disturbances (including insomnia, an inability to fall asleep; and morning waking, awakening in the early morning and being unable to return to sleep).

Depression is one of the more commonly experienced mental disorders. For example, in

1985, psychologists John Wing and Paul Bebbington examined research that used psycho-logical tests to measure the prevalence of (or lifetime risk for) depression in the general population. They found that estimates of the prevalence of depression generally ranged from about 5 to 10 percent. Interestingly, all the studies examined by Wing and Bebbington agreed that depression was more common in women than in men. Estimates of the prevalence of depression ranged from 2.6 to 4.5 percent in men and from 5.9 to 9.0 percent in women.

Depression is also related to other characteristics. Risk for depression increases with age. The evidence is clear that depression is more common in adults and the elderly than in children or adolescents. Interest in childhood depression has increased since the early 1970's, however, and the number of children and adolescents who have been diagnosed as depressed has increased since that time. Depression is also related to socioeconomic status. In general, people who are unemployed and who are in lower income groups have higher risks for depression than others. This may be a result of the higher levels of stress experienced by individuals in lower-income groups. Finally, family history is related to depression. That is, clinical depression tends to run in families. This is consistent with both biological and psychological theories of depression.

Psychologists face several difficulties when attempting to determine the prevalence of depression. First, the symptoms of depression range in severity from mild to severe. It may not always be clear at which point these symptoms move from the mild nuisances associated with "normal" levels of sadness to significant symptoms associated with clinical depression. Since the early 1970's, clinical psychologists have devoted an increased amount of attention to depressions that occur at mild to moderate levels. Even though these milder depressions are not as debilitating as clinical depression, they produce significant distress for the individual and so warrant attention. In 1980, the term "dysthymic disorder" was introduced to describe depressions which, although mild to moderate, persist chronically.

Another complication in determining the prevalence of depression is that it may occur either as a primary or as a secondary problem. As a primary problem, depression is the initial or major disorder which should be the focus of clinical intervention. On the other hand, as a secondary problem, depression occurs in reaction to or as a consequence of another disorder. For example, many patients experience such discomfort or distress from medical or mental disorders that they eventually develop the symptoms of depression. In this case, the primary disorder and not depression is usually the focus of treatment.

There are several major approaches to the treatment of clinical depression, each focusing on one of the four classes of symptoms of depression. Psychoanalytic therapists believe that the cause of depression is emotional: underlying anger which stems from some childhood loss and which has been turned inward. Psychoanalysts therefore treat depression by helping the client to identify the cause of the underlying anger and to cope with it in a more effective manner.

Psychiatrist Aaron T. Beck views depression primarily as a cognitive disorder. He holds that depressives have negative views of self, world, and future, and that they interpret their experiences in a distorted fashion so as to support these pessimistic views. A related cognitive model of depression is that of Martin E. P. Seligman. He argues that depression results from the perception that one is helpless or has little or no control over the events in one's life. Seligman has shown that laboratory-induced helplessness produces many of the symptoms of depression. Cognitive therapy for depression, which Beck described in 1979, aims at helping depressed clients identify and then change their negative and inaccurate patterns of thinking.

Behavioral therapists view depression as the result of conditioning. Psychologist Peter Lewinsohn suggests that depression results from low amounts of reinforcement. His behavioral therapy for depression aims at increasing reinforcement levels, through scheduling pleasant activities and improving the client's social skills.

Biologically oriented therapies exist as well. Two classes of antidepressant medications, monoamine oxidase (MAO) inhibitors and tricyclics, are effective both in treating clinical depression and in preventing future episodes of depression. Electroconvulsive (shock) therapy (ECT) has also been found to be effective in treating severe depression. Although the reasons the biological treatments work have not been conclusively identified, it is thought that they are effective because they increase the activity or amount of norepinephrine and serotonin, two neurotransmitters which are important in the transmission of impulses in the nervous system.

Applications

In 1983, Eugene Levitt, Bernard Lubin, and James Brooks reported the results of the National Depression Survey, which attempted to determine the prevalence and correlates of depression in the general population. They interviewed more than three thousand people, including 622 teenagers, who were randomly selected to be a representative sample of the entire United States population. Subjects completed a brief self-report measure of depression and answered questions concerning their age, occupation, education, religion, and other variables.

Levitt, Lubin, and Brooks found that slightly more than 3 percent of the population was experiencing depression that was severe enough to warrant clinical intervention and so could be termed clinical depression. This figure is similar to that found by other investigators. In addition, Levitt, Lubin, and Brooks found that depression was related to sex, age, occupational status, and income. Depression was higher for subjects who were female, older, lower in occupational status, and either low or high in income (earning less than $6,000 or more than $25,000).

One of the most widely used measures of depression is the Beck Depression Inventory (BDI). Beck introduced this test in 1961 to assess the severity of depression in individuals who are known or suspected to have depression. The BDI has twenty-one items, each concerning a symptom of depression (for example, weight loss, suicidal thinking) which is rated for severity. The BDI can be self-administered or can be completed by an interviewer.

Since its introduction, the BDI has become one of the most widely used measures of depression for both research and clinical purposes. Many studies have shown that the BDI is an accurate and useful measure of depression. For example, BDI scores have been found to be related to both clinicians' ratings of the severity of a client's depression and clinical improvements during the course of treatment for depression, and to be able to discriminate between the diagnosis of clinical depression and other conditions.

Psychologist Maria Kovacs developed the Children's Depression Inventory (CDI) by modifying the BDI for use with children. Similar in format to the BDI, the CDI contains twenty-eight items, each of which concerns a symptom of depression that is rated for severity. Research has supported the utility of the CDI. CDI ratings have been found to be related to clinicians' ratings of childhood depression. CDI scores have also been found to discriminate children hospitalized for depression from children hospitalized for other disorders. The CDI (along with other recently developed measures of childhood depression) has contributed to psychology's recent research on and understanding of the causes and treatment of childhood depression.

Many research projects since the 1970's have examined the effectiveness of cognitive and behavioral treatments of depression. Beck and his colleagues have demonstrated that cognitive therapy for depression is superior to no treatment whatsoever and to placebos (inactive psychological or medical interventions which should have no real effect but which the client believes have therapeutic value). In addition, this research has shown that cognitive therapy is about as effective as both antidepressant medications and behavior therapy. Similarly, Lewinsohn and others have shown the effectiveness of behavior therapy on depression by demonstrating that it is superior to no treatment and to placebo conditions.

One of the most important studies of the treatment of depression is the Treatment of Depression Collaborative Research Program, begun by the National Institute of Mental Health (NIMH) in the mid-1980's. A group of 250 clinically depressed patients was randomly assigned to four treatment conditions: interpersonal psychotherapy, cognitive behavioral psychotherapy, tricyclic antidepressant medication, and placebo medication. Treatment was presented over sixteen to twenty sessions. Patients were assessed by both self-report and a clinical evaluator before treatment, after every fourth session, and at six-, twelve-, and eighteen-month follow-ups after the end of treatment.

This study found that patients in all four treatment conditions improved significantly over the course of therapy. In general, patients who received antidepressant medication improved the most, patients who received the placebo improved the least, and patients who received the two forms of psychotherapy improved to an intermediate degree (but were closer in improvement to those receiving antidepressant medication than to those receiving the placebo). This study also found that, for patients in general, there was no significant difference between the effectiveness rates of the antidepressant medication and the two forms of psychotherapy.

For severely depressed patients, however, antidepressant medication and interpersonal psychotherapy were found to be more effective than other treatments; for less severely depressed patients, there were no differences in effectiveness across the four treatment conditions.

Context

Clinical depression is one of the most prevalent psychological disorders. Because depression is associated with an increased risk for suicide, it is also one of the more severe disorders. For these reasons, psychologists have devoted much effort to determining the causes of depression and developing effective treatments.

Theories and treatments of depression can be classified into four groups: emotional, cognitive, behavioral, and physical. In the first half of the twentieth century, the psychoanalytic theory of depression, which emphasizes the role of the emotion of anger, dominated clinical psychology's thinking about the causes and treatment of depression. Following the discovery of the first antidepressant medications in the 1950's, psychologists increased their attention to physical theories and treatments of depression. Since the early 1970's, Beck's and Seligman's cognitive approaches and Lewinsohn's behavioral theory have received increased amounts of attention. By the 1990's, the biological, cognitive, and behavioral theories of depression had all surpassed the psychoanalytic theory of depression in terms of research support for their respective proposed causes and treatments.

Another shift in emphasis in psychology's thinking about depression concerns childhood depression. Prior to the 1970's, psychologists paid relatively little attention to depression in children; classical psychoanalytic theory suggested that children had not yet completed a crucial step of their psychological development that psychoanalysts believed was necessary for a person to become depressed. Thus, many psychologists believed that children did not experience depression or that, if they did become depressed, their depressions were not severe. Research in the 1970's demonstrated that children do experience depression and that, when depressed, children exhibit symptoms similar to those of depressed adults. Since the 1970's, psychologists have devoted much effort to understanding the cause and treatment of childhood depression. Much of this work has examined how the biological, cognitive, and behavioral models of depression, originally developed for and applied to adults, may generalize to children.

Another shift in psychology's thinking about depression concerns the attention paid to mild and moderate depressions. Since the 1960's, clinical psychology has been interested in the early detection and treatment of minor conditions in order to prevent the development of more severe disorders. This emphasis on prevention has influenced the field's thinking about depression. Since the early 1970's, psychologists have applied cognitive and behavioral models of depression to nonpatients who obtain high scores on measures of depression. Even though these individuals are not clinically depressed, they still experience significant distress and so may benefit from the attention of psychologists. By using cognitive or behavioral interventions with these individuals, psychologists may prevent the development of more severe depressions.

Bibliography

Beck, Aaron T., A. J. Rush, B. F. Shaw, and G. Emery. *Cognitive Therapy of Depression.* New York: Guilford Press, 1979. Summarizes the cognitive theory of depression and describes how this model can be applied in the treatment of depressed clients.

Beckham, Ernest Edward, and William R. Leber, eds. *Handbook of Depression: Treatment, Assessment, and Research.* Homewood, Ill.: Dorsey Press, 1985. Presents a comprehensive overview of depression. Presents the major approaches to explaining, diagnosing, and treating depression, along with the research evidence concerning each.

Levitt, Eugene E., Bernard Lubin, and James M. Brooks. *Depression: Concepts, Controversies, and Some New Facts.* 2d ed. Hillsdale, N.J.: Lawrence Erlbaum, 1983. Reviews the symptoms, theories, and epidemiology of depression. Also describes the results of a national survey of depression.

Lewinsohn, Peter M., R. F. Munoz, M. A. Youngren, and A. M. Zeiss. *Control Your Depression.* Englewood Cliffs, N.J.: Prentice-Hall, 1978. A self-help book written for a general audience. Describes Lewinsohn's behavioral therapy, which has been found to be an effective treatment for depression.

Rehm, Lynn P., ed. *Behavior Therapy for Depression: Present Status and Future Directions.*

New York: Academic Press, 1981. An overview of behavioral and cognitive behavioral models of depression.

Reynolds, W. M., and H. F. Johnston, eds. *Handbook of Depression in Children and Adolescents*. New York: Plenum Publishing, 1994.

Rush, A. John, and Kenneth Z. Altshuler, eds. *Depression: Basic Mechanisms, Diagnosis, and Treatment*. New York: Guilford Press, 1986. Presents research concerning the biological models of the cause and treatment of depression.

Rutter, Michael, Carroll E. Izard, and Peter B. Read, eds. *Depression in Young People: Developmental and Clinical Perspectives*. New York: Guilford Press, 1986. Presents research on many aspects of the problem of depression in children, which had not received much attention from psychologists until the 1970's.

Seligman, Martin E. P. *Helplessness: On Depression, Development, and Death*. San Francisco: W. H. Freeman, 1987. Seligman explains the learned helplessness theory of depression, describing his early research and comparing the symptoms of laboratory-induced helplessness to those of clinical depression.

Michael Wierzbicki

See also:

Abnormality, 1; Anxiety Disorders, 65; Bipolar Disorder, 104; Cognitive Behavior Therapy, 128; Depression: Theoretical Explanations, 200; Learned Helplessness, 359; Obsessions and Compulsions, 427; Phobias, 459; Psychosurgery, 490; Substance Abuse, 604; Suicide, 610.

DEPRESSION
Theoretical Explanations

Type of psychology: Psychopathology
Field of study: Depression

Depression is seen in all social classes, races, and ethnic groups; it is so pervasive that it has been called the "common cold of mental illness." The study of depression has focused on biological underpinnings, cognitive concomitants, stress and coping style precursors, and interpersonal context.

Principal terms

BIPOLAR DISORDER: a disorder characterized by the occurrence of one or more manic episodes, usually interspersed with one or more major depressive episodes

MAJOR DEPRESSIVE EPISODE: a disorder of mood and functioning, meeting clearly specified criteria and present for at least two weeks, which is characterized by dysphoric mood or apathy

MANIC EPISODE: a distinct period of mood disturbance, meeting clearly specified criteria, which is characterized by abnormally and persistently elevated, expansive, or irritable mood

UNIPOLAR DEPRESSION: a disorder characterized by the occurrence of one or more major depressive episodes but no manic episodes

Overview

Almost everyone gets "down in the dumps" or has "the blues" sometimes. Feeling sad or dejected is clearly a normal part of the spectrum of human emotion. This situation is so common that a very important issue is how to separate a normal "blue" or "down" mood or emotion from an abnormal clinical state. Most clinicians use measures of intensity, severity, and duration of these emotions to separate the almost unavoidable human experience of sadness and dejection from clinical depression.

Depression is seen in all social classes, races, and ethnic groups. It is so pervasive that it has been called "the common cold of mental illness" in the popular press. It is approximately twice as common among women as it is among men. Depression is seen among all occupations, but it is most common among people in the arts and humanities. Famous individuals such as Abraham Lincoln and Winston Churchill had to cope with depression; Churchill called the affliction "the black dog." More recently, United States senator Thomas Eagleton and astronaut Edwin Aldrin were known to have bouts of serious depression.

Of all problems that are mentioned by patients at psychological and psychiatric clinics, some form of depression is most common. It is estimated that approximately 25 percent of women in the United States will experience at least one significant depression during their lives. Contrary to a popular misconception that depression is most common among the elderly, it is actually most common in twenty-five- to forty-four-year-olds. About 10 percent of the college population report moderate depression, and 5 percent report severe depression. Suicidal thoughts are common in depressive clients. In long-term follow-up, it has been found that approximately 15 percent of depressed individuals eventually kill themselves. Alternatively viewed, approximately 60 percent of suicides are believed to be caused by depression or by depression in association with alcohol abuse. As has been vividly portrayed in the media, teenage suicide in the United States has increased in recent years at an alarming rate.

The role of family or genetic factors in depression was addressed long ago by Robert Burton in *The Anatomy of Melancholy* (1621), in which he noted that the "inbred cause of melancholy is our temperature, in whole or part, which we receive from our parents" and "such as the temperature of the father is, such is the son's, and look what disease the father had when he begot him, his son will have after him." More than 350 years later, the role of family factors in depression was addressed in a major collaborative study in the United States. In what was called the National Institute of Mental Health Collaborative Study of the Psychobiology of Depression, a large number of standardized instruments were developed to assess prevalence and incidence of depression, life histories, psychosocial stressors, and outcome of depression. The family members of depressed persons were assessed along with the depressed individual. It was found that bipolar depression was largely confined to relatives of individuals with bipolar disorder. Unipolar depression, however, was common among relatives of both unipolar and bipolar-depressed individuals. The different patterns of familial transmission for bipolar and unipolar disorders strengthen the general conviction that these two disorders should be kept distinct from each other.

One explanation for increased vulnerability to depression in close relatives of depressed individuals is an inherited deficiency in two key components of brain chemistry: norepinephrine and serotonin, both of which are neurotransmitters. If depressions could be reliably subtyped according to the primary neurotransmitter deficiency, the choice of antidepressant medication would logically follow. Research is conflicting, however, on whether there is one group of depressed individuals who are low in norepinephrine and normal in serotonin, and another group of depressives who are low in serotonin and normal in norepinephrine. Future developments in the study of neurotransmitters may have practical implications for the matching of particular pharmacotherapy interventions with particular types of depression. Evidence does indicate that for many depressed patients, substantial alteration in neurotransmitter activity occurs during their depression. This altered activity may directly mediate many of the disturbing symptoms of depression.

A different approach to understanding depression has been put forward by cognitive theorists. According to Aaron Beck, in *Cognitive Therapy and the Emotional Disorders* (1976), cognitive distortions cause many if not most of a person's depressed states. Three of the most important cognitive distortions are arbitrary inference, overgeneralization, and magnification and minimization. Arbitrary inference refers to the process of drawing a conclusion from a situation, event, or experience when there is no evidence to support the conclusion or when the conclusion is contrary to the evidence. For example, an individual concludes that his boss hates him because he seldom says positive things to him. Overgeneralization refers to an individual's pattern of drawing conclusions about his or her ability, performance, or worth based on a single incident. An example of overgeneralization is an individual concluding that she is worthless because she is unable to find her way to a particular address (even though she has numerous other exemplary skills). Magnification and minimization refer to errors in evaluation that are so gross as to constitute distortions. Magnification refers to the exaggeration of negative events; minimization refers to the underemphasis of positive events.

According to Beck, there are three important aspects of these distortions or depressive cognitions. First, they are automatic—that is, they occur without reflection or forethought. Second, they appear to be involuntary. Some patients indicate that these thoughts occur even though they have resolved not to have them. Third (interestingly), the depressed person accepts these thoughts as plausible, even though others would clearly not view them in the same manner.

While there is ample empirical support for the association of depression and negative cognitive factors such as cognitive distortions, irrational beliefs, and negative statements about oneself, only now is there beginning to be research that demonstrates the ability of cognitive variables to predict subsequent depression. It appears that a cognitive vulnerability plays a role in symptom formation for at least some individuals and in the maintenance of ongoing episodes of depression for many, if not all, depressed persons.

Yet another approach to understanding depression focuses on stress and coping. James Coyne (in a 1991 article) suggests that depression may be understood as a failure to cope with ongoing life problems or stressors. It has been hypothesized that coping effectively with problems and stressors can lessen the impact of these problems and help prevent them from becoming chronic. Depressed patients show slower recovery if they display poor coping skills. Avoidance coping strategies appear to be particularly likely in depression and are one example of poor coping. Depressed persons also show elevated levels of emotion-focused coping strategies, such as wishful thinking, distancing, self-blame, and isolation. These strategies also tend to be ineffective. While most forms of coping are impaired during an episode of depression, only self-isolation, an interpersonal avoidance strategy, appears to be an enduring coping style of persons vulnerable to depression. Thus, coping processes appear to change for the worse during an episode of depression, and poor coping helps to maintain the episode. In particular, depressed persons appear likely to avoid problem situations and to engage in strategies with a low likelihood of resulting in problem resolution or an enhanced sense of personal control.

Interpersonal approaches to understanding depression are related to stress and coping models but highlight the interpersonal environment as particularly important in depression. There is considerable evidence that low levels of social support are related to depression. Perhaps the relationship between social support and depression results from the fact that depressed persons do not seek social support; however, there is also evidence that poor social support leads to or maintains depressive symptomatology. In particular, evidence links the absence of close relationships with the development of depressive symptomatology. Accordingly, the work on general social support and depression can be seen as pointing in the direction of direct consideration of intimate relationships and their role in depression. Since the strongest family ties are usually in the marital relationship, it is natural to look to the marital relationship for particularly powerful opportunities to provide social support. Indeed, there is considerable evidence of an association between marital discord and depression. It had been expected by some that the association between marital discord and depression would be greater for women than men; however, it is generally equivalent between sexes when one looks across studies. Indeed, the risk of having a major depressive episode is approximately twenty-five times higher for both males and females if they are in a discordant marital relationship than if they are in a nondiscordant marital relationship.

Applications

There are a number of ways to understand depression, and each approach appears to have something to offer. Given the distressing nature of depression, it is not surprising that these differing approaches to understanding depression have led in turn to several different effective ways of treating depression.

Pharmacological interventions for unipolar depression have sometimes been held to normalize a genetically determined biochemical defect; the evidence, however, does not support this extreme biological characterization of unipolar depression. Yet neurotransmitters may directly mediate many of the behaviors affected in depression (for example, sleep, appetite, and pleasure), and neurotransmitter level and activity are disturbed as a concomitant of many episodes of depression; hence, the use of antidepressant agents that influence neurotransmitter level or activity should be helpful in reducing or eliminating symptoms of depression even if the disturbance in neurotransmitter level or activity is itself the result of environmental or cognitive changes. In addition, there is considerable direct evidence that antidepressants can be useful in the treatment of depression in many cases. In controlled trials, both more recently developed and older forms of antidepressants provided improvement rates of 66 to 75 percent, in contrast to placebos, which showed improvement rates of 30 to 60 percent. Exactly for whom they will work, however, and exactly how or why they work are still not entirely clear.

A second effective approach to the treatment of depression can be found in cognitive therapy. It has become clear that altering cognitions and behavior in a cognitive behavioral format can work to relieve an ongoing episode of depression and may reduce the likelihood of relapse more than the use of psychopharmacology alone. Thus, cognitive processes are, at a minimum, reasonable targets of intervention in the treatment of many depressed patients. In addition, cognitive therapy appears to work well at decreasing depressive symptomatology even in the context of ongoing marital discord. Thus, for many depressed patients, interventions targeted at altering dysfunctional, negative automatic thoughts are likely to be useful.

Finally, interpersonal psychotherapy (IPT) has been developed by Gerald Klerman. This successful approach emphasizes abnormal grief, interpersonal disputes, role transitions, loss, and interpersonal deficits, as well as social and familial factors. Results of a large, multicenter collaborative study conducted by the National Institute of Mental Health indicated that IPT can work as well as antidepressant medication for many depressed patients. In addition, earlier research indicated that IPT can improve the social functioning of depressed patients in a manner not typically produced by antidepressant medications alone. Given the interpersonal problems which are often part of a depressive episode, these improvements in social functioning and interpersonal environment appear to be particularly important for depressed persons. In a related development, marital therapy has been tested as a treatment for depressed persons who are maritally discordant, and it appears to be successful.

Context

The identification of depression as a recognizable state has a very long history. Clinical depression was described as early as the eighth century B.C., in the biblical descriptions of Saul. During the fourth century B.C., Hippocrates coined the term "melancholy" to describe one of the three forms of mental illness he recognized. Later, Galen attempted to provide a biochemical explanation of melancholy based on the theory of "humors." Indeed, repeated descriptions and discussions of depression are present from classical times through the Middle Ages and into modern times.

The first comprehensive treatment of depression in English was provided by Timothy Bright's *Treatise of Melancholia* (1586). In 1624, Robert Burton provided his own major work on depression, *The Anatomy of Melancholy*. Most of the credit for developing the modern understanding of affective disorders, however, is given to Emil Kraepelin, a German psychiatrist. It was in Kraepelin's system that the term "depression" first assumed importance.

Since classical times, there have been debate and controversy over whether depression is best considered an illness or a response to an unhappy situation. Indeed, it is obvious to the most casual observer that sadness is a normal response to unhappy events. Even now, there is less than complete agreement on when fluctuations in mood should be considered pathological and when they are within normal limits. To help resolve this problem, diagnostic criteria have been developed, and structured interview procedures are often used to determine whether a particular individual should be considered depressed.

While many attempts have been made to divide the depressive disorders into subtypes, only the bipolar versus unipolar distinction has been widely accepted around the world. Unipolar depression is much more common than bipolar depression and so will continue to attract a larger share of research attention in the future. In most articles, the term "depression" refers to unipolar depression only. Models of depression have become increasingly sophisticated, progressing from Hippocrates' theory that depression was produced by an excess of black bile to modern biochemical, cognitive, coping, stress, and interpersonal models. It seems likely that even more sophisticated models of depression may provide guidance for the next great challenge facing clinical psychology: reversing the trend in Western societies toward ever-increasing rates of depression.

Bibliography

Beach, Stephen R. H., E. E. Sandeen, and K. D. O'Leary. *Depression in Marriage*. New York: Guilford Press, 1990. Summarizes the literature on basic models of depression. Provides the basis for understanding the important role of marriage in the etiology, maintenance, and treatment of depression.

Beck, Aaron T. *Cognitive Therapy and the Emotional Disorders*. New York: International Universities Press, 1976. Clearly lays out the basics of the cognitive model of depression. An important start for those who wish to understand the cognitive approach more thoroughly.

Burns, David D. *Feeling Good: The New Mood Therapy*. New York: William Morrow, 1980. Provides a very entertaining and accessible presentation of the cognitive approach to depression. Presents basic results and the basics of cognitive theory, as well as a practical set of suggestions for getting out of a depression.

Coyne, James C., ed. *Essential Papers on Depression*. New York: New York University Press, 1985. Includes representatives of every major theoretical position advanced between 1900 and 1985. Each selection is a classic presentation of an important perspective. This source will acquaint the reader with the opinions of major theorists in their own words.

Coyne, James C., and G. Downey. "Social Factors and Psychopathology: Stress, Social Support, and Coping Processes." *Annual Review of Psychology* 42 (1991): 401-426. This influential chapter ties together stress and coping with interpersonal processes to provide a deeper understanding of the nature of depression. Also provides an account of advances in the way both depression and interpersonal processes related to depression may be studied.

Kleinman, Arthur, and Byron Good. *Culture and Depression*. Berkeley: University of California Press, 1985. This exceptional volume examines the cross-cultural research on depression. Authors from anthropology, psychiatry, and psychology attempt to address the diversity that exists across cultures in the experience and expression of depression. The persevering reader will be rewarded with a journey through time and across many societies.

Paykel, Eugene S. *Handbook of Affective Disorders*. New York: Guilford Press, 1982. Provides comprehensive coverage of depression, mania, and anxiety in relation to depression. Includes detailed descriptions of symptoms, assessment procedures, epidemiology, and treatment procedures.

Reynolds, W. M., and H. F. Johnston, eds. *Handbook of Depression in Children and Adolescents*. New York: Plenum Publishing, 1994.

Stephen R. H. Beach

See also:

DREAM ANALYSIS

Type of psychology: Personality
Fields of study: Classic analytic themes and issues; personality theory; psychodynamic therapies

Dream analysis refers to efforts to understand the meaning of dreams by closely examining, or analyzing, their content. Freudian psychoanalysis and Carl Jung's analytic psychology present differing views on dream interpretation.

Principal terms

ANALYTIC PSYCHOLOGY: the depth psychology developed by Carl Jung

ARCHETYPES: as described in analytic psychology, universal themes that originate in the collective unconscious

COMPENSATION: the idea that dream events psychologically adjust (compensate) for waking imbalances

CONDENSATION: the collection in a single dream image of several different sources

DISPLACEMENT: the shifting of intense emotion away from its real source in the dream to a less important object

DREAM WORK: work with dreams in psychotherapy or for personal growth and understanding

FREE ASSOCIATION: the psychoanalytic method of talking without restriction

LATENT CONTENT: according to psychoanalytic theory, the hidden content of a dream, camouflaged by the manifest content

MANIFEST CONTENT: the content of a dream just as it is experienced

PSYCHOANALYSIS: the psychological theory and therapeutic method developed by Sigmund Freud and his followers

Overview

Today there are a variety of theories of the nature of dreams and dreaming. Sigmund Freud, however, was the first to investigate the meaning of dreams systematically and, in the broad sense, scientifically. The "analytic" approach to dreams began with Freud and was later modified, particularly by his younger colleague Carl G. Jung. Freud's early study *Die Traumdeutung* (1900; *The Interpretation of Dreams*, 1913) is considered by many to have been one of the most influential books in the history of Western thought. The importance of the book is attributable not solely to his theory of dreams and their interpretation but also to the implications his theory carried for human nature itself. It suggests that many of the most important themes in the human psyche (a term used to mean the entire psychological life of the individual) are unconsciousness and, moreover, represent desires that are unacceptable to traditional social value systems.

Freud considered the content of dreams to be symbolic. This was not a new idea in and of itself, as witnessed by Joseph's well-known biblical interpretation of the pharaoh's dreams. What was new was that the symbolic nature of the dream content concerned deep, taboo impulses within the unconscious mind. Such impulses were often of a forbidden sexual nature, dealing, for example, with incestuous impulses or homosexuality. They might also contain aggressive material unacceptable to the waking mind, such as a "death wish"—that is, a desire for the death of someone well known to the dreamer. In all events, Freud considered the dream enactment to be carried out in the service of wish fulfillment, though often such wishes were repressed and thus unconscious.

According to Freud, each dream must be understood on two distinct levels. First is the manifest content of the dream. This is the dream simply as it appears, and as it might be related to another person or written down. The manifest content, however, is not the true subject of the dream; it serves to camouflage a deeper meaning, while at the same time presenting it in a morally acceptable way. The true meaning of the dream is to be found only in its hidden, or latent content—for example, in the sexual or aggressive material that the manifest content symbolically hides.

In terms of Freud's theory of personality, the dream is a creation of the infantile unconscious, seeking fulfillment for desires or impulses too morally painful to be entertained consciously by the ego. The moral aspect of the personality censors the dream content, allowing it expression only in the symbolic or manifest form experienced by the dreamer. Rather than dreaming directly about sexual intercourse, for example, a woman might dream that she is riding bareback on a horse, because the rhythmic motion of the horse resembles that of intercourse. She might awaken surprised to find herself sexually aroused. Many such dreams were recorded by Freud and his followers.

Freud was a shrewd observer of dreams, and he noticed that the vast majority of objects seen in them represent things seen in waking life during the day or two immediately preceding the dream. For example, after dreaming of a train with a steam engine, one might recall that on the previous day he or she had parked near a toy store that displayed an electric train in the window—one that resembled in general form the train later seen in the dream. Subsequent investigations of this idea have confirmed that this is indeed true. Freud also noted that a single object in a dream—a person, for example—could represent several objects, a process that he called condensation. A man might see an attractive woman in a dream and on later reflection realize that she had the hair of one woman he had known in the past, the eyes of another, and so on, all in a perfectly natural alliance.

Other important dream processes include dramatization, by which dream content represents its basic themes involving wish fulfillment, in imagistic form, usually in concrete pictorial representations. In other words, dreams present their stories largely in picture form. Another important process in Freudian dream theory is displacement, the idea that some object or event of relatively little importance in terms of the actual latent meaning of the dream takes on intense emotional meaning, acting as a decoy, as it were, for the emotion connected with a far more sinister theme.

Carl G. Jung, Freud's younger contemporary, at first supported Freud's ideas with great enthusiasm but later developed a psychology of his own quite independent of Freud. This came to be termed analytic psychology, in contrast to Freudian psychoanalysis. Freud had stressed the importance of individual biographical material in the dreams of his patients, whereas Jung tended to stress the importance of universal themes. He believed that such themes, or archetypes, appear not only in dreams but also in mythic stories from all over the world, as well as in art and literature—and in the delusional symptoms of psychotic patients. Such themes include water (as symbolic of the spirit or the collective unconscious), the great mother, the hero, the king, and so on. Many are seen among the pantheon of ancient Greek gods. The most important archetype is the self, which represents the integration or unity of the psyche. It is symbolized by many round or symmetrical images, termed mandalas. Examples include the rose, the lotus flower, starbursts such as those seen in the stained glass windows of Gothic cathedrals, the solar disk, and so on.

While such images are taken in analytic psychology to be symbolic in the sense that they represent truths greater than themselves, they in no sense are thought to camouflage any kind of latent content in the dream. In other words, Jungians believe in the transparency of dreams, in the sense that they hide nothing but make the most direct symbolic expression of the disposition of the unconscious. They function both as a communication from the deep collective unconscious and as compensation for events and dispositions of waking life. A lonely man may dream of women, for example, not simply as a sexual fulfillment, but as a compensation for the absence of the feminine in his waking life. Thus, from the Jungian perspective, dreams represent to the dreamer a side of life often overlooked during waking existence.

Applications

The term "dream work" refers to the use of dreams as an adjunct to psychotherapy; more recently, it has come into common use as any systematic effort to work with dreams as part of personal exploration or growth. Both Freud and Jung utilized dream interpretation in psychotherapy. Even today, psychoanalysis (Freudian therapy) as well as Jungian analysis rely heavily on it for providing insights into unconscious processes.

To begin with a simple example of a dream understood from a Freudian perspective, suppose that a man argues with his mother in the afternoon and that night dreams he is at a funeral. The atmosphere is unusual for a funeral, however, as no one seems unhappy. Indeed, the ambience is like that of a cocktail party. He does not know whom the funeral is for, so he asks one of the guests. The answer is, "your mother." He wakes up.

This dream thinly disguises a death wish toward the mother. This is not necessarily as bad as it may seem. It simply means that on some irrational level he "wishes she were dead." Notice, however, that the man himself appears in the dream only in the third person—that is, he does not actually attack and kill his mother. The superego, or moral aspect of the personality, would not allow such an act even in the dream. Rather, this individual simply arrives somehow at a funeral and discovers that it is his mother who has died. Thus, he has no sense of guilt to connect with the event, yet the death wish is satisfied.

To take a more complex example, suppose that a young woman preparing to enter college dreams that she is presented with a nurse's cap and a piece of chalk of the type used for writing on blackboards. After some consideration, she picks up the piece of chalk and holds it above her head. A crowd of students sitting in the background gives her a rousing cheer, and the chalk turns to gold in her hands.

From a Freudian point of view, the nurse's cap and the piece of chalk are both sexual symbols. The cap represents female genitalia (as do jewelry boxes, orchids, and many other symbols), while the stick of chalk is a standard phallic symbol, representing the penis. What one would seem to have, from this perspective, is a sexual struggle in which heterosexuality wins out over homosexuality. The analyst would not, however, proceed by simply interpreting the dream to the patient. Rather, he or she would encourage the patient to free associate on the events and objects of the dream. In free association, one is asked to let one's mind move freely and without inhibition or intentional direction across the material of the dream, voicing all thoughts that come to mind. If this process is continued for long enough, and over sufficient therapeutic sessions, the patient may come to the real meaning of the dream, bringing the latent content into consciousness. In the process of free associating, the analyst may make occasional interpretations to the patient, but only after sensing that the patient is prepared to accept and understand the nature of the threatening material at hand.

In thinking about and discussing a dream, certain aspects of the dream may become more important, while other parts may recede into the background of memory. These transformations are termed secondary revision or elaboration, and may themselves become the object of examination in the therapeutic session.

For an example of a Jungian approach to dream interpretation, one could return to the above dream of the nurse's cap and the chalk. To begin with, the Jungian analyst would not use free association, but would engage the patient in an active dialogue about the dream. Of particular importance, he or she would be less likely to stress sexual issues and more likely to look at the apparent career choice poised by the dream. Indeed, Jungian psychology views the psyche as drawn toward a purposeful future rather than being, as in the case of Freudian theory, driven inexorably from the past. The selection of the chalk, and particularly the fact that the chalk is transformed in the end to gold, a universal symbol for that which is of ultimate value, are key considerations. Notice that an interpretation of this type implies no hidden agenda for the dream beyond the full connotations of the content itself. In this sense, the Jungian interpretation views the meaning of the dream as transparent, though not necessarily obvious.

An example typical of the Jungian approach is a dream that was experienced by a middle-aged man shortly after entering analysis. It was a simple dream in which he found himself traveling to the ocean and preparing to go scuba diving, something he had never done in waking life. In this dream the ocean represents the spirit, or the collective unconscious, in which the rich variety of deep-sea life exemplifies the archetypal life of the unconscious. This is what the man hopes to be able to experience in his analysis. In the Jungian perspective, consciousness ultimately derives its life-giving energy from the collective unconsciousness. For this reason, dreams of such things as water and fish are often considered good, since they depict the active life of the unconscious. In the early years of Christianity, for example, Christ was frequently symbolized by a fish, the creature of the spirit, or water.

Context

Freud's approach to dreams was the first to place dream activity squarely in the context of a unified theory of the mind. Earlier efforts at understanding the meaning of dreams had derived from religious or mythological contexts, as was the case in much of the ancient world and in Europe during the Middle Ages. The ancient Greeks wrote at some length about dreams, usually insisting that they had some literal meaning. In the "dream incubation," conducted at special temples dedicated to that purpose, dreams were associated with healing.

Freud's early writing was unique in that it emphasized the biological roots of the mind, and thus of dreams, in concepts such as instincts, drives, and psychic energy (libido). He believed that the entire structure of dreams, with their manifest content produced by censorship of their latent content by the moral agency of the personality, was fundamentally biological. This stress on biological foundations eventually decreased in importance as psychoanalytic thinkers, including Freud, began to recognize the importance of social influences on the personality, especially during infancy. Freud, for example, came to recognize a class of dreams that did not seem to operate in the service of wish fulfillment at all, but seemed to be an attempt of the mind in fantasy to resolve pressing emotional issues. An example that was discussed in the 1920's dealt with "war neurosis," an emotionally distraught state brought about by traumatic events experienced on the battlefield or elsewhere during war. Victims are later prone to repetitious dreams that seem again and again to enact the terror of these traumatic events.

Ego psychology, a more recent school of psychoanalytic thought, especially practiced in the United States, tends to stress the autonomy of the ego rather than the instinctual unconscious. It emphasizes the importance of early childhood experiences. Object relations theory, on the other hand, stresses the importance of "objects" of attachment, especially the mother, during the first ten years of life. The basic agenda of dream analysis, however, remains central to psychoanalytic dream work in virtually all of its forms, namely the notion that latent dream content must be made manifest.

The basic notion of a division of dream content into latent and manifest meaning has come increasingly under attack by dream theorists and researchers of a variety of persuasions, including a number of neuroscientists working on the nature of dreaming as a natural activity of the brain. The latter tend to view dreaming as a fundamentally biological event that incidentally reflects the concerns of waking life. Such reflections represent a more or less straightforward chewing over of the individual's daily concerns. Thus, while not subscribing to Jung's ideas concerning archetypes and the collective unconscious, such an approach agrees that the real meaning of the dream is not actively hidden from view.

Bibliography

Alvarez, Alfred. *Night: Night Life, Night Language, Sleep, and Dreams*. New York: W. W. Norton, 1995.

Foulkes, William David. *A Grammar of Dreams*. New York: Basic Books, 1978. While not a general introduction to dream analysis, this formally written book is a landmark study which argues that dream events are essentially grammatical in form.

Freud, Sigmund. *The Interpretation of Dreams*. Translated by James Strachey. New York: Avon Books, 1965. One of the most influential books in Western history, this book describes in detail Freud's original theory of dreams. Those who have not previously read Freud in the original will be delighted to discover that he was a superb writer. This book was first published in German in 1900.

Gardner, Richard A. *Dream Analysis in Psychotherapy*. Cresskill, N.J.: Creative Therapeutics, 1996.

Hillman, James. *The Dream and the Underworld*. New York: Harper & Row, 1979. The most prominent of the neo-Jungians, Hillman views the dream as an experience of the underworld of traditional mythology.

Hobson, J. Allan. *The Dreaming Brain*. New York: Basic Books, 1988. This highly readable book is an excellent general introduction to the study of dreams from a historical and scientific point of view, with special emphasis on Hobson's own area of study, the biological understanding of the dreaming brain.

Jung, Carl Gustav. *Dreams.* Translated by R. F. C. Hull. Princeton, N.J.: Princeton University Press, 1974. This is number 20 in the Bollingen Series; the volume contains papers taken from vols. 4, 8, 12, and 16 of *The Collected Works of C. G. Jung.* Jung discusses his views of dreams as communications of the unconsciousness, as well as the role of archetypes in dreams and dreams as compensation.

Van de Castle, Robert L. *Our Dreaming Mind.* New York: Ballantine Books, 1994.

Allen L. Combs

See also:

Analytical Psychology: Carl G. Jung, 49; Consciousness, Levels of, 165; Dreams, 212;Psychoanalytic Psychology and Personality: Sigmund Freud, 478.

DREAMS

Type of psychology: Consciousness
Fields of study: Classic analytic themes and issues; sleep

Dreams provide a unique window into psychological life. The dream's presentation of a story, experienced as meaningful in its own right, is a real and original form of human existence; it also discloses unrealized possibilities in the dreamer's waking life.

Principal terms

ACTIVATION-SYNTHESIS HYPOTHESIS: a theory that dreams are the brain's attempt to make sense of random and meaningless nervous system activity

EXISTENCE: as a psychological term, refers to the uniquely human existence of a person; a person's own standing forth or involvement in a personal history

LATENT CONTENT: in Freudian theory, the unconscious meaning of the dream, which has been disguised

MANIFEST CONTENT: in Freudian theory, the actual events of the dream, which are taken as symbolic of other, unconscious meanings

PHENOMENOLOGY: a philosophical approach used by some psychologists to understand meanings as they appear in actual experience

PSYCHOANALYSIS: Freud's label for his psychology in general as well as its distinctive type of psychotherapy; psychoanalysis emphasizes the determining role of unconscious desires

RAPID EYE MOVEMENT (REM) SLEEP: a distinct phase of sleep characterized by rapid eye movements of the sleeper; it has been reliably correlated with occasions when dreaming is occurring

UNCONSCIOUS: in Freudian psychology, that part of psychological life unavailable to awareness, repressed because of the anxiety that the unconscious desires would arouse if known

Overview

Dreaming is a state of consciousness wherein a sleeping person experiences a real involvement with objects, events, or other people that are not objectively present in that location at that time. Dreams may also incorporate an item that is actually present, such as a ringing alarm clock, but it will not be the objective clock in the bedroom with which the dreaming person is involved. In the dream, for example, it might be experienced as a telephone. The allure of dreams is precisely their providing an experience of something beyond objective presences. Furthermore, this "beyond" is not usually something the dreamer can choose in advance. Even a person who goes to sleep seeking to have a specific question answered in a dream experiences it as arising from an unforeseen depth. Because dreams "take" the person, it is more accurate to describe the experience of dreaming, as Medard Boss does, in terms of "it dreamt me." The only exception is the rare experience in a lucid dream (that is, one in which the dreamer is aware that it is a dream) of deliberately choosing how to interact with events in the dream.

Two different approaches have dominated twentieth century psychology's understanding of dreams, both of which are rooted in much older assumptions about dreaming. One explains dreaming as a neurophysiological event, while the other understands dreaming as a meaningful expression of the dreamer's waking life. Neurophysiological psychology takes the position that the dream is not a reflection of waking life, but of nervous system activity within the brain: nonsensical "noise" unrelated to any personally lived meaning. In the 1970's, J. Alan Hobson and Robert W. McCarley proposed the activation-synthesis hypothesis, which theorized that dreams are merely the brain's attempt to make sense of random activity by neurons (nerve cells) in the brain stem (the most phylogenetically primitive brain structure). According to their view, this random neuronal discharge stimulated or "activated" the cortex part of the brain, which then formed a dream in order to synthesize, or make sense of, that stimulation. In 1991, their theory was updated with the more recently developed "connectionist" view of the brain's neuronal activity.

Such theories may provide an explanation of the brain structure and activity necessary for dreaming to occur; however, they do not offer a basis for comprehending the experienced meaning of dreams. Specifying what happens physiologically during dreaming is not the same as understanding the dream itself, any more than an analysis of ink, paper, and the printing process could account for the plot of a book. By dismissing in advance the meaningfulness of dreams, neurophysiological psychology cannot address the question of why a dream should form precisely the particular synthesis it does, rather than some other. The understanding of the dream itself requires a different level of psychological investigation.

It was this sort of study that Sigmund Freud pioneered with his psychoanalytic theory of dreams. In his key book *Die Traumdeutung* (1900; *The Interpretation of Dreams*, 1913), Freud interpreted the meaningfulness of dreams as fulfillments of repressed, unconscious wishes, usually originating in childhood and mostly of a sexual nature. His claim that the apparently unreal consciousness of dreams masked a real unconsciousness effected a major breakthrough. This theory required a split in the reality status of the dream, however, since what it interpreted as real (the dream's disclosure of an unconscious desire) was not part of the actually dreamed story. Because of this discrepancy, Freud viewed the plot of the dream, its "manifest content," as a disguise, as a merely symbolic substitution of something else that remained concealed (the "latent content" of the dream). He saw the dream as a compromise solution by which an unconscious desire could be expressed while still remaining protected from full disclosure. Similarly, the disguised dream also guards the dreamer's sleep from being disrupted by the anxiety of fully facing repressed desires.

A variety of subsequent psychoanalytic theorists modified Freud's original insight. Carl Jung developed the most richly elaborated view of dream symbolization. He considered dreams as originating not in one's individual unconscious but from a "collective unconscious," and understood them as compensations for imbalances within one's waking life. Other psychoanalysts departed from Freud on more basic grounds, influenced by the existential phenomenological philosophy of Martin Heidegger.

Ludwig Binswanger and Medard Boss, independently, were the first psychoanalysts to explore dreaming phenomenologically. In doing so, they established a decisive advance beyond the Freudian interpretation of dreams. Rather than searching behind or beneath the dream for a symbolized reality cut off from the dreamer's experience, Binswanger and Boss recognized the imaginative power of dreams as the dreamer's movement into the real. They understood how the dream itself is meaningful to the dreamer—not as a symbol for something else, but as an original mode of existing on its own terms. They saw dreams as a movement by which dreamers imaginatively project themselves toward the truth of their personal histories. In other words, a phenomenology of dreaming takes dreams as "allusions" pointing to reality, rather than as "illusions" pointing away from it. Any discussion of a latent content is seen as a shift away from the dream itself, to waking associations about it. Thus, no approach based on latent contents could ever more than hypothetically disclose the meaningfulness of a dream. Instead of interpreting dream phenomena as symbols, Boss recommended "explicating" them within their array of spontaneous references and relationships in the dream itself.

Applications

The possibility that dreams may provide knowledge of the dreamer's own existence makes them useful for psychotherapy and personal growth. This application has been especially characteristic of Freudian psychoanalysis, a form of therapy devoted to helping patients become conscious of previously unconscious material. Because Freud regarded dreams as the "royal road" to the unconscious, dream interpretation became a principal technique in psychoanalysis. The psychoanalyst strives, like a detective, to decode the dream's disguised symbols and bring to light the patient's unconscious desires.

Other types of therapy use dream interpretation differently, depending on their view of the role of the unconscious in the patient's illness. For example, in Gestalt therapy, developed by Fritz Perls, the patient might "act out" the role of a person (or even object) in the dream, based on the theory that each character in the dream represents some aspect of the dreamer's own self. If, for example, a man dreamed of being frightened by a viciously snarling dog, he may be asked to assume the position of the dog and to describe that perspective.

It is not only in psychotherapy that dream work can be valuably applied. A growing movement emphasizes how individuals, alone or in dream groups, can benefit from attending to their dreams. Psychologists such as Stanley Krippner, Henry Reed, Gayle Delaney, Montague Ullman, and Alvin Mahrer have devised methods of working with one's own dreams to achieve personal growth.

Phenomenological psychology's understanding of dreams as imaginative enactments of the real provides support for both therapeutic and personal applications. As Boss has noted, certain "possibilities to be" may address themselves to people for the first time in their lives through dreams. Erik Craig calls these "larval" possibilities, for they become realized first in dreaming. Craig points out that within the sanctuary of their dreaming mode of existence, people are often open to possibilities that are ignored while awake. In dreaming, these "disenfranchised possibilities" appear with striking clarity as the real and meaningful features of one's existence that they are. Dreaming anticipates the realization of one's possibilities by allowing them to emerge within the dream state. In working phenomenologically with a dream, one aims to clarify the imaginative, allusive power of the dream by making these emerging possibilities explicit.

As an imaginative arc toward the actual achievement or realization of one's possibilities, a dream can be a decisive point in the life of the dreamer. It may be the very point at which one can either embrace the authentic existence to which the dream alludes or shrink from it, psychopathologically alienating oneself from one's own possibilities. The dream faces the dreamer with the choice between freedom and inauthenticity. The following two illustrations (taken from research on transformative dream experiences) show this liberating value of the dream's imaginative capacity.

Ellen, a sixty-three-year-old woman, dreams of walking sturdily up a mountain, following a much younger man. She finds that she simply cannot keep up with his pace; she begins to walk slower, then stops and sits upon a rock outcropping. She looks up for the first time and is struck by the beauty of the view. She sees an eagle fly and observes the younger man reassuringly continuing his walk over the next mountain. At that time in her waking life, Ellen was struggling to realize that it was time to slow down the very busy pace of her professional work. She had been unable, however, to resist the temptations of taking on additional commitments, until the dream presented her with another possibility. Afterward, she realized that sitting, reflecting, and observing was the new way for her to be. She saw that the work would get done: The journey would be continued by other, younger people. Through her dream, Ellen was able to make the difficult passage from the productive, generative stage of middle age to the reflective, integrative stage of old age.

At other times, a dream may finally resolve a long-standing constriction from an earlier stage of life. For example, in her early forties, Betty dreamed of being confronted in a tunnel by hideous monsters, the most terrifying of which appeared as "the evil one." He came right up to her, threatening to contaminate her with his evil, yet she could not face him. Finally, sensing a fate worse than death if she continued to avoid this monstrous other, she looked him in the eye and told him he was evil. She demanded that he respect her, and he did, backing off and letting her pass. In waking life, Betty had been living with the conviction of her own evilness ever since she had been told she was a devil by a relative who had repeatedly sexually abused her as a child. She was afraid of virtually everything. After the dream, she felt released from this fear and no longer believed that her own powers were evil. She began doing things, such as walking alone at night, that would have been impossible before. Taking hold of her new possibilities, Betty could live an expanded existence, made real for her for the first time in her dream.

Context
Ancient peoples understood their dreams as portraits of a meaningful reality—not as something made up by their minds, but as actual experiences of their souls' communication with the divine. Already in A.D. 140, however, the Greek philosopher Artemidorus of Daldi had proposed that dreams revealed not divine nature but the human nature of the dreamer.

Scientific psychology, limited by its model of the experiment as its research methodology, was slow to study dreaming. Indeed, Edwin Boring's highly regarded *A History of Experimental Psychology* (1929, rev. 1950) did not even mention dreaming in its expansive review of psychology. This began to change in the 1950's, with studies at the University of Chicago by Nathaniel Kleitman and Eugene Aserinsky, who discovered a phase of sleep characterized by rapid eye movement (REM). Using recording equipment to detect the onset of this phase of sleep, they were able to discover its correlation to dreaming. By waking subjects in REM sleep, they found that the vast majority could remember a dream, even those who had been unable previously to recall dreams. Since normal sleep patterns involve

REM phases every ninety minutes or so, it was concluded that people dream several times each night, despite their wide variations in ability to remember dreams.

This ability to scientifically detect the apparent occurrence of dreaming has inspired, in the decades since then, many laboratory studies of sleep and dreaming. Two unsettled issues cloud much of this research. One is the unknown representativeness of dreams in laboratory conditions as compared with those dreamed in one's own home. Calvin Hall, who has collected thousands of dreams from ordinary life, notes that laboratory dreams tend to be more mundane, home dreams more dramatic. A second problem is that the precise relation of REM sleep to dreams remains unsettled. Unable to specify whether REM sleep caused dreaming or dreaming caused REM sleep, early researchers had simply stated that REM signaled the occurrence of dreaming. Recent research shows, however, that dreaming can also occur apart from REM sleep. Other research shows that REM sleep is present even in those considered unable to dream. These include anencephalic infants (who lack most of their brain, except for the brain stem) and cats that have had the brain structures deemed essential for dreaming surgically disconnected.

Despite these theoretical problems, the scientific study of dreaming is now a flourishing subdiscipline in theoretical and research psychology. The trend to approach dreams as meaningful is also thriving, not only within theoretical and research psychology, but also in psychotherapeutic applications. The many books, journals, and conferences devoted to dreaming indicate it will continue to be one of psychology's growing edges in the near future. Additionally, dream work has overflowed the discipline of psychology altogether and is gathering momentum among the general public. This movement is supported by a number of thoughtful how-to books and by an enduring interest in the personal transformation afforded by plumbing the depths of one's psychological life.

Bibliography

Alvarez, Alfred. *Night: Night Life, Night Language, Sleep, and Dreams*. New York: W. W. Norton, 1995.

Boss, Medard. *I Dreamt Last Night. . . .* New York: Gardner Press, 1977. Boss forcefully argues for his phenomenological approach to understanding dreams. He describes dreaming as a mode of existing that can be understood as such directly on its own terms, without the need to interpret it symbolically. He clearly demonstrates that position by his analysis of many dreams.

Craig, P. Erik. "Dreaming, Reality, and Allusion: An Existential-Phenomenological Inquiry." In *Advances in Qualitative Psychology*, edited by Florence Van Zuuren, Frederick J. Wertz, and Bep Mook. Berwyn, Pa.: Swets North America, 1987. Craig provides a masterfully stated argument for the appreciation of the real experience of the dreamer. His careful example also shows the relevance of dreaming to waking life.

Delaney, Gayle. *Living Your Dreams*. New York: Harper & Row, 1979. Delaney has developed and popularized a means of dream interpretation for personal growth, in which dreams are used as sources of insight for solving personal life problems. This book offers an easily accessible manual for applying her approach.

Freud, Sigmund. *The Interpretation of Dreams*. Translated by James Strachey. New York: Avon Books, 1965. This challenging book is an English translation of Freud's pioneering study of dreams, which was first published in German in 1900. It revolutionized psychological thought and contains, by Freud's own acknowledgment, his most valuable discoveries.

Hall, Calvin Springer, and Robert L. Van de Castle. *The Content Analysis of Dreams*. New York: Appleton-Century-Crofts, 1966. An extremely comprehensive collection of dreams. It features more than a thousand, collected from college students and sorted for the statistical frequency of contents such as setting, character traits, mood, and relationships.

Jung, Carl. *Dreams*. Translated by R. F. C. Hull. Princeton, N.J.: Princeton University Press, 1974. This book assembles some of Jung's basic writings on dreams published earlier (from volumes 4, 8, 12, and 16 in his collected works). It offers a sampling of his views on the relation of dreams and psychoanalysis, psychic energy, alchemy, and the practical use of dream symbols.

LaBerge, Stephen. *Lucid Dreaming*. Los Angeles: J. P. Tarcher, 1985. By experimentally demonstrating lucid dreaming (the awareness, while dreaming, that one is dreaming), LaBerge's research has opened a new wave of theory, research, and applications.

Mahrer, Alvin. *Dream Work in Psychotherapy and Self-Change*. New York: W. W. Norton, 1989. This book is directed both to psychotherapists and laypersons. To the first group, it offers a new experiential approach to dream work. To the second, it offers a complete instructional guide to using dreams to promote self-change.

Van de Castle, Robert L. *Our Dreaming Mind*. New York: Ballantine Books, 1994.

Christopher M. Aanstoos

See also:

DRIVE THEORY

Type of psychology: Motivation
Field of study: Motivation theory

A drive is a state influenced by an animal's need; the animal is motivated to reduce tension or to seek a goal. Drive theory is concerned with the nature of the internal forces that compel an animal to behave.

Principal terms

BEHAVIOR: responses and activities of an animal that usually lead to a changed relationship between it and its environment

DRIVE: an intervening process referring to the behavioral energy originating from a need; a drive is directly related to behavior

DRIVE REDUCTION: behaviors that result in the animal encountering certain environmental resources; such behaviors will be repeated when the drive state recurs

LAW OF EFFECT: a term describing the concept that responses which are followed by a reward will tend to be repeated

NEED: a state of an organism attributable to deprivation of a biological or psychological requirement; it is related to a disturbance in the homeostatic state

REINFORCEMENT: a situation that occurs when a stimulus closely following a behavior makes the behavior likely to recur

Overview

One goal of science is to understand, predict, or manipulate natural events. A scientist may start by observing an event of interest and measuring it as precisely as possible to detect any changes. In experimental research, scientists systematically manipulate various other events to see whether the event of interest also varies. In survey research, various events are measured to see whether they vary with the event of interest. Understanding is achieved when the relationship between the event of interest (the dependent variable) and other events (independent variables) is established. One can then predict and/or manipulate the event of interest. A theory provides a guideline to organize the variables into a system based upon some common properties that they share. To a psychologist, the dependent variable is the behavior of all animals and humans. The independent variable (also called a determinant) may be any other variable related to behaviors. Psychological research aims to discover the determinants of certain behavior; some of them are motivational variables. The field of motivation examines why particular behavior occurs, why it is so strong, and why it is so persistent.

A drive is a process related to the source of behavioral energy originating from within the body that is created by disturbances in homeostasis. A homeostatic imbalance creates a state of need for certain stimuli from the environment which can restore the balance. For example, abnormal body temperature and hyperosmolality of the body fluid (electrolyte concentration outside cells that is higher than that of the intracellular fluid, resulting in cell dehydration) are disturbances in homeostasis. The homeostatic balance can be restored through two means. Physiological means such as vasodilation, sweating, and panting serve to reduce body temperature; concentration of electrolytes in the urine by the kidneys reduces hyperosmolality. Second, behavioral means such as taking off clothes, turning on an air conditioner, and drinking cold liquid lower body temperature; drinking water would also result in reducing the hyperosmolality. One may examine a case of homeostatic imbalance in detail to illustrate how the two means function to restore the balance.

When the body fluid volume is reduced (hypovolemia) because of loss of blood or body fluid from intense sweating, the body responds immediately by vasoconstriction, reducing urine volume (through vasopressin release), and conserving sodium (through aldosterone release). Those are physiological means that will restore the blood pressure and prevent circulatory failure. Eventually, however, the body must get back the lost fluid from the environment via behavior (water seeking and drinking) to achieve long-lasting homeostasis. The physiological means are immediate and effective, but they are only stopgap measures. Behavior is the means with which the animal interacts with its environment to get back the lost resource.

The concept of drives is very important to the theories of Clark L. Hull, a neo-behaviorist. According to Hull, a drive has at least two distinct functions as far as behavioral activation is concerned. Without drives there could be no reinforcement and thus no learning, because drive reduction is the reinforcement. Without drives there could be no response, for a drive activates behavioral potentials into performance. Drive theory maintains that a state named "drive" (or D) is a necessary condition for behavior to occur; however, D is not the same as the bodily need. D determines how strongly and persistently a behavior is to occur; it connects the need and behavior. This distinction between need and drive is necessary, because while the state of need serves as the source of behavior, the intensity of behavior is not always related to the intensity of need. There are cases in which the need increases but behavior does not, or in which the need is still there but behavior is no longer manifested. Prolonged deprivation, for example, may not result in a linear or proportional increase in behavior. A water-deprived animal may stop drinking even before cellular dehydration is restored to the normal state; the behavior is changing independent of homeostatic imbalance. Cessation of behavior is seen as being attributable to drive reduction.

Hull uses D to symbolize drive and sHr (H is commonly used to denote this, for convenience) to symbolize a habit which consists of an acquired relationship between stimulus (S) and response (R). It represents a memory of experience in which certain environmental stimuli and responses were followed by a reward. An effective reward establishes an S-R relationship; the effect is termed reinforcement. One example of an H would be an experience of maze stimuli and running that led to food. H is a behavioral potential, not a behavior. Food deprivation induces a need state that can be physiologically defined; then D will energize H into behavior. The need increases monotonically with hours of deprivation, but D increases only up to three days without food. A simplified version of the Hullian formula for a behavior would be "behavior = H × D," or "performance = behavioral potential × energizer." The formula indicates that learning, via establishing behavioral potential, and D, via energizing the potential, are both necessary for performance to occur. This is a multiplicative relationship; that is, when either H or D is zero, a specific performance cannot occur.

Sigmund Freud proposed, in his psychoanalytical approach to behavioral energy, that psychic energy is the source of human behaviors. The id is the reservoir of instinctual energy presumed to be directly from the somatic processes. This energy is unorganized, illogical, timeless, knowing "no values, no good or evil, no morality" (according to Freud in 1933). The id operates according to the pleasure principle, using the primary process to discharge its energy as soon as possible, with no regard for reality. When the discharge is hindered by reality, however, the ego handles the situation according to the reality principle, using a secondary process to pursue realistic gratification. The ego mediates between the id on one hand and reality on the other.

Freud thus conceptualized the id to be the energy source, and the ego to manage behavior in terms of reality. Learning is manifested in the way the ego manages behavior for gratification under restriction of the environment and the superego. In this model, the drive is seen as the energizer of behavior. The similarity between the Freudian and Hullian concepts of drive is obvious. Food deprivation would generate homeostatic imbalance, which is the somatic process, and the need, which is similar to the energy of the id. The organism cannot obtain immediate gratification because of the environmental constraints to obtain food, so behavior is generated to negotiate with the environment. Drive is much like the ego, since it energizes the behavioral potentials into behaviors to seek reality gratification, which is equivalent to drive reduction. The concept of pleasure and behavioral changes commonly appears in various theories that incorporate a subtle influence of Freudian thought.

Applications

In one classic experiment, Carl J. Warden studied the persistence of behavior as a function of various sources, including the strength of a drive, using an apparatus called a Columbia obstruction box. He demonstrated that a rat without food would cross an electrified grid to reach a goal box that held food. When the rat was immediately brought back from the goal box to the start box, it would cross the grid again and again. The number of grid crossings was positively related to the number of days without food for up to three days. From the fourth day without food, however, the number of crossings slowly decreased. When baby rats were placed in the goal box, a mother rat would cross the grid repeatedly. When a male or female rat was placed in the goal box, a rat of the opposite sex would cross repeatedly. The number of crossings by the male rat was positively related to the duration it spent without a female companion.

These animals were all manifesting the effect of different drives: hunger, maternal instinct, or sex. It was shown that the maternal drive was associated with the greatest number of crossings (twenty-two times in twenty minutes), followed by thirst (twenty times), hunger (seventeen), female sex drive (fourteen), male sex drive (thirteen), and exploration (six). Warden demonstrated that various internal forces, created by deprivation and hormonal state, and external forces, created by different goal objects, together determine the grid-crossing behavior. The level of deprivation induces drive motivation; the reward in the goal box induces incentive motivation. In this example, the focus is on drive motivation.

If one were to place a well-trained rat into a maze, it might or might not run to the goal box. Whether it would run, how fast it would run, and how well (in terms of errors) it would run would depend upon whether the subject were food-deprived. With food deprivation, the well-trained rat would run to the goal box with few errors. If it had just been fed, it would not run; it would simply wander, sniff at the corner, and go to sleep. The environmental stimuli (the maze) are the same; the rat's behavior is different because the internal force—the drive created by food deprivation—is different. A need state produces D, and D then triggers behavior. The behavior that will occur is determined jointly by the past experience of learning, which is termed H, as well as stimuli, S, from the environment. An inexperienced rat, without the H of maze running, will behave differently from a well-trained rat in a maze. D is an intervening variable: It connects need and behavior, so one must consider both the source (need) and the consequence (behavior) to define D. When D is zero, there will be no maze running, no matter how well-trained the rat is. On the other hand, if there is no H (training), the proper maze-running behavior will not occur, no matter how hungry the rat is. An animal must be exposed to a maze when hungry to learn to negotiate the various turns on the way to the goal box containing food. Without food deprivation (and the resultant D), the animal would not perform even if it could; one cannot tell whether an animal has the knowledge to run the maze until one introduces a D variable. H is a potential of behavior, and D makes the potential into the observable reality of performance. Motivation turns a behavior on.

These ideas can be applied to countless real-life examples. If a person is not very good at playing tennis (has a low H), for example, no matter how motivated (high D) he is, he will not be able to beat a friend who is an expert at the game. If a person is very good at tennis (high H) but does not feel like playing (low D), perhaps because of a lack of sleep, she will not perform well. The same situation would apply for taking a test, delivering a speech, or running a marathon.

In another experiment involving drive, Edward L. Thorndike put a cat into a puzzle box. The cat attempted to get out via various behaviors (mewing, scratching, and so on). By chance, it stepped on a plate that resulted in the door opening, allowing the cat to escape. The cat was repeatedly returned to the box, and soon it would escape right away by stepping on the plate; other, useless behaviors were no longer manifested. The source of D in this case was the anxiety induced by confinement in the box, which could be measured by various physiological changes, such as heart rate and hormonal levels. Escaping would make the anxiety disappear; D is reduced. D reduction results in an increase in the probability that the behavior immediately preceding it (stepping on the plate) will recur. Thorndike describes this puzzle-box learning as trial and error, implying a blind attempt at various means of escape until one happens to work. He states that a "satisfying effect" will create repetition, calling this the law of effect; the essence of the satisfying effect appears to be drive reduction. A five-stage learning cycle is then complete: It consists of need, drive, behavior, drive reduction, and behavior repetition.

Context

Research on how a habit (H) is formed and how it is stored in the brain is a lively research topic in the field of psychobiology of learning, memory, and cognition, as well as in neuropsychology, which deals with learning deficit and loss of memory. Drive and reinforcement are important variables that determine whether learning will succeed and whether past learning will be manifested as behaviors. Research on hunger and thirst forms one subfield of psychobiology.

If D is the common energizer of various behaviors, then all sources of D—hunger, thirst, sex, mothering, exploration—should have something in common physiologically. The so-called central motive state is hypothesized to be such a state. It is known that arousal is common to the sources of D. Research involves biological delineation of the sources of D; researchers are studying the mechanisms of hunger, for example. There has been insufficient attention paid to the physiological processes by which hunger may motivate various behaviors and by which drive reduction would serve as a reinforcement in learning. Extreme lack of motivation can be seen in some depressed and psychotic patients, which results both in a lack of new learning and in a lack of manifesting what is already known. The neuronal substrates of this "lack of energy" represent one problem under investigation in the area of drive and motivation.

Bibliography

Bolles, Robert C. *Theory of Motivation*. 2d ed. New York: Harper & Row, 1975. This standard text in motivation reviews the concepts of motivation and drive and present pros and cons of the drive concept. The author is a contemporary psychological theoretician.

Freud, Sigmund. *New Introductory Lectures on Psychoanalysis*. New York: W. W. Norton, 1933. Freud explains his theory of the workings of the id, ego, and superego. His concept of behavioral energy is described in this book.

Hull, Clark Leonard. *Principles of Behavior*. New York: Appleton-Century, 1943. This bible of the Hullian neobehavioristic theory delineates the concepts of D and H and the philosophical bases of behavioral study. The theory has excited many students into studying psychology; it has gone through many revisions and additions.

Logan, Frank A., and Douglas P. Ferraro. *Systematic Analyses of Learning and Motivation*. New York: John Wiley & Sons, 1978. Logan, who was a student of Hull, describes how motivation is involved in learning.

Petri, Herbert L. *Motivation: Theory, Research, and Application*. 4th ed. Belmont, Calif.: Wadsworth, 1996.

Pfaff, Donald W., ed. *The Physiological Mechanisms of Motivation*. New York: Springer-Verlag, 1982. Various authors describe the physiological substrates of different sources of drive and motivation in terms of the nervous system, hormones, and body fluid parameters.

Stellar, James R., and Eliot Stellar. *The Neurobiology of Motivation and Reward*. New York: Springer-Verlag, 1985. Eliot Stellar, one of the best known theorists in biopsychology of motivation, along with his son, describes how biological antecedents of motivation can be found to explain various behavior.

Warden, Carl John. *Animal Motivation: Experimental Studies on the Albino Rat*. New York: Columbia University Press, 1931. This was the first research attempting to compare different sources of drive using various reward substances.

Sigmund Hsiao

See also:

EGO PSYCHOLOGY
Erik Erikson

Type of psychology: Personality
Fields of study: Personality theory; psychodynamic and neoanalytic models

Erik Erikson emphasized the importance of social, rather than sexual, factors in the development of personality; he also expanded the number of stages of development to eight in order to cover the entire life span. It was Erikson who introduced the notion of the identity crisis.

Principal terms

BASIC ANTIPATHY/CORE PATHOLOGY: the negative personality characteristic developed when the individual experiences mostly the dystonic (disruptive) element of a psychosocial crisis; the antithesis of a basic strength

BASIC STRENGTH: the positive personality characteristic developed when the individual experiences mostly the syntonic (harmonious) element of a psychosocial crisis

PLAY CONSTRUCTION: a projective personality test technique developed by Erikson to reveal unconscious memories and concerns of patients who are too young to express themselves in other ways

PSYCHOHISTORY: a technique of analysis in which the actions of the subject are examined in the light of the social and historical forces that affect the psychological makeup and personality of the subject

PSYCHOSOCIAL CRISIS: a turning point in the process of development precipitated by the individual having to face a new set of social demands and new social relationships

PSYCHOSOCIAL STAGES OF DEVELOPMENT: sequential and specific periods of life during which crises precipitated by changing social demands and relationships necessitate personality changes and new attitudes in the individual

Overview

Erik Erikson was born in 1902. Some reports suggest that he was born out of wedlock; others suggest that his mother was married but that his father had abandoned her. Still other reports suggest that Erikson's father died shortly before or immediately after his birth. Whatever the exact circumstances of his conception and birth, it is known that his mother married young Erik's pediatrician three years after his birth. Erik grew up in comfortable surroundings as Erik Homburger in southern Germany and was expected to become a doctor like his stepfather. Both his mother and his stepfather were from Jewish families, but Erik was considered an outsider when he attended temple because of his blond hair and blue eyes. Ironically, at school he was also considered an outsider despite his Aryan features and was referred to by his classmates as a Jew. It is generally believed that his unknown paternal lineage and his religious heritage were underlying causes of his later focus on the concept that he is most famous for developing: the identity crisis typically experienced in adolescence.

Erik Homburger, in his late teens, abandoned his family's plans for him to become a doctor; he opted for traveling throughout southern Germany and northern Italy and exercising his talent for sketching, both in his travels and in art school. Erikson himself has described those years as a time of discontent, rebellion, and confusion, the same feelings experienced by many teenagers as they try to come to grips with the need to establish their own sense of identity.

During his late twenties, he worked for, and was psychoanalyzed by, Anna Freud, another of the leaders of the ego psychology movement and the daughter of Sigmund Freud. He was graduated from the Vienna Psychoanalytic Institute in 1933 and emigrated to the United States a year later. He became a U.S. citizen and changed his name to Erik Homburger Erikson. He never fully explained why he chose Erikson for his last name, but the most interesting suggestion is that his sons wanted to be known as "Erik's son."

In the 1940's, Erikson began to develop his own theory of personality development. He always believed that his theory, while separate and different from Freud's psychoanalysis, was not incompatible with Freud's. He had become acquainted with Freud, and had come to admire him greatly, while undergoing personal analysis by Anna Freud in Vienna. From the beginning of his theorizing, Erikson identified himself as a post-Freudian rather than as anti-Freudian or neo-Freudian. In 1950, Erikson published _Childhood and Society_, the first major book that explained the theory he was in the process of developing. Erikson subsequently authored several books, as well as chapters in books edited by others, elaborating his theory and applying his concepts.

Erikson's theory differs from Freud's psychoanalytic theory in many respects. While Freud viewed the ego as a relatively weak portion of the personality, barely able to control the much stronger id, Erikson viewed it as a more positive, powerful, and adaptive force. Erikson's theory therefore exemplifies a branch of personality theories classified as ego psychology. Further, Erikson emphasized the importance of social interactions in the development of the individual's personality, while Freud emphasized unconscious sexual factors.

Erikson's theory provides a much more positive, hopeful perspective on the human condition than is found in traditional psychoanalytic theory. Freud believed that either overindulgence or excessive conflict during any of the early psychosexual stages of development could cause the individual either to fixate in that stage or to regress back to an earlier stage. Erikson believed that the individual would adopt a negative characteristic, but would also move on to the next psychosocial stage of development. Freud also believed that, without therapy, the person who fixated or regressed would be unable to develop further, because he or she would not have the opportunity to work through the psychosexual tasks of the remaining stages. Erikson, however, believed that since each psychosocial stage of development demands a different pattern of social relationships, the person has a chance to begin anew in each stage. In addition, he believed that a particularly good situation in a later stage could result in the reversal of the negative characteristic adopted in an earlier stage.

Erikson concluded that personality develops over the entire life of the individual. He postulated the existence of eight psychosocial stages of development, the last of which encompasses the period of old age. Freud, on the other hand, proposed five psychosexual stages of development and focused on only the periods of infancy and early childhood. In Freud's theory, all the important parts of the personality are in place, and all the most significant events have been experienced, by the time the individual is six years of age.

In addition to those theoretical differences with Freud, Erikson emphasized the need to develop in either a positive or a negative direction during each of the psychosocial stages of development. In his view, each new set of social demands sets up a new crisis for the individual to resolve. The best known of these crises occurs in adolescence, when the individual must either develop a positive sense of identity or experience role confusion. Today it is widely recognized that "crisis" was probably a bad choice of terminology, because common use of that term implies negative connotations Erikson never intended. He meant for the term to denote an important, even essential, turning point, but not necessarily one that was traumatic or difficult. Later researchers, in fact, have found that most teenagers are able to establish their identity without undue difficulties; only about 20 to 25 percent of teenagers experience the degree of difficulty that would be implied by the common usage of the term "crisis."

Applications

In describing the development of personality, Erikson identified eight stages of psychosocial development, each of which covers a specific period of time and is biologically based. At each stage, the individual encounters a different kind of social situation, is expected to meet different social demands, and experiences different social relationships. Different opportunities for personality development are offered, and new elements are added to the individual's personality at each stage. One element is syntonic (harmonious or positive), while the other is dystonic (disruptive or negative); together they constitute the psychosocial crisis faced by the individual. The conflict between the two elements produces either a basic strength or its basic antipathy or core pathology.

During the first year of life, the infant experiences the psychosocial conflict Erikson identified as trust versus mistrust. The infant is essentially helpless and is dependent upon others for satisfaction of its basic needs. The degree to which its needs are met will determine whether the infant develops the basic strength of hope, or its antipathy and core pathology, withdrawal. Both the syntonic and dystonic elements of trust and mistrust must be experienced by the infant in order for optimum development to occur. If the infant's needs were so well anticipated and perfectly met that the infant never experienced frustration, the result would be an extreme form of trust, and the infant would become too gullible. On the other hand, if the infant's needs were rarely or never met, the result would be an extreme form of mistrust, and the infant would become excessively suspicious and cynical. Optimum development requires a favorable balance of trust and mistrust, which leads to the development of hope. The same principle holds true for optimum development at each of the remaining stages, and the balance must favor the syntonic elements.

During early childhood, the second and third years of life, the child experiences the psychosocial conflict of autonomy versus shame and doubt. As his or her body continues to develop, the child is able to do things he or she was incapable of doing before, and his or her relationships with others change. The cognitive development of the child allows him or her to begin to differentiate between himself or herself and the rest of the world. The negativism of the period, known as the "terrible twos," results from this cognitive development. Now the child can say "No" to mother without denying himself or herself. Many parents perceive the negativism of this period as evidence of disrespect and willfulness, and they try to teach the child "proper respect" for elders. Such parents might teach a child to be ashamed of his or her natural desire to be a separate, independent, autonomous person. Parents who understand the cognitive development that is going on can understand that the child is simply becoming his or her own person, and allow the child the freedom necessary to begin to become an effective, self-sufficient individual. If the child is allowed to express freely his or her efforts at developing independence of action, he or she is able to develop a sense of autonomy and will develop the basic strength of will. If, on the other hand, the child is punished or made to feel ashamed of these efforts to express independence, the child will experience shame and doubt and develop the basic antipathy of compulsion.

Early childhood is followed by a period Erikson called the play age. Between the ages of three and six, the child faces the psychosocial crisis of initiative versus guilt. After developing the capacity for autonomous activity, the child can now develop the capacity to initiate purposefully that autonomous behavior in an effort to attain his or her own goals. If the child is able to initiate successfully purposeful activities that lead to the attainment of his or her desired goals, he or she will develop purpose, the basic strength of the play age. If the child's goals are forbidden, or if he or she must delay seeking those goals on a regular basis, the child can experience guilt for desiring those goals and develop inhibition, the core pathology of the play age.

School age extends from about the age of six to about the time of puberty, usually at twelve or thirteen. The psychosocial task of the school age is to confront the issue of industry versus inferiority. Industry refers to the willingness of the child to stick with a task and finish it. If he or she is unable to complete tasks successfully or to reach goals, the dystonic attitude of inferiority results. While industry leads to the development of the basic strength of competence, inferiority leads to the basic antipathy of inertia, and the child may give up and regress to the more infantile, nonproductive play characteristic of the play age.

During adolescence, from puberty to the late teens or early twenties, the individual is faced with the need to develop a stable, secure sense of identity and the basic strength of fidelity. The alternative is to experience role confusion and the core pathology of repudiation. Adolescence is a time for the individual to try different roles and ideologies in the search for meaning in his or her own life. The intense concern for fitting in with an in-group, copying the clothing styles that are popular, and using the currently popular vocabulary are all the result of the effort to find one's place in the world. It seems that in every successive generation, teenagers must go through this trial-and-error method of finding out who they are, what they want to do, and how best to accomplish their goals.

Young adulthood is the stage that has the greatest variability in length. Traditionally, it has been described as the middle to late twenties, but some individuals may not complete this stage until they are in their thirties, or even later. The young adult must face the psychosocial conflict Erikson identified as intimacy versus isolation. To develop intimacy and the basic strength of love, the young adult must be able to merge his or her identity with the identity of another without fear of losing his or her own identity. If the young adult is unable to take a chance risking his or her identity by sharing intimacy, he or she will experience isolation and develop the core pathology known as exclusivity.

Adulthood, which encompasses the fourth, fifth, and part of the sixth decade of life, is the time for the individual to generate or produce. The desire to produce and rear children, to produce works that will last beyond one's own lifetime, to help the next generation to develop, and to build a better world all result from the psychosocial crisis Erikson called generativity versus stagnation. Generativity leads to the basic strength of care. If the adult is unable to become generative, the alternative is to stagnate, become self-absorbed, and develop the core pathology of adulthood, rejectivity. According to Erikson, rejectivity leads to some of the worst aspects of what others call human nature: hatred of individuals and groups, wars, and the resulting destruction and atrocities.

Old age is the time for the individual to experience the psychosocial conflict of ego integrity versus despair. This final stage of development lasts from the sixties until the individual's death. For the individual who has mostly experienced the syntonic developments of trust, autonomy, initiative, industry, identity, intimacy, and generativity, the characteristic of integrity will predominate. That person will develop the basic strength Erikson called wisdom. Wisdom enables the person to maintain an informed and detached concern with life while facing the inevitability of death. The individual who has mostly experienced the dystonic developments of mistrust, shame and doubt, guilt, inferiority, ego confusion, isolation, and stagnation will develop the basic antipathy Erikson called disdain.

Context

Erik Erikson made a number of significant contributions to the field of psychology and to the ways in which the lay public both views and describes the world. Many people, in fact, use ideas advanced by Erikson without being aware of whose ideas they are.

Erikson moved the focus of attention in developmental theories from the sexual domain into the social domain. He introduced the notion of identity crisis into the common vocabulary. He also expanded the time span of personality development to cover the entire life of the individual. Like many other psychologists, he added to the repertoire of clinical techniques available for both investigation and therapy. His theory also offers a more positive, hopeful view of the human condition than did Sigmund Freud's psychoanalysis.

Finally, one must include among Erikson's contributions to the field of psychology play construction and psychohistorical analysis. Play construction is a projective technique Erikson developed to explore the unconscious processes of children. A child is given a random selection of toys and is asked to construct a scenario using those toys. The scenario that is constructed is, according to Erikson, an unconscious expression of the child's life history that reveals hidden needs and motives.

Psychohistorical analysis refers to an approach pioneered by Erikson in which the investigator examines the role that historical factors and personal experiences play in the personality development of the individual. While Freud argued that "anatomy is destiny," Erikson countered that "anatomy, history, and personality are our combined destiny." A psychohistory is similar to a case history, except that psychohistories usually involve individuals who are essentially emotionally stable, while case histories are developed for persons who experience emotional difficulties. Erikson published psychohistorical biographies of Mahatma Gandhi and Martin Luther.

Bibliography

Coles, Robert. *Erik H. Erikson: The Growth of His Work*. Boston: Little, Brown, 1970. A well-written biography, though Coles has been criticized by some as too friendly toward his subject; some reviewers have gone so far as to accuse him of hero worship.

Erikson, Erik Homburger. *Childhood and Society*. New York: W. W. Norton, 1950. The first major book that explained the theory Erikson was in the process of developing. Republished in 1963 and again in 1985, this remains one of the most popular, and most frequently recommended, psychology books ever published.

_____. *Gandhi's Truth: On the Origins of Militant Nonviolence*. New York: W. W. Norton, 1969. The better of Erikson's psychohistorical biographies. Erikson examines in detail the historical period in which Gandhi grew up, and the personal experiences that eventually led Gandhi to become one of the world's most influential religious and spiritual leaders. Erikson believes that the writer of a psychohistory should become emotionally involved with the subject; his emotional attachment to Gandhi is apparent. Erikson attributes that attachment to his own lifelong search for the father he had never known.

Evans, Richard Isadore. *Dialogue with Erik Erikson*. Reprint. Northvale, N.J.: Jason Aronson, 1995.

_____. *The Making of Psychology: Discussions with Creative Contributors*. New York: Alfred A. Knopf, 1976. An excellent compilation of interviews with many of the major forces in the history of psychology. The chapter on Erikson includes not only a discussion of the eight psychosocial stages but also a psychohistorical discussion comparing Adolf Hitler's and Mahatma Gandhi's lives and contributions to the world (Hitler does not fare well in the comparison).

Psychoanalysis and Contemporary Thought 19, no. 2 (1996). A special issue entitled "Ideas and Identities: The Life and Work of Erik Erikson," edited by Robert S. Wallerstein. A variety of insightful perspectives on Erikson; includes a selection of photographs.

Roazen, Paul. *Erik H. Erikson: The Power and Limits of a Vision*. New York: Free Press, 1976. Although Roazen is more critical of Erikson than Coles is, he finds Erikson's approach more likely than Freud's to be helpful in therapeutic encounters. This biography, coupled with Coles's, is likely to produce a more balanced view of Erikson's place in the history of psychology than if either book is read alone.

Tribe, Carol. *Profile of Three Theories: Erikson, Maslow, Piaget*. Dubuque, Iowa: Kendall Hunt Publishing, 1995.

John W. Nichols

See also:

DEVELOPMENT OF EMOTION

Type of psychology: Emotion
Field of study: Infancy and childhood

The development of emotions is intertwined with all aspects of human development; understanding how and when to express emotions, for example, is an essential component of personality and normal developmental processes.

Principal terms

EMOTIONAL ELICITOR: a stimulus event that is necessary for an emotion to occur

EMOTIONAL EXPERIENCE: the background needed for the interpretation and evaluation of an emotional state and expression

EMOTIONAL EXPRESSIONS: the observable behaviors, such as facial expressions, changes in heart rate, and vocalizations, that often accompany emotional states

EMOTIONAL RECEPTORS: certain cells or structures in the brain that detect and respond to events

EMOTIONAL STATE: a set of changes in somatic and/or neurophysiological activity that occur when emotional receptors are activated

STRANGER ANXIETY: a common phenomenon that generally occurs during the end of the first year of life in which the elicitor of a stranger tends to produce the emotion of anxiety

TEMPERAMENT: an inborn set of moods and patterns of reacting

Overview

In their book entitled *Children's Emotions and Moods: Developmental Theory and Measurement* (1983), Michael Lewis and Linda Michalson outline a model of the development of emotion. According to Lewis and Michalson, emotion consists of five components: elicitors, receptors, states, expressions, and experiences.

An elicitor is a stimulus event that is necessary for an emotion to occur. The stimulus may be either external or internal to the individual. Some elicitors are assumed to produce emotion almost automatically. In other words, little experience is needed for emotion to result once the elicitor is presented. Other types of elicitors produce different results as the individual develops. For example, the elicitor of a stranger tends to produce the emotion of fear in most infants. This phenomenon, which generally occurs during the end of the first year of life, is called "stranger anxiety." As children get older, this fear tends to decrease. The influence of an elicitor may change over time for several reasons. For example, as children develop, their cognitive capacities increase. Thus, in order for a child to be afraid of a stranger, he or she must first gain the ability to tell the difference between a stranger and a parent. Therefore, some elicitors change in their relation to emotion as children develop.

Receptors are cells or structures in the brain that detect and respond to events. There is debate as to the specificity of these receptors—that is, whether there are specific receptors for specific emotions or more general receptors that activate overall arousal. There is limited information available about how development relates to these receptors. It is possible that the receptors can change in sensitivity over time through either biological development, social experiences, or a complex interaction between biological growth and learning experiences.

In the third component of Lewis and Michalson's model, emotional states involve a set of changes in somatic and/or neurophysiological activity that occur when emotional receptors are activated. These emotional states have been conceptualized in two ways. In one view, emotional states are thought to be inborn and development does not play a particularly important role. An alternative view is that the newborn infant has two general emotional states: negative and positive. As the child develops, these states become more differentiated. That is, whereas an infant of three months may experience a limited number of emotional states, including distress, excitement, and delight, a two-year-old child can experience a wider (more differentiated) variety of emotions, including fear, anger, jealousy, joy, and affection.

The fourth component of this developmental model concerns the expression of emotion. Emotional expressions differ from emotional states in that they are the observable behaviors (such as facial expressions, posturing, and vocalizations) that often accompany emotional states. Some researchers have examined facial expression in infants to provide evidence of discrete emotional expressions at a very young age. For example, psychologists have been able to distinguish eight different emotions in the facial expression of twelve-month-old children. It is unknown, however, whether these observed expressions in infants truly represent separate internal emotional states.

The fifth component of emotion, emotional experience, involves the interpretation and evaluation by the child of an emotional state. As the child develops, he or she gradually gains the ability to experience a broad range of emotions. Whereas a newborn is capable of experiencing distress, the older child has the ability to evaluate his or her own behavior and emotional state as well as the situational context in order to experience an emotion such as embarrassment.

It should be clear from the above discussion that the child's experience and expression of emotion change considerably as the child develops. As early as three to four months, infants display patterns of behaviors that suggest emotional states of distress, gratification, and excitement. An infant who displays increased motor movement and heart rate, closes the eyes, and cries in response to pain, cold, or hunger is showing distress. When an infant experiences gratification, he or she displays behaviors such as decreased muscle tension and closing of the eyes after feeding.

At around six months of age, infants appear to experience new emotions, including fear and anger. When infants of this age are confronted with a new or unfamiliar situation, they often respond by retracting their mouths, widening their eyes, and raising their brows; they may also cry. Prior to this time, infants may attend to unfamiliar events but do not appear to be frightened by them. Six-month-old infants also seem to experience anger in response to frustrating situations, such as the removal of an interesting toy. As early as the first year, infants are able to respond to certain emotions displayed by other people. For example, one-year-old children tend to become upset when they witness someone being angry.

The sequence of the development of emotions and their universality has led psychologists to postulate that emotions may develop because they serve an adaptive purpose for survival. Children early display emotions that tend to keep the caretaker nearby, such as crying at separation. Children's fearfulness of the unfamiliar may protect them from approaching situations that they are as yet unable to handle.

Children's inferences about others' emotions also develop over time. Preschool children can correctly interpret facial expressions of emotions in others and can make accurate predictions about how other people will feel in certain situations. While young children are able to infer whether someone feels "good" or "bad," older children are able to make more refined evaluations of others' emotions, differentiating "bad" feelings into "mad," "scared," or "sad." With maturation, children become able to tell when people are hiding their feelings or are pretending to feel a certain way.

Finally, unlike very young children, older children learn to use labels to describe their internal states. As children become more verbal and reflective, they learn from others how to label their own emotional states in a variety of situations. With age, children are also better able to monitor and modify the expression of their own emotional experience.

Applications

The role of emotional states, expressions, and experiences is pertinent to many aspects of psychology, particularly the study of personality and psychopathology. Emotional expression is a fundamental aspect in the way one relates to and communicates with others. Thus, psychologists who are interested in almost any aspect of normal or abnormal development find an understanding of emotional development essential.

Stella Chess and Alexander Thomas conducted pioneering studies in the area of infant temperament. The term "temperament" describes infants' inborn moods and activity levels. For example, some babies are easily soothed, while others are irritable and cry much more. Individual differences in temperament play a role in the way an infant's emotional state is related to the environment (elicitors). Based on their observations of infants, Thomas and Chess described a child with a difficult temperament as one who shows intense irritability and withdrawal regarding new situations. Infants with difficult temperaments are more likely than infants with easy temperaments to react negatively to certain elicitors. For example, an infant with an easy temperament may be pleasantly surprised when opening a jack-in-the-box, whereas an infant with a difficult temperament may be startled and upset. Chess and Thomas' research, as well as the research of many other psychologists who have built on their work, suggests that early temperament is predictive of later social competence—children with difficult temperaments are more likely to have problems with peers later in life.

Differences among children in their emotional expression and their ability to regulate their own emotions have an effect on later emotional and social development. For example, children who are extremely fearful of new situations are less likely to approach unfamiliar situations or people, and thus are less likely to explore and gain new information about the world. In addition, the ways in which children express themselves and regulate their emotions can have enormous impact on the reactions and behaviors of significant others. When a father and infant interact, they communicate with each other through facial expressions and bodily movements. Although a father cannot know for certain what his child is feeling, he makes inferences based on the baby's expressions. Fathers are delighted by their child's smiles and cooing noises. These behaviors keep the father engaged and encourage him to continue these satisfying interactions with the child. Thus, the child who smiles and coos will be more likely to receive the father's attention than a child who is more subdued and withdrawn. Given the countless interactions that a father and infant have, the temperament style of the child can have a powerful influence on the social environment experienced by the child.

One area in the field of emotional development is "attachment." John Bowlby, a British psychiatrist, proposed that infants are born with the capacity for certain behaviors (such as crying, smiling, and cooing) that help keep adults close. According to Bowlby, being able to keep adults in close proximity is adaptive in that it ensures the infant will be cared for and will be more likely to survive. Through repeated interactions between parent and child, an attachment is formed. Bowlby, as well as Mary Ainsworth, who expanded on Bowlby's ideas and tested them empirically, proposed that all normal infants form attachments. These attachments are thought to provide the basis for healthy emotional and social development. It is within the context of a healthy attachment with a caregiver that the infant is able to feel safe in exploring his or her surroundings. If a child develops unhealthy or insecure emotional attachments, social and emotional development suffers.

Mothers who form "anxious attachments" with their children are unable to evaluate and react to their children's needs and behaviors effectively. For example, a mother may misinterpret her child's reaction to seeing a large dog as fear (as opposed to interest). When the mother communicates to the child her own anxiety about the child's safety, the child is likely to reinterpret his or her own emotional state as fearful. The child might then learn that all dogs are dangerous. Psychologists are studying the relation between the quality of early parent/child attachments and the child's later ability to form healthy relationships in adulthood.

As it becomes increasingly clear that the ability to regulate one's emotions plays an important role in development, clinical psychologists have incorporated this information into various aspects of therapy. Children, as do adults, experience different emotions in part because of their interpretations and explanations of their own and other people's behavior. For example, if a child thinks that another child bumped into her by accident, she is less likely to be mad or upset than if she made the interpretation that the child bumped her intentionally. Children who are aggressive may lack basic skills in understanding the behavior of others and in dealing with interpersonal relations. Thus, a clinical psychologist might help aggressive children by teaching them to be aware of others' feelings and reactions. When children are able to interpret nonhostile behavior appropriately, they are less likely to become angry and retaliate.

Similarly, overly anxious and fearful children can be taught to make more reasonable evaluations about their environment and the consequences of certain behaviors. For example, a child who has an abnormal fear of new situations can learn to confront new situations with the help of a trusted person. By confronting these fearful situations, and learning that there are no negative consequences, the child develops self-confidence and can become less fearful.

Context
Although the study of emotion dates back to Plato and Aristotle, a comprehensive formulation of how emotions develop is far from complete. In fact, compared to the study of other areas of development, such as cognition, language, and memory, the development of

emotion has received limited attention.

The study of most aspects of psychology has been subject to debates about the relative importance of biological factors versus learning or socialization. The study of emotional development is no exception. At the extremes, there are two interpretations of the development of emotion. The biological model of the development of emotion is based on Charles Darwin's ideas that emotional expressions are biologically determined and have adaptive value. According to this model, the components of emotion (elicitors, receptors, states, and expressions) are biologically determined and are relatively unaffected by learning.

The socialization or interactive model of emotion focuses on the ways in which emotions are learned. This model does not disregard the role of biological factors in the development of emotions; rather, it emphasizes the importance of the environmental influences of emotional development. In this model, the connections between elicitors, emotional states, and experiences are based on one's experiences with parents and peers. This model provides an understanding of the ways children learn how and when to express their emotions.

Most psychologists today recognize that the biological model and the socialization model provide information about different aspects of emotional development. As in other areas of child development, emotional development is understood to be the result of the interaction of biological and socialization factors; although the complex interaction between biological and social influences on emotional development is poorly understood. Today, emotional development is viewed in the context of the child's social, psychological, and physical development. Psychologists are interested in understanding how infants begin to make sense of the world around them and how infants experience early emotions. It has been found that infants have enormous capacities very early in life. They are able to perceive differences in the world around them, act upon the external world, and experience a wide variety of emotions and sensations.

Understanding the intricacies of emotional development is a challenging task. One difficulty in this area of research is that infants are unable to talk about (and indeed, even to know) what they are feeling. Therefore, researchers must rely on external signs such as crying and smiling as indicators of emotion as well as on physiological changes that can be reliably measured. As psychologists become more creative in their research and continue to develop more sophisticated tools for investigating emotions, they will continue to piece together the puzzle of emotional development.

Bibliography

Bower, T. G. R. *A Primer of Infant Development*. San Francisco: W. H. Freeman, 1977. Describes the process and features of development during the first two years of life. Presents basic information regarding infant emotional, social, motor, language, perceptual, and cognitive development. Provides a basis for placing emotional development in the context of other areas of development.

Emde, Robert N., T. J. Gaensbauer, and R. J. Harmon. *Emotional Expression in Infancy: A Biobehavioral Study*. New York: International Universities Press, 1976. In this research monograph in the "Psychological Issues" series, Emde and his colleagues report on their study of normal infant development during the first year of life. Their research involves the longitudinal study of emotional expression in sixteen infants using a variety of investigative techniques.

Flavell, J. H. *Cognitive Development*. 2d ed. Englewood Cliffs, N.J.: Prentice-Hall, 1985. This classic book, in its second edition, provides a comprehensive overview of the contemporary field of cognitive development. The chapter on social cognition provides interesting examples and descriptions of research evidence on social-cognitive development during infancy.

Lewis, Michael, and Linda Michalson. *Children's Emotions and Moods: Developmental Theory and Measurement*. New York: Plenum Press, 1983. Examines emotional development from its theoretical perspective and, through a structural analysis of the meaning of emotion, outlines a theory of emotional development. Presents a measurement system for assessing emotional development in young children that is based on situation-specific assessments of children's emotional behaviors.

Lewis, Michael, and Leonard A. Rosenblum, eds. *The Development of Affect*. New York: Plenum Press, 1978. Presents the work of more than twenty-five contributors, including Harry Harlow, Jerome Kagan, L. Alan Sroufe, and Robert Emde. It is the first volume in a series edited by Michael Lewis and Leonard Rosenblum entitled "Genesis of Behavior." Surveys advances in methodology and theory which have promoted understanding of the meaning and development of affect.

Newsweek. "Your Child from Birth to Three." (Spring/Summer, 1997). Special child development issue.

Laurence Grimm
Laurie S. Miller

See also:

Aggression, 31; Attachment and Bonding in Infancy and Childhood, 71; Attraction Theories, 77; Emotion, Functions of, 235; Emotion: Definition and Assessment, 242.

FUNCTIONS OF EMOTION

Type of psychology: Emotion
Field of study: Motivation theory

Scientists have explored the possibility that emotion has an adaptive purpose; that is, it may increase the ability of a species to survive. Various theorists have suggested that emotion may serve important functions in social communication, the warding off of aggression, the exercise of power and maintenance of status, and the direction of attention to important events.

Principal terms

ADAPTATION: the process of adjusting to certain relatively constant conditions in the environment; certain traits may allow the organism to fit the demands and opportunities presented by the environment better, and these tend to be preserved in the species

EMOTION: a state often associated with goal-directed behavior and often marked by peripheral physiological arousal, such as increased heart rate; expressive behaviors, such as facial expression; and subjective experience, such as feelings of pleasure or displeasure

ETHOLOGY: a branch of zoology that studies animals in their natural environments; it is often concerned with investigating the adaptive significance and innate basis of behaviors

EXPRESSION OF EMOTION: the use of any channels or means for communicating emotion, such as facial expression, voice, and body position

FUNCTION: something that serves a purpose, especially the purpose of enhancing the ability of the species to survive; an action that is part of or contributes to a larger action

MOTIVATION: processes that energize, maintain, and direct behavior; the potential for energizing behavior built into a behavioral regulation system

NATURAL SELECTION: the process by which those characteristics of a species that help it to survive or adapt to its environment tend to be passed along by members that live long enough to have offspring

Overview

Two primary meanings of the word "function" have concerned emotion theorists in search of the functions of emotion. The first and most important has concerned finding the possible purposes served by emotion or emotions, especially those functions that might enhance the ability of the organism to adapt to its environment and hence to survive. This notion of emotions as serving an adaptive function was first introduced and investigated by Charles Darwin, the great English naturalist of the nineteenth century. A second, more recent sense of the word "function" used by emotion theorists concerns the question of how emotion fits or works within the larger behavioral control system—that is, the function of emotion as a component of a behavioral regulation system.

In 1872, Darwin published *The Expression of the Emotions in Man and Animals*. In this work Darwin provided many examples of how the expressions of both animals and humans serve to signal their intentions. Darwin provides an example of a dog approaching another dog or human in a hostile or aggressive manner. The dog approaches stiffly, with its head held erect or slightly lowered, the hair on its back bristling, its eyes in a fixed stare, its ears flattened against its head, and its teeth bared in a snarl. Darwin argued that it is not difficult to infer the intentions of the animal—it is ready to attack; furthermore, he argued that this signals the hostile frame of mind of the animal. Darwin contended that some of these patterns of expression and the muscle movement patterns are habits that developed to serve a purpose through learning; however, most of the movements of expression are innate or inherited. Another of Darwin's examples illustrates this. A hungry baby does not need to learn how to cry and move its facial muscles in an expression of distress. Rather, the behavior has been inherited. The baby's expression of distress functions for the welfare of the baby by communicating to its mother its need for food.

This expression is an adaptive response that will make it more likely that the baby will get what it needs to survive. According to Darwin's notion of natural selection, infants or young that cannot get their own food but can signal their need state in this way would be more likely to receive adequate nutrition and would therefore be more likely to live long enough to pass this trait or behavioral disposition to their own offspring. In other words, infants who cried to communicate their distress from hunger would have a selective advantage over infants who did not or could not show this expression of their motivational state.

In spite of Darwin's great contribution to understanding the functions of motives, emotions, and expressive tendencies, the preceding arguments can be criticized on two counts. First, as with most arguments using natural selection and evolutionary theory, the reasoning proceeds backward from the fact to the occurrence. In other words, the argument proceeds in the following manner: Since many surviving and apparently prospering animals have the ability to cry in distress from what humans suppose to be a hungry state, this behavior must have been adaptive for the organism. It is difficult to do experiments to test the assumption of natural selection with higher organisms, because the time between generations is too long to detect much effect of pressures from the environment.

A second criticism concerns the quality of the inferences made about animals' motivational and emotional states. From the evidence that Darwin provided on the expression of motivation and emotion in humans and other animals, it has been argued that there is continuity between humans and other animals in the inheritance of certain expressions that signal similar internal states in both humans and animals. For example, although humans less often bare their teeth in anger than dogs, they often have a similar fixed stare as the dog cited in the previous example. The assumption is that the dog is also experiencing anger. This is an error called anthropomorphism, which is the act of attributing characteristics of humans to animals. Unlike humans, other animals cannot say what it is that they are feeling. Many researchers in emotion forgive Darwin for this error, since there is converging evidence to support the notion that there are similarities in the underlying states that correspond to similar expressions for at least some expressions.

If there is continuity between the species in the expression of internal motivated states, then, according to Darwin's theory, it would be expected that humans would likely show more similarities in expression of emotions with nearer relatives (for example, other primates, such as monkeys and chimpanzees) than with organisms that are not as closely related to humans, such as dogs. William Redikan in 1982 reviewed research on the evolution of human facial expressions or displays, discussing the possible functions of those displays. For example, he argues that a sadness display in the chimpanzee may be signaled by a low-intensity silent pout, while laughter may be signaled by what is termed the "play face" of the chimpanzee. The tense-mouth display is found in several species of primates, including humans, and is thought to signal anger or imminent attack. In it, the lips are compressed tightly together and the eyes are fixed and staring. In some species, the ears are flattened against the head. Parts of this display are similar to that of Darwin's example of the dog.

What is the function of these expressive displays? The tense-mouth display may function as protective movements prior to attack, especially one that might involve biting. The ears pressed against the head would serve to protect them from injury.

Nico Frijda has suggested that all expressive movements may have a functional explanation in terms of the organism's relationship to some aspect of its environment. For Frijda, emotions are tendencies toward specific modes of interaction with others, objects, and the environment. The expression of these tendencies is the embodiment of the emotion. For example, the hiding and crouching movements associated with fear serve to reduce the chances of being seen or hurt; the pattern of movement of the mouth in the display of disgust serves to eject distasteful substances from the mouth. According to Frijda, these expressive movements that embody the emotion are ways of contacting the environment.

In general, a primary function of the expression of emotion is to communicate to others the motivational-emotional state or situation of the organism. These can serve important social functions that enhance the survivability of individuals and members of the group. The ethologist Irenaus Eibl-Eibesfeldt has argued that several expressions may serve to diffuse possible aggression in potentially aggressive encounters for both humans and other animals. Smiles in humans and perhaps smilelike displays for some other primates may help control aggression. Also, facial displays that signal potential aggression or threat may serve to warn other individuals so they can adopt some strategy to avoid aggressive confrontation, thus preserving the individuals. As Robert Plutchik has noted, however, if the prediction process of an organism leads it to conclude that another individual is threatening, then the appropriate feeling may be anger, with an appropriate behavior being attack for the purpose of injuring or destroying the other individual. According to Plutchik, emotions function as bodily reactions to survival-related problems.

The sociologist Theodore Kemper has further argued that emotions are adaptive for group survival. He describes social structure as depending on power and status. For him, emotions result from outcomes of power and status relations. Religion, for example, can use emotions such as guilt and joy to maintain a particular pattern of power and status relations within the society and thus preserve the social order and the individuals that depend on it for survival.

Other emotion theorists have examined the function of emotion in terms of how emotion operates within systems for the regulation of behavior. For example, Klaus Scherer has noted that often emotion theorists view the function of emotion as a disruption of behavioral sequences that allows the organism to redirect its attention to some important or survival-related event in the environment. He further argues that emotions are adaptive motivating mechanisms and that mild emotional states can be present without disrupting ongoing behavior. In this view, emotions are a part of the behavioral regulation system, and they allow organisms to adapt more flexibly to their environments.

Applications

One of the many possible applications of the research on the functions of emotion is the possibility of improving the nonverbal communication of emotion in both clinical and nonclinical settings. Another is improving communication and understanding between humans and other animal species by better comprehending the motives and emotions of animals.

Plutchik has pointed out that while people often think they understand much about emotions at an implicit or intuitive level, there are gaps in this knowledge—concerning questions about the functions of emotions, for example. In fact, there is no formal instruction on the purposes behind emotional expression. Attention to this kind of knowledge could be useful in contributing to what Ross Buck has termed "emotional education." In addition, a better understanding of the adaptive functions of particular emotional displays could help clinicians, such as psychiatrists and clinical psychologists, to understand the meaning and purposes of expressions of emotion in their clients.

The evidence for continuity in the expressions of emotion in humans and other animals has definite implications for those who work with animals, such as animal trainers, police, pet owners, and researchers. Understanding the purposes behind particular motivated behaviors can be very important for success in attempts to train animals. Research on animal learning contains many examples of failures to train certain behaviors because the animals were motivated for some other purpose; sometimes these other motives are revealed in their expressions.

Much of the interest in examining the functions of emotion, especially the role of expressive behaviors, came directly from Darwin's own work on the expression of emotion in humans and animals. Darwin's careful research was seminal in developing many lines of research concerning the biological basis of expressive behaviors, especially facial expression. For example, considerable research has been done by Paul Ekman, Carroll Izard, and others that shows that the same facial expressions for a small set of primary emotions such as joy, sadness, anger, disgust, and fear can be found universally in the human species. These "core" facial expressions are essentially unlearned (innate) and can be elicited almost reflexively and automatically under the appropriate stimulus conditions. Since the facial expression for each of the primary emotions has a unique pattern of facial muscle activity that can be discriminated and perceived, this can provide the basis for communicating specific emotions. Furthermore, many theorists (such as Frijda) have argued that each emotion has a specific function that relates the organism to the environment in a particular way. According to Frijda, each emotion corresponds to a particular action-readiness tendency. In other words, the emotion prepares the organism to contact the environment in a specific, often adaptive, manner.

Darwin's notions of the natural selection of behaviors and the continuity of mental and behavioral processes among species have been instrumental in unifying constructs within a single theoretical framework. These should continue to be important to behavioral scientists in explaining the functions of emotion.

Context

The modern study of the functions of emotion began with the evolutionary theory of Charles Darwin. He argued that, just as some physical traits might be adaptive, some behaviors, behavioral patterns, or their dispositions might enhance the ability of organisms to live long enough to pass along the behaviors to their offspring. In other words, those behaviors that would enhance the ability of a species' members to survive would be preserved in their offspring through natural selection. On the other hand, behaviors that would reduce an individual's ability to survive would probably be selected against.

Darwin's evolutionary theory had important implications for areas of science other than biology, especially psychology. First of all, the theory emphasized the continuity among species. According to Darwin's view, the differences between humans and other animals are not so much differences of kind as differences of degree. This contradicted the teachings of the Judeo-Christian tradition, which argued that humans are a special part of creation and are to have dominion over the other animals or lesser creatures.

A second implication of the theory related to both the passing along of adaptive behaviors and the continuity of humans and other animals is the notion that mental abilities could develop through natural selection. Darwin argued that perhaps human intellectual abilities increased through natural selection. According to this view, other behaviors and psychological states and dispositions, such as motives and emotions, might change through natural selection and would be expected to show some similarities when closely related species were compared. In other words, as Lewis Petrinovich has noted, Darwin suggested a "mental continuity" among species.

This assumption of continuity had a profound influence on the development of behavioral science. In biology, the field of ethology came to rely heavily on Darwin's evolutionary theory to explain patterns of animal behavior, especially innately based behaviors, reviving the idea of instincts. In psychology, the assumption of continuity legitimized interest in animal behavior at the end of the nineteenth century. Moreover, early influential psychologists such as William James and other functionalists assumed that mental processes are useful to an organism in helping it adapt to its environment. Petrinovich has further argued that, in general, the James-Lange theory of emotion views the organism within its total situation or environment. William McDougall, also influenced by Darwinian theory, argued that instincts are associated with specific emotions. As Robert Franken has noted, McDougall thought the instinct of flight corresponded to the emotion of fear; repulsion to disgust; and curiosity to wonder. So, according to McDougall, an adaptive response such as fleeing from a threatening situation was associated with an emotional state.

Bibliography

Atkinson, Rita, Richard Atkinson, Edward Smith, and Daryl Bem. "Emotion." In *Introduction to Psychology*. 10th ed. San Diego: Harcourt Brace Jovanovich, 1990. This general psychology text provides a sophisticated and detailed treatment of various issues and phenomena in the study of emotion, including the function of particular displays in the aggressive behavior of animals.

Buck, Ross. *Human Motivation and Emotion*. 2d ed. New York: John Wiley & Sons, 1988. This is a comprehensive textbook on emotion that places emotion within a model including motivation and cognition, while thoroughly exploring biological aspects as well.

Darwin, Charles. "The Expression of the Emotions in Man and Animals." In *What Is an Emotion? Classic Readings in Philosophical Psychology*, edited by Cheshire Calhoun and Robert Solomon. New York: Oxford University Press, 1984. The authors include excerpts from the writings of some of the most important thinkers in the development of emotion theory, such as René Descartes, Charles Darwin, William James, Sigmund Freud, and Walter B. Cannon. Also included are introductory and summary comments about the passages.

Eibl-Eibesfeldt, Irenaus. "Strategies of Social Interaction." In *Emotion: Theory, Research, and Experience*, edited by Robert Plutchik and Henry Kellerman. Vol. 1. New York: Academic Press, 1980. The famous ethologist examines the function of expressions in the development of basic social strategies involved in sharing, giving, taking, friendly encounters, and so on.

Franken, Robert E. *Human Motivation.* 2d ed. Pacific Grove, Calif.: Brooks/Cole, 1988. This text on motivation offers a good historical introduction to the field of motivation, summarizing the major theories and influences.

Frijda, Nico. *The Emotions.* Cambridge, England: Cambridge University Press, 1986. Frijda discusses emotion in terms of expressive behaviors, physiology, experience, regulation, and so on in a detailed yet readable account. At the same time, he develops a model of motivation and emotion, emphasizing their function.

Kemper, Theodore D. "Power, Status, and Emotions: A Sociological Contribution to a Psychophysiological Domain." In *Approaches to Emotion*, edited by Klaus R. Scherer and Paul Ekman. Hillsdale, N.J.: Lawrence Erlbaum, 1984. Kemper takes a sociological approach to what is often thought to be a psychological domain. He argues that strong emotions often arise when there are changes in a group or in a group member's power and status as compared to the larger social surround.

Lazarus, Richard S., and Bernice N. Lazarus. *Passion and Reason: Making Sense of Our Emotions.* New York: Oxford University Press, 1994.

Ono, Taketoshi. *Perception, Memory, and Emotion: Frontiers in Neuroscience.* New York: Elsevier Science, 1996.

Petrinovich, Lewis. "Darwin and the Representative Expression of Reality." In *Darwin and Facial Expression: A Century of Research in Review*, edited by Paul Ekman. New York: Academic Press, 1973. The author traces the far-reaching influence of Darwin's theory of evolution on the development of various psychological theories and approaches including animal psychology, structuralism, functionalism, learning theory, social psychology, and ethology.

Plutchik, Robert. "A General Psychoevolutionary Theory of Emotion." In *Emotion: Theory, Research, and Experience*, edited by Robert Plutchik and Henry Kellerman. Vol. 1. New York: Academic Press, 1980. Plutchik summarizes his theory of emotion, placing it within evolutionary theory and discussing various theoretical and methodological problems encountered in the study of emotion.

Redikan, William K. "An Evolutionary Perspective on Human Facial Displays." In *Emotions in the Human Face*, edited by Paul Ekman. 2d ed. Cambridge, England: Cambridge University Press, 1982. Redikan reviews the evidence for the functions of various emotional displays in humans and other animals.

Scherer, Klaus R. "On the Nature and Function of Emotion: A Component Process Approach." In *Approaches to Emotions*, edited by Klaus R. Scherer and Paul Ekman. Hillsdale, N.J.: Lawrence Erlbaum, 1984. Scherer proposes a theory of emotion that examines the function of emotion as a component in a behavioral regulation process.

D. Alan Bensley

See also:

Emotion, Development of, 229; Emotion: Definition and Assessment, 242.

EMOTION
Definition and Assessment

Type of psychology: Emotion
Field of study: Motivation theory

Emotion is a basic aspect of human functioning. Emotions are personal experiences that arise from a complex interplay among physiological, cognitive, and situational variables. Theories and measurement of emotion allow psychologists to understand diverse expressions of behavior, and they form the cornerstone of many approaches to the treatment of psychological problems.

Principal terms

COGNITIVE APPRAISAL: a person's interpretation of a situation; cognitive appraisal influences what emotion the person experiences

EMOTIONAL INTENSITY: the strength with which a person experiences positive and negative emotions

PRIMARY EMOTIONS: basic, innate emotions

PSYCHOSOMATIC DISORDERS: physical disorders that are a result of chronic, negative emotions

SECONDARY EMOTIONS: emotions that derive from the combination of primary emotions

STATE EMOTION: the momentary experience of an emotion

TRAIT EMOTION: the frequency that a person experiences a given emotional state; a person that exhibits the trait of hostile emotion is one who frequently shows hostility

VISCERAL RESPONSES: internal, physiological responses such as heart rate and blood pressure

Overview

An emotion is a valenced experience that is felt with some degree of intensity, involves a person's interpretation of the immediate situation, and is accompanied by learned and unlearned physical responses. Emotions are transitory states, and they have five characteristics. First, emotions are experiences, not specific behaviors or thoughts. Although thoughts can sometimes lead to emotions, and behaviors can sometimes be caused by emotions, an emotion is a personal experience. Second, an emotional experience has "valence," meaning that the emotion has a positive or negative quality. Because emotions have valence, they often motivate people toward action. People tend to seek activities, situations, and people that enhance their experience of positive emotional states, and they tend to avoid situations that are connected with the experience of negative emotions.

Third, emotions involve cognitive appraisals. That is, one's interpretation of the immediate situation influences which emotion is experienced. For example, a child may experience either joy or fear when being chased, depending on whether the child interprets the chase as playful or dangerous. Fourth, emotions involve physical responses. Physical responses may be internal, such as changes in heart rate, blood pressure, or respiration (called visceral responses); physical responses can also be external, such as facial expressions. In addition, the bodily responses that characterize emotions are partly reflexive (unlearned) and partly learned. An increase in heart rate is a reflexive response that accompanies intense fear. That which a person fears, however, and his or her accompanying bodily response, may be the product of learning; crying when afraid is an emotional expression that is subject to learning experiences. Fifth, emotions can vary in intensity: Anger can become rage, amusement can become joy, and fear can be heightened to a state of terror.

Psychologist Robert Plutchik contends that there are eight innate, primary emotions: joy, anticipation, anger, disgust, sadness, surprise, fear, and acceptance. Like the colors of a color wheel, primary emotions can combine to produce secondary emotions. For example, surprise plus sadness can produce disappointment; anger plus disgust can produce contempt; and fear plus surprise can produce awe. Since each primary emotion can vary in intensity, and each level of intensity for one emotion can combine with some other level of intensity of another emotion, the total number of possible emotions runs to the hundreds. Although many psychologists agree that there exist primary emotions, there is no way that a person could distinguish such a large number of personal emotional experiences. Moreover, psychologists have not even attempted to measure such an unwieldy array of secondary emotions.

Nevertheless, psychologists have developed numerous assessment instruments to study common emotions. (An assessment instrument is simply a method used to measure something.) Since there are several different emotions, the study of emotion requires the development of specific methods that can accurately measure each of the common emotions. The most popular method of measuring an emotion is a self-report questionnaire in which a person answers questions relevant to a particular emotion. When measuring emotions, researchers make a distinction between "state" and "trait" emotion. An emotional state refers to what a person is experiencing at the moment. If one were interested in assessing how anxious someone currently is, one might use a questionnaire that asks the person to respond to several anxiety-related statements, using a scale from 1 ("not at all") to 5 ("very much"). Some examples of relevant statements are "I feel tense," "I feel nervous and shaky inside," "My heart is beating rapidly," and "I feel a sense of foreboding." The higher the total score on the questionnaire, the more anxiety the person is experiencing at the moment.

Trait emotion refers to how often an emotion is experienced. An "anxious person" is someone who frequently experiences the state of anxiety. Moreover, one would call someone a "hostile person" if one determined that he or she frequently exhibits states of anger. Examples of statements that assess trait anxiety are "I frequently become tense," "I often feel afraid for no apparent reason," "I am bothered by dizzy spells," and "I tend to worry a lot."

Psychologists have developed numerous questionnaires to assess emotions. There are self-report measures to assess anxiety, anger, guilt, happiness, and hopelessness, to name a few. In addition to measures of specific emotions, researchers have developed methods for assessing emotional intensity. Emotional intensity refers to the strength with which a person experiences both positive and negative emotions. It has been found that people who are emotionally intense report a feeling of well-being as "exuberance, animated joyfulness, and zestful enthusiasm." On the other hand, people who score low on a measure of emotional intensity experience a state of well-being as "serenity, contentment, tranquil calmness, and easygoing composure."

In addition to the use of self-report measures of emotion, psychologists often use physiological measures. Using sophisticated biological measuring instruments, psychologists are able to assess emotional arousal by measuring, for example, heart rate, skin sweating, respiration, blood pressure, and muscle tension. By examining the amount these measures change in response to a stimulus, researchers are able to infer emotional arousal. For example, it has been found that people who have the type of personality that puts them at risk for heart attacks show greater increases in blood pressure when trapped in a traffic jam, in comparison to those people who have personality characteristics that do not predispose them to heart attacks. In this instance, the psychologist uses the measure of blood pressure to infer a negative emotion, such as anger or frustration.

One question that arises when using physiological measures to assess emotions is whether each emotion has a specific pattern of physiological responses. For example, blood pressure appears to be particularly responsive to anger-inducing situations. People's heart rates, however, increase during emotional states of excitement, anxiety, anger, and sexual arousal. For this reason, researchers may use multiple measures of emotion, assessing self-reports of emotion while physiological responses are being recorded. Another way of assessing emotions is by direct observation of overt behavior. Approach behavior can indicate acceptance, and avoidance behavior can reflect fear or disgust. In addition, facial expressions have been used to assess various emotional states.

The experience of emotion involves psychological, physiological, and behavioral components. Different emotions are assessed using a variety of questionnaires, physiological indices, and observational methods. The study of emotion has far-reaching implications for the understanding of human functioning and has important applications in many fields of psychology.

Applications

When researchers developed means for measuring visceral responses and discovered that these responses are associated with emotions, it was not long before the question arose, "Is it possible to detect when someone is lying?" The use of a polygraph to detect lying is based on the assumption that people will feel anxious or guilty when asked a question that has personal, emotional significance to past deeds. The polygraph tester measures and compares physiological responses to both control questions and relevant questions to infer lying. For example, suppose someone is suspected of murdering John Smith on May 16. The tester may ask the following control question: "Have you ever hurt someone?" Since everyone has hurt someone at one time or another, and probably feels guilty about it, some level of emotional response will be registered as changes in heart rate and respiration. The relevant question is "Did you kill John Smith on May 16?" Supposedly, the innocent person will show a greater emotional response to the control question than the relevant question. The perpetrator of the crime should show a greater emotional response to the relevant question because of its extreme emotional significance.

The use of polygraph testing is surrounded by controversy. Although some liars can be detected, what if a perpetrator does not feel guilty about the crime—or does not believe that the polygraph can measure lying? These people will not show the expected response to the critical questions about the crime. In addition, research has shown that some innocent people will become so anxious when asked "relevant" questions that they are mistakenly viewed as guilty. The American Psychological Association has expressed grave concern over the validity of polygraph testing. The U.S. Congress has outlawed the use of preemployment testing to predict who might, for example, steal inventory. Despite the reservations of the American Psychological Association, however, security agencies and defense industries are allowed to use polygraph testing.

The development of theories of emotion and of methods for measuring emotions has wide application in the field of clinical psychology. Many psychological disorders are defined by emotional problems. People with phobias exhibit excessive anxiety in situations that offer little or no possibility of harm. Strong fears of water, heights, insects, closed spaces, flying, and social situations are common examples of phobias. Theories of emotion provide a framework within which clinicians can understand the development of phobias. Measures of anxiety can be used to help diagnose those people who suffer from phobias.

Depression is another example of a psychological disorder that has a strong emotional component. Twenty percent of females and 10 percent of males will experience a major depression at some time in their lives. This complex disorder is manifested by distorted thinking (such as self-critical thinking), physical difficulties (such as fatigue), and an array of emotions. Some of the emotional symptoms of depression include sadness, anxiety, and guilt. Thus, when psychologists assess the emotional aspects of depression, they use questionnaires that include items that address several different emotions.

Not only does the study of emotion help psychologists to understand psychological disorders, but methods of treatment also have been developed based on the understanding of emotion. For example, psychological research has shown that emotional responses, such as anxiety, can be learned. Consequently, treatment strategies have been developed to help people "unlearn" their anxiety reactions. As a result, many people who suffer from simple phobias can be effectively treated in a short period of time. Theories of emotion that examine the relation between thinking and emotion have led to therapies to alleviate depression. Aaron Beck has shown that the sadness, anxiety, and guilt that accompany depression can be treated by helping people change their styles of thinking.

Another topic area within clinical psychology that has benefited by the increasing understanding of emotion is psychosomatic disorders. A psychosomatic disorder (also called a psychophysiological disorder) is an abnormal physical condition brought about by chronic negative emotions. Ulcers, hypertension, headaches, and arthritis are examples of conditions that can be brought about or worsened by negative emotions. The emotions that are most often implicated in the development of psychosomatic disorders are anger and anxiety. For example, researchers have discovered that prolonged anxiety induced by internal conflict can cause ulcers in susceptible people. In addition, researchers now have evidence that chronic hostility is a risk factor for the development of heart disease.

Social psychologists study the influence of social factors on behavior. Theories of emotion have been a focus of social psychologists because one's experience of emotion is in part determined by the immediate situation, and the immediate situation often includes the behavior of others. Indeed, Stanley Schachter, a social psychologist, is responsible for the development of a theory of emotion that underscores the importance of one's cognitive appraisal of the social context in determining what emotion one experiences. For example, when people experience physiological arousal, their own emotional experience will most likely be consistent with their interpretation of the social context. If they are with a happy person, they will experience happiness; if they are in the presence of an angry person, they will experience anger. Theories of emotion have increased understanding of many social phenomena, such as aggression and interpersonal attraction.

Context

Emotions and their expression have been of interest to philosophers and theologians for more than two thousand years. In the fifth century B.C., the Greek physician Hippocrates classified people on the basis of emotional temperament. The view that people differ in temperament remains today. Arnold Buss and Robert Plomin have hypothesized that newborns differ in their susceptibility to distress, fear, and anger. Everyday descriptions of people as "happy-go-lucky," "stoic," and "volatile" represent the tendency to group people according to characteristic styles of emotional expression. Clinical psychologists speak of the "hysterical personality" as exhibiting excessive emotional lability and the "schizoid personality" as showing emotional indifference toward others. Thus, for centuries, philosophers and psychologists have recognized the importance of understanding personality differences based on the type and degree of emotional expression.

Theologians have traditionally approached emotion as representing the dark side of human nature. What elevates humans above other animals has been thought to be the capacity to overcome passion with reason. Even this seemingly archaic view of emotion has its counterpart in modern psychology. Psychoanalysts help people gain control of their feelings through understanding the unconscious roots of their emotions. Cognitive therapists attempt to alleviate emotional dysfunctions by teaching clients to "think more rationally."

The modern era of research on emotion can be traced to Charles Darwin's 1872 book, *The Expression of the Emotions in Man and Animals*. Darwin believed that emotional displays evolved as a means of communication and had adaptive significance for the survival of the species. Indeed, there is some scientific support for the assertion that emotional expressions are basic biological responses: Newborn infants show expressions of emotions that closely match the expressions of adults; all infants, including those born deaf and blind, exhibit similar facial expressions in similar situations; very young babies can tell the difference between different emotional expressions; and there is considerable similarity in the expression of emotions across diverse cultures.

In the last half of the twentieth century, psychologists have made important advances in formulating theories of emotions and devising assessment instruments to measure emotions. Scientists have arrived at the point where they recognize many of the fundamental aspects of emotion: the nervous system, thought, behavior, and the immediate situation. The challenge for the future is to map the intricate interplay among these variables and achieve a thorough understanding of this basic facet of human functioning.

Bibliography

Arnold, Madga B., ed. *The Nature of Emotion*. Harmondsworth, Middlesex, England: Penguin Books, 1968. Reprints a number of classic articles published before 1960. Valuable for gaining insight into the historical sweep of the topic of emotion. Some chapters are largely philosophical or theoretical, yet not too difficult to understand. Other chapters require some knowledge of physiology. This volume is not an introductory treatment of theories of emotion, and thus should be consulted only after gaining a knowledge base of the field.

Barlow, David H. *Anxiety and Its Disorders*. New York: Guilford Press, 1988. In the early part of the book, the author reviews basic aspects of emotion. The remainder is devoted to the emotion of anxiety, and how anxiety forms the basis of many clinical disorders. Some of the disorders addressed are panic disorder, obsessive-compulsive disorder, phobias, and post-traumatic stress disorder. A very comprehensive treatment of anxiety disorders. Barlow takes a strong research orientation and presents the material at a college level.

Bernstein, Douglas A., E. F. Roy, Thomas K. Srull, and D. C. Wickens. *Psychology*. 2d ed. New York: Houghton Mifflin, 1991. Chapter 12 presents an introduction to the topic of emotion. Covers a wide range of areas: definition of emotion, physiology of emotion, major theories, social aspects of emotion, and facial expressions. The authors do not assume that the reader has any background in psychology, and they write in a clear, concise manner, providing interesting examples and graphics. Indeed, most college textbooks that cover an introduction to psychology have a chapter on emotion.

Corcoran, Kevin J., and Joel Fischer. *Measures for Clinical Practice: A Sourcebook*. New York: Free Press, 1987. Reprints more than one hundred self-report assessment instruments. Among them are numerous measures of various emotions and psychological problems in which emotional dysfunction is prominent; there are instruments to measure anxiety, guilt, anger, hostility, depression, stress, and mood. An excellent source for learning how researchers measure emotions, and can be used should one want to conduct a study. Bear in mind, however, that this book does not include some of the most commonly used questionnaires for measuring emotions.

Goleman, Daniel. *Emotional Intelligence*. New York: Bantam Books, 1995.

Ono, Taketoshi. *Perception, Memory, and Emotion: Frontiers in Neuroscience*. New York: Elsevier Science, 1996.

Laurence Grimm

See also:

Emotion, Development of, 229; Emotion, Functions of, 235.

THE ENDOCRINE SYSTEM

Type of psychology: Biological bases of behavior
Field of study: Endocrine system

Behavior, by definition, includes physiological events which are responses to internal and external stimuli; the endocrine system, through the action of hormones and in cooperation with the nervous system, plays a necessary role in bringing about these reactions in animals and humans.

Principal terms

ADRENAL GLANDS: endocrine glands located above the kidney consisting of a medulla and cortex area, each of which is under pituitary control and which functions in response to stress

BEHAVIOR: a physiological response made by an organism to internal or external stimuli

BIOPSYCHOLOGY: a branch of psychology that uses data from biology, endocrinology, genetics, and neuroscience in order to understand the mechanisms of behavior

ENDOCRINE SYSTEM: a series of ductless glands that secrete chemicals called hormones

ETHOLOGY: a science that studies animal behavior

HORMONE: a chemical messenger secreted by endocrine tissue that causes biochemical reactions

HYPOTHALAMUS: the area of the brain that interacts with the pituitary gland in executing control over the physiology of the body

PITUITARY: an endocrine gland located in the brain that controls several other endocrines and that cooperates with the hypothalamus of the nervous system in controlling physiology

Overview

A subdivision of biopsychology known as physiological psychology studies animal and human responses to internal and external stimuli. Much of the research in physiological psychology has focused on the role of the nervous system in determining behavior. As more was learned about nervous system activities and resulting behaviors, it was realized that the nervous system does not act independently of the endocrine system: The systems cooperate in providing the biological bases for behavior.

The endocrine system essentially consists of ductless glands that produce chemical substances called hormones. The hormones elicit physiological reactions, either locally or at some distant target site. When acting at a distance, the hormones travel to the site by way of the circulatory system.

Among most invertebrates, animals without backbones, endocrine glands are not in evidence. Specialized cells known as neurosecretory cells serve as endocrine tissue. The cells, which resemble the neuron or functional cell of the nervous system, are hormone producers. In invertebrate animals such as the hydra and planaria, the secretions (hormones) of the neurosecretory cells seem to influence growth and may be the underlying cause of the tremendous powers of regeneration possessed by the animals. There are indications that the development of sexuality, the laying of eggs, and the release of sperm may be under hormonal control. Attempts to establish the link between hormones and invertebrate behavior when the hormones are produced by neurosecretory cells have inherent problems. A common method of studying hormone influence involves removal of the secreting organ, which causes a hormone deficit. Changes in physiology and/or behavior are observed. Hormone is then provided to the animal to see if the original condition can be restored. Utilization of this method is complicated by the difficulty in removing all the functioning neurosecretory cells. In addition, the cells regenerate rapidly. This prevents an accurate assessment of the effects of hormone deficit.

Hormone effects are observable and measurable in the more developed invertebrates such as the *Arthropoda*. Studies carried out on insects and crustaceans indicate the presence of both neurosecretory cells and endocrine glands. Among the behaviors and activities which are controlled by the hormones released from either the cells or the glands are molting, sexual differentiation, sexual behavior, water balance, and diapause. Since arthropods are encased in an outer skeletal structure, it is necessary for the animals to shed their outer structure in order to grow. During the growth years, the animals go through cycles of shedding the outer skeleton or molting, growing, and reforming an outer coat. There is evidence that insects are under hormonal control when they enter a state of diapause, or arrested behavior in adverse times.

All vertebrates, animals with backbones, have a well-developed and highly organized endocrine system. The system consists of the following glands: the pituitary, the pineal, the thyroid, the thymus, the pancreas, a pair of adrenals (each adrenal actually acts as two glands—the adrenal cortex produces unique hormones and functions independently of the adrenal medulla), a pair of parathyroids, and a pair of ovaries or testes. Endocrine tissue in the gastrointestinal tract readies the system for the digestive process. During a pregnancy, the placental tissue assumes an endocrine function. Although the kidneys do not produce a hormone directly, they release an enzyme which converts a blood protein into a hormone that stimulates red blood cell production.

All vertebrates have a pituitary. The pituitary is a small, round organ found at the base of the brain. This major endocrine gland interacts with the hypothalamus of the nervous system. Together they control behavior. The hypothalamus is kept aware of physiological events in the body by monitoring the composition of the blood. In turn, the hypothalamus signals the pituitary by either nerve impulse or chemical messenger. The pituitary responds by releasing or ceasing to release hormones which will have a direct effect on physiology or will stimulate other endocrines to release their hormones in order to alter the physiological event and influence behavior. The endocrine system exerts its effects on a biochemical level.

The human endocrine system is typical of vertebrate endocrine systems and their effect on behavior, although certain hormones may have a more pronounced and obvious effect in other vertebrates. For example, melanocyte-stimulating hormone, which is generated by the anterior lobe of the pituitary, greatly increases skin pigmentation in amphibians. This creates a protective coloration. In humans, the darkening effect is not achieved unless excessive hormone is administered. The protective function is not apparent. There are enough similarities among human and animal endocrine functions and effects, however, to warrant the use of data from both ethology and human behavioral studies in determining the biological bases for behavior.

Applications

The influence of the endocrine system on behavior has been studied on many levels. Much of the work has been done on animals; laboratory rats have been the most frequently used subjects. There is, however, a growing body of information on hormonal effects on a variety of human behaviors, including reproductive and developmental behavior, reaction to stress, learning, and memory. Studies carried out in reproductive and developmental biology on both animal and human subjects have substantiated the belief that hormones influence mating behavior, developmental events including sexual differentiation, and female and male sexuality.

Castration experiments have linked the testes with a male mating behavior pattern in animals. The sexually active adult male animal aggressively seeks and attempts to mount the female whether she is receptive or not. The castrated male retains the ability to mount and impregnate a female but loses the aggressiveness and persistent pursuit of females. The male may assume the more submissive, female behavior and even engage in homosexual encounters. Normally, the release of reproductive hormones in the male is noncyclic, whereas in the female, it is cyclic. Castrated animals begin to exhibit the female, cyclic-pattern hormone release. The hormonal influence is confirmed by administering androgens (male hormones) to the castrated animals. Male mating behavior and the noncyclic release of hormones returns.

The presence of male hormones has an effect on the female cycle and sexual receptivity. Pheromones are substances secreted on the body of one individual which influence the behavior of another. These chemical messengers function during mate attraction, territoriality, and episodes of fear. Their existence and functions are well documented throughout the animal kingdom, especially among insects and mammals. In experiments using rats, it was shown that the pheromones act in conjunction with male hormones in bringing the female to a state of receptivity. The urine of noncastrated male rats contains androgens. When a male rat is introduced into a cage of sexually inactive females, the male sends off chemical signals by way of pheromones and the androgen-containing urine. The result is the accelerated onset of estrus, or sexual receptivity, on the part of the females. Castrated males produce pheromones but do not have androgens in the urine. When castrated males are introduced into a cage of inactive females, the estrous cycle is not affected.

Female mammals, with the exception of monkeys, apes, and humans, experience a reproductive cycle known as estrus. Under hormonal control, the female is receptive to the male once or twice a year, when her eggs are available for fertilization. This period of receptivity is known as the estrous phase, or heat. Research shows that the particular female hormone which induces estrus is progesterone.

The work done by researchers in developing contraceptives clarified the role of hormones in the functioning of the human female reproductive system. The system operates in a monthly cycle during which ovarian and uterine changes occur under hormonal control. These hormones do not affect the human female's receptivity, which is not limited to fertile periods.

Testosterone derivatives known as anabolic steroids are illegally used by some athletes in an attempt to increase muscularity, strength, and performance. While both sexes do experience the desired effects, long-term, high dosage usage has undesirable consequences. This is particularly true in the female, who begins to exhibit a deepening of the voice, a male body shape, and increased body and facial hair. Both males and females can become sterile. Psychotic behaviors such as depression and anger have been recorded.

Developmental biologists indicate that hormones exert their influence as early as six or seven weeks into embryonic development. At this point, undifferentiated tissue with the potential of developing into either a female or a male reproductive system will develop into a male system in the presence of testosterone, and into a female system in its absence. There is some evidence that the embryonic hormones have an effect on the developing brain, producing either a male or female brain. Functionally, this may account for the cyclic activity of female reproductive hormones and the noncyclic activity of the male. A few anatomical differences between male and female brains have been observed in both rats and humans. In the hypothalamus of the brain, there are cell bodies called nuclei. In rats and in humans, these nuclei are larger in males than in females.

Learning and memory can be experimentally affected by hormones. Experiments reveal that chemicals which resemble adrenocorticotropic hormone (ACTH) can extend the memory time of rats. Rats, stimulated by electric shock and provided with an avoidance possibility such as moving into another chamber of a cage or climbing a pole in the center of the cage, were administered ACTH-like molecules. The treated rats were able to remember the appropriate reaction to the stimulus for a longer period of time. In other experiments, rats in a maze were administered vasopressin, a posterior pituitary hormone, which increased their frequency in selecting the correct pathway through the maze.

The effect of vasopressin on human memory is not as clearly defined. There have been positive results with schizophrenic patients and patients with alcohol-induced amnesia. In these cases, memory has been enhanced to a limited degree. There is no solid evidence that learning and memory in humans will be greatly improved by the administration of vasopressin. Areas such as eating disorders, psychotic behavior, hormone therapy, behavior modification, and biological clocks and rhythms challenge the physiological psychologist to further research to test hormonal influences.

Context

Curiosity about behavior, both animal and human, is of long standing. The suspicion that substances in the body contribute to behavior also has a long history. During the fifth century B.C., Hippocrates suggested, in his humoral theory, that personality was determined by four body fluids: phlegm, black bile, yellow bile, and blood. The dominance of one or another of the fluids was associated with a behavior pattern. A proportionate distribution of the fluids resulted in a balanced personality. This theory has contributed terms such as phlegmatic, sanguine, bilious, and good- or bad-humored to describe personality types and states of mind.

Aristotle (384-322 B.C.) is reported to have performed castration experiments on both fowl and men in order to alter behavior. He believed that something produced by the testes caused male behavior. Several nineteenth century researchers continued the study of the connection between the testes and male reproductive behavior. In 1849, Arnold Adolphe Berthold initiated a series of experiments on cockerels. He removed the testes from six birds and noted their loss of "male" behavior. Testes were transplanted into the abdomen of half the castrated birds. Successful transplantation restored the typical male crowing and combativeness.

During the late nineteenth and early twentieth centuries, sciences became more organized. Interest in behavior and its causes continued. The science of ethology, which focuses on animal behavior, came into existence. In the early 1900's, John B. Watson founded a branch of psychology that became known as behavior science. This area of psychology concentrated on human behavioral studies. Eventually, ethology and behavior science contributed to a new branch of psychology, biopsychology, which incorporates and applies data from neuroscience, genetics, endocrinology, and physiology in the quest for biological explanations of behavior. Biopsychology embraces several subdivisions. Physiological psychology focuses on nervous system and endocrine system research. Psychopharmacology specializes in the effects of drugs on the nervous system and ultimately on behavior. The development of therapeutic drugs is a goal of this discipline. The neuropsychologist studies the effects of brain damage on behavior. Psychophysiology differs from physiological psychology in that the psychophysiologist uses only human subjects while the physiological psychologist experiments on laboratory animals, especially rats.

Early research in physiological psychology focused on the nervous system, but it soon became evident that the endocrine system also influenced behavior and that the effects of the two systems were interrelated contributors to behavior. Hans Selye, a Canadian scientist, proposed a direct connection between the endocrine system and behavior. In 1946, he described physiological events that were triggered by stress. This set of bodily changes became known as the general adaptation syndrome. The syndrome involved the mobilization of the autonomic nervous system, the adrenal glands, and the anterior lobe of the pituitary.

As research continued, data on the role of the endocrine system in determining behavior began to accumulate. Researchers continue to look to the endocrine system to provide clues about the causes of psychiatric diseases and the efficacy of hormone therapy in treating the diseases, as well as in altering behavior patterns.

Bibliography

Bioscience 33 (October, 1983). The entire issue is devoted to the effects of hormones on behavior. Includes an article on invertebrates in general, followed by articles on fish through primates. Written in nonesoteric language.

Brennan, James F. *History and Systems of Psychology*. Englewood Cliffs, N.J.: Prentice-Hall, 1982. Readable presentation of the history and development of psychology. Covers the highlights of the discipline from the time of ancient Greece up to the early 1980's. Good background material for those not well grounded in psychology, and interesting reading for those with a historical leaning.

Donovan, Bernard T. *Hormones and Human Behavior*. Cambridge, England: Cambridge University Press, 1985. An excellent compilation of the information available on hormones and behavior up to 1985. Uses technical language, but one who reads on a high-school level and has had some exposure to science will find the book informative and interesting. Focuses on the pituitary, the gonads, and the adrenals, and their effect on human behavior.

Drickamer, Lee C., and Stephen H. Vessey. *Animal Behavior*. 3d ed. Dubuque, Iowa: Wm. C. Brown, 1991. Intended for undergraduate students who are interested in animal behavior. Of particular interest is chapter 10, which deals with hormones and behavior.

Presents a clear explanation of the endocrine system and the mechanism of hormone action. Avoids highly technical language. The effect of hormones on behavior of invertebrates and vertebrates is well illustrated with many interesting examples from the animal world.

Highnam, Kenneth Charles, and Leonard Hill. *The Comparative Endocrinology of the Invertebrates*. New York: American Elsevier, 1969. The various types of invertebrate endocrine systems are described in this book. Although the book was published in 1969, it is a valuable source of information, especially on the insect and crustacean hormones. Technical language is used but is clearly explained in layperson's terms. Drawings and charts contribute to the understanding of the material.

Johnson, Michael L., and Johannes D. Veldhuis, eds. *Quantitative Neuroendocrinology*. San Diego, Calif.: Academic Press, 1995.

Pinel, John P. J. *Biopsychology*. Boston: Allyn & Bacon, 1990. A textbook intended for use by the undergraduate college student. There are two chapters of particular interest. Chapter 1 defines the position of biopsychology within the larger field of psychology, delineates the subdivisions of biopsychology, and describes the type of research carried out in each area. An account of research involving the human reproductive hormones and their effects is found in chapter 10. Both chapters are interesting and well written. The author makes use of good examples, drawings, and charts.

Rosemary Scheirer

See also:

The Autonomic Nervous System, 88; The Central and Peripheral Nervous Systems, 115; The Cerebral Cortex, 121; Reflexes, 507.

GENDER-IDENTITY FORMATION

Type of psychology: Developmental psychology
Fields of study: Cognitive development; infancy and childhood

Gender-identity formation refers to the complex processes through which young children come to incorporate their gender into their behavior, attitudes, and self-understanding. This includes the development of an inner sense of one's femaleness or maleness; the acquisition of knowledge about cultural expectations for females and males; and the development of attitudes, interests, and behavior that reflect these expectations.

Principal terms

GENDER CONSTANCY: the understanding that gender is a permanent characteristic of the self and other people

GENDER IDENTITY: a child's accurate labeling of himself or herself by gender; also, a person's inner sense of femaleness or maleness

GENDER SCHEMA: a general knowledge framework that organizes information and guides perceptions related to males and females

SEX ROLE: the set of expectations about a person's attitudes and behavior that is culturally assigned based on one's gender

SEX-ROLE SOCIALIZATION: the process of teaching children to conform to gender-linked social rules and expectations

SEX TYPING: the process of acquiring traits, attitudes, and behaviors seen culturally as appropriate for members of one's gender; gender-role acquisition

Overview

The first question that is usually asked about a newborn baby is whether it is a boy or a girl. The single fact of the child's gender has enormous implications for the course of his or her entire life. Gender-identity formation refers to the complex processes through which children incorporate the biological and social fact of their gender into their behavior, attitudes, and self-understanding.

This area includes ideas about two major interrelated processes: gender-identity development and sex typing. The term "gender-identity development," used in its narrower sense, refers to the process through which children come to label themselves cognitively as boys or girls and to have an inner sense of themselves as male or female. "Sex typing," also called gender-role acquisition, refers to the processes through which children learn what is expected of members of their gender and come to exhibit primarily those personality traits, behaviors, interests, and attitudes.

Social-learning theorists such as Walter Mischel have described mechanisms of learning through which children come to exhibit sex-typed behavior. Boys and girls often behave differently because they are rewarded and punished for different behaviors. In other words, they receive different conditioning. In addition, children's behavior becomes sex typed because children observe other males and females regularly behaving differently according to their gender, and they imitate or model this behavior.

Parents are especially important in the process of learning one's gender role, both as models for gender-appropriate behavior and as sources of rewards or reinforcement. Because parents become associated with positive experiences (such as being fed and comforted) early in life, children learn to look to them and other adults for rewards. Parents and other adults such as teachers often react differentially to gender-typed behaviors, rewarding gender-appropriate behavior (for example, giving praise or attention) and punishing gender-inappropriate behavior (for example, frowning, ignoring, or reprimanding).

As children become more involved with their peers (children their own age), they begin to influence one another's behavior, often strongly reinforcing traditional gender roles. The fact that children are usually given different toys and different areas in which to play based on their gender is also important. Girls are given opportunities to learn different behaviors from those of boys (for example, girls learn nurturing behavior through playing with dolls) because they are exposed to different experiences.

Using what is called a cognitive developmental perspective, Lawrence Kohlberg described developmental changes in children's understanding of gender concepts. These changes parallel the broad developmental changes in the way children's thinking is organized, first described by Jean Piaget and Barbel Inhelder. Children mature naturally through stages of more and more complex cognitive organization. In the area of understanding gender, the first stage is the acquisition of a rudimentary gender identity, the ability to categorize oneself correctly as a boy or a girl.

Children are able to apply gender labels to themselves correctly by about age three. At this stage, young children base gender labeling on differences in easily observable characteristics such as hairstyle and clothing, and they do not grasp the importance of genital differences in determining gender. As children's thinking about the physical world becomes more complex, so does their understanding of gender. Gradually, by about age seven, children enter a second stage and acquire the concept known as gender constancy.

Gender constancy refers to the understanding that gender is a stable characteristic that cannot change over time and that is not altered by superficial physical transformations such as wearing a dress or cutting one's hair. As children come to see gender as a stable, important characteristic of themselves and other people, they begin to use the concept consistently to organize social information. They learn societal expectations for members of each gender by watching the actions of the people around them.

Kohlberg proposed that children use their developing knowledge of cultural gender expectations to teach themselves to adopt culturally defined gender roles (self-socialization). He argued that children acquire a strong motive to conform to gender roles because of their need for self-consistency and self-esteem. A young boy says to himself, "I am a boy, not a girl; I want to do boy things, play with boy toys, and wear boy clothes."

Children hold more rigid gender stereotypes before they acquire gender constancy (ages two through seven); once gender constancy is achieved, they become more flexible in their adherence to gender roles. As children enter adolescence, their thinking about the world again enters a new stage of development, becoming even more complex and less rigid. As a result, they may be able to achieve what Joseph Pleck has called "sex-role transcendence" and to choose their interests and behaviors somewhat independent of cultural expectations.

Gender-schema theory is a way of explaining gender-identity formation, which is closely related to the cognitive developmental approach. The concept of a schema or a general knowledge framework comes from the field of cognitive psychology. Sandra Bem proposed that each person develops a set of gender-linked associations, or a gender schema, as part of a personal knowledge structure. This gender schema filters and interprets new information, and as a result, people have a basic predisposition to process information on the basis of gender. People tend to dichotomize objects and attributes on the basis of gender, even including things such as colors, which have no relevance to biological sex.

Bem proposed that sex typing develops as children learn the content of society's gender schema and as they begin to link that schema to their self-concept or view of themselves. Individuals vary in the degree to which the gender schema is central to their self-concept; it is central to the self-concept of highly sex-typed individuals (traditionally masculine males or traditionally feminine females).

Applications

Ideas about gender-identity formation have important implications for child rearing and education. Most parents want to help their child identify with and feel positive about his or her own gender. Those few children who fail to develop a clear inner sense of themselves as male or female that is consistent with their biological sex may have significant social adjustment difficulties; they are sometimes given psychological treatment for a condition called "gender-identity disorder." Adults who continue to have a gender identity that is inconsistent with their biological sex desire surgery and hormonal treatments to change their sex. This rare condition is called transsexualism, and it is more common among biological males than females. Although many people have interests, personality characteristics, or sexual preferences commonly associated with the other gender, they are not transsexuals; their inner sense of their gender is consistent with their biological sex.

Often, parents and educators want to help children avoid becoming strongly sex typed. They do not want children's options for activities, interests, and aspirations to be limited to those traditionally associated with their gender. Adopting strongly sex-typed interests may be especially problematic for girls, because the traditional female role and the qualities associated with it (that is, emotionality, nurturance, and dependence) tend to be devalued in American culture. Traditionally masculine interests and behaviors are usually tolerated in girls before puberty; it is all right to be a "tomboy." Traditionally feminine interests and behaviors, however, tend to be discouraged in boys; it is not acceptable to be a "sissy."

Considerable research has focused on whether and how socializing agents, including parents, teachers, peers, and media such as children's books and television, reinforce gender stereotypes and teach children to exhibit sex-typed behaviors. Researchers have been concerned both with how gender roles are modeled for children and with how sex-typed behavior is rewarded. A study by Lisa Serbin and her colleagues is an example. These researchers observed teachers' interactions with children in a preschool setting and recorded their observations in a standardized way. They found that teachers gave more attention to girls when they were physically close to them than when they were farther away; however, teachers' attention to boys did not vary with the child's proximity. This finding suggests that teachers reinforce girls more than boys for "dependent" behavior without necessarily meaning to do so.

Parents often report that they try to treat their children the same regardless of their gender. Many of the most powerful influences parents exert result from behaviors of which they are probably unaware. Research studies have shown that parents consistently interact differently with male and female children in areas such as engaging in gross motor play (for example, running, jumping, throwing), encouraging children's sex-typed play (particularly, discouraging doll-play among boys), demanding effort and giving help with problem-solving tasks, and allowing children to have independence and freedom from supervision.

Children's peers have been shown to play an important role in sex-role socialization. Particularly in early childhood, when children's gender concepts tend to be far more rigid than those of adults, peers may be the source of misinformation (for example, "girls can't be doctors; girls have to be nurses") and of strong sanctions against behavior that is inconsistent with one's gender role.

Laboratory studies have shown that exposure to gender stereotypes in books and on television tends to have a measurable effect on children's sex-typed behavior. For example, children are more likely to play with a "gender-inappropriate" toy after reading a story in which a child of their gender played with that toy. In addition, these media may be important in the development of a child's gender schema because they provide a rich network of information and associations related to gender. Extensive studies of the gender-related content of children's books and children's television were conducted in the 1970's, and this led to reform efforts by some textbook publishers and television producers.

One influential study by a group called Women on Words and Images analyzed the contents of 134 grade-school readers and found gender-stereotypic portrayals of male and female characters, gender-stereotypic themes, and male dominance to be the rule. Boys outnumbered girls as major characters by five to two; in 2,760 stories examined, only three mothers were shown working outside the home. Systematic studies of children's television have produced similar results.

Context

Psychologists have been interested in gender-identity formation since the work of Sigmund Freud and other early theorists in the beginning of the twentieth century. Since the early 1970's, however, there has been a major shift in thinking about this topic, largely as a result of the women's movement. Early work in this area considered sex typing to be a healthy and desirable goal for children. Since the 1970's, much research has been based on the assumption that rigid adherence to traditional gender roles is restrictive and undesirable.

Freud's theory of psychosexual development was the first to attempt to explain gender-identity formation. Freud believed that sex-typed behavior results primarily from girls identifying with (wanting to be like) their mothers and boys identifying with their fathers; however, he believed that during infancy both boys and girls form strong sexual feelings for their mothers and identify with them. Thus, Freud tried to explain how boys come to identify with their fathers and how girls transfer their sexual feelings to their fathers.

Freud believed that the discovery that girls and women do not have penises leads the three- to five-year-old boy to develop great fear that he will lose his own penis (castration anxiety). As a result, the boy begins to identify with his father out of fear that the father will take away the penis. He gives up his identification with his mother and suppresses his sexual feelings toward her. For a little girl, the same discovery leads to penis envy and to blaming the mother for her lack of this desired organ. Because of her disappointment, she transfers her sexual feelings from her mother to her father, and she fantasizes that her father will give her a penis substitute—a baby.

Freud's theory was an important inspiration for much of the work done on gender identity prior to the late 1960's. Since that time, however, developmental psychologists have not often used Freud's theory because most of its concepts rely on the idea of unconscious forces that cannot be evaluated scientifically.

Freud's idea that "anatomy is destiny"—that profound psychological differences between the sexes are inevitable—has met with strong criticism with the rise of the women's movement. The issue of the relative importance of biological, genetic factors (or "nature") compared with experiential, social factors (or "nurture") in gender-identity formation has been a major source of controversy in psychology. Most psychologists acknowledge a role for both nature and nuture in forming differences in the behavior of boys and girls. Psychologists are interested in understanding how inborn capacities (such as cognitive organization) interact with environmental experiences in forming a person's identity as a male or a female.

The twentieth century has experienced a great upheaval in thinking about gender roles, and this has been mirrored by changes in psychological research and theory about gender. The growing scientific understanding of gender identity may help to form future societal attitudes as well as being formed by them.

Bibliography

Bem, Sandra L. "Gender Schema Theory and Its Implications for Child Development: Raising Gender-Aschematic Children in a Gender-Schematic Society." *Signs* 8, no. 4 (1983): 598-616. Introduction to gender-schema for nonpsychologists. Provides an in-depth discussion of this approach to gender-identity formation and compares it to other major psychological theories. Bem also suggests practical applications of her perspective to child rearing.

Brooks-Gunn, Jeanne, and Wendy Schempp Matthews. *He and She: How Children Develop Their Sex-Role Identity*. Englewood Cliffs, N.J.: Prentice-Hall, 1979. Provides a clear, thorough description of children's sex-role development for parents, educators, and students. Also provides research evidence and anecdotal examples describing sex-role acquisition from the prenatal period through adolescence. A good, usable reference for high school students.

Burke, Phyllis. *Gender Shock: Exploding the Myths of Male and Female*. New York: Doubleday & Company, 1996.

Hughes, Fergus, and Lloyd Noppe. "Gender Roles and Gender Differences." In *Human Development Across the Life Span*. St. Paul, Minn.: West, 1985. Presents an overview of gender-identity formation across the entire life span, including information about gender roles in old age. Provides extensive information about gender from a developmental perspective. Easily accessible to beginning college students.

Huston, A. C. "Sex-Typing." In *Handbook of Child Psychology*, edited by Paul H. Mussen. Vol. 4, edited by E. Mavis Hetherington. 4th ed. New York: John Wiley & Sons, 1983. Relatively technical, but provides a masterful organization and in-depth analysis of theory and research relevant to sex typing. Also includes a long and thorough bibliography.

Lieblich, Amia, and Ruthellen Josselson, eds. *Exploring Identity and Gender*. Thousand Oaks, Calif.: Sage Publications, 1994.

Lott, Bernice E. *Women's Lives: Themes and Variations in Gender Learning*. Monterey, Calif.: Brooks/Cole, 1987. Frequently used textbook for college classes on the psychology of women. Chapters 3 and 4 present an accessible, entertaining account of gender-identity formation from a social-learning perspective, integrating research evidence. Other chapters explore implications of gender-role acquisition for women in adult life. Helpful for those who are interested in gender-related topics in psychology.

Ruble, D. N. "Sex-Role Development." In *Developmental Psychology: An Advanced Textbook*, edited by Marc H. Bornstein and Michael E. Lamb. Hillsdale, N.J.: Lawrence Erlbaum, 1984. Presents a comprehensive discussion of gender-identity formation and related issues in developmental psychology. Includes research evidence for sex differences in behavior and biological, social, and cognitive factors in sex-role development. Clearly written, scholarly in tone, and presupposes some prior familiarity with the field.

Lesley A. Slavin

See also:

Adolescence: Sexuality, 19; Attachment and Bonding in Infancy and Childhood, 71; Cognitive Development Theory: Jean Piaget, 135; Homosexuality, 278; Moral Development, 399; Motor Development, 410.

GENERATIVITY IN ADULTHOOD

Type of psychology: Developmental psychology
Field of study: Adulthood

Generativity describes the task of Erik Erikson's seventh stage of the life cycle, which occurs at about age forty. Individuals who have achieved generativity show a concern for the next generation and engage in activities that will leave the world a better place for others. Those who ignore the needs of others and focus on their own needs experience stagnation and meaninglessness.

Principal terms

GENERATIVITY: the need to take care of future generations through the experiences of caring, nurturing, and education

ID: the powerful basic drives (such as the need to express anger) that motivate individuals to behave with little awareness of the reasons for their behavior

IDENTITY: the establishment of a distinctive personality based on the foundation laid in childhood and the expectations associated with reaching adulthood

MIDLIFE TRANSITION: a stage occurring around the age of forty marked by physical changes associated with aging as well as thoughts about death

SELF-ABSORPTION: the inability to show concern for the well-being of others; synonymous with stagnation

SELF-CENTEREDNESS: an attitude in which an individual views the world from his or her own perspective, with a focus on what he or she can get from the world

STAGNATION: a preoccupation with self that may lead to feelings of insecurity and a failure to take responsibility for one's life

SUPEREGO: the collection of moral behaviors learned from parents, teachers, and other authority figures that, without awareness, affect the decisions a person makes

UNCONSCIOUS MOTIVES: forces underlying behavior of which individuals are usually unaware; they are probably the result of the desires of the id and/or the superego

Overview

Caring, nurturing, and educating form the basis for generativity. The need to give something to or leave something for the next generation helps give meaning and purpose to the middle-aged adult. The failure to find effective ways of assisting the next generation may lead to a sense of uselessness and stagnation.

According to Erik Erikson, individuals go through a series of stages as they grow into adulthood and approach their death. By the time adults reach their forties, they have passed through six stages of development centered on the individual's interaction with his or her environment. The seventh stage of the life cycle is called the generativity-versus-stagnation stage. The stage begins at about age forty and lasts ten to thirty years.

The generativity-versus-stagnation stage is characterized by a need to begin a review of one's life, with the focus of that review centering on the care received as a child and the care given to the generation to come. Individuals in this stage are busy with careers, parenting, and the care of their own parents. In a work entitled *Vital Involvement in Old Age* (1986), Erik Erikson, his wife Joan Erikson, and their coauthor Helen Kivnick indicate that individuals in the middle-adulthood period of development have a responsibility for the "maintenance of the world." They must give birth to, rear, and mentor the people who will survive them. They must see to it that social institutions such as schools and governments are strong, and they have an obligation to make others aware of the importance of preserving natural resources and leaving the environment intact for the next generation.

If individuals relinquish their responsibilities to care for the next generation, they are likely to feel stagnated. The stagnated person may eventually experience despair and a sense of meaninglessness. Individuals who do not develop a sense of concern for the next generation are often self-indulgent. They want to take from the world and the people around them what they think they deserve, rather than return what they have gained in wisdom and resources in an effort to preserve the world. The self-indulgent adult will often seek intimate relationships but will not bring to those relationships enough care and concern. Consequently, the self-indulgent adult will fail to find the intimacy he or she seeks or will develop a false sense of intimacy, usually with another person who is unable to convey genuine concern for others.

The stagnated person conveys a sense of self-centeredness. Often, these individuals are obsessed with cleanliness and order. They are rigid and unable to tolerate a change in plans or a new approach to solving problems. They pamper themselves and find little comfort in sharing with others.

Though it might appear that an individual who has reached middle age must either have a caring, giving personality or must be selfish and unconcerned about the welfare of others, it is the case that most people between the ages of forty and sixty have moments of genuine concern for others as well as moments of extreme selfishness. No caring person has achieved generativity without moments of stagnation. Caring individuals may get angry at the many needs put before them. They may, at times, resent the efforts they have put into child rearing, education, or providing for the next generation. There may be times when caring parents, teachers, or artists grow bitter because their efforts go unrewarded or, worse yet, unnoticed. Truly caring persons use these moments of selfishness to evaluate their motives and check their priorities. They often emerge with purer motives and a stronger need to make the world a better place without expecting so much in return. They then move into the next stage of development, integrity versus despair, with a good sense of purpose and meaningfulness.

Finally, it is important to note that not all manifestations of generativity occur through parenting and grandparenting. An individual's concern for the next generation may come through the world of work or through the world of ideas. Erikson has noted that this type of generativity is accompanied by a sense of playfulness and is present in the most creative individuals. People such as Albert Einstein, Mahatma Gandhi, and George Bernard Shaw showed their generativity through their creative and often ingenious approaches to ideas and to the people those ideas touch. What these creative people share is their deep and genuine concern for others. The teacher, the compassionate politician, and the environmental activist also share this concern for others and for the world people share, and in doing so express their generativity.

The generativity-versus-stagnation stage of the life cycle is characterized by the struggle between giving of oneself to the next generation and stealing moments of selfishness in which one keeps one's resources for oneself. The adult who successfully reaches a balance between the need to serve others and the need to serve the self will enter the final stage of development with few regrets.

Applications

Erikson first introduced the concept of generativity in his book *Childhood and Society* (1950). Though first introduced as an approach to understanding continuing development through adulthood, Erikson's ideas have been used by therapists as well as research scientists in a variety of situations to explain a variety of behaviors.

Therapists concerned about the psychological trauma associated with the midlife transition rely heavily on Erikson's theory of adult development to help clients understand and overcome many of their fears and reservations about reaching the midpoint of their lives. Marriage and family counselors often guide their clients through the difficult process of acknowledging that their lives are half over by helping them see where they have come and what they have done to ensure a better life for their children and for the rest of the next generation.

Those individuals seeking counseling during their forties and fifties are often concerned that their lives are meaningless. Therapists, using Erikson's ideas about the need to give something to future generations, can guide their clients toward giving back some of what they have learned from their lives thus far. This giving may take many forms and may include monetary gifts to charities, educational trust funds, or children and grandchildren. The gift of time can be given through established volunteer programs such as Retired Seniors Volunteer Programs, Foster Grandparents, VISTA, or the Peace Corps. Time can be spent serving the needs of local charities or schools. Letters to politicians and other types of political involvement may often help persons who suffer from a lack of meaning find purpose and direction in their lives.

Thus, the therapist confronted with a client who appears apathetic and directionless may rely heavily on the ideas of Erikson to lead the client away from the slow-moving, stale life of self-centeredness to the more exciting, creative world of generativity. In so doing, the therapist may be paving the way for the next stage of the life cycle, in which individuals review their life in an attempt to make peace with themselves before they die. Those individuals who can identify how and where they have created a better world for the next generation will find the integrity they seek and avoid the despair of a life not given to the service of others.

Many other therapeutic applications of Erikson's work are possible. One particularly interesting application involves work with incest victims. According to Sebastian Mudry in an article published in 1986 in the *Journal for Specialists in Group Work*, incest victims have many developmental crises to resolve. Those who reach the generativity-versus-stagnation stage may be able to help the next generation by sharing their experiences with others. They may become professionally trained therapists specializing in the treatment of incest victims. They will most likely work hard to ensure that their own children do not become incest victims. They may volunteer to help other incest victims learn to cope with their victimization. If, however, they are unable to resolve the crisis present during the generativity stage of adult development, they may turn toward nurturing themselves at the expense of others. They may focus on self-preservation, refusing to share with others the many insights they have to offer because of their life experiences. On the other hand, incest victims who have successfully resolved the generativity-versus-stagnation crisis are likely to discover a way to nurture themselves in appropriately selfish ways while simultaneously giving of themselves to others without giving themselves away.

Clearly, the need to achieve some sense of generativity is important, and a failure to do so may send an individual to a therapist for assistance. Therapeutic intervention, however, is not the only use for Erikson's theory. Research scientists, in an effort to determine how well individuals have resolved the conflicts important in each of Erikson's stages of the life cycle, have developed a series of questionnaires. The most commonly used measure is called the Self-Description Questionnaire, developed by Robert Boyd in 1970. Individuals are asked to say whether they are like or not like a person who would make a statement such as "I express the belief that adults should leave teenagers to work out their own problems." While most teenagers would like most adults to agree with such statements, the adult who is concerned about the next generation would most likely say he or she was not like someone who would make such a statement. Those same adults would, however, probably agree with statements such as "I express enjoyment in working with and guiding the development of young people."

Scores on the Self-Description Questionnaire can be used in a variety of ways. Organizations seeking volunteers or employees to work with youth in programs such as the Boy Scouts or Campfire Girls, or as parole officers, might want to screen applicants using the questionnaire before offering them positions.

In a direct application to the Self-Description Questionnaire, the measure has been modified to be used with low-literate adults as a tool to assist in the development of individually tailored educational programs. Robert Boyd and Larry Martin, in an article published in *Adult Education Quarterly* (1984), suggest that teachers of adult students administer the questionnaires to determine why adult learners have returned to school. They argue that understanding the motivation of the students may help create a more enjoyable learning environment. They also suggest that teachers use the questionnaire to identify their own motives for being teachers.

Context

The roots of Erikson's theory of development across the life span are deep and complex. According to Robert Coles, author of *Erik H. Erikson: The Growth of His Work* (1970), the philosopher Søren Kierkegaard had a tremendous influence on Erikson's thinking. Of particular importance were Kierkegaard's ideas about the mind. He claimed that the mind is a battleground in which the selfish desires of the individual fight against the need to survive with other individuals and eventually face a judgmental God who expects selflessness. Clearly, Erikson's work reflects pieces of Kierkegaard's thinking.

Though the philosopher's influence was substantial, the work of Sigmund Freud was instrumental in the development of Erikson's theory. From Freud's theory, Erikson retained the idea of unconscious motives for behavior and the important interplay between one's selfish desires (represented by the id) and one's moral conscience (represented by the superego). Erikson enhanced Freud's work by introducing the need to be aware of the environmental and cultural climate in which an individual develops. He also argued that the culture can determine what needs are most important to the id, as well as the values that will be incorporated into the superego.

The foundations for the proposal of the generativity-versus-stagnation stage of the life cycle can be found in Erikson's extensive observations of American Indian culture as well as veterans returning from World War II. After the war, American society was in need of a review of its goals and what kind of world it was leaving for the next generation. In the postwar nuclear age, Erikson's ideas about leaving the world a better place developed and helped shape a generation of young thinkers who devoured his book *Childhood and Society*. In the book, they found permission to question the direction in which American society was heading and affirmation of the need to attend to one's place in the world order.

The ideas about development set forth in Erikson's work were quietly revolutionary. He was the first to propose that development is a lifelong process culminating only in death. He was the first to incorporate the needs of and important influence of the culture into a theory of development. He was one of the first to expand Freud's clinical observational techniques to normal individuals and to those from a variety of economic and ethnic backgrounds.

Despite these important contributions, Erikson's theory, like most theories of personality, is difficult to test using the well-established methods of science. Some success at defining and measuring identity (Erikson's fifth stage of development) has been achieved. Such accomplishments suggest that future work with each of the remaining seven stages will be fruitful. Therapists and scientists alike are beginning to put Erikson's notion of generativity to the test. The importance of resolving the crisis that occurs during middle adulthood is likely to continue to attract the attention of therapists. In addition, research scientists depend on theories to explain their observations. Erikson's developmental theory provides a fertile ground for testing new ideas and explaining findings, and it is likely to continue to be one of the most important theories of adult development, if for no other reason than that it was the first.

Bibliography

Elkind, David. "Erik Erikson's Eight Ages of Man." In *Readings in Human Development: Contemporary Perspectives*, edited by David Elkind and D. C. Hetzel. New York: Harper & Row, 1977. In an easy-to-read, conversational style, Elkind presents the eight stages of Erikson's developmental theory. Intermingles descriptions of Erikson's theory with pieces of his life story in a manner that brings his work to life. An excellent starting point for a basic understanding of Erikson's developmental theory that also provides good insight into Erikson himself.

Erikson, Erik H. *Childhood and Society*. New York: W. W. Norton, 1950. Lays the foundation for and explains Erikson's theory of development. Erikson's psychological training, his artistic background, and his excellent command of the language are evident throughout the book. The clinical method of study is described and then applied to children and to Native Americans. The concept of the ego is developed and explored through biography and literature as well as clinical case histories. Well written; should be read by anyone with an interest in personality or development.

Evans, Richard I. *Dialogue with Erik Erikson*. New York: Harper & Row, 1967. Reprint. Northvale, N.J.: Jason Aronson, 1995. As the title suggests, this work is the result of several hours of conversation with Erikson, conducted for a film series of discussions with major personality theorists. Has appeal for the novice reader, who will discover Erikson's warmth and humanness in the dialogue. Also has appeal for those familiar with Erikson's theories in that it helps put his ideas into the context of the human condition. Discusses at length the eight stages of development, as well as Erikson's ideas on the application of his theories in the therapeutic environment. Some readers may find the question-and-answer format difficult to follow, but their efforts will be worth the insights they gain from reading the book.

Green, Michael. *Theories of Human Development: A Comparative Approach.* Englewood Cliffs, N.J.: Prentice-Hall, 1989. Crucial for anyone who wants to put Erikson's ideas in the broader context of developmental theories. From the chart comparing seven theorists on sixteen characteristics to the final chapter on the compatibility of the theories, the author encourages a critical comparison of ideas about development. The eight stages of development are described, as are the influences of culture and history on the development of individuals. The book is a textbook designed for courses in development; most readers will find it well written, easy to read, and complete with summaries and thought-provoking questions about human development. Highly recommended for those contemplating future study of developmental theories.

Psychoanalysis and Contemporary Thought 19, no. 2 (1996). A special issue entitled "Ideas and Identities: The Life and Work of Erik Erikson," edited by Robert S. Wallerstein. A variety of insightful perspectives on Erikson; includes a selection of photographs.

Schlein, Stephen, ed. *A Way of Looking at Things: Selected Papers from 1930 to 1980, Erik H. Erikson.* New York: W. W. Norton, 1987. The selected papers of Erikson chosen for this work reflect five decades of thought about development and the human condition. Works included are among the best from Erikson's writings and are organized topically, adding to readability. The chapter entitled "The Human Life Cycle" eloquently describes and provides examples of each of Erikson's proposed developmental stages, complete with graphs and charts to assist the reader in comprehending the theory. Difficult reading for the novice, but well worth the effort. Of special interest are the sketches by Erikson distributed throughout the book.

Tribe, Carol. *Profile of Three Theories: Erikson, Maslow, Piaget.* Dubuque, Iowa: Kendall Hunt Publishing, 1995.

Lori L. Temple

See also:

Aging: Cognitive Changes, 37; Cognitive Development Theory: Jean Piaget, 135; Ego Psychology: Erik Erikson, 223; Identity Crises, 284; Integrity, 315; Intimacy in Adulthood, 340; Moral Development, 399; Trust, Autonomy, Initiative, and Industry, 633.

HABITUATION AND SENSITIZATION

Type of psychology: Learning
Field of study: Biological influences on learning

Habituation is a decrease in behavioral response that results from repeated presentation of a stimulus, whereas sensitization is a heightened behavioral response that results from a stronger stimulus. These two processes differ physiologically and are the most fundamental and widespread forms of learning in the animal kingdom.

Principal terms

ADAPTATION: a heritable characteristic that presumably has developed as a result of natural selection and thus increases an animal's ability to survive and reproduce

INNATE: a term describing any inborn characteristic or behavior that is determined and controlled largely by the genes

LEARNING: a modification in behavior that involves changes in the nervous system that are not caused by fatigue, maturation, or injury

NEURON: a single nerve cell responsible for transmission of a nervous impulse

NEUROTRANSMITTER: a chemical released at the terminal end of one neuron that moves across the synapse and stimulates or inhibits another neuron

STIMULUS: an environmental cue that can potentially modify an animal's behavior via its nervous system

SYNAPSE: the junction between two neurons over which a nervous impulse is chemically transduced

Overview

Habituation and sensitization are the two most fundamental and widespread forms of learning in the animal kingdom. According to ethologists, learning is any modification in behavior that results from previous experience and in some way involves the nervous system, and is not caused by development, fatigue, or injury. More advanced forms of learning include association, perceptual or programmed learning, and insight; the two simplest (nonassociative) forms are habituation and sensitization. These two processes can be characterized as behavioral modifications that result from repeated presentation of simple environmental stimuli.

Habituation is a decrease in response to repeated presentation of a stimulus. One of the most widely cited examples of this kind of learning involves the startle response exhibited by young nestling birds in response to potential predators such as hawks. A young duck, for example, will exhibit an innate startle response whenever a hawk-shaped model or silhouette is passed overhead. With repeated presentation of the model, however, the intensity of the bird's response will decline as the animal becomes habituated, or learns that the stimulus bears no immediate significance.

Common throughout the animal kingdom and even among some groups of protozoans, habituation is important for preventing repeated responses to irrelevant environmental stimuli that could otherwise overwhelm an organism's senses and interfere with other critical tasks. In the case of a young nestling bird, there is a clear advantage to an alarm response in the presence of a potential predator; however, a continued fixed response would result in an unnecessary expenditure of energy and distraction from other important activities such as feeding.

In identifying a habituation response, it is necessary to distinguish between true habituation and sensory adaptation and fatigue. These latter two phenomena involve a waning in responsiveness that is caused by temporary insensitivity of sense organs or muscle fatigue, and thus are not considered forms of learning. In contrast, habituation results in a drop in responsiveness even though the nervous system is fully capable of detecting a signal and eliciting a muscle response.

In contrast to habituation, sensitization is the heightened sensitivity (or hypersensitivity) that results from initial or repeated exposure to a strong stimulus. Examples of sensitization include the increased sensitivity of humans to soft sounds following exposure to a loud startling noise, such as a gunshot, or the increased responsiveness and sensitivity of a laboratory animal to mild (usually irrelevant) tactile stimulation after an electric shock. Sensitization increases an organism's awareness and responsiveness to a variety of environmental stimuli, thereby preparing it for potentially dangerous situations.

At first glance, habituation and sensitization seem to be opposite behavioral responses—one simply a decrease in responsiveness and the other an increase—but, in fact, they are physiologically different processes, each with its own set of unique characteristics.

At the physiological level, the two responses are determined by contrasting neurological processes that take place in different parts of the nervous system. Habituation is thought to take place primarily in the reflex arc (or SR) system, which consists of short neuronal circuits between sense organs and muscles. In contrast, sensitization is assumed to occur in the state system, or that part of the nervous system that regulates an organism's state of responsiveness. The SR system controls specific responses, whereas the state system determines an organism's general level of readiness to respond. The interaction between habituation and sensitization and these systems determines the exact outcome of a response. At the cellular level, habituated sensory neurons produce fewer neurotransmitters on the postsynaptic membrane, and sensitized neurons are stimulated by other neurons to increase neurotransmitter production and hence, responsiveness of the nerves. Thus, while their ultimate neurological effects are somewhat opposite, the mechanisms by which such effects are achieved are quite different.

Other important differences between habituation and sensitization include contrasting recovery times, opposite patterns of stimuli specificity, and differences in responsiveness to stimuli intensity. Sensitization is generally characterized by a short-term or spontaneous recovery, as are some cases of habituation. In certain situations, however, recovery from habituation may take several days, and even then it may result in incomplete or less intensive responses.

In comparison to sensitization, habituation is usually elicited by very specific sign stimuli such as certain colors, shapes, or sounds. Thus, even after complete habituation to one stimulus, the organism will still respond fully to a second stimulus. Sensitization, on the other hand, can be characterized as a more generalized response, one in which a single stimulus will result in complete sensitization to a variety of stimuli. Such fundamental differences between these two learning processes reflect differences in their function and survival value. It is a clear advantage to an organism to increase its general awareness to a variety of stimuli (such as occurs in sensitization) once it is alarmed. A similar generalized pattern of habituation, however, would shut down the organism's sensitivity to many important stimuli and possibly put the organism in danger.

A final important difference between habituation and sensitization is the manner in which the two processes are affected by stimulus strength. Habituation is more likely to occur if the repeated stimulus is weak, and sensitization will occur when the stimulus is strong.

These various characteristics have important survival implications, especially for species that rely on stereotypic responses to avoid predation and other life-threatening situations. They ensure that the response is elicited in a timely fashion, that the animal is returned to a normal state in a relatively short period of time, and that the animal is not overwhelmed with sensory input.

Applications

Habituation and sensitization have been studied in a variety of contexts and in a number of organisms, from simple protozoans (such as stentor) to human subjects. Such studies have focused on the adaptive significance of these simple learning processes, their neurological control, and the range of behavioral responses that result from interaction between these two forms of learning.

One particular organism in which the neurological basis of habituation and sensitization has been extensively studied is the marine slug *Aplysia*. Eric Kendel and his associates at Columbia University have shown that when the mantle of this organism is prodded, the slug quickly withdraws its gills into a central cavity; but, after repeated prodding, it learns to ignore the stimulus (that is, it becomes habituated). Conversely, when the slug is stimulated with an electric shock, its sensitivity to prodding increases greatly, and it withdraws its gills in response to even the slightest tactile stimulation (that is, it becomes sensitized).

Because *Aplysia* possesses only a few, large neurons, it is an excellent organism in which to study the physiological basis of learning. Capitalizing on this unique system, Kendel and his colleagues have been able to establish the neurological changes that accompany simple forms of learning. In the case of habituation, they have shown that repeated stimulation interferes with calcium ion channels in the nerve, which under normal circumstances, causes synaptic vesicles to release neurotransmitters, which in turn relay a nervous impulse between two neurons. Thus, habituation results in a blocking of the chemical signals between nerves and thereby prevents gill withdrawal.

When *Aplysia* is stimulated (or sensitized) by an electric shock, an interneuron (a closed nerve circuit contained within one part of the nervous system) stimulates the sensory neuron by opening calcium ion channels, increasing neurotransmitter production and promoting gill withdrawal. Thus, the proximate neurological changes that take place during sensitization and habituation are nearly opposite, but they are achieved by very different neurological circuits.

A second area in which habituation and sensitization responses have been the subject of extensive investigation is the sucking reflex exhibited by human infants. When the cheek or lips of a young child are touched with a nipple or finger, they will automatically begin sucking. In a study designed to explore how various stimuli affect this reflex, it was shown that babies respond much more vigorously to a bottle nipple than to the end of a piece of rubber tubing. In addition, repeated presentation of a bottle nipple causes an increase in sucking response, whereas repeated stimulation with rubber tubing causes a decline in sucking. The sensitized or elevated response to a rubber nipple is a result of activation of the state system, which increases the baby's awareness and readiness to respond. Sensitization, however, does not occur when the baby is stimulated with rubber tubing, and instead the child habituates to this stimulus.

In addition to influencing these simple innate behaviors such as sucking reflexes and withdrawal responses, habituation is believed to be responsible for a number of more complex emotional reactions in humans. Explanations for the effects of habituation on emotions are derived primarily from the opponent process theory of motivation.

The opponent process theory holds that each emotional stimulation (or primary process) initiated by an environmental stimulus is opposed by an internal process in the organism. The emotional changes that actually occur in the organism are predicted to result from the net effect of these two processes. The opponent process detracts from the primary process, and summation of the two yields a particular emotional response. It is hypothesized that when the organism is repeatedly stimulated, the primary process is unaffected but the opponent process is strengthened, which results in a net reduction in the overall emotional response. In other words, repeated presentation of an emotion-arousing stimulus results in habituation in the emotional response, primarily as a result of the elevated opponent response.

An increase in drug tolerance, which results from repeated usage of a drug, is best explained by this kind of habituation. Habitual users of alcohol, caffeine, nicotine, and various opiate derivatives must consume greater quantities of such drugs each time they are ingested in order to achieve the same emotional stimulation. Thus, with repeated usage, there is a decline in the overall emotional response. This decline in the euphoric effects of a drug is primarily the result of an increase in the opponent process, which can be characterized as the negative effects of the drug. This is presumably why habitual users experience more severe physiological problems (for example, headaches or delirium tremens) upon termination of a drug.

Similar patterns of habituation have also been suggested to explain the human emotional responses associated with love and attachment, and the extreme feelings of euphoria derived from various thrill-seeking activities such as skydiving. Thus, while habituation and sensitization are simple forms of learning, they may be involved in a variety of more complex behaviors and emotions as well.

Context

Studies of habituation and sensitization have been especially helpful in clarifying the physiological and genetic mechanisms that control various forms of learning. Such investigations have also shown that habituation and sensitization are widespread phenomena with tremendous adaptive significance throughout the animal kingdom.

Ethologists, in marked contrast with psychologists (especially behaviorist psychologists), have historically emphasized the importance of underlying physiological mechanisms in regulation of various behavioral phenomena. Traditionally, they argued that many forms of behavior are not only genetically determined, or innate, but further constrained by the physiological hardware of the organism. They held that psychologists completely ignored these factors by focusing on only the input and output of experiments. Psychologists, on the other hand, have maintained that nearly all forms of behavior are influenced in some way by learning. These contrasting views, which developed largely as a result of different experimental approaches, eventually gave way to a more modern and unified picture of behavior.

One area of research that greatly facilitated this unification was the study of habituation and sensitization. By discovering the chemical and neurological changes that take place during these simple forms of learning, neurobiologists succeeded in demonstrating how the physiological environment is modified during the learning process and that such modifications are remarkably similar throughout the animal kingdom. Thus, it became quite clear that an understanding of proximate physiological mechanisms was central to the study of behavior and learning.

In addition, other studies on sensitization and habituation helped establish the generality of these processes among various groups of animals. They showed that simple forms of learning can occur in nearly all major animal phyla, and that these learning processes often result in modification of simple innate behaviors as well as a variety of more complex responses. From these and other studies, it was soon evident that learning and instinct are not mutually exclusive events, but two processes that work together to provide animals with maximum flexibility to their environment. The kind of learning that occurs during habituation and sensitization allows animals to modify simple, fixed behaviors in response to repeated exposure to environmental stimuli. Habituation allows an organism to filter irrelevant background stimuli and prevent sensory overload and interference of normal activities critical to its survival. Sensitization helps increase an organism's awareness to stimuli in the face of potentially dangerous situations.

These two forms of learning represent important behavioral adaptations with tremendous generality in the animal kingdom. Even in humans, a variety of seemingly complex behaviors can be attributed to interactions between sensitization and habituation, and the simple neurological changes that accompany them.

Bibliography

Domjan, Michael, and Barbara Burkhard. *Principles of Learning and Behavior*. Monterey, Calif.: Brooks/Cole, 1982. Provides a complete treatment of the psychological basis and mechanisms of learning. Chapter 3 is devoted entirely to habituation and sensitization, and it provides several specific examples of these processes in both human and animal subjects. Includes many original data tables and graphs and a thorough review of the literature.

Grier, James W. *Biology of Animal Behavior*. St. Louis: Times Mirror/Mosby, 1984. This college-level text provides comprehensive treatment of the study of animal behavior. Clearly written and well illustrated; should provide a good introduction for the layperson. Integrates information from a variety of disciplines including ethology, behavioral ecology, psychology, and neurobiology. Six chapters are devoted to the physiological control of behavior, and one chapter deals entirely with learning and memory.

McFarland, David, ed. *The Oxford Companion to Animal Behavior*. Rev. and enl. ed. New

York: Oxford University Press, 1987. Intended as a reference guide, this comprehensive survey of behavior was written by a team of internationally known biologists, psychologists, and neurobiologists, and it contains more than two hundred entries covering a variety of topics. Provides a detailed summary of various forms of learning, including habituation and sensitization. The index provides cross-references organized by both subject and species lists.

McSweeney, Frances K., John M. Hinson, and Cari B. Cannon. "Sensitization-Habituation May Occur During Operant Conditioning." *Psychological Bulletin* 120, no. 2 (September, 1996): 256-272.

Manning, Aubrey. *An Introduction to Animal Behavior*. 3d ed. Reading, Mass.: Addison-Wesley, 1979. A concise handbook offering a light introduction to many general aspects of animal behavior and learning. Provides a discussion on stimulus filtering, an entire chapter on the physiological basis of behavior and motivation, and a complete summary of various forms of learning. Well researched, clearly written, and effectively illustrated.

Raven, Peter H. *Biology*. St. Louis: Times Mirror/Mosby, 1989. Chapter 56 of this general text on the science of biology offers an excellent first introduction to the general concepts of ethology and animal behavior. Includes a brief summary of learning and detailed coverage of habituation, sensitization, and conditioning in *Aplysia*. A concise summary, suggestions for additional reading, and review questions appear at the end of the chapter.

Shepherd, Gordon Murray. *Neurobiology*. Oxford, England: Oxford University Press, 1983. This somewhat advanced college-level volume on neurobiology offers an in-depth account of the physiological basis of learning and memory. A portion of chapter 30 is devoted specifically to the neurological changes associated with habituation and sensitization. Detailed diagrams, data summaries, and complete literature reviews are provided.

Michael A. Steele

See also:

HELPING
Bystander Intervention

Type of psychology: Social psychology
Fields of study: Group processes; prosocial behavior

The study of the psychology of bystander intervention has led to an understanding of the processes that often prevent witnesses to an incident from offering needed assistance, even if an emergency is involved; such events may have tragic consequences, and knowledge of the dynamics of these situations may sometimes keep them from occurring.

Principal terms

AUDIENCE INHIBITION: a tendency to be hesitant to act in front of others

BYSTANDER EFFECT: the tendency to be less likely to help when other people are present; also referred to as the social inhibition of helping

CONFEDERATE: in a social psychological experiment, a person who is "part of the act" and is instructed to behave in a certain way

DIFFUSION OF RESPONSIBILITY: the tendency to share the obligation to help in an emergency with the other people present

SOCIAL INFLUENCE: as applied to bystander intervention, the process whereby each bystander is led by the inaction of others to conclude that no emergency is really occurring

Overview

In early 1964, Kitty Genovese was stabbed to death in front of her New York City apartment building as she returned from work around 3:30 A.M. The assault was particularly brutal, actually consisting of three separate attacks stretching over a period of more than a half hour. Perhaps most shocking about this tragedy, however, was a troubling fact that emerged in the police department's subsequent investigation: Thirty-eight of the woman's neighbors had witnessed the incident without intervening. No one had even called the police during the episode.

This case was only one of several similar occurrences that took place in the mid-1960's, attracting considerable attention and prompting much commentary. The remarks of newspaper columnists, magazine writers, and the like focused on such notions as "alienation," "apathy," "indifference," and "lack of concern for our fellow humans." Bibb Latané and John Darley, social psychologists who at the time were professors at universities in New York City, reasoned that ascribing personality characteristics such as these to bystanders who fail to help is not the key to understanding how onlookers can remain inactive while another individual is victimized. Rather, one must look to the situation itself to uncover the powerful social forces that inhibit helping.

Latané and Darley thus embarked on a program of research that culminated in their classic 1970 book *The Unresponsive Bystander: Why Doesn't He Help?* They began their analysis of the "bystander effect" by recognizing that there are usually several good reasons that one should not necessarily expect bystanders to offer help in an emergency. For example, most people are not prepared to deal with emergencies, which tend to happen quickly and without warning. In addition, direct intervention may involve real physical danger, as in the Genovese incident. Finally, becoming involved in such situations may lead to court appearances or other legal consequences.

Latané and Darley also proposed a model describing a sequence of cognitive events that must occur before a bystander will offer assistance in an emergency. First, a bystander must notice the event; second, he or she must interpret that event as an emergency; third, the bystander must decide that it is his or her responsibility to do something. At this point, two steps in the process still remain: The bystander must decide exactly what to do; then he or she must successfully implement that decision. It is important to recognize that a negative outcome at any of these steps in the decision-making process will prevent helping. In the light of the cognitive process just described and the other reasons that people fail to intervene in emergencies, it is perhaps surprising, Latané and Darley suggested, that bystanders ever help.

Remarkably (and ironically), one situational factor is primarily responsible for the social inhibition of helping: the presence of other people. Latané and Darley proposed three social psychological processes to explain precisely how the presence of others inhibits helping. Each of these operates within the decision-making framework described earlier, and all three appear to be necessary to account completely for the bystander effect.

The first of these processes is audience inhibition, which refers to people's general reluctance to do things in front of others. When people are aware that their behavior is on public display and are concerned about what other people think, they may be hesitant to offer help for fear of appearing incompetent. Furthermore, a bystander who decides to offer help will be embarrassed if it turns out that he or she has misinterpreted the situation when it is not really an emergency. For example, how might a person feel if he or she stepped out of the crowd to administer CPR to a man lying unconscious on the ground, only to roll him over and realize that he is merely intoxicated? Risks of this sort are greater the larger the number of other people present.

The second process, social influence, frequently contributes to the social inhibition of helping by leading bystanders to misinterpret the event. Emergencies are often ambiguous, and a person confronted with ambiguity will look to the behavior of other people for clues about how to behave. While the person is attempting to appraise the reactions of other people, he or she will probably attempt to remain calm. That person, then, is likely to see a group of others doing exactly the same: appearing calm and doing nothing while trying to figure out whether a true emergency is taking place. Each person will be fooled by the inaction of everyone else into thinking that the situation is less serious than it really is and that not intervening is the appropriate course of action. The ultimate result is a sort of group behavioral paralysis, and the victim goes without help.

The final process, the most powerful of the three, was probably the main force at work in the Genovese incident (social influence was probably not involved, since witnesses remained isolated from one another in their own apartments). This phenomenon, known as diffusion of responsibility, occurs when an individual knows that others are available to help. While a lone bystander at an emergency bears the total responsibility for helping, those in a group share the responsibility equally with the others present. Thus, the larger the number of other witnesses, the smaller is each individual's obligation to act. As a result, individuals in groups are likely to assume that someone else will intervene.

Applications

Latané and Darley tested their ideas in a number of ingenious experiments, several of which are considered classic examples of social psychological research. In one of these, Columbia University students arrived individually at a laboratory to take part in a study that they believed would involve an interview. Each subject was sent to a waiting room to complete a preliminary questionnaire. Some of them found two other people already seated in the room, while others sat down alone.

Soon after the subject began working on the questionnaire, smoke began filling the room through a wall vent. The smoke could hardly be ignored; within four minutes the room contained enough smoke to interfere with vision and breathing. Latané and Darley were primarily interested in how frequently subjects simply got up and left the room to report the emergency. Most (75 percent) of the subjects who were waiting alone reported the smoke, but those in groups were far less likely to do so. Groups consisting of three naïve subjects reported it only 38 percent of the time; when the subject waited (unknowingly, of course) with two confederates who were instructed to do nothing, only 10 percent responded.

Observations of the unresponsive subjects supported the researchers' notion that the social influence process in groups would inhibit helping by leading people to misinterpret the situation. Interviews with these participants revealed that they had produced a variety of explanations for the smoke: air conditioning vapor, steam, smog, and even "truth gas." In other words, lone subjects for the most part behaved responsibly, but those in groups were generally led by the inaction of others to conclude almost anything but the obvious—that a legitimate emergency was taking place. It is important to realize that social influence, as demonstrated in this experiment, is most potent when bystanders in groups do not communicate with one another; such was the case in this experiment, and such tends to be the case with analogous groups in real life. Simply talking to the others present can clarify what really is happening, thus eliminating the bystander effect.

A second classic study demonstrates the power of the diffusion-of-responsibility process. In this experiment, college students thought they were participating in a group discussion about the difficulties of adjusting to college. In order to reduce the discomfort that could be associated with discussing personal matters, each subject was ushered to a private cubicle from which he or she would communicate with other group members through an intercom system. In each case, however, there was only one actual subject; the other "group members" had been previously tape recorded. Thus, Latané and Darley were able to manipulate the size of the group as perceived by the subject.

Each "member" of the group talked for two minutes, with the actual subject speaking last. A second round then began, and the first "group member" to speak began suffering a frighteningly severe epileptic seizure, choking and pleading for help. Since the subject had no idea where the other "group members" were located, the only available course of helping action was to leave the cubicle and report the emergency to the person in charge.

On the basis of the diffusion-of-responsibility concept, Latané and Darley expected that the likelihood of helping would decrease as the perceived size of the group increased. When the subject was part of a two-person group (only him or her and the victim, thus making the subject the only person available to help), 85 percent of the participants reported the seizure. When the subject believed that he or she was in a group of three, 62 percent responded. Only 31 percent of those who thought they were in a six-person group offered help. Without question, the responsibility for acting in this emergency was perceived to be divided among everyone believed to be available to help.

The circumstances of this experiment correspond directly to those of the Kitty Genovese murder. Most important, the subjects in this study were not in a face-to-face group, just as the witnesses to the Genovese murder were isolated in their own apartments; consequently, social influence could not lead to a misinterpretation of the event (which was not ambiguous anyway). In short, simply knowing that others are available to respond acts as a powerful deterrent to helping. It is also significant that this experiment demonstrated that bystanders who fail to intervene are usually not the least bit apathetic or indifferent. Rather, the typical unresponsive subject showed clear signs of distress over the plight of the victim; nevertheless, the belief that others were present still tended to suppress intervention.

Diffusion of responsibility is a very common social force and is not at all restricted to situations as serious as those that have been discussed here. Anyone who has failed to work as hard as possible on a group task, heard a doorbell go unanswered at a party, or experienced a telephone ringing seven or eight times even though the entire family is at home has probably fallen victim to the same process.

Context

The work of Latané and Darley attracted much attention and acclaim. From a methodological standpoint, their experiments are still regarded as some of social psychology's most clever and intriguing. Their findings, however, were even more remarkable: Demonstrating consistently the social inhibition of helping, they destroyed the common belief in "safety in numbers." This research also provides a powerful illustration of one of the major lessons of social psychology—that situational forces affecting behavior can be overpowering, eliminating at least temporarily the influence of personality. The work of Latané and Darley showed convincingly that a person cannot rely on human nature, kindness, or any other dispositional quality if he or she should become the victim of an emergency.

This program of research also provided the impetus for much work on helping that has been conducted by other investigators. Various kinds of precipitating incidents were examined, as were differences between experiments conducted in laboratories and those performed in natural settings. Other studies investigated the effects of a wide range of different characteristics of the subjects, victims, and other bystanders involved. It was discovered, for example, that people are more likely to offer assistance when someone else has already modeled helping behavior and if the victim is particularly needy, deserving, or somehow similar to the helper; certain transitory mood states, such as happiness and guilt, were also found to increase helping. The research findings mentioned here are only a sample, as helping behavior continued to be a popular topic among social psychologists throughout the 1970's.

Despite the large assortment of factors investigated, many of these other studies included a manipulation of the variable that had been the principal concern of Latané and Darley: group size. Two major articles published by Latané and his colleagues in 1981 reviewed nearly one hundred different instances of research comparing helping by individuals in groups with that by lone bystanders. They found, almost without exception in these studies, that people were less likely to help in groups than when they were alone, suggesting that the bystander effect is perhaps as consistent and predictable as any within the domain of social psychology.

Although incidents such as the murder of Kitty Genovese do not occur every day, it is important to recognize that scores of them have been reported over the years, and they continue to occur regularly. Unfortunately, the understanding provided by the research has not led to strategies for avoiding these tragedies. (Considering the ability of situational forces to override personality influences, one should not be too surprised by this.) There is, however, one bit of hope: At least one study has demonstrated that students who have learned about the bystander effect in a psychology class are more likely to intervene in an emergency than those who have not been exposed to that material.

Bibliography

Batson, C. D. "Prosocial Motivation: Is It Ever Truly Altruistic?" In *Advances in Experimental Social Psychology*, edited by Leonard Berkowitz. San Diego: Academic Press, 1987. A very thorough examination of what happens psychologically within the person who helps, with a special focus on the role of empathy in determining the helping response. This chapter is somewhat high-level, but it does convey the flavor of this area of research.

Cialdini, Robert B. *Influence: Science and Practice*. 2d ed. Glenview, Ill.: Scott, Foresman, 1988. An extremely interesting book dealing generally with the issue of social influence. Contains an excellent chapter analyzing the bystander effect, with emphasis on the role of other people in helping to define a social situation. Cialdini presents some provocative examples and offers advice about how to prevent oneself from becoming a victim.

Latané, Bibb, and John M. Darley. *The Unresponsive Bystander: Why Doesn't He Help?* New York: Appleton-Century-Crofts, 1970. The classic source on bystander intervention in emergencies, detailing all of Latané and Darley's original research on the problem. The clever methodology of many of their experiments and their engaging writing style make this a fascinating and readable book.

Latané, Bibb, S. A. Nida, and D. W. Wilson. "The Effects of Group Size on Helping Behavior." In *Altruism and Helping Behavior: Social, Personality, and Developmental Perspectives*, edited by J. Phillipe Rushton and Richard M. Sorrentino. Hillsdale, N.J.: Lawrence Erlbaum, 1981. Reviews the research examining the relationship between group size and helping, including a discussion of the methodological problems involved. Contains not only a good summary of Latané and Darley's original theoretical ideas but also some subsequent developments, such as Latané's general model of group behavior known as social impact theory.

Macaulay, Jaqueline, and Leonard Berkowitz, eds. *Altruism and Helping Behavior: Social Psychological Studies of Some Antecedents and Consequences*. New York: Academic Press, 1970. A classic volume reporting much of the earliest work on the social psychology of helping. Not all the chapters deal directly with bystander intervention, but the book does contain two separate chapters by Latané and Darley that provide excellent summaries of much of their original work.

Rushton, J. Phillipe, and Richard M. Sorrentino, eds. *Altruism and Helping Behavior: Social, Personality, and Developmental Perspectives*. Hillsdale, N.J.: Lawrence Erlbaum, 1981. Presents a range of articles reflecting the different directions established in the study of helping behavior following the initial exploration of bystander intervention in emergencies. Some of the chapters deal not with bystander intervention per se but with helping or altruism in the broader sense (such as how altruism is learned).

Staub, Ervin. "Helping a Distressed Person: Social, Personality, and Stimulus Determinants." In *Advances in Experimental Social Psychology*, edited by Leonard Berkowitz. New York: Academic Press, 1974. Another important and frequently cited chapter from an earlier point in the history of research in this area. Although social psychologists rarely take issue with Latané and Darley's analysis of bystander intervention, Staub offers a somewhat different perspective, placing more emphasis on personality influences. He also presents some interesting research with children.

Weiner, Bernard. *Judgments of Responsibility: A Foundation for a Theory of Social Conduct*. New York: Guilford Press, 1995.

Steve A. Nida

See also:

Affiliation and Friendship, 25; Aggression, 31; Cognitive Dissonance Theory, 141; Crowd Behavior, 182; Self: Definition and Assessment, 524.

HOMOSEXUALITY

Type of psychology: Motivation
Fields of study: Attitudes and behavior; interpersonal relations; physical motives

Sexuality is one of the most complex and individual attributes of the human psyche. There are four types of theories with regard to the development of sexual orientation, but as of the mid-1990's none seemed sufficient to explain the huge diversity to be found in sexual expression across ages and cultures.

Principal terms

ANDROGYNY: the expression of both traditionally feminine and traditionally masculine attributes

GAY: a term that is usually, but not exclusively, used to describe a homosexual male who is open about his sexual orientation

HOMOPHOBIA: a fear of, prejudice against, or hatred toward homosexuals, usually based upon irrational stereotyping

HOMOSEXUAL: a person who is attracted to members of the same sex; of or relating to sexual activity with a member of the same sex

LESBIAN: a female homosexual; often used in association with the term "gay," which usually refers to males

PEDOPHILE: an adult who is sexually aroused by children; about 90 percent of pedophiles are males with a heterosexual orientation

TRANSSEXUAL: someone who feels like he or she is trapped in the body of a member of the wrong sex; sometimes gender-change surgery is sought

TRANSVESTITE: a person who, for fun or sexual arousal, often dresses and acts like a member of the opposite sex (going "in drag"); most are heterosexual males

Overview

Theories on the origin and development of homosexual orientation can be categorized into four groups: psychoanalytic, biological, social learning, and sociobiological theories. Psychoanalytic theories are based on the Freudian model of "psychosexual stages" of development, developed by Austrian psychiatrist Sigmund Freud. According to this model, every child goes through several stages, including the "phallic stage," during which he or she learns to identify with his or her same-sex parent. For boys, this is supposed to be particularly difficult, since it requires redefining the strong bond that they have had with their mother since birth. According to Freudian theorists, homosexuality is an outcome of the failure to resolve this developmental crisis: If a boy's father is absent or "weak," and his mother is domineering or overprotective, the boy may never come to identify with his father; for a girl, having a "cold" or rejecting mother could prevent her from identifying with the female role.

Research has found that homosexuals are, in fact, more likely to feel an inability to relate to their same-sex parent than heterosexuals are and to report that the same-sex parent was "cold" or "distant" during their childhood. Some studies have suggested, however, that this psychological distance between parent and offspring is found mostly in families with children who show cross-gender behaviors when very young and that the distancing is more likely to be a result of preexisting differences in the child than a cause of later differences.

Biological theories suggest that homosexuality is genetic, is a result of unusual hormone levels, or is a result of prenatal maternal effects on the developing fetus. Although there may be genes which predispose a person to become homosexual under certain circumstances, as of 1997 no specific genes had definitively been linked to homosexuality. Similarly, there do not seem to be consistent differences between levels of hormones in homosexual and heterosexual adults. The possibility remains that subtle fluctuations of hormones during critical periods of fetal development may influence brain structures which regulate sexual arousal and attraction.

Social-learning models suggest that homosexual orientation develops as a response to pleasurable homosexual experiences during childhood and adolescence, perhaps coupled with unpleasant heterosexual experiences. Many boys have homosexual experiences as part of their normal sexual experimentation while growing up. According to the model, some boys will find these experiences more pleasurable or successful than their experiments with heterosexuality and will continue to seek homosexual interactions. Why only certain boys find their homosexual experiences more pleasurable than their heterosexual experiences could be related to a variety of factors, including age, family dynamics, the child's social skills, and personality. Young girls are less likely to have early homosexual experiences but may be "turned off" from heterosexuality by experiences such as rape, abuse, or assault.

Sociobiological models are all based on the assumption that common behaviors must have evolved because they were somehow beneficial, or related to something beneficial, which helped the individuals who performed them to pass their genes to the next generation. From this perspective, homosexuality seems incongruous, but since it is so common, researchers have tried to find out how homosexual behavior might in fact increase a person's ability to pass on genes to subsequent generations. Theorists have come up with three possible explanations—the parental manipulation model, the kin selection model, and the by-product model.

The parental manipulation model suggests that homosexuals do not directly pass on more of their genes than heterosexuals, but that their parents do. According to this model, parents subconsciously manipulate their child's development to make him or her less likely to start a family; in this way, the adult child is able to contribute time, energy, and income to brothers, sisters, nieces, and nephews. In the end, the parents have "sacrificed" one child's reproduction in exchange for more grandchildren—or, at least, for more indulged, more evolutionarily competitive grandchildren.

The kin selection model is similar, but in it, the homosexual individual is not manipulated but is sacrificing his or her own reproduction willingly (although subconsciously) in exchange for more nieces and nephews (that is, more relatives' genes in subsequent generations). According to this model, individuals who are willing to make this sacrifice (no matter how subconscious) are either those who are not likely to be very successful in heterosexual interactions (and are thus not actually making much of a sacrifice) or those who have a particular attribute that makes them especially good at helping their families. As an analogy, theorists point out how, through much of human history, reproductive sacrifice in the form of joining a religious order often provided income, protection, or status for other family members.

The by-product model suggests that homosexuality is an inevitable outcome of evolved sex differences. According to this model, the facts that, overall, men have a higher sex drive than women and that, historically, most societies have allowed polygyny (where one man has more than one wife) will result in many unmated males who still have an urge to satisfy their high sex drive. Thus, men will become (or will at least act) homosexual when male partners are easier to find than females. This model is the one most likely to explain "facultative homosexuality," that is, homosexual behavior by people who consider themselves basically heterosexual.

Applications

Prior to the gay liberation movement, homosexuality was classified as a mental disorder. In the 1970's, however, when psychiatrists were revising the American Psychiatric Association's *Diagnostic and Statistical Manual of Mental Disorders* (DSM), they removed homosexuality from the list of illnesses. The third edition of the manual (DSM-III), published in 1980, reflected this change. Homosexuality is not associated with disordered thinking or impaired abilities in any way. Therefore, counseling or therapy for the purpose of changing sexual orientation is not recommended. Even when sought, such therapy is rarely successful. On the other hand, many gays, especially adolescents, find benefit from counseling in order to find information, support, and ways to cope with their sexuality.

For men, sexual orientation seems to be fixed at an early age; most gay men feel as though they were "always" homosexual, just as most heterosexual men feel they were "always" heterosexual. In women, however, sexual orientation is less likely to be fixed early; some women change from a heterosexual to homosexual orientation (or vice versa) in adulthood. In such cases, sexual orientation is better seen as a choice than as an acting out of something preexisting in the psyche, and often such changes are made after a woman has left an unhealthy or abusive relationship or has experienced some other sort of emotional or psychological awakening that changes her outlook on life. In these cases, counseling for the sake of changing sexual orientation per se is not recommended, but it may be appropriate for the woman to seek help dealing with the other changes or events in her life. Most women in this circumstance find that a same-sex, even lesbian, therapist is most helpful, since she will be more likely to empathize with her client.

Many women who change sexual orientation in mid-life already have children, and many who are lesbian from adolescence choose to have children (by artificial insemination or by having intercourse with a male friend). Often, such women have found a lack of support for their parenting and sometimes even experience legal problems retaining custody rights of their children. Gay men, too, have had difficulty retaining parental rights or becoming foster or adoptive parents.

Psychological research shows, however, that homosexuals are as good at parenting as heterosexuals and that they are as effective at providing role models. Homosexuals are more likely than heterosexuals to model androgyny—the expression of both traditionally masculine and traditionally feminine attributes—for their children. Some research has shown that an androgynous approach is more healthy and more successful in American society than sticking to traditionally defined roles. For example, sometimes women need to be assertive on the job or in relationships, whereas traditionally men were assertive and women were passive. Similarly, men are less likely to experience stress-related mental and physical health problems if they learn to express their emotions, something only women were traditionally supposed to do.

Neither modeling androgyny nor modeling homosexuality is likely to cause a child to become homosexual, and children reared by homosexual parents are no more likely to become homosexual than children reared by heterosexual parents. Similarly, modeling of androgyny or homosexuality by teachers does not influence the development of homosexuality in children and adolescents. Having an openly homosexual teacher may be a stimulus for a gay child to discover and explore his or her sexuality, but it does not create that sexuality.

Other variations in adult sexual expression, sometimes associated with, or confused with, homosexuality, are transvestism and transsexuality. Transvestism occurs when a person enjoys, or gets sexually excited by, dressing as a member of the opposite sex. Some gay men enjoy cross-dressing, and others enjoy acting feminine. The majority of homosexuals, however, do not do either; most transvestites are heterosexual. Transsexuality is different from both homosexuality and transvestism; it is categorized by a feeling that one is trapped in the body of the wrong sex. Transsexuality, unlike homosexuality or transvestism, is considered a mental disorder; it is officially a form of gender dysphoria—gender confusion. Transsexuals may feel as though they are engaging in homosexual activity if they have sexual relations with a member of the opposite sex. Some transsexuals decide to cross-dress and live as a member of the opposite sex. They may have hormone treatments and surgery to change legally into a member of the opposite sex. Transsexuality, unlike homosexuality or transvestism, is very rare.

Context

The word "homosexual" is usually used in everyday language as a noun, referring to someone who is sexually attracted to, and has sexual relations with, members of the same sex. As a noun, however, the word is misleading, since few people who call themselves homosexual have never engaged in heterosexual activity; similarly, many people who call themselves heterosexual have at some time engaged in some sort of homosexual activity. Therefore, many sex researchers (sexologists) use a seven-point scale first devised for the Alfred Kinsey surveys in the 1940's, ranging from 0 (exclusively heterosexual) to 6 (exclusively homosexual). Others prefer to use the words "heterosexual" and "homosexual" as adjectives describing behaviors rather than as nouns.

Homosexual behavior has been documented in every society that sexologists have studied; in many societies it has been institutionalized. For example, the ancient Greeks believed that women were spiritually beneath men and that male-male love was the highest form. In Melanesian societies, homosexual activity was thought to be necessary for young boys to mature into virile, heterosexual adults. Homosexuality as an overall preference or orientation is harder to study, but it is thought that between 5 and 10 percent of adult males, and between 2 and 4 percent of females, have a predominantly homosexual orientation.

In Western, Judeo-Christian culture, homosexual behavior has long been considered taboo or sinful. Thus, in the United States and other predominantly Christian cultures, homosexuality has been frowned upon, and homosexuals have been ostracized, being seen as perverted, unnatural, or sick. In 1974, however, the American Psychiatric Association determined that homosexuality was not indicative of mental illness. In contrast to early twentieth century studies of homosexuals who were either psychiatric patients or prison inmates, later studies of a representative cross-section of people showed that individuals with a homosexual orientation are no more likely to suffer from mental illness than those with a heterosexual orientation.

In spite of these scientific data, many heterosexuals (especially males) still harbor negative feelings about homosexuality. This phenomenon is called homophobia. Some of this fear, disgust, and hatred is attributable to the incorrect belief that many homosexuals are child molesters. In fact, more than 90 percent of pedophiles are heterosexual. Another source of homophobia is the fear of acquired immune deficiency syndrome (AIDS). This deadly sexually transmitted disease is more easily transmitted through anal intercourse than through vaginal intercourse and thus has spread more rapidly among homosexuals than heterosexuals. Education about "safe sex" practices, however, has dramatically reduced transmission rates in homosexual communities.

Sexologists have not been able to avoid the political controversies surrounding their field—making the study of a difficult subject even harder. Research will continue, but no one should expect fast and simple explanations. Sexuality, perhaps more than any other attribute of the human psyche, is personal and individual. Questions about sexual orientation, sexual development, and sexual behavior are all complex; it will take a long time to unravel the answers.

Bibliography

Bell, Alan P., and Martin Weinberg. *Homosexualities: A Study of Diversity Among Men and Women*. New York: Simon & Schuster, 1978. This official Kinsey Institute publication presents the methods and results of the most extensive sex survey to focus specifically on homosexual behavior. Presents descriptions of homosexual feelings, partnerships, and lifestyles, based on intensive interviews with more than fifteen hundred men and women.

Bell, Alan P., Martin S. Weinberg, and Sue Kiefer Hammersmith. *Sexual Preference: Its Development in Men and Women*. Bloomington: Indiana University Press, 1981. In a follow-up to Bell and Weinberg's first book (described above), this volume compares the childhood and adolescent experiences of male and female homosexual and heterosexual adults. Organized in a question-and-answer format, this book explores possible explanations for homosexual versus heterosexual development.

Blumstein, Philip W., and Pepper Schwartz. *American Couples: Money, Work, Sex*. New York: William Morrow, 1983. Part 1 presents statistical data on the lifestyles and interpersonal relationships of more than five thousand married, heterosexual cohabiting, homosexual, and lesbian couples. Part 2 presents interviews with selected couples from each of the four groups, along with a follow-up study on each several years later. Many user-friendly charts for comparison.

Koertge, Noretta, ed. *Nature and Causes of Homosexuality: A Philosophic and Scientific Inquiry*. New York: Haworth Press, 1981. This volume is the third in an ongoing monograph series entitled "Research on Homosexuality," each volume of which was originally published as an issue of the *Journal of Homosexuality*. All volumes are valuable, although somewhat technical. This one is a good place to start; others cover law, psychotherapy, literature, alcoholism, anthropology, historical perspectives, social sex roles, bisexuality, and homophobia.

McNaught, Brian. *A Disturbed Peace: Selected Writings of an Irish Catholic Homosexual.* Washington, D.C.: Dignity, 1981. A very personal viewpoint from an advocate of gay rights. The publisher, Dignity, is an organization of gay Catholics (and their friends and relatives) who feel rejected by their church but who still feel a need to exercise both their religion and their sexual feelings.

Marmor, Judd, ed. *Homosexual Behavior: A Modern Appraisal.* New York: Basic Books, 1980. For those interested in a clinical perspective on homosexuality, this is the book. It puts the early twentieth century psychoanalytic viewpoint in context after presenting late twentieth century information from both the biological and social sciences. Collectively, the contributors' expertise is quite vast.

Sullivan, Andrew. *Virtually Normal: An Argument About Homosexuality.* New York: Alfred A. Knopf, 1995.

Tripp, C. A. *The Homosexual Matrix.* New York: McGraw-Hill, 1975. For those who want to sit down and read for pleasure as well as for information. Tripp covers fact, culture, and mythology, both historical and modern. A good representative of the "gay liberation" era books on homosexuality, most of the text is as valid as when it was written (though it clearly does not cover post-AIDS changes in homosexual culture and behavior).

Whitham, Frederick L. "Culturally Invariable Properties of Male Homosexuality: Tentative Conclusions from Cross-Cultural Research." *Archives of Sexual Behavior* 12 (1983): 40. Unlike much of the cross-cultural literature on homosexuality, this article focuses specifically on cross-cultural prevalence and attributes of those with a homosexual orientation, rather than on the institutionalized and ritual forms of homosexual behavior found in many non-Western cultures.

Linda Mealey

See also:

Drive Theory, 218; Gender Identity Formation, 254; Instinct Theory, 303; Sexual Variants and Paraphilias, 541.

IDENTITY CRISES

Type of psychology: Developmental psychology
Fields of study: Adolescence; adulthood

Identity crises are the internal and external conflicts faced by the adolescent/young adult when choosing an occupation and coming to terms with a basic ideology. Development of a personal identity is a central component of psychosocial maturity.

Principal terms

IDENTITY: a configuration of occupational, sexual, and ideological commitments; according to Erikson, the positive pole of the fifth stage of psychosocial development

IDENTITY CONFUSION/DIFFUSION: an incomplete or inadequate sense of self, which can range from a state of occasional uncertainty to a psychotic state

IDENTITY STATUS: a description of one's self-structure based on evidence of exploration of alternatives and commitments to a career and a basic set of values

NEGATIVE IDENTITY: a self-structure that reflects a deviant lifestyle such as that taken on by a delinquent

PSYCHOSOCIAL MATURITY: the completion of development in those areas that include both psychological and social aspects, such as identity and sexuality

PSYCHOSOCIAL MORATORIUM: a period during which the adolescent is free from responsibilities and obligations in order to explore the meaning of life

Overview

Identity crises are an integral phase in human development. According to Erik Erikson, successful resolution of the identity crisis is contingent on the earlier resolution of the crises associated with infancy and childhood, such as trust, autonomy, initiative, and industry. Further, the extent to which the conflict surrounding identity is resolved will influence how the individual will cope with the crises of adulthood.

According to Erikson's model of the human life cycle, an identity crisis is one of the psychosocial conflicts faced by the adolescent. In Erikson's model, which was published in the 1960's, each age period is defined by a certain type of psychosocial crisis. Adolescence is the life stage during which acquiring an identity presents a major conflict. Failure to resolve the conflict results in identity confusion/diffusion—that is, an inadequate sense of self.

Identity implies an existential position, according to James Marcia, who construes identity as a self-structure composed of one's personal history, belief system, and competencies. One's perception of uniqueness is directly related to the development of this self-structure. A somewhat similar position has been taken by Jane Kroger, who views the identity crisis as a problem of self-definition. The resulting identity is a balance between self and others. Erikson defines identity as the belief that one's past experiences and identity will be confirmed in the future—as exemplified in the choice of a career. Identity is a composite of one's sexuality, physical makeup, vocation, and belief system. Identity is the pulling together of who one is and who one can become, which involves compositing one's past, present, and future. It is a synthesis of earlier identifications. Successfully resolving the identity crisis is contingent on the interactions that the adolescent/young adult has with others. Erikson contends that interacting with others provides the needed feedback about who one is and who one ought to be. These interactions with others enable the adolescent/young adult to gain a perspective of self that includes an evaluation of his or her physical and social self. Identity acquisition is cognitive as well as social.

From Erikson's perspective, as discussed by James Cote and Charles Levine (1987), four conditions are necessary for an identity crisis: Puberty has been reached; the requisite cognitive development is present; physical growth is nearing adult stature; and societal influences are guiding the person toward an integration and resynthesis of identity. The dialectics of society and personality, implicit in the last condition, are given the most attention by Erikson, according to Cote and Levine, because the other three conditions are part of normative development. Developmental level of the individual and societal pressures combine to elicit an identity crisis; but Cote and Levine note that timing of this crisis is contingent on factors such as ethnicity, gender, socioeconomic status, and subculture, as well as personality factors (for example, authoritarianism or neuroticism) and socialization practices. The severity of the identity crisis is determined by the extent to which one's identity portrayal is interfered with by the uncertainty inherent in moving toward self-definition and unexpected events.

An integral part of the identity crisis is the psychological moratorium, a time during which society permits the individual to work on crisis resolution. During this moratorium, the adolescent/young adult has the opportunity to examine societal roles, career possibilities, and values, free from the expectation of commitments and long-term responsibilities. Although some individuals choose to remain in a moratorium indefinitely, Erikson contends that there is an absolute end to the recognizable moratorium. At its completion, the adolescent/young adult should have attained the necessary restructuring of self and identifications so that he or she can find a place in society which fits this identity.

Based on Erikson's writings, Cote and Levine identify two types of institutionalized moratoria: the technological moratorium, which is highly structured, and the humanistic moratorium, which is less highly structured. The technological moratorium is the product of the educational system, which is charged by society with socializing youth to fit in adult society. Individuals in this moratorium option experience less difficulty in resolving the identity crisis because they move into occupations and societal roles for which they have been prepared with significantly less intrapsychic trauma in accepting an ideology. The school takes an active role in easing this transition by providing vocational and academic counseling for students, facilitating scheduling so that students can gain work experience while enrolled in school, and encouraging early decision making as to a future career.

The identity crisis for individuals in the humanistic moratorium is more stressful, painful, and of longer duration than for those in the technological moratorium. The focal concern of the adolescent/young adult in the humanistic moratorium is humanistic values, which are largely missing from the technological moratorium. There is more variability in this concern for humanistic values, which is reflected in the moratorium that is chosen and the commitments that are made. These conditions elicit an alternation between progressive and regressive states, with the individual making commitments at one time and disengaging at another. The character Holden Caulfield in J. D. Salinger's classic novel *The Catcher in the Rye*

(1951) is an example of this type of identity problem. More extreme identity confusion is found among individuals in this moratorium. According to Cote and Levine, social support is often lacking, which hinders formation of a stable identity. Family and community support is especially important for these individuals. Yet these are the adolescents/young adults who, because their lifestyle departs from the societal mold, are often ostracized and denied support. Individuals may promote a cause of some type. Those who choose a humanistic moratorium are more likely to be intellectual, artistic, antiestablishment, and ideologically nonconforming. After a time, some of these individuals accept technological values and roles.

Individuals whose identity seeking is not influenced by technological or humanistic moratoria face a rather different situation. Some remain in a constant state of flux in which choices are avoided and commitments are lacking. Others take on a negative identity by accepting a deviant lifestyle and value system (for example, delinquency or gang member-ship). In this instance, the negative elements of an identity outweigh the positive elements. This type of identity crisis resolution occurs in an environment which precludes normative identity development (for example, excessively demanding parents, absence of an adequate role model).

Applications

Erikson's writings on identity crises have been responsible for an extensive literature, consisting of conceptual as well as empirical articles. Perhaps the most widely used application is Marcia's identity status paradigm, in which he has conceptualized and operationalized Erikson's theory of identity development in terms of several statuses which result from exploration and commitment. More than one hundred empirical studies have been generated from this paradigm, according to a review by Cote and Levine (1988). The identity status paradigm provides a methodological procedure for determining identity statuses based on resolution of an identity crisis and the presence of commitments to an occupation and an ideology.

According to the Marcia paradigm, an ego identity can be one of several statuses consisting of achievement, foreclosure, moratorium, or diffusion. An achievement status indicates resolution of the identity crisis and firm commitments to an occupation and an ideology. In a foreclosure status, one has formed commitments but has not experienced a crisis. The moratorium status denotes that an identity crisis is currently being experienced, and no commitments have been made. The diffusion status implies the absence of a crisis and no commitments. Much of the research has focused on identifying the personality characteristics associated with each of these statuses. Other studies have examined the interactional patterns as well as information-processing and problem-solving strategies. Achievement and moratorium statuses seek out, process, and evaluate information in their decision making. Foreclosures have more rigid belief systems and conform to normative standards held by significant others, while those in the diffusion status delay decision making. Significant differences have been found among the statuses in terms of their capacity for intimacy, with diffusions scoring lowest, followed by foreclosures. Achieve-ment and moratorium statuses have a greater capacity for intimacy.

Two areas of research that continue to attract attention are parental socialization patterns associated with crisis resolution, and identity crises in females. The findings to date reveal distinctive parental patterns associated with each status. Positive but somewhat ambivalent relationships between parents and the adolescent/young adult are reported for achievement status. Moratorium-status adolescents/young adults also seem to have ambivalent relationships with their parents, but they are less conforming. Males in this status tend to experience difficulty in separating from their mothers. Foreclosures view their parents as highly accepting and encouraging. Parental pressure for conformity to family values is very evident. Diffusion-status adolescents report much parental rejection and detachment from parents, especially from the father. In general, the data from family studies show that the same-sex parent is an important figure in identity resolution.

The interest in female identity has arisen because different criteria have been used to identify identity status based on the Marcia paradigm. Attitudes toward premarital sexual relations is a major content area in status determination. The research in general shows that achievement and foreclosure statuses are very similar in females, as are the moratorium and diffusion statuses. This pattern is not found for males. It has been argued by some that the focal concerns of females, in addition to concerns with occupation and ideology, involve interpersonal relationships more than do the concerns of males. Therefore, in forming a self-structure, females may examine the world outside for self-evaluation and acceptance in addition to the internal examination of self which typically occurs in males. The effect of an external focus on identity resolution in females is unknown, but this type of focus is likely to prolong the identity crisis. Further, it is still necessary to determine the areas in which choices and commitments are made for females.

The concept of negative identity has been used frequently in clinical settings to explain antisocial acts and delinquency in youth, as well as gang-related behavior. Randall Jones and Barbara Hartman (1988) found that the use of substances (for example, cigarettes, alcohol, and other drugs) was higher and more likely in youths of identity-diffusion status. Erikson and others have argued that troubled youths find that elements of a negative identity provide them with a sense of some mastery over a situation for which a positive approach has been continually denied them. In the examples cited, deviant behavior provided this sense of mastery and an identity.

Context

The identity crisis is the major conflict faced by the adolescent. Erikson's theorizing about the identity crisis made a major contribution to the adolescent literature. Marcia's reconceptualization of ego identity facilitated identity research and clinical assessment by providing a methodological approach for determining identity development and the psychological concomitants of identity. As a result, the study of identity and the awareness of the psychological impact on the individual has become a major research area and has provided a basis for clinical intervention.

The concept of identity crises originated with Erikson, based on the clinical experiences which he used to develop a theory of ego identity development. Explication of this theory appeared in his writings during the 1950's and 1960's. Erikson's theory of the human life cycle places identity resolution as the major crisis faced by the adolescent. The success of this resolution is determined by the satisfactory resolution of crises in the stages preceding adolescence.

Identity formation is a major topic in most textbooks on adolescence, and it is a focal concern of practitioners who treat adolescents with psychological adjustment problems. Until the appearance of Erikson's writings, the field of adolescence was mostly a discussion of physical and sexual development. His focus on psychosocial development, especially the emergence of a self-structure, increased immeasurably the understanding of adolescent development and the problems faced by the adolescent growing up in Western society. As Cote and Levine have noted, identity is a multidimensional construct, consisting of sociological perspectives, specifically the social environment in which the individual interacts, as well as psychological processes. Thus, a supportive social environment is critical to crisis resolution. The absence of this supportive environment has frequently been cited as an explanation for identity problems and the acquisition of a negative identity.

It is important to realize that identity has a temporal element as well as a lifelong duration. That is, identity as a personality characteristic undergoes transformations throughout the life cycle. While crisis resolution may be achieved during adolescence/young adulthood, this self-structure is not permanent. Crises can reemerge during the life span. The midlife crises of middle adulthood, written about frequently in the popular press, are often viewed as a manifestation of the earlier identity crisis experienced during adolescence/young adulthood.

A future role for identity crises is difficult to forecast. The psychological moratorium will continue to be an important process. Given the constant change in American society, the moratorium options available for youth may be more restricted, or more ambiguous and less stable. This scenario is more probable for humanistic moratoria as society moves toward more institutional structure in the form of schools taking on increased responsibility for the socialization of children and youth. The provision of child care before and after school is one example of the school's increased role. The erosion which has occurred in family structure presents another problem for identity crisis resolution.

Bibliography

Cote, James E., and Charles Levine. "A Critical Examination of the Ego Identity Status Paradigm." *Developmental Review* 8 (June, 1988): 147-184. Critiques the Marcia identity-status paradigm and notes several areas of divergence from Erikson's conceptualization theory of identity. Advances the argument for an interdisciplinary approach to understanding identity, and identifies several questions about identity crises that need to be considered.

_____. "A Formulation of Erikson's Theory of Ego Identity Formation." *Developmental Review* 7 (December, 1987): 209-218. A comprehensive review of Erikson's theory of ego identity and the role of psychological moratoria in the resolution of identity crises. Discusses Erikson's concepts of value orientation stages and the ego-superego conflict over personality control. Offers criticisms of Erikson's work and suggests cautions for the researcher.

Erikson, Erik Homburger. *Childhood and Society.* 2d ed. New York: W. W. Norton, 1963. A presentation of case histories based on Erikson's clinical experiences, as well as a discussion of Erikson's lifecycle model of human development. One section of the book is devoted to an examination of youth and identity. Clinical studies are used to illustrate the problems youth face in identity resolution.

_____. *Identity, Youth, and Crisis.* New York: W. W. Norton, 1968. A theoretical discussion of ego identity formation and identity confusion, with special attention given to issues such as womanhood, and race and identity. Erikson relies heavily on his vast clinical experiences to illustrate the concepts that he discusses. The life cycle as it applies to identity is examined from an epigenetic perspective.

Evans, Richard I. *Dialogue with Erik Erikson.* Reprint. Northvale, N.J.: Jason Aronson, 1995.

Kroger, Jane. *Identity in Adolescence.* London: Routledge & Kegan Paul, 1989. A presentation of identity development as conceptualized by Erikson and others. Each approach is criticized, and the empirical findings generated by the approach are summarized. The first chapter of the book is devoted to an overview of identity from a developmental and sociocultural perspective. The final chapter presents an integration of what is known about identity.

Marcia, James E. "Identity in Adolescence." In *Handbooks of Adolescent Psychology,* edited by Joseph Adelson. New York: John Wiley & Sons, 1980. A discussion of the identity statuses developed by Marcia, based on a paradigm derived from Erikson's conceptualization of ego identity. Reviews the research literature on personality characteristics, patterns of interaction, developmental studies, identity in women, and other directions in identity research. Ends with a discussion of a general ego-developmental approach to identity.

Psychoanalysis and Contemporary Thought 19, no. 2 (1996). A special issue entitled "Ideas and Identities: The Life and Work of Erik Erikson," edited by Robert S. Wallerstein. A variety of insightful perspectives on Erikson; includes a selection of photographs.

Tribe, Carol. *Profile of Three Theories: Erikson, Maslow, Piaget.* Dubuque, Iowa: Kendall Hunt Publishing, 1995.

Joseph C. LaVoie

See also:

Adolescence: Cognitive Skills, 13; Adolescence: Sexuality, 19; Attachment and Bonding in Infancy and Childhood, 71; Cognitive Development Theory: Jean Piaget, 135; Ego Psychology: Erik Erikson, 223; Gender-Identity Formation, 254; Generativity in Adulthood, 260; Integrity, 315; Intimacy in Adulthood, 340; Psychoanalytic Psychology, 471; Trust, Autonomy, Initiative, and Industry, 633.

IMPRINTING AND LEARNING

Type of psychology: Learning
Fields of study: Biological influences on learning; endocrine system

Imprinting is an endogenous, or inborn, animal behavior by which young mammals and birds learn specific, visible physical patterns to associate with important concepts such as the identification of one's mother, navigation routes, and danger. The phenomenon, which relies primarily upon visual cues and hormonal scents, is of high survival value for the species possessing it.

Principal terms

CONDITIONING: a type of learning in which an animal understands a concept by associating it with some object or by the administration of rewards and/or punishments

CRITICAL PERIOD: a specific time period during an animal's development during which a certain type of learning such as imprinting must occur if it is to be successfully incorporated into the animal's psyche

ENDOGENOUS BEHAVIOR: an innate, or inborn, behavior that is established by the animal's inherited genetic code (DNA) and that is not influenced by the animal's experiences or environment

ETHOLOGY: the study of animal behavior, psychology, and biology and the theories describing such behaviors

EXOGENOUS BEHAVIOR: a behavior that an animal acquires by learning, experience, and direct contact with its environment

IMPRINTING: a type of endogenous animal behavior by which a young individual mentally "photographs" a pattern and associates that pattern with a specific concept; the phenomenon occurs primarily in mammals and birds

PHEROMONE: a hormone or other chemical that is produced and released from the tissues of one individual and targets tissues in another individual, usually with a consciously or unconsciously detectable scent

PLASTICITY: a phenomenon of neuronal growth in the cerebral cortex of higher vertebrate animals that is associated with an animal's memory, learning capacity, and intelligence

VISUAL CUES: specific visible physical objects or patterns that an animal learns to associate with certain concepts

VOCAL CUES: specific sounds, frequency, and language that an animal learns to associate with certain concepts

Overview

Imprinting is an important type of behavior by which an animal learns specific concepts and identifies certain objects or individuals that are essential for survival. Imprinting events almost always occur very early in the life of an animal, during critical periods or time frames when the animal is most sensitive to environmental cues and influences. The phenomenon occurs in a variety of species, but it is most pronounced in the homeothermic (warm-blooded) and socially oriented higher vertebrate species, especially mammals and birds.

Imprinting is learned behavior. Most learned behavior falls within the domain of exogenous behavior, or behavior that an animal obtains by its experiences with fellow conspecifics (members of the same species) and the environment. Imprinting, however, is predominantly, if not exclusively, an endogenous behavior, which is a behavior that is genetically encoded within the individual. An individual is born with the capacity to imprint. The animal's cellular biochemistry and physiology will determine when in its development that it will imprint. The only environmental influence of any consequence in imprinting is the object of the imprint during the critical period. Ethologists, scientists who study animal behavior, debate the extent of endogenous and exogenous influences upon animal behavior. Most behaviors involve a combination of both, although one type may be more pronounced than the other.

The capacity for an animal to imprint is genetically determined and, therefore, is inherited. This type of behavior is to the animal's advantage for critical situations that must be correctly handled the first time. Such behaviors include the identification of one's parents (especially one's mother), the ability to navigate, the ability to identify danger, and even the tendency to perform the language of one's own species. Imprinting behaviors generally are of high survival value and hence must be programmed into the individual via the genes. Biological research has failed to identify many of the genes that are responsible for imprinting behaviors, although the hormonal basis of imprinting is well understood. Most imprinting studies have focused upon the environmental signals and developmental state of the individual during the occurrence of imprinting.

These studies have involved mammals and birds, warm-blooded species that have high social bonding, which seems to be a prerequisite for imprinting. The most famous imprinting studies were performed by the animal behaviorists and Nobel laureates Konrad Lorenz and Nikolaas Tinbergen. They and their many colleagues have detailed analyses of imprinting in a variety of species, in particular waterfowl such as geese and ducks. The maternal imprinting behavior of the newborn gosling or duckling upon the first moving object that it sees is the most striking example of imprinting behavior.

The maternal imprint is the means by which a newborn identifies its mother and the mother identifies its young. In birds, the newborn chick follows the first moving object that it sees, an object that should be its mother. The critical imprinting period is within a few hours after hatching. The chick visually will lock in on its moving mother and follow it wherever it goes until the chick reaches adulthood. The act of imprinting not only allows for the identification of one's parents but also serves as a trigger for all subsequent social events with members of one's own species. As has been established in numerous experiments, a newborn gosling that first sees a female duck will imprint on the duck and follow it endlessly. Upon reaching adulthood, the grown goose, which has been raised in the social environment of ducks, will attempt to behave as a duck, even to the point of mating. Newborn goslings, ducklings, and chicks can easily imprint on humans.

In mammals, imprinting relies not only upon visual cues but also on physical contact and smell. Newborn infants imprint upon their mothers, and vice versa, by direct contact, sight, and smell during the critical period, which usually occurs within twenty hours following birth. The newborn and its mother must come into direct contact with each other's skin and become familiarized with each other's smell. The latter phenomenon involves the release of special hormones called pheromones from each individual's body. Pheromones trigger a biochemical response in the body of the recipient individual, in this case leading to a locked identification pattern for the other involved individual. If direct contact between mother and infant is not maintained during the critical imprinting period, then the mother may reject the infant because she is unfamiliar with its scent. In such a case, the infant's life would be in jeopardy unless it were claimed by a substitute mother. Even in this situation, the failure to imprint would trigger subsequent psychological trauma in the infant, possibly leading to aberrant social behavior in later life.

Although maternal imprinting in mammal and bird species represents the best-documented studies of imprinting behavior, imprinting may be involved in other types of learned behavior. In migratory bird species, ethologists have attempted to explain how bird populations navigate from their summer nesting sites to their wintering sites and back every year without error. Different species manage to navigate in different fashions. The indigo bunting, however, navigates via the patterns of stars in the sky at night. Indigo bunting chicks imprint upon the celestial star patterns for their summer nesting site during a specific critical period, a fact that was determined by the rearrangement of planetarium stars for chicks by some nefarious research scientists.

Further research studies on birds also implicate imprinting in danger recognition and identification of one's species-specific call or song. Young birds of many species identify predatory birds (for example, hawks, falcons, and owls) by the outline of the predator's body during flight or attack and by special markings on the predator's body. Experiments also have demonstrated that unhatched birds can hear their mother's call or song; birds may imprint on their own species' call or song before they hatch. These studies reiterate the fact that imprinting is associated with a critical period during early development in which survival-related behaviors must become firmly established.

Applications

Imprinting is of considerable interest to psychologists because of its role in the learning process for humans. Humans imprint in much the same fashion as other mammals. The extended lifetime, long childhood, and great capacity for learning and intelligence make imprinting in humans an important area of study. Active research on imprinting is continually being conducted with humans, primates, cetaceans (such as dolphins, whales, and seals), and many other mammals, as well as with a large variety of bird species. Comparisons among the behaviors of these many species yield considerable similarities in the mechanisms of imprinting. These similarities underscore the importance of imprinting events in the life, survival, and socialization of the individual.

With humans, maternal imprinting occurs much as in other mammals. The infant and its mother must be in direct contact during the hours following birth. During this critical period, there is an exchange of pheromones between mother and infant, an exchange that, to a large extent, will bond the two. Such bonding immediately following birth can occur between infant and father in the same manner. Many psychologists stress the importance of both parents being present at the time of a child's delivery and making contact with the child during the critical hours of the first day following birth. Familiarization is important not only for the child but for the parents as well because all three are imprinting upon one another.

Failure of maternal or paternal imprinting during the critical period following birth can have drastic consequences in humans. The necessary, and poorly understood, biochemical changes that occur in the bodies of a child and parent during the critical period will not occur if there is no direct contact and, therefore, no transfer of imprinting pheromones. Consequently, familiarization and acceptance between the involved individuals may not occur, even if intense contact is maintained after the end of the critical period. The psychological impact upon the child and upon the parents may be profound, perhaps not immediately, but in later years. Studies on this problem are extremely limited because of the difficulty of tracing cause-and-effect relationships over many years when many behaviors are involved. There is some evidence, however, which indicates that failure to imprint may be associated with such things as learning disabilities, child-parent conflicts, and abnormal adolescent behavior. Nevertheless, other cases of imprinting failure seem to have no effect, as can be seen in tens of thousands of adopted children. The success or failure of maternal imprinting in humans is a subject of considerable importance in terms of how maternal imprinting affects human behavior and social interactions in later life.

Different human cultures maintain distinct methods of child rearing. In some cultures, children are reared by family servants or relatives from birth onward, not by the actual mother. Some cultures wrap infants very tightly so that they can barely move; other cultures are more permissive. Child and adolescent psychology focuses attention upon early life experiences that could have great influence upon later social behavior. The success or failure of imprinting, along with other early childhood experiences, may be a factor in later social behaviors such as competitiveness, interaction with individuals of the opposite sex, mating, and maintenance of a stable family structure. Even criminal behavior and psychological abnormalities may be traceable to such early childhood events.

Imprinting studies with mammal and bird species are much easier, because the researcher has the freedom to conduct controlled experiments that test many different variables, thereby identifying the factors that influence an individual animal's ability to imprint. For bird species, a famous experiment is the moving ball experiment. A newly hatched chick is isolated in a chamber within which a suspended ball revolves around the center of the chamber. The researcher can test not only movement as an imprinting trigger but also other variables, such as critical imprinting time after hatching, color as an imprinting factor, and variations in the shape of the ball as imprinting factors. Other experiments involve switching eggs between different species (for example, placing a duck egg among geese eggs).

For mammals, imprinting has been observed in many species, such as humans, chimpanzees, gorillas, dolphins, elephant seals, wolves, and cattle. In most of these species, the failure of a mother to contact her newborn almost always results in her rejection of the child. In species such as elephant seals, smell is the primary means by which a mother identifies its pups. Maternal imprinting is of critical importance in a mammalian child's subsequent social development. Replacement of a newborn monkey's natural mother with a "doll" substitute leads to irreparable damage; the infant is socially and sexually repressed in its later life encounters with other monkeys. These and other studies establish imprinting as a required learning behavior for the successful survival and socialization of all birds and mammals.

Context

Animal behaviorists and psychologists attempt to identify the key factors that are responsible for imprinting in mammalian and avian species. Numerous factors, including vocal and visual cues, probably are involved, although the strongest two factors appear to be direct skin contact and the exchange of pheromones that are detectable by smell. The maternal imprinting behavior is the most intensively studied imprinting phenomenon, though imprinting appears to occur in diverse behaviors such as mating, migratory navigation, and certain forms of communication.

Imprinting attracts the interest of psychologists because it occurs at critical periods in an individual's life; because subsequent developmental, social, and behavioral events hinge upon what happens during the imprinting event; and because imprinting occurs at the genetic or biochemical level. Biochemically, imprinting relies upon the production and release of pheromones, molecules that have a specific structure and that can be manufactured in the laboratory. The identification and mass production of these pheromones could possibly produce treatments for some behavioral abnormalities.

As an endogenous (instinctive) form of learning, imprinting relies upon the highly complex nervous and endocrine systems of birds and mammals. It also appears limited to social behavior, a major characteristic of these species. The complex nervous systems involve a highly developed brain, vocal communication, well-developed eyes, and a keen sense of smell. The endocrine systems of these species produce a variety of hormones, including the pheromones that are involved in imprinting, mating, and territoriality. Understanding the nervous and endocrine regulation of behavior at all levels is of major interest to biological and psychological researchers. Such studies may prove to be fruitful in the discovery of the origin and nature of animal consciousness.

Imprinting may be contrasted with exogenous forms of learning. These other learning types include conditioning, in which individuals learn by repeated exposure to a stimulus, by association of the concept stimulus with apparently unrelated phenomena and objects, or by a system of reward and punishment administered by parents. Other exogenous learning forms include habituation (getting used to something) and trial and error. All learned behaviors are a combination of endogenous and exogenous factors.

Imprinting occurs at critical time periods during an individual's life, especially during early childhood. Maternal imprinting usually occurs between ten and thirty hours after birth or hatching for most species, with optimum imprinting occurring around twenty hours after birth. The imprinting event serves as a lock onto a specific behavior pattern and triggers subsequent behavioral events, including social interactions and sexual behavior. It is important for the individual that the imprinting events occur properly, or subsequent developmental and behavioral events could be affected drastically.

Bibliography

Beck, William S., Karel F. Liem, and George Gaylord Simpson. *Life: An Introduction to Biology*. 3d ed. New York: HarperCollins, 1991. Introduction to biology for the beginning student. Contains a clear text, many strong diagrams and illustrations, and beautiful photographs. Contains a thorough discussion of animal behavior, famous experiments, and various types of animal learning, including imprinting, and describes the studies of Konrad Lorenz and others.

Klopfer, Peter H., and Jack P. Hailman. *An Introduction to Animal Behavior: Ethology's First Century*. Englewood Cliffs, N.J.: Prentice-Hall, 1967. An excellent and well-organized introduction to the history of animal behavior research. Presents major themes and models, and cites many important studies. Chapters 3 and 12 discuss instinctive and learned aspects of behavioral development.

Manning, Aubrey. *An Introduction to Animal Behavior*. Reading, Mass.: Addison-Wesley, 1979. Concise, detailed, and thorough presentation of animal behavior research. Encompasses all major behavioral theories and supporting experiments. Includes a good discussion of imprinting studies, particularly with reference to maternal imprinting, and describes the biological bases behind imprinting and other behaviors.

Marler, Peter, and William J. Hamilton III. *Mechanisms of Animal Behavior*. New York: John Wiley & Sons, 1966. A detailed and comprehensive introduction to animal behavior, theories of behavior, and behavior research. Cites hundreds of case studies. Discusses imprinting, including maternal and sexual imprinting, and the biological bases behind imprinting behavior. Several chapters deal with imprinting-related phenomena.

Raven, Peter H., and George B. Johnson. *Biology*. 2d ed. St. Louis: Times Mirror/Mosby, 1989. A strong presentation of all aspects of biology for the beginning student. Includes excellent diagrams and illustrations. Summarizes the major theories and classic experiments of animal behavior research, including imprinting studies.

Wallace, Robert A., Gerald P. Sanders, and Robert J. Ferl. *Biology: The Science of Life*. 3d ed. New York: HarperCollins, 1991. An outstanding book for beginning students that describes all major concepts in biology with great clarity, using numerous examples, good illustrations, and beautiful photographs. Discusses behavioral research, including studies of maternal imprinting.

Wilson, Edward Osborne. *Sociobiology: The New Synthesis*. Cambridge, Mass.: The Belknap Press of Harvard University Press, 1975. An incredibly comprehensive study of sociobiology, a perspective which maintains that animal behavior is a driving force in animal species evolution. The author, a prominent entomologist, is the leading proponent of this controversial theory, which he defends with hundreds of case studies. Describes the biological basis of behavior during all stages of animal development.

David Wason Hollar, Jr.

See also:

Avoidance Learning, 93; Habituation and Sensitization, 266; Instrumental Conditioning: Acquisition and Extinction, 309; Learned Helplessness, 359; Learning: Generalization and Discrimination, 370; Learning, 364; Pavlovian Conditioning, 433.

INDIVIDUAL PSYCHOLOGY
Alfred Adler

Type of psychology: Personality
Fields of study: Personality theory; psychodynamic and neoanalytic models

Individual psychology is the personality theory that was developed by Alfred Adler after he broke from Freudian psychoanalytical ideas. Adler emphasized the importance of childhood inferiority feelings and stressed psychosocial rather than psychosexual development.

Principal terms

COMPENSATION: a defense mechanism for overcoming feelings of inferiority by trying harder to excel

INFERIORITY: a feeling of being less strong, knowledgeable, talented, and privileged than others that is universal for all people; the unique way an individual copes with this is the key to his or her style of life

MASCULINE PROTEST: the denying of inferiority feeling through rebelliousness, violence, or maintaining a tough exterior

PRIVATE LOGIC: an individual's techniques for coping with the feeling of inferiority by unconsciously redefining himself or herself in a way not compatible with social interest

SOCIAL INTEREST: a communal feeling which is engendered by fulfilling contacts with friends, family, and career; it overcomes feelings of inferiority

STYLE OF LIFE: an individual's unique and holistic way of coping with life

Overview

Individual psychology is the name of the school of personality theory and psychotherapy developed by Alfred Adler (1870-1937), a Viennese general-practice physician turned psychiatrist. The term "individual" has a dual implication: It implies uniqueness (each personality exists in a person whose distinctiveness must be appreciated); also, the personality is an indivisible unit that cannot be broken down into separate traits, drives, or habits which could be analyzed as if they had an existence apart from the whole.

The essence of a person's uniqueness is his or her style of life: a unified system which provides the principles that guide everyday behavior and gives the individual a perspective with which to perceive the self and the world. The style of life is fairly stable after about age six, and it represents the individual's attempt to explain and cope with the great problem of human existence: the feeling of inferiority.

All people develop a feeling of inferiority. First of all, they are born children in an adult world and realize that they have smaller and weaker bodies, less knowledge, and virtually no privileges. Then people start to compare themselves and realize that there are other people their own age who are better athletes, better scholars, more popular, more artistically talented, wealthier, more socially privileged, more physically attractive, or simply luckier. If one allows the perception of one's own self-worth to be influenced by such subjective comparisons, then one's self-esteem will be lowered by an inferiority complex.

Adler believed that since one's style of life was largely determined early in life, certain childhood conditions made individuals more vulnerable to feelings of inferiority. For example, children born into poverty or into ethnic groups subjected to prejudice may develop a heightened sense of inferiority. Those children with real disabilities (learning or physical disabilities, for example) would also be more susceptible to devaluing their own worth, especially when others are excessively critical or mocking.

Adler looked inside the family for the most powerful influences on a child's developing style of life. Parents who treat a child harshly (through physical, verbal, or sexual abuse) would certainly foster feelings of inferiority in that child. Similarly, parents who neglect or abandon their children contribute to the problem. (Adler believed that such children, instead of directing their rage outward against such parents, turn it inward and say, "There must be something wrong with me, or they would not treat me this way.") Surprisingly, Adler also believed that those parents who pamper their children frustrate the development of positive self-esteem, for such youngsters conclude that they must be very weak and ineffectual in order to require such constant protection and service. When such pampered children go out into the larger world and are not the recipients of constant attention and favors, their previous training has not prepared them for this; they rapidly develop inferior feelings.

The impact of the family on the formulation of one's style of life also includes the influence of siblings. Adler was the first to note that a child's birth order contributed to personality. Oldest children tend to be more serious and success-oriented, because they spend more time with their parents and identify more closely with them. When the younger children come along, the oldest child naturally falls into a leadership role. Youngest children are more likely to have greater social skills and be creative and rebellious. Regardless of birth order, intense sibling rivalries and comparisons can easily damage the esteem of children.

Adler was not fatalistic in discussing the possible impact on style of life of these congenital and environmental forces; he held that it is neither heredity nor environment which determines personality, but rather the way that individuals interpret heredity and environment. These furnish only the building blocks out of which the individual fashions a work of art: the style of life. People have (and make) choices, and this determines their own development; some people, however, have been trained by life to make better choices than others.

All individuals have the capacity to compensate for feelings of inferiority. Many great athletes were frail children and worked hard to develop their physical strength and skills. Great painters overcame weak eyesight; great musicians overcame poor hearing. Given proper encouragement, people are capable of great accomplishments.

The healthy, normal course of development is for individuals to overcome their feeling of inferiority and develop social interest. This involves a feeling of community, or humanistic identification, and a concern with the well-being of others, not only one's own private feelings. Social interest is reflected in and reinforced by cooperative and constructive interactions with others. It starts in childhood, when the youngster has nurturing and encouraging contacts with parents, teachers, and peers.

Later, the three main pillars of social interest are friends, family, and career. Having friends helps one to overcome inferiority, because it allows one to be important in the eyes of someone else. Friends tell one their problems, so one does not feel that one is the only person who has self-doubt and frustration. Starting one's own family reduces inferiority feeling in much the same way. One feels loved by spouse and children, and one is very important to them. Having an occupation allows one to develop a sense of mastery and accomplishment and provides some service to others or to society at large. Therefore, those people who have difficulty establishing and maintaining friendships, succeeding as a spouse or parent, or finding a fulfilling career will have less opportunity to develop a healthy social interest and will have a greater susceptibility to lingering feelings of inferiority.

The alternatives to developing social interest as a way of escaping from feelings of inferiority are either to wallow in them or to explain them away with private logic. Such individuals retreat from meaningful interpersonal relationships and challenging work because it might threaten their precariously balanced self-esteem. Private logic convinces these individuals to seek a sham sense of superiority or notoriety in some way that lacks social interest.

One such approach in private logic is what Adler termed masculine protest (because Western patriarchal culture has encouraged such behavior in males and discouraged it in females). The formula is to be rebellious, defiant, even violent. Underlying all sadism, for example, is an attempt to deny weakness. The gangster wants more than money, the rapist more than sex: They need a feeling of power in order to cover up an unresolved inferiority feeling. The prostitute wants more than money; she needs to have the power to attract and manipulate men, even though she herself may be totally dependent on her pimp or on drugs.

Applications

Adler's theory, like Freud's psychoanalysis and B. F. Skinner's radical behaviorism, is a flexible and powerful tool for understanding and guiding human behavior. The first and foremost applications of individual psychology have been in the areas of child rearing, education, and guidance. Because the first six years of life are formative, the contact that children have during this time with parents, teachers, siblings, and peers will influence that child's later decisions in the direction of social interest or private logic. Adlerians recommend that parents and teachers be firm and fair, and above all, encouraging. One should tell children that they can overcome their disabilities and praise every progress toward accomplishment and social interest. One should avoid excessive punishments, for this will only convince children that others are against them and that they must withdraw into private logic.

After World War I, the new Social Democratic government of Austria gave Adler the task of developing a system of youth guidance clinics throughout the nation. Each child age six to fourteen was screened, then counseled, if necessary. In the 1920's, the rates of crime and mental disorders among young people declined dramatically.

A second example of the applicability of Adler's theory would be at the other end of the life cycle: old age. Late life is a period in which the incidence of mental disorder, especially depression, increases. This can be understood in terms of diminished opportunity to sustain social interest and increased sources of inferiority feeling.

Recall that social interest has three pillars: career, friends, and family. Traditionally, one retires from one's career at about age sixty-five. Elders who do not develop satisfying new activities (especially those activities which involve a sense of accomplishment and contribution to others) adjust poorly to retirement and tend to become depressed. Old friends die or move into retirement communities. Sometimes it is harder to see and talk with old friends because of the difficulty of driving or using public transportation as one ages, or because one or one's friends become hard of hearing or experience a stroke that impairs speech. By far the greatest interpersonal loss of later life is the loss of a spouse. When adult children move away in pursuit of their own lives, this may also give an elder the perception of being abandoned.

Conditions that can rekindle old feelings of inferiority abound in later life. Real physical inferiorities arise. The average elder reports at least two of the following chronic conditions: impaired vision, impaired hearing, a heart condition, stroke, or arthritis. The United States is a youth- and body-oriented culture that worships physical attractiveness, not wrinkles and fat. Some elders, especially those who have had the burdens of long-term illness, feel inferior because of their reduced financial resources.

A third area of application is social psychology, especially the study of prejudice. Gordon Allport suggested that those people who exhibit racial or religious prejudice are typically people who feel inferior themselves: They are trying to feel better about themselves by at least feeling superior to someone else. Typically, prejudice against African Americans has been greatest among whites of low socioeconomic status. Prejudice against new immigrants has been greatest among the more poorly skilled domestic workers. Another example of prejudice would be social class distinctions. The middle class feels inferior (in terms of wealth and privilege) to the upper class. Therefore, the middle class responds by using its private logic to demean the justification of wealth: "The rich are rich because their ancestors were robber barons or because they themselves were junk bond traders in the 1980's." The middle class feels superior to the lower class, however, and again uses private logic to justify and legitimize that class distinction: "The poor are poor because they are lazy and irresponsible." In order to solidify its own identity as hardworking and responsible, the middle class develops a perception of the poor that is more derogatory than an objective analysis would permit.

The most telling application of the theory of individual psychology to prejudice occurred in the first part of the twentieth century in Germany. The rise of Nazi anti-Semitism can be associated with the humiliating German defeat in World War I and with the deplorable economic conditions brought about by hyperinflation and depression. Adolf Hitler first blamed the Jews for the "November treason" which stabbed the German army in the back. (This private logic allowed the German people to believe that their defeated army would have achieved an all-out victory at the front had it not been for the Jewish traitors back in Berlin.) All the problems of capitalism and social inequality were laid at the feet of Jewish financiers, and every fear of rabble-rousing Communists was associated with Jewish radicals. Since everything bad, weak, cowardly, or exploitive was labeled "Jewish," the Germans could believe that they themselves were everything good. The result of the institutionalization of this private logic in the Third Reich led to one of the most blatant examples of masculine protest that humankind has witnessed: World War II and the Holocaust.

A fourth application is associated with management and sales. Management applies interpersonal relations to subordinates; sales applies interpersonal relations to prospective customers. Adler's formula for effective interpersonal relations is simple: Do not make the other person feel inferior. Treat workers with respect. Act as if they are intelligent, competent, wise, and motivated. Give subordinates the opportunity and the encouragement to do a good job, so that they can nurture their own social interest by having a feeling of accomplishment and contribution. Mary Kay Ash, the cosmetics magnate, said that she treated each of her employees and distributors as if each were wearing a sign saying, "make me feel important." A similar strategy should apply to customers.

Context

The idea of the inferiority complex bears some similarity to the writings of many previous thinkers. Nineteenth century French psychologist Pierre Janet came closest by developing a theory of perceived insufficiency as a root of all neurosis. American psychologist William James spoke of an innate craving to be appreciated. Adler's emphasis on the individual's capacity of striving for compensation and on masculine protest has parallels in the writings of philosopher Friedrich Nietzsche.

Yet the optimistic, simplified, psychosocial approach of Alfred Adler can only be understood as a reaction to the pessimistic, esoteric, psychosexual approach of Sigmund Freud. Adler was a respected general practitioner in Vienna. He heard his first lecture on psychoanalysis in 1899 and was fascinated, although he never regarded himself as a pupil or disciple of Freud. He was invited to join the Vienna Psychoanalytic Society, and did so in 1902, but he was never psychoanalyzed himself. By the end of the decade, he had become president of the society and editor of its journal. As Adler's own theories developed, and as he voiced them within the psychoanalytic association, Freud became increasingly defensive.

Adler came to criticize several underpinnings of psychoanalytic theory. For example, he suggested that the Oedipus complex was merely the reaction of a pampered child, not a universal complex. Adler saw dysfunctional sexual attitudes and practices as a symptom of underlying neurosis, not as its underlying cause. When Adler would not recant his heresy, the Vienna Psychoanalytic Society was split into a Freudian majority and an Adlerian minority. For a brief period, the Adlerians retained the term "psychoanalysis," only later defining their school as individual psychology.

Freud's influence on Adler can be seen in the emphasis on the importance of early childhood and on the ideas that the motives that underlie neurosis are outside conscious awareness (private logic) and that it is only through insight into these motives that cure can be attained. It is largely in Adler's reaction against Freud, however, that Adler truly defined himself. He saw Freud as offering a mechanistic system in which individuals merely react according to instincts and their early childhood environment; Adler believed that individuals have choices about their futures. He saw Freud as emphasizing universal themes that are rigidly repeated in each patient; Adler believed that people fashion their unique styles of life. Adler saw Freud as being focused on the intrapsychic; Adler emphasized the interpersonal, social field.

While Freud's personality theory has been the best remembered, Adler's has been the most rediscovered. In the 1940's, holistic theorists such as Kurt Lewin and Kurt Goldstein reiterated Adler's emphasis on the individual's subjective and comprehensive approach to perceptions. In the 1960's, humanistic theorists such as Abraham Maslow and Carl Rogers rediscovered his emphasis on individuals overcoming the conditions of their childhood and striving toward a self-actualization and potential to love. In the 1980's, cognitive theorists such as Albert Ellis, Aaron Beck, and Martin E. P. Seligman emphasized how individuals perceive and understand their situation as the central element underlying psychopathology.

An evaluation of individual psychology must necessarily include some enumeration of its weaknesses as well as its strengths. The positives are obvious: The theory is easy to comprehend, optimistic about human nature, and applicable to the understanding of a wide variety of issues. The weaknesses would be the other side of those very strengths. If a theory is so easy to comprehend, is it not then simplistic—or merely a reformulation of common sense? This may explain why so many other theorists "rediscovered" Adler's ideas throughout the twentieth century. If a theory is so optimistic about human potential, can it present a balanced view of human nature? If a theory is flexible and broad enough as to be able to explain so much, can it be precise enough to explain anything with any depth? Although everything in individual psychology fits together as a unified whole, it is not always clear what the lines of reasoning are. Does excessive inferiority feeling preclude the formulation of social interest, or does social interest assuage inferiority feeling? Does inferiority feeling engender private logic, or does private logic sustain inferiority feeling? At different times, Adler and Adlerians seem to argue both sides of these questions. The Achilles heel of individual psychology (and of psychoanalysis) is prediction. If a given child is in a situation that heightens feelings of inferiority, will that child overcompensate effectively and develop social interest as an adult, or will private logic take over—if it does, will it be in the form of self-brooding or masculine protest?

Although the fuzziness of Adlerian concepts will preclude individual psychology from being a major force in academic psychology, it is safe to predict that future theorists will again rediscover many of Alfred Adler's concepts.

Bibliography

Adler, Alfred. *The Individual Psychology of Alfred Adler*. Edited by Heinz L. Ansbacher and Rowena R. Ansbacher. New York: Basic Books, 1956.

_____. *Superiority and Social Interest*. Edited by Heinz L. Ansbacher and Rowena R. Ansbacher. Evanston, Ill.: Northwestern University Press, 1964. There is no standard edition or comprehensive collection of Adler's writings. He wrote many books, but unlike Sigmund Freud or Carl Jung, he essentially said the same thing over and over (especially after 1913, when his theory congealed). Any of Adler's later books will give a good sense of his theory. The above two edited works by the Ansbachers take representative excerpts from Adler's numerous books and, together with editorial comments, give a good picture of the development of Adler's thought.

Bottome, Phyllis. *Alfred Adler: A Biography*. New York: G. P. Putnam's Sons, 1939. This classic biography was written only two years after Adler's death. It gives much insight into the man and his theory, but the book is a bit too laudatory.

Dreikurs, Rudolf. *Fundamentals of Adlerian Psychology*. New York: Greenberg, 1950. The author was an Adlerian disciple who became the leader of the Adlerian movement in the United States after World War II. His simple style and straightforward advice are very much in keeping with the style of Adler himself. Dreikurs' own expertise was in the area of child development.

Hoffman, Edward. *The Drive for Self: Alfred Adler and the Founding of Individual Psychology*. Foreword by Kurt A. Adler. Reading, Mass.: Addison-Wesley, 1994.

Mosak, Harold H. *Alfred Adler: His Influence on Psychology Today*. Park Ridge, N.J.: Noyes Press, 1973. This edited volume covers Adlerian applications to understanding education, social issues, and the humanities, as well as discussing the clinical aspects of the theory.

Mosak, Harold H., and Birdie Mosak. *A Bibliography of Adlerian Psychology*. Washington, D.C.: Hemisphere, 1975. This is a very comprehensive bibliography covering individual psychology up through the early 1970's. Even articles appearing in newsletters are included. It is organized by authors' last names but has a subject index.

Stepansky, Paul E. *In Freud's Shadow: Adler in Context*. New York: Analytic Press, 1983. This is one of the more recent biographies of Adler. It does an excellent job of considering Adler's sociohistorical context and his interpersonal struggles with Freud. True Adlerians will maintain that this book does not do Adler justice.

T. L. Brink

See also:

Analytical Psychology: Carl G. Jung, 49; Dream Analysis, 206; Ego Psychology: Erik Erikson, 223; Personality Theory: Major Issues, 453; Psychoanalytic Psychology, 471; Psychoanalytic Psychology and Personality: Sigmund Freud, 478; Radical Behaviorism: B. F. Skinner, 501; Social Learning: Albert Bandura, 559; Social Psychological Models: Erich Fromm, 565; Social Psychological Models: Karen Horney, 571.

INSTINCT THEORY

Type of psychology: Motivation
Fields of study: Biological influences on learning; motivation theory

Until behaviorism, which rejected instincts, became the dominant theoretical model for psychology during the early decades of the twentieth century, instinct theory was often used to explain both animal and human motivation. As behaviorism faded, aspects of instinct theory returned to psychology—modernized, but still recognizable as parts of the oldest theory of motivation.

Principal terms

BEHAVIORISM: a school of psychology that had a commanding influence on American psychology from the 1920's to the 1950's; it dictated that scientific psychology could work only with directly measurable factors

INSTINCT: an inherited, unlearned, complex sequence of behaviors, uniform in their expression and universal in a species

MOTIVATION: an inferred inner force that instigates, directs, and sustains behavior, as opposed to the "outside" environmental forces that influence actions

REFLEX: an inherited simple response of one part of the body to a specific stimulus, made without thought—for example, closing the eye when a flying insect hits the eyeball

SCIENTIFIC METHOD: an approach to gaining knowledge that involves proposing a hypothesis, rejecting or accepting it on the basis of evidence gathered, and sharing what was learned with others

TROPISM: an inherited, fairly complex behavior of an entire organism—for example, a moth's being attracted to light

Overview

When instinct theory was incorporated into the new scientific psychology of the late nineteenth century, it was already centuries old. In its earliest form, instinct theory specified that a creature's essential nature was already established at birth and that its actions would largely be directed by that nature. A modern restatement of this notion would be that creatures are already programmed, as computers are, at birth and that they must operate according to their programs. Charles Darwin's theory of evolution through natural selection, first published in 1859, led to great controversy in the late nineteenth and early twentieth centuries. It also fostered speculation that, if humans were evolved from earlier forms and were therefore more closely related to other animals than had once been believed, humans might have instincts—inherited behaviors—as other animals were observed to have. William McDougall was one of the main early instinct theorists; he suggested a list of human instincts in 1908 that included such varied behaviors as repulsion, curiosity, self-abasement, and gregariousness. Many researchers came up with their own lists of human instincts; by the 1920's, more than two thousand had been suggested.

A computer program can be printed out and studied, but an instinct in the original sense cannot so easily be made explicit. At best, it can be inferred from the behavior of an animal or person after other explanations for that behavior have been discounted. At worst, it is simply assumed from observing behavior. That a person has, for example, an instinct of argumentativeness could be assumed from the person's arguing; arguing is then "explained" by declaring that it comes from an instinct of argumentativeness. Such circular reasoning is unacceptable in scientific analyses, but it is very common in some early scientific (and many modern, popular) discussions of instinct.

As is often the case with ideas that have long been believed by both scientists and the general public, instinct theory has separated into several theories. The earliest form, mentioned above, was accepted by Aristotle, the ancient Greek philosopher/scientist. He wrote in his *Politics* that "a social instinct is implanted in all men by nature" and stated that "a man would be thought a coward if he had no more courage than a courageous woman, and a woman would be thought loquacious if she imposed no more restraint on her conversation than the good man." The first comment declares an inherent quality of people; the second, inherent qualities of men and women. Very likely, Aristotle's beliefs were based on careful observation of people around him—a good beginning, but not a sufficient basis for making factual comments about people in general.

Aristotle's views were those of a scientist of his day. Centuries later, a scientist would not hold such views, but a layperson very well might. Over the many centuries since Aristotle expressed his views on instinct theory, "popular" versions of it have been more influential than the cautious versions offered by later scientists.

Modern science reaches conclusions based, to the greatest extent possible, on evidence gathered and interpreted along lines suggested by theories. Traditional instinct theory is especially weak in suggesting such lines; usually it put early psychologists in the position of trying to support the idea that instinct had caused a behavior by demonstrating that nothing else had caused it. Rather than supporting one possibility, they were attempting to deny dozens of others. Even worse, they were forcing thought into an "either-or" pattern rather than allowing for the possibility that a behavior may be based on inherited influences interacting with learned ones.

For example, to try to evaluate the possibility that people are instinctively afraid of snakes, one could begin by finding a number of people afraid of snakes, followed by an attempt to discount all the ways in which those individuals might have learned their fear—that they had never been harmed by a snake, never been startled, never been told that snakes are dangerous, and so on. The task is all but impossible, almost guaranteeing that a researcher will conclude that there are several ways that the fear could have been learned, so there is no need for an instinct explanation. The fact that people who fear snakes can learn not to fear them can be offered as further evidence that they had learned their original fear—not a particularly compelling argument, but a good enough approach for a researcher who wants to discount instinct.

When behaviorism became the predominant theoretical stance of psychology in the 1920's, the problems with instinct as an explanation of motivation were "resolved" simply by sidestepping them. Instincts were discarded as unscientific, and other concepts—such as needs, drives, and motives—were substituted for them. Psychology's dropping the term instinct from its jargon did not, either for lower animals or for people, eliminate the behaviors it had originally labeled; dropping the term did, however, separate even further the popular views of instinct from the scientific ones.

Applications

Instinct theory's purpose in psychology's infancy was the same as it had once been in the distant past: to explain motivation of a variety of species, from the simplest creatures up through people. Unfortunately, it had also served other purposes in the past, purposes which often proved unwelcome to early behavioral scientists. To declare people superior to other animals, or men superior to women, or almost any target group better or worse than another was not a goal of psychology.

Worse than the heritage of centuries of misuse of the concept of instinct, however, was the accumulation of evidence that instincts (as originally defined, as completely unlearned behavior) were limited to simple creatures and were virtually nonexistent in people. Psychology and related sciences virtually eliminated instinct as a motivational concept for decades, yet they could not avoid bringing back similar notions. The term "instinct" was gone, but what it tried to explain was not. For example, social psychologists, working in the 1940's to find alternatives to the belief that aggression is instinctive in humans, proposed that frustration (goal blocking) is a major cause. When pressed to explain why frustration led to aggression, many indicated that this is simply part of human nature. Some years later, it was demonstrated that the presence of some sort of weapon during a frustrating experience enhanced the likelihood of aggression, apparently through a "triggering effect." Instinct as a concept was not invoked, but these ideas came very close.

Even closer was the work of another group of scientists, ethologists, in their explanations of some animal behaviors. Evaluating what might be thought a good example of instinct in its earliest definition, a duckling following its mother, they demonstrated that experience with a moving, quacking object is necessary. In other words, learning (but learning limited to a very brief period in the duckling's development) led to the behavior. Many other seemingly strong examples of instinct were demonstrated to be a consequence of some inner predisposition interacting with environmental circumstances. A new, useful rethinking of the ancient instinct concept had begun.

A 1961 article by Keller and Marian Breland suggested that instinct should still be a part of psychology, despite its period of disgrace. In training performing animals, they witnessed a phenomenon they termed "instinctive drift." (It is interesting to note that although other terms, such as "species-specific behavior," were at that time preferred to "instinct," the Brelands stated their preference for the original label.) Instinctive drift refers to the tendency of a creature's trained behavior to move in the direction of inherited predispositions.

The Brelands tried to teach pigs to place coins in a piggybank; they found that although the pigs could easily be taught to pick up coins and run toward the bank, they could not be stopped from repeatedly dropping and rooting at them. Raccoons could be taught to drop coins in a container but could not be stopped from "dipping" the coins in and rubbing them together, a drift toward the instinctive washing of food. Several other species presented similar problems to their would-be trainers, all related to what the Brelands willingly called instinct.

Preparedness is another example of an instinct/learning relationship. Through conditioning, any creature can be taught to associate some previously neutral stimuli with a behavior. Dogs in Ivan Pavlov's laboratory at the beginning of the twentieth century readily learned to salivate at the sound of a bell, a signal that food would appear immediately. While some stimuli can easily serve as signals for a particular species, others cannot. It seems clear that they are prepared by nature for some sorts of learning but not others. Rats can readily be trained to press a lever (a bar in a Skinner box) to obtain food, and pigeons can readily be trained to peck at something to do so, but there are some behaviors that they simply cannot learn to serve that purpose.

Conditioned taste aversion is yet another example of an instinctive influence that has been well documented by modern psychology. In people and other animals, nausea following the taste of food very consistently leads to that taste's becoming aversive. The taste/nausea combination is specific; electric shock following a taste does not cause the taste to become aversive, nor does a visual stimulus followed by nausea cause the sight to become aversive. Researchers theorize that the ability to learn to detect and avoid tainted food has survival value, so it has become instinctive.

Context

In popular use, belief in instincts has confused and hurt people more than it has enlightened or helped them. Instinct theory often imposes a rigid either-or form on people's thinking about human motivation. That is, people are encouraged by the notion of instinct to wonder if some behavior—aggression, for example—is either inherent in people or learned from experience.

Once one's thoughts are cast into such a mold, one is less likely to consider the strong likelihood that a behavior has multiple bases, which may be different from one person to the next. Instead of looking for the many possible reasons for human aggression—some related to inherent qualities and some related to learned qualities—one looks for a single cause. Often, intently focusing on one possibility to the exclusion of all others blinds people to the very fact that they are doing so. Searching for "the" answer, they fail to recognize that their very method of searching has locked their thinking onto a counterproductive track.

Instinct theory has been invoked to grant people special status, above that of other animals. Generally, this argument states that people can reason and rationally control their actions, while lower animals are guided solely by instincts. At best, this argument has been used to claim that people are especially loved by their God. At worst, the idea that lower animals are supposedly guided only by instinct was used by René Descartes to claim that animals are essentially automata, incapable of actually feeling pain, and that therefore they could be vivisected without anesthesia.

Instinct theory has also been used to support the claim that some people are more worthy than other people. Those with fewer "base instincts," or even those who by their rationality have overcome them, are supposedly superior. Acceptance of such nonsense has led to very real errors of judgment and considerable human suffering. For example, over many centuries, across much of the world, it was believed that women, simply by virtue of being female, were not capable of sufficiently clear thinking to justify providing them with a formal education, allowing them to own property, or letting them hold elected office or vote. Anthropologist Margaret Mead, in her 1942 book *And Keep Your Powder Dry: An Anthropologist Looks at America,* reports reversal of the foolish claim that women inherently lack some important quality. Young women in her classes, when told the then-prevailing view that people had no instincts and therefore that they had no maternal instinct, according to Mead, became very upset, believing that they lacked something essential. Many minority racial or ethnic groups have suffered in similar fashion from claims that, by their unalterable nature, they are incapable of behaving at levels comparable to those in the majority.

Instinct theory has been used to suggest the absolute inevitability of many undesirable behaviors, sometimes as a way of excusing them. The ideas that philandering is part of a man's nature or that gossiping is part of a woman's are patently foolish uses of the concept of instinct.

Bibliography

Birney, Robert Charles, and Richard C. Teevan. *Instinct: An Enduring Problem in Psychology*. Princeton, N.J.: Van Nostrand, 1961. A collection of readings intended for college students. Contains fourteen articles, ranging from William James's 1887 discussion of instinct to Frank Beach's 1955 "The Descent of Instinct," in which Beach traces the idea of instinct from the time of the ancient Greeks up to the 1950's and concludes that "the instinct concept has survived in almost complete absence of empirical validation."

Breland, Keller, and Marian Breland. "The Misbehavior of Organisms." *American Psychologist* 16 (November, 1961): 681-684. In the process of training performing animals, the Brelands were forced to contend with inherited behaviors of their pupils. This article alerted a generation of psychologists to the possibility that instinct had been inappropriately eliminated from their thinking. The writing is clear and amusing, and the article should be fairly easy to locate; most college and university libraries will have the journal.

Cherry, Andrew L., Jr. *The Socializing Instincts: Individual, Family, and Social Bonds*. Westport, Conn.: Praeger, 1994.

Cofer, Charles Norval, and M. H. Appley. *Motivation: Theory and Research*. New York: John Wiley & Sons, 1964. Long regarded as a classic on the topic of motivation, this book includes (in chapter 2, "Motivation in Historical Perspective") thirty-two pages of material that traces instinct through the centuries. Chapter 3, "The Concept of Instinct: Ethological Position," discusses ways the once discredited concept was returning to psychology in the early 1960's.

Hilgard, Ernest Ropiequet. *Psychology in America: A Historical Survey*. San Diego: Harcourt Brace Jovanovich, 1987. The material Hilgard covers is often complex, but his clear organization and writing make it accessible to most readers. Material related to instinct in several chapters (for example, those on motivation, comparative psychology, and social psychology) can help a reader gain further background on instinct's place in psychology.

Petri, Herbert L. *Motivation: Theory, Research, and Application*. 4th ed. Belmont, Calif.: Wadsworth, 1996.

Watson, John Broadus. *Behaviorism*. Rev. ed. Chicago: University of Chicago Press, 1930. The fifth chapter of Watson's popular presentation of the new psychology he was sponsoring ("Are There Any Human Instincts?") nicely illustrates how behaviorism handled instinct. This chapter contains Watson's famous declaration, "Give me a dozen healthy infants, well-formed, and my own specified world to bring them up in and I'll guarantee to take any one at random and train him to become any type of specialist I might select. . . . " Watson's writing is still charming, but his position is today mainly a curiosity.

Weiten, Wayne. *Psychology: Themes and Variations*. 2d ed. Pacific Grove, Calif.: Brooks/ Cole, 1991. Introductory psychology texts all have some coverage of instinct's return to psychology and, more important, describe how several other concepts have been introduced to deal with topics with which instinct was once inappropriately linked. Weiten's text is one of the best: easy and interesting to read, yet strong in its coverage of scientific psychology.

Harry A. Tiemann, Jr.

See also:

Achievement Motivation, 7; Drive Theory, 218; Homosexuality, 278; Imprinting and Learning, 290; Motivational Constructs, 404.

INSTRUMENTAL CONDITIONING
Acquisition and Extinction

Type of psychology: Learning
Field of study: Instrumental conditioning

Unlike Pavlovian conditioning, which deals with reflexive behaviors, instrumental conditioning deals with learned behaviors that are nonreflexive. The consequences of responding and how those consequences are presented to the organism determine how these behaviors are learned and maintained. Instrumental conditioning techniques have been successfully applied to a wide variety of areas, including classroom learning and treatment of mental disorders.

Principal terms

EXTINCTION: the removal of reinforcement and the subsequent ceasing of the instrumental response

INSTRUMENTAL CONDITIONING: a type of conditioning in which the organism is the agent or instrument in causing behavior to occur; differs from Pavlovian conditioning, in which the organism plays a passive role

LAW OF EFFECT: Thorndike's basic law of instrumental conditioning, which holds that responses followed by certain events will be either more or less likely to recur

OPERANT: the basic response unit in instrumental conditioning; a response which, when emitted, operates upon its environment and is instrumental in providing some consequences

PUNISHER: a possible consequence of emitting a response which reduces the likelihood of repeating the response and can be positive or negative

REINFORCER: a possible consequence of emitting a response which increases the likelihood of repeating the response and can be positive or negative

SHAPING: the acquiring of instrumental behavior in small steps or increments by reinforcing successively closer approximations to the desired final behavior

SKINNER BOX: the most commonly used apparatus for studying instrumental conditioning; manipulation of a lever (for rats, monkeys, or humans) or an illuminated disk (for pigeons) produces consequences

Overview

Instrumental, or operant, conditioning is involved with the acquisition and maintenance of responses that, unlike the responses of Pavlovian conditioning, are nonreflexive. Instrumental responses appear to be flexible, intelligent, complex, farsighted, and controlled by their consequences. This is in marked contrast to the rigid, simple, and automatic appearance of Pavlovian responses, which are elicited by preceding (rather than consequent) stimuli. Although instrumental conditioning has been used since ancient times, its identification and discovery are credited to the psychologist Edward L. Thorndike.

At the end of the nineteenth century, Thorndike confined hungry cats in a puzzle box and placed food outside the box. A cat could get to the food by correctly manipulating a latch inside the box, which opened the door. Thorndike showed that with repeated trials, the time it took the cat to press the latch decreased. Thus, through repeated trials, the cat acquired a new behavior and became increasingly efficient at performing it. From these experiments, Thorndike formulated his law of effect in 1911. Responses which are followed by a particular consequence become connected to the situations, so that when the situation recurs, the response is more or less likely to recur. If the response is more likely to recur, the consequence is called a reinforcer. If it is less likely to recur, the consequence is called a punisher. When a cat pressed the latch, it obtained food. Pressing the latch became associated with the box and with obtaining food. The cat was more likely to press the latch and press it quickly upon being reintroduced to the box. (Food is thus a reinforcer.) If the cat had instead received an electric shock, it would likely have ceased responding. (Electric shock would be a punisher.)

As Thorndike so ably demonstrated with his puzzle box experiments and law of effect, the hallmark of instrumental conditioning is that the response must first occur before the consequence can be given and eventually exert control over the behavior. That is, a contingency or association between the behavior and what follows must be developed. If the response is simple, as with Thorndike's puzzle box, the organism can usually acquire the correct response through trial and error without assistance. If the response is more complex, however, or if rapid acquisition of a simple response is desired, then assistance will be required. If the organism is a human, verbal instruction or modeling the correct behavior may be sufficient.

If the organism is not human, or if the behavior cannot be adequately described verbally or modeled, shaping will have to be used. With this procedure, the desired behavior is acquired by successively reinforcing small steps, or increments, of behavior which increasingly approximate the final behavior. The size of the steps is small enough to ensure a smooth transition from one response to the next. For example, if the task were to cause a rat to press on a bar to receive food in a Skinner box, the researcher could shape the rat by first reinforcing responses that are oriented toward the bar, then reinforcing movements toward the bar, then reinforcing the placing of the rat's paws on the bar, and finally reinforcing the pressing of the bar.

Shaping is made possible by the processes of differential reinforcement and induction. By differentially reinforcing the desired response and not reinforcing incorrect responses, the researcher causes the desired response to become more frequent. As the correct response becomes more frequent, similar responses which have not previously occurred also become more probable. These new responses are natural variations of the correct response, and some of these responses will be even closer approximations of the desired behaviors. This process is called induction. These new responses can then be differentially reinforced until the final desired behavior is shaped.

Reinforcement is critical to the successful acquisition, and then maintenance, of instrumental behavior. If reinforcement is withdrawn, the behavior will undergo extinction; that is, it will cease to occur. All instrumental behavior will extinguish if it is not reinforced. The important question then becomes how long it takes the behavior to extinguish. The most important factor determining the course of extinction is the schedule of reinforcement that is used to maintain the behavior. Each correct response can be either reinforced or not reinforced every single time it occurs during maintenance. It is well established that behavior that is only intermittently or partially reinforced is much more resistant to extinction than behavior that is reinforced every time. A good example of this partial-reinforcement extinction effect is provided in a study done by Donald J. Lewis. Five groups of college students were permitted to play a slot machine. Depending upon the group, the slot machine was rigged to pay off on either one, two, four, six, or all eight (continuous reinforcement) of the initial plays. The machine then stopped paying off altogether (extinction). Lewis found that the one-, two-, four-, and six-payoff groups all continued to pull the handle more often and longer than did the eight-payoff group before they finally stopped responding. Furthermore, resistance to extinction was inversely related to the number of payoffs; that is, the one-payoff group took longest to extinguish and made the most pulls, and the eight-payoff group made the least.

During the acquisition of instrumental behaviors, each correct response should be reinforced so that correct behavior will not have a chance to extinguish. Once the behavior is acquired, however, not every occurrence of the correct response need be reinforced. Fewer reinforcers will be required, and the behavior will be stronger.

Applications

Since instrumental (operant) conditioning stresses the control of behavior by the consequences produced by that behavior, it provides a powerful tool for teaching new behaviors.

Animal trainers rely on it to teach their animals new tricks. For example, Gunther Gebel-Williams, the legendary animal trainer with the Ringling Bros. and Barnum & Bailey Circus, used shaping with his lions and tigers. Unlike rats or pigeons, lions and tigers must begin learning their routines when they are young, around fifteen months old ("You can't take a grown-up lion and say, 'Come on, get on the horse,' " Gebel-Williams wryly observed). In one instance, lion cubs learn tiny bits of behavior that might later be integrated into a routine. For example, the cubs are urged to run across the center ring, jump onto a small platform, and then jump onto a dummy horse that a circus hand is pulling about the ring. When each phase is performed correctly, the cub receives meat, petting, and praise. Mild aversive stimuli are sometimes used, too. A cub learns to stand on its hind legs when meat is held above its head. Additionally, short, sharp taps from a stick help the cub assume the right position. Once this is done, however, the aversive stimulus ceases (a behavior is strengthened through removal of a consequence, or negative reinforcer), and the cub receives affection and food (a behavior is strengthened through presentation of a consequence or positive reinforcer).

Mild aversive stimulation can also be useful for teaching tricks to killer whales. Since killer whales have no natural enemies, force cannot be used to get them to do a trick. Rather, food and affection are used as the primary reinforcers. The whales, not their trainers, design the activities that are eventually performed. The routines consist of movements that are natural to the whale. Each day, the trainer gets in the water and plays with the whale. When the trainer sees a behavior that could be part of the routine, the behavior is reinforced. Killer whales are highly intelligent, so they readily repeat the behavior. If the whale performs incorrect responses during acquisition, however, affection is withheld; the trainer simply walks away (negative punishment, in which a behavior is suppressed through removal of a consequence). The whale must ask the trainer to come back. If the whale performs properly, then affection is restored (positive reinforcement). Through this method, the whale quickly picks up the appropriate routine.

Instrumental conditioning procedures have also been used extensively to facilitate new behaviors in individuals with severe mental disorders. Theodore Allyon and Nathan Azrin provided schizophrenic and mentally disordered hospital patients with candy, cigarettes, or extra coffee or milk if they picked up a knife, fork, or spoon while passing by the service counter. The reward procedure had no noticeable effect; the frequency of the desired behavior remained very low. Then, as the patients passed in line, the attendant verbally instructed them to "please pick up your knife, fork, and spoon, and you have a choice of extra milk, coffee, cigarettes, or candy." The addition of these verbal instructions produced an immediate increase in the desired behavior. It is likely that picking up the silverware could have been shaped in successive approximations without the verbal instructions; however, this experiment shows how effective verbal instructions can sometimes be with humans. The verbal instructions act as a controlling stimulus to call attention to the desired behavior.

As a last example, instrumental procedures have been used in classrooms to help promote and maintain discipline. David R. Adamson has offered a number of tips for both correcting misbehaviors and promoting good behaviors. Simple solutions should be sought. If students return late from recess, the teacher should time exactly how late the last person arrives and deduct that amount of time (negative punishment) from the whole class's next recess. Tighter rules should be imposed. The teacher should list the consequences for breaking rules and follow through consistently from the first moment if those rules are broken.

Good behavior should be rewarded. This helps disruptive students identify appropriate behaviors. The teacher should write out behavior contracts listing the desired instrumental behavior (for example, raising one's hand before talking), how often the behavior must occur (for example, 100 percent of the time), the positive reinforcers the student will receive for behaving appropriately (for example, a ten-minute recess from class each day), and the length of the contract (for example, one week or less). The teacher should use unexpected reinforcers occasionally when the students behave appropriately. For example, a special film can be shown. The teacher should be certain that the students know the reinforcer is a direct result of their good behavior.

Context

Learning became a central part of American psychology with the development of Pavlovian conditioning and Watsonian behaviorism in the late nineteenth and early twentieth centuries. Interest focused on how behavior was modified in response to ever-changing conditions in an organism's environment. John B. Watson adopted Pavlovian conditioning as his model of learning. Watson discarded instincts and other inherited behaviors, leaving as the remaining unit of unlearned behavior the unconditioned reflex (UR), which was elicited by the unconditioned stimulus (US). The unit of habit or learning was the conditioned reflex (CR). Human behavior was the product of conditioning of URs. Animals and people were born with a limited number of US-UR relationships. By conditioning and association of USs with conditioned stimuli (CSs), these CSs produced the more complex, learned behaviors of the adult. Watson ignored the implications of Thorndike's instrumental conditioning as a model for a second type of learning.

In two important articles published in 1935 and 1937, however, B. F. Skinner convincingly argued that Thorndike's law of effect described most of the behavior of organisms. Skinner further demonstrated the powerful effect of the consequences rather than antecedents of behavior in modifying and strengthening behavior by forming a contingency, or connection, between the response and its consequence. Skinner referred to this behavior as produced by operant conditioning (a term he preferred to instrumental conditioning), which, he argued, should be the concern of psychologists; Pavlovian conditioning should be the concern of physiologists.

In the beginning of his 1979 book, *The Road Less Traveled,* M. Scott Peck states, "Life is difficult. This is a great truth, one of the greatest truths. . . . Life is a series of problems." The solutions for which people strive to resolve life's problems describe how well they fit or match with their world, how able they are to change or modify their behavior successfully in response to a changing environment, and how well they control their environment in order to enhance their lives.

Instrumental conditioning is a better model than Pavlovian conditioning for explaining how most changes in behavior occur. This is not to deny the importance of Pavlovian conditioning. Nevertheless, most of people's adaptations to their changing world require the acquisition of behaviors that are spontaneous, modifiable, intelligent, goal-oriented, and farsighted, rather than rigidly controlled or elicited by definite external events. It is the instrumental conditioning model that captures these characteristics.

Bibliography

Baldwin, John D., and Janice I. Baldwin. *Behavior Principles in Everyday Life.* Englewood Cliffs, N.J.: Prentice-Hall, 1981. A very readable introductory text which presents a lucid discussion of instrumental/operant conditioning, as well as numerous examples of it in everyday life.

Ferster, Charles B., and Stuart A. Culbertson. *Behavior Principles.* 3d ed. Englewood Cliffs, N.J.: Prentice-Hall, 1982. Similar in orientation to the Baldwin and Baldwin book cited above, but more advanced in its discussion of instrumental/operant conditioning and presentation of examples.

Lutz, John. *Introduction to Learning and Memory.* Pacific Grove, Calif.: Brooks/Cole, 1994.

Ormrod, Jeanne E. *Human Learning: Principles, Theories, and Educational Applications.* Columbus, Ohio: Charles E. Merrill, 1990. Another very enjoyable and readable presentation of instrumental/operant conditioning, with specific applications to the classroom.

Skinner, B. F. *Cumulative Record: A Selection of Papers.* 3d ed. New York: Appleton-Century-Crofts, 1972. A varied selection of important papers on instrumental/operant conditioning by the most important and influential psychologist in this area. Presents both theoretical and applied papers.

_____. *Science and Human Behavior.* New York: Macmillan, 1953. A thoughtful and thought-provoking discussion of instrumental/operant conditioning from the perspective of its usefulness in improving life on the individual and societal levels.

Smith, Terry L. *Behavior and Its Causes: Philosophical Foundations of Operant Psychology.* Boston: Kluwer Academic Publishers, 1994.

Ullman, Leonard P., and Leonard Krasner. *Case Studies in Behavior Modification*. New York: Holt, Rinehart and Winston, 1965. A thorough treatment of the application of instrumental/operant conditioning to the understanding and treatment of mental disorders.

Laurence Miller

See also:

Avoidance Learning, 93; Habituation and Sensitization, 266; Imprinting and Learning, 290; Instrumental Conditioning: Learned Helplessness, 359; Learning: Generalization and Discrimination, 370; Learning, 364; Pavlovian Conditioning, 433.

INTEGRITY

Type of psychology: Developmental psychology
Fields of study: Adulthood; aging

"Integrity," as used by Erik Erikson, refers to a sense of wholeness and completeness. According to Erikson, the task of the last stage of development is to achieve integrity and overcome the despair that can be associated with the review of one's life. The attainment of wisdom is the final outcome of the struggle between integrity and despair and can be achieved through life review.

Principal terms

DESPAIR: the feeling that life has been full of too many regrets and too many lost opportunities

ID: the part of the mind containing powerful basic drives, such as the need to express anger

IDENTITY: a distinctive personality established over time, based on the foundation laid in childhood and the expectations associated with reaching adulthood

INTEGRITY: the need to integrate life events into a complete picture of the self that begins around the age of seventy and ends at death

LIFE REVIEW: the process of reviewing one's life to achieve a better understanding of its meaning

REMINISCENCE: the process of thinking or talking about the past

SUPEREGO: the collection of moral behaviors learned from parents, teachers, and other authority figures that affect the decisions people make

UNCONSCIOUS MOTIVES: the forces of which individuals are usually unaware, that underlie behavior; they have been said to result from the desires of the id and/or the superego

WISDOM: as defined by Erikson, an informed and detached concern for life in the face of death

Overview

The concept of integrity is a difficult one to define. For most people, it means honesty and good character. According to Erik Erikson, in his work *Childhood and Society* (1950), integrity means a sense of wholeness and completeness. Individuals who fail to find integrity in their lives may be left with feelings of despair and worthlessness. The conflict between integrity and despair occurs, according to Erikson, in the final stage of development. Individuals who are approaching the last part of their lives have already gone through seven stages of development and have resolved or have failed to resolve issues such as trust, identity, and intimacy. The final stage of development is called the integrity-versus-despair stage. It begins at about age seventy and lasts for the rest of an individual's life.

This last stage of life is characterized by a need to review one's life and make sense out of the events that have occurred in earlier stages of growth. Individuals looking back over their lives may need to make peace with their past, accept some events as unchangeable, acknowledge their mistakes, and seek reconciliation with significant others in their lives. In the last stage, unlike earlier stages in which the focus of an individual's life is on others, individuals turn inward. More time is spent alone, reviewing the past, looking for themes that tie a person's life together, and finding ways to make sense of all the good and bad things that have occurred.

The end result of the struggle toward integrity is wisdom. Older persons who have looked back over their lives, acknowledged their failings, and made peace with their past have a depth of understanding that others can only achieve when they too approach the end of their lives. A sense of dignity is achieved and maintained despite the physical and sometimes financial problems that often accompany the aging process. The wisdom attained during this period of development is often shared with the next generation, adding even more worth and completeness to a person's life.

Not everyone is able to look back over his or her life and put things together to create the wholeness that characterizes the wise and dignified individual. Those who have made mistakes that they have been unable to forget or for which they have been unable to make amends are likely to experience feelings of despair. Those who dwell on missed opportunities may experience a sense of worthlessness. Those who are unable to reconcile broken relationships may experience feelings of anxiety and restlessness. There may be a sense that important activities have been left undone and that there is no time left to complete them. Physical deterioration and social isolation may add to the feelings of despair and increase the desire to hurry the arrival of death. The increase in depression and suicide rates that accompanies the aging process attests the fact that not all older individuals resolve the integrity-versus-despair conflict successfully.

It might be tempting to conclude that a person who appears to have the wisdom associated with successful resolution of the final stage of development has no self-doubt or uncertainty; wisdom, however, is not gained without moments of despair. The dynamic interplay between finding meaning in one's life and grieving over unfulfilled goals is at the center of wisdom. Learning to acknowledge the moments of despair and finding ways to reconcile relationships and overcome or accept the mistakes in one's life serve as the foundation for the integrity that is developed. Often the deepest moments of despair can make individuals aware of the need to come to terms with the past in order to make the most of the time they have left.

Clearly, not every individual reaches the final stage of development. Some are cut short by untimely death; others suffer from diseases that render them incapable of remembering their past. Still others fail to acknowledge that they are going to die and remain in earlier stages of development until they are too sick to do the hard work associated with life review. Most individuals who survive into their seventies, however, acknowledge their mortality; they understand that their lives will end sooner rather than later. This realization often comes because physical impairments and chronic illnesses remind them of their approaching death. Those who do accept the reality that they are in the final stages of life, no matter how physically impaired they might be, have an opportunity to accept their lives and, in so doing, approach their pending deaths with dignity.

Applications
Increasing interest in adult development, particularly in aging, has led to several investigations involving the application of the concept of integrity. One of the most common applications of Erikson's ideas concerning the final stage of life can be found in the use of

autobiographical, biographical, and even fictional information to provide insight into the process of aging. In a book he edited entitled *Adulthood* (1978), Erikson devotes a chapter he himself wrote to a review of Ingmar Bergman's film *Smultronstället* (1957; *Wild Strawberries*, 1959). In the review, Erikson uses his ideas about integrity and despair to find meaning and purpose in the life of the film's central character, Dr. Isak Borg, a retired Swedish doctor.

This process of using life reviews found in biographical works to identify the development of integrity in a person's life has been applied to many famous and some not-so-famous individuals. An extensive description of the application of Erikson's ideas to the understanding of the life of Vera Brittain, a British feminist and pacifist, was written by Abigail J. Stewart, Carol Franz, and Lynne Layton and published in *Journal of Personality* 56 (March, 1988). A similar technique has been applied to study the lives of Augusta Turnley (a fictional character from the 1975 novel *Perilous Voyage*, written by Lael Wertenbaker), Florida Scott-Maxwell (an author and psychologist), and Arie Carpenter (a woman born and reared in rural North Carolina). This type of application is described in an article in *International Journal of Aging and Human Development* 27, no. 1 (1988), written by Natalie Rosel. The reviews of the lives of these individuals show the universality of Erikson's ideas and the diverse ways in which people reach and maintain a sense of dignity in their lives. The concepts of dealing with despair and the achievement of wisdom are made concrete through examples from the biographies and autobiographies that serve as the database for the studies.

Though a clearer understanding of the attainment of integrity is achieved by applying Erikson's theory to biographical sketches, there is much to be gained by applying his ideas to the lives of those who are still living. In a study involving a group of elderly nursing home residents, published in 1990, Lois Taft and Milton F. Nehrke explored the development of integrity. The authors wanted to discover whether people whose conversations about the past (a phenomenon called reminiscence) involved a review of their lives would have a stronger sense of integrity than those who used reminiscence as a tool for education or as a way to discover solutions for problems. Those nursing home residents who reported spending more time reviewing their lives when reminiscing about the past agreed more strongly with statements indicating the presence of integrity, such as "I am proud of what I have done" and "I am satisfied with my life so far." The authors of the study concluded that people benefit from reminiscing about their past and that the listeners also benefit from the wisdom, knowledge, and insight that emerges from those actively involved in the life-review process.

The results of the nursing home study suggest two things. First, even people who are no longer able to take care of all their daily needs (for example, meal preparation, housekeeping, and monitoring medication) may benefit from the life-review process. They may be able to achieve a sense of dignity despite their impairments. The results obtained in the nursing home study also suggest that therapists who work with clients in the final stage of development might use life review as a way to help them deal with many of the issues that arise during the integrity-versus-despair stage of development.

Studies such as the one done with the nursing home residents continue to show the importance of Erikson's developmental theory. His work has led to improved therapeutic interventions for older adults. Counselors are incorporating the idea that development continues throughout the life span into their treatments. They have recognized that older individuals can and do benefit from therapeutic interventions designed to deal with their specific needs. The symptoms of depression and the emotions associated with losing a spouse are being identified and treated in the older population. Negative feelings arising from the adjustments required during retirement are also being identified, and therapists are responding with interventions unique to an older population. Counselors are in the process of helping older adults deal with their pending deaths and are helping them make the most of what remains of their lives. Social workers in nursing homes are helping residents remain oriented to time and place and are working with them to improve the quality of their lives. Clearly, Erikson's identification of the conflict between integrity and despair in the final stage of life has contributed to the enhancement of the therapeutic interventions for older adults.

Context

Erikson's thoughts on the development of wisdom emerging from the struggle between integrity and despair have roots in the philosophy of Søren Kierkegaard. Robert Coles, the author of *Erik H. Erikson: The Growth of His Work* (1970), argues that Kierkegaard's concept of the mind as a battleground in which selfish desires of individuals fight against the needs of society may have been one of the foundations of Erikson's conceptualization of the eight stages of development.

In each of the proposed developmental stages, the actions of the individual in the context of the society in which he or she is reared plays a central role in the conflict that must be resolved in that stage. In the integrity-versus-despair stage, individuals fight to maintain their dignity in a body that is failing them in the context of a society that may not value their insight and experience.

Erikson's ideas were also heavily influenced by one of his teachers, Sigmund Freud. Like Freud, Erikson believed in the existence of unconscious motives that could be responsible for behavior. The conflict between the desires of the individual (represented by the id) and the standards set by parents, teachers, and the culture (represented by the superego) is at the heart of both Freud's and Erikson's work. Erikson, in contrast to Freud, put more emphasis on the importance of the environment and was more interested in development across the life span than was his teacher.

Building on the foundation laid by Kierkegaard and Freud, Erikson spent many years studying American Indians, veterans returning from World War II, and children and adults from diverse backgrounds. His development of the ideas concerning integrity and despair were derived from these experiences but were particularly influenced by his interest in people such as Martin Luther, Albert Einstein, and Mahatma Gandhi. In studying their lives, he saw the development of integrity out of despair. He argued that in all people's lives there are moments of regret and lost opportunities that they must accept and from which they must learn; in so doing, they can attain wisdom.

Erikson's theory of development, as introduced in his book *Childhood and Society*, is explained in more detail in several subsequent works. His most detailed discussion of the final stage of life is developed in a book coauthored with Joan Erikson, his wife, and Helen Kivnick entitled *Vital Involvement in Old Age* (1986). Through the information obtained from clients (called informants), the authors provide examples from each of the conflicts that are present in each of the eight stages of development. The emphasis is on the importance of the struggles encountered in earlier stages and their influence on the development of integrity in the final stage.

Erikson's thoughts about development are important in a variety of ways. He was one of the first theorists to propose a developmental theory acknowledging that growth occurs across the life span, culminating only in death. Furthermore, his work expanded on Freud's by including the important role that the culture in which individuals are reared plays in development.

Despite these important contributions, Erikson, like most developmental and most personality theorists, has been criticized. The most frequently cited problems with the theory involve the difficulty that investigators have in testing the concepts it proposes. Investigators cannot easily define integrity or wisdom, or measure integrity or despair. These are difficult but not insurmountable problems.

The work done with life review suggests that some progress is being made in understanding the final stage of development, and it provides hope that more of Erikson's ideas will be tested in the laboratory and used in the therapist's office in the future. Despite the many problems with testing Erikson's assumptions about development, his theory continues to play a vital role in the understanding of personality across the life span.

Bibliography

Coles, Robert. *Erik H. Erikson: The Growth of His Work*. Boston: Little, Brown, 1970. A definitive work on the historical and psychological roots of Erikson's theory and on his writings. Fascinating reading for those who attempt to understand a theory by understanding the person who developed it. Some background in philosophy and some prior exposure to Freud are helpful.

Erikson, Erik H., ed. *Adulthood*. New York: W. W. Norton, 1978. The first chapter, written by Erikson, uses the life of the Swedish doctor portrayed in Ingmar Bergman's film *Wild Strawberries* to highlight the concepts of integrity and despair. Both the film and the chapter are highly recommended. The remainder of the work is also well presented but not as relevant to the concepts of integrity and despair as the first chapter.

_____. *Childhood and Society*. New York: W. W. Norton, 1950. Lays the foundation for and explains Erikson's theory of development. Erikson's psychological training, his artistic background, and his excellent command of the language are evident throughout the book. The clinical method of study is described and then applied to children and to Native Americans. The concept of the ego is developed and explored through biography and literature as well as clinical case histories. Should be read by anyone with an interest in personality or development.

_____. *Identity and the Life Cycle*. New York: International University Press, 1959. Reprint. New York: W. W. Norton, 1980. Expands on the earlier thoughts communicated in *Childhood and Society*. Thoughts about the importance of the historical backdrop in which people develop are more fully expressed than in earlier works. The growth of the individual as reflected in the healthy personality is described in some detail. The writing is dense and may be difficult for the reader who has not had much exposure to Erikson's work.

Erikson, Erik H., Joan M. Erikson, and Helen Q. Kivnick. *Vital Involvement in Old Age*. New York: W. W. Norton, 1986. Published when Erikson was well into his eighties. Describes the stages of the life cycle in reverse chronological order, emphasizing the importance of and dependence on earlier stages of development in successful aging. Clinical examples are abundant and help illustrate the many nuances of Erikson's theory. Not an easy read for those unfamiliar with Erikson's ideas, but a delightful and telling example of Erikson's own generativity and integrity.

Evans, Richard I. *Dialogue with Erik Erikson*. Reprint. Northvale, N.J.: Jason Aronson, 1995.

Gross, Francis L., Jr. *Introducing Erik Erikson: An Invitation to His Thinking*. Lanham, Md.: University Press of America, 1987. Introduces the thoughts of Erikson through brief historical excerpts and anecdotes from Erikson's life. Explanations of his theory are also included. Written for the novice and enhanced by frequent examples from classic and popular literature. The writing style is engaging and frequently humorous.

Psychoanalysis and Contemporary Thought 19, no. 2 (1996). A special issue entitled "Ideas and Identities: The Life and Work of Erik Erikson," edited by Robert S. Wallerstein. A variety of insightful perspectives on Erikson; includes a selection of photographs.

Tribe, Carol. *Profile of Three Theories: Erikson, Maslow, Piaget*. Dubuque, Iowa: Kendall Hunt Publishing, 1995.

Lori L. Temple

See also:

Adolescence: Cognitive Skills, 13; Adolescence: Sexuality, 19; Ego Psychology: Erik Erikson, 223; Generativity in Adulthood, 260; Identity Crises, 284; Intimacy in Adulthood, 340; Moral Development, 399; Psychoanalytic Psychology, 471; Trust, Autonomy, Initiative, and Industry, 633.

INTELLIGENCE
Definition and Theoretical Models

Type of psychology: Intelligence and intelligence testing
Fields of study: General issues in intelligence; intelligence assessment

Intelligence is a hypothetical concept, rather than a tangible entity, that is used by psychologists and other scientists to explain differences in the quality and adaptive value of the behavior of humans and, to some extent, animals. Its meaning and the theoretical models used to explore it are as varied as the field of psychology itself.

Principal terms

COGNITIVE PSYCHOLOGY: an area of psychology that deals with all aspects of experience that pertain to the process of knowing

CORRELATION: the degree of correspondence between two variables, which is usually expressed by a coefficient that can range from +1.00 to -1.00; 0.00 signifies no correspondence

FACTOR: a purely descriptive and hypothetical entity that is identified by examining the pattern of results of a factor analysis

FACTOR ANALYSIS: a statistical technique wherein a set of correlated variables can be regrouped in terms of the degree of commonality they share

HERITABILITY: the quality that allows a given characteristic or trait to be passed on through genes from one generation to another

Overview

The idea that human beings differ in their capacity to adapt to their environments, to learn from experience, to exercise various skills, and in general to succeed at various endeavors has existed since ancient times. Intelligence is the quality most often singled out as responsible for successful adaptations. Up to the end of the nineteenth century, notions about what constitutes intelligence and how differences in intelligence arise were mostly speculative. In the late 1800's, several trends converged to bring about an event that would change the way in which intelligence was seen and dramatically influence the way it would be studied. That event, which occurred in 1905, was the publication of the first useful instrument for measuring intelligence, the Binet-Simon scale, which was developed in France by Alfred Binet and Théodore Simon.

Although the development of intelligence tests was a great technological accomplishment, it occurred, in a sense, somewhat prematurely, before much scientific attention had been paid to the concept of intelligence. This circumstance tied the issue of defining intelligence and a large part of the research into its nature and origins to the limitations of the tests that had been devised. In fact, the working definition of intelligence that many psychologists have used either explicitly or implicitly in their scientific and applied pursuits is the one expressed by Edwin Boring in 1923, which holds that intelligence is whatever intelligence tests measure. Most psychologists realize that this definition is redundant and inadequate in that it erroneously implies that the tests are perfectly accurate and able to capture all that is meant by the concept. Nevertheless, psychologists and others have proceeded to use the tests as if the definition were true, mainly because of a scarcity of viable alternatives. The general public has also been led astray by the existence of "intelligence" tests and the frequent misuse of their results. Many people have come to think of the intelligence quotient, or IQ, not as a simple score achieved on a particular test, which it is, but as a complete and stable measure of intellectual capacity, which it most definitely is not. Such misconceptions about what intelligence-test scores represent also have led to an understandable resistance toward and resentment of intelligence tests.

Boring's semifacetious definition of intelligence may be the best known and most criticized one, but it is only one among many that have been offered. Most experts in the field have defined the concept at least once in their careers. Two of the most frequently cited and influential definitions are the ones provided by Alfred Binet himself and by David Wechsler, author of a series of "second-generation" individual intelligence tests that over-took the Binet scales in terms of the frequency with which they are used. Binet believed that the essential activities of intelligence are to judge well, to comprehend well, and to reason well. He stated that intelligent thought is characterized by direction, knowing what to do and how to do it; by adaptation, the capacity to monitor one's strategies for attaining a desired end; and by criticism, the power to evaluate and control one's behavior. In 1975, almost sixty-five years after Binet's death, Wechsler defined intelligence, not dissimilarly, as the global capacity of the individual to act purposefully, to think rationally, and to deal effectively with the environment.

In addition to the testing experts (psychometricians), developmental, learning, and cognitive psychologists, among others, are also vitally interested in the concept of intelligence. Specialists in each of these subfields emphasize different aspects of it in their definitions and research.

Representative definitions were sampled in 1921, when the *Journal of Educational Psychology* published the views of fourteen leading investigators, and again in 1986, when Robert Sternberg and Douglas Detterman collected the opinions of twenty-four experts in a book entitled *What Is Intelligence? Contemporary Viewpoints on Its Nature and Definition.* Most of the experts sampled in 1921 offered definitions that equated intelligence with one or more specific abilities. For example, Lewis Terman equated it with abstract thinking, which is the ability to elaborate concepts and to use language and other symbols. Others proposed definitions that emphasized the ability to adapt and/or learn. Some definitions centered on knowledge and cognitive components only, whereas others included nonintellectual qualities, such as perseverance. In comparison, Sternberg's and Detterman's 1986 survey of definitions, which is even more wide ranging, is accompanied by an organizational framework consisting of fifty-five categories or combinations of categories under which the twenty-four definitions can be classified. Some theorists view intelligence from a biological perspective and emphasize differences across species and/or the role of the central nervous system. Some stress cognitive aspects of mental functioning, while others focus on the role of motivation and goals. Still others, such as Anne Anastasi, choose to look upon intelligence as a quality that is inherent in behavior rather than in the individual. Another major perspective highlights the role of the environment, in terms of demands and values, in defining what constitutes intelligent behavior. Throughout the 1986 survey, one can find definitions that straddle two or more categories.

A review of the 1921 and 1986 surveys shows that the definitions proposed have become considerably more sophisticated and suggests that, as the field of psychology has expanded, the views of experts on intelligence may have grown farther apart. The reader of the 1986 work is left with the clear impression that intelligence is such a multifaceted concept that no single quality can define it and no single task or series of tasks can capture it completely. Moreover, it is clear that in order to unravel the qualities that produce intelligent behavior one must look not only at individuals and their skills but also at the requirements of the systems in which people find themselves. In other words, intelligence cannot be defined in a vacuum.

Applications

The lack of a universally accepted definition has not deterred continuous theorizing and research on the concept of intelligence. The central issue that has dominated theoretical models of intelligence is the question of whether it is a single, global ability or a collection of specialized abilities. This debate, started in England by Charles Spearman, is based on research that uses the correlations among various measures of abilities and, in particular, the method of factor analysis, which was also pioneered by Spearman. As early as 1904, Spearman, having examined the patterns of correlation coefficients among tests of sensory discrimination and estimates of intelligence, proposed that all mental functions are the result of a single general factor, which he later designated g. Spearman equated g with the ability to grasp and apply relations. He also allowed for the fact that most tasks require unique abilities, and he named those *s*, or specific, factors. According to Spearman, to the extent that performance on tasks was positively correlated, the correlation was attributable to the presence of g, whereas the presence of specific factors tended to lower the correlation between measures of performance on different tasks. By 1927, Spearman had modified his theory to allow for the existence of an intermediate class of factors, known as group factors, which were neither as universal as g nor as narrow as the *s* factors. Group factors were seen as accounting for the fact that certain types of activities, such as tasks involving the use of numbers or the element of speed, correlate more highly with one another than they do with tasks that do not have such elements in common.

Factor-analytic research has undergone explosive growth and extensive variations and refinements in both England and the United States since the 1920's. In the United States, work in this field was influenced greatly by Truman Kelley, whose 1928 book *Crossroads in the Mind of Man* presented a method for isolating group factors, and L. L. Thurstone, who by further elaboration of factor-analytic procedures identified a set of about twelve factors that he designated as the "primary mental abilities." Seven of these were repeatedly found in a number of investigations, using samples of people at different age levels, that were carried out by both Thurstone and others. These group factors or primary mental abilities are verbal comprehension, word fluency, speed and accuracy of arithmetic computation, spatial visualization, associative memory, perceptual speed, and general reasoning.

As the search for distinct intellectual factors progressed, their number multiplied, and so did the number of models devised to organize them. One type of scheme, used by Cyril Burt, Philip Vernon, and others, is a hierarchical arrangement of factors. In these models, Spearman's g factor is placed at the top of a pyramid and the specific factors are placed at the bottom; in between, there are one or more levels of group factors selected in terms of their breadth and arranged according to their interrelationships with the more general factors above them and the more specific factors below them. In Vernon's scheme, for example, the ability to change a tire might be classified as a specific factor at the base of the pyramid, located underneath an intermediate group factor labeled mechanical information, which in turn would be under one of the two major group factors identified by Vernon as the main subdivisions under g—namely, the practical-mechanical factor. The hierarchical scheme for organizing mental abilities is a useful device that is endorsed by many psychologists on both sides of the Atlantic. It recognizes that very few tasks are so simple as to require a single skill for successful performance, that many intellectual functions share some common elements, and that some abilities play a more pivotal role than others in the performance of culturally valued activities.

Another well-known scheme for organizing intellectual traits is the structure-of-intellect (SOI) model developed by J. P. Guilford. Although the SOI is grounded in extensive factor-analytic research conducted by Guilford throughout the 1940's and 1950's, the model goes beyond factor analysis and is perhaps the most ambitious attempt to classify systematically all the possible functions of the human intellect. The SOI classifies intellectual traits along three dimensions—namely, five types of operations, four types of contents, and six types of productions, for a total of 120 categories ($5 \times 4 \times 6$). Intellectual operations consist of what a person actually does (for example, evaluating or remembering something), the contents are the types of materials or information on which the operations are performed (for example, symbols, such as letters or numbers), and the products are the form in which the contents are processed (for example, units or relations). Not all the 120 categories in Guilford's complex model have been used, but enough factors have been identified to account for about 100 of them, and some have proved very useful in labeling and understanding the skills that tests measure. Furthermore, Guilford's model has served to call attention to some dimensions of intellectual activity, such as creativity and interpersonal skills, that had been neglected previously.

Contemporary theorists in the area of intelligence have tried to avoid the reliance on factor analysis and existing tests that have limited traditional research and have tried different approaches to the subject. For example, Howard Gardner, in his 1983 book *Frames of Mind: The Theory of Multiple Intelligences*, starts with the premises that the essence of intelligence is competence and that there are several distinct areas in which human beings can demonstrate competence. Based on a wide-ranging review of evidence from many scientific fields and sources, Gardner has designated seven areas of competence as separate and relatively independent "intelligences." His list includes some familiar categories, such as linguistic, spatial, and logical-mathematical intelligences, as well as the more unusual categories of musical, bodily-kinesthetic, and personal intelligences.

Another theory is the one proposed by Robert Sternberg in his 1985 book *Beyond IQ: A Triarchic Theory of Human Intelligence*. Sternberg defines intelligence, broadly, as mental self-management and stresses the "real-world," in addition to the academic, aspects of the concept. He believes that intelligent behavior consists of purposively adapting to, selecting, and shaping one's environment and that both culture and personality play significant roles in such behavior.

Theories of intelligence are still grappling with the issues of defining its nature and composition. Generally, newer theories do not represent radical departures from the past. They do, however, emphasize examining intelligence in relation to the variety of environments in which people actually live rather than to only academic or laboratory environments. Moreover, many investigators, especially those in cognitive psychology, are more interested in breaking down and replicating the steps involved in information processing and problem solving than they are in enumerating factors or settling on a single definition of intelligence. These trends hold the promise of moving the work in the field in the direction of devising new ways to teach people to understand, evaluate, and deal with their environments more intelligently instead of simply measuring how well they do on intelligence tests.

Context

The most heated of all the debates about intelligence is the one regarding its determinants, often described as the "nature-nurture" controversy. The "nature" side of the debate was spearheaded by Francis Galton, a nineteenth century English scientist who had become convinced that intelligence was a hereditary trait. Galton's followers tried to show, through studies comparing identical and nonidentical twins reared together and reared apart and by comparisons of people related to each other in varying degrees, that genetic endowment plays a far larger role than the environment in determining intelligence. Attempts to quantify an index of heritability for intelligence through such studies abound, and the estimates derived from them vary widely. On the "nurture" side of the debate, massive quantities of data have been gathered in an effort to show that the environment, including factors such as prenatal care, social-class membership, exposure to certain facilitative experiences, and educational opportunities of all sorts, has the more crucial role in determining a person's level of intellectual functioning.

Many critics, such as Anastasi (in a widely cited 1958 article entitled "Heredity, Environment, and the Question 'How?' ") have pointed out the futility of debating how much each factor contributes to intelligence. Anastasi and others argue that behavior is a function of the interaction between heredity and the total experiential history of individuals and that, from the moment of conception, the two are inextricably tied. Moreover, they point out that, even if intelligence were shown to be primarily determined by heredity, environmental influences could still modify its expression at any point. Most psychologists now accept this "interactionist" position and have moved on to explore how intelligence develops and how specific genetic and environmental factors affect it.

Bibliography

Fancher, Raymond E. *The Intelligence Men: Makers of the IQ Controversy*. New York: W. W. Norton, 1985. Presents the history of the various debates on intelligence in a highly readable fashion. The lives and ideas of the pioneers in the field, such as Alfred Binet and Francis Galton, are described in some detail.

Gardner, Howard. *Frames of Mind: The Theory of Multiple Intelligences*. New York: Basic Books, 1983. Gardner's description of the talents he designates as "intelligences" and explanation of the reasons for his selections provide a fascinating introduction to many of the most intriguing aspects of the field, including the extremes of prodigies and idiots savants.

Guilford, Joy Paul. *The Nature of Human Intelligence*. New York: McGraw-Hill, 1967.

Guilford describes the foundation of his theory of the structure of the intellect and in the process reviews the history of research into and theorizing about intelligence. This volume is an important contribution to the field.

Li, Rex. *A Theory of Conceptual Intelligence: Thinking, Learning, Creativity, and Giftedness*. Westport, Conn.: Praeger, 1996.

Sternberg, Robert J. *The Triarchic Mind: A New Theory of Human Intelligence*. New York: Viking Penguin, 1988. Sternberg reviews and criticizes the limitations of traditional views of intelligence and presents his own variations on that theme. The book is addressed to a general audience and contains a number of intellectual exercises aimed at enhancing the reader's performance on cognitive tests.

Vernon, Philip Ewart, *Intelligence: Heredity and Environment*. San Francisco: W. H. Freeman, 1979. Presents a thorough and thoughtful review of research on both sides of the "nature-nurture" debate on the development of intelligence. The issue of racial differences in intelligence is also discussed at length.

Wagman, Morton. *Human Intellect and Cognitive Science: Toward a General Unified Theory of Intelligence*. Westport, Conn.: Praeger, 1996.

Susana P. Urbina

See also:

Creativity and Intelligence, 176; Intelligence: Giftedness and Retardation, 327; Intelligence Tests, 333; Race and Intelligence, 495.

INTELLIGENCE
Giftedness and Retardation

Type of psychology: Intelligence and intelligence testing
Field of study: General issues in intelligence

Giftedness and retardation can be seen as occupying two extremes of the continuum of intelligence. The two conditions may be diagnosed through intelligence testing; each of them presents its own needs and dilemmas.

Principal terms

ADAPTIVE BEHAVIOR: certain common skills and abilities—such as eating, communicating, dressing, grooming, shopping, and working—that enable one to function in the world

GIFTEDNESS: a marked ability to learn more rapidly, perform intricate problems, and solve problems with a higher degree of rapidity; operationally defined as an IQ score above 130 on an individually administered test

INTELLIGENCE: as David Wechsler defines it, the aggregate or global capacity of an individual to act purposefully, think rationally, and deal effectively with his or her environment

PRODIGY: a very gifted child whose skills and abilities are readily apparent early in life

RELIABILITY: the ability of a test to measure a construct or skill with a high degree of consistency

RETARDATION: a condition, measured by an IQ score of less than 70, wherein a person has mental abilities that are far below average; other skills and abilities, such as adaptive behavior, may also be marginal

VALIDITY: the extent to which a test measures what it purports to measure

Overview

The terms "giftedness" and "retardation" are frequently used to identify opposite ends of the spectrum of intelligence. These two categories reflect two extremes of the population, and they embody different, disparate domains. Giftedness has typically been defined by using intelligence quotient (IQ) scores from an individually administered intelligence test given by a school psychologist or other professional. Although there is some variation from state to state and from program to program, the generally accepted cut-off point is an IQ score of 130 or above for placement in a gifted program or recognition as a gifted student.

Gifted individuals generally show greater problem-solving skills, manifest a greater degree of insight, and tend to learn more rapidly than the average person. They may show greater interest and curiosity in the world and may have been identified as "more intelligent" early in their lives. There are also many children, however, who drift through school (and do quite well) without being recognized as gifted until they find a subject in which they become passionately interested; their giftedness then becomes manifested.

Some gifted children, seen by their peers as outsiders, may be taunted or ostracized; this situation can leave lifelong emotional scars. Another problem is that parents may put unrealistic expectations on gifted children or try to live vicariously through them; these situations also create emotional problems for the children.

The Wechsler Intelligence Scale for Children-Revised (WISC-R), developed by David Wechsler in 1974, is generally the most commonly used IQ test for the determination of giftedness, although other tests, such as the Stanford-Binet test, are used for placement. Much concern has been voiced about the reliability and validity of intelligence tests; some tests that are administered in groups, for example, may be less reliable or valid than individually administered tests, which require a highly trained examiner. Individual tests yield clinical, educational, and other information. It should also be noted that there has been much discussion and theorizing concerning what, exactly, "intelligence" is. Some theorists hold that it reflects the speed of information processing—that is, how fast one learns and processes new information. Others believe that it is the difficulty of the problems that one can solve that more accurately reflects one's intelligence. Still others believe that the interaction of one's personality, environment, motivation, and natural skills makes up the construct of intelligence.

In some school districts, achievement test scores are used for placing children in gifted-student programs. Such children may show exceptional talents or skills in one or a variety of areas—mathematics, science, reading, spelling, and so on. Teachers often nominate students for inclusion in gifted programs. Parents, too, may believe their child to be gifted and expect the school system to provide the enrichment that they think is necessary for the child to develop fully.

On the other end of the intelligence spectrum is mental retardation. While the causes of mental retardation vary, the intellectual and cognitive deficiencies do not; there is a marked deficiency in intellectual thinking processes. There are several classifications of mental retardation, based primarily on IQ scores. In a general sense, these classifications are borderline mental retardation (IQ of 70-79), mild mental retardation (IQ of 50-55 to 70), moderate mental retardation (IQ of 35-40 to 50-55), severe mental retardation (IQ of 20-25 to 35-40), and profound mental retardation (IQ below 20 or 25). These scores should be viewed with some caution, however, as different IQ tests vary greatly in their theoretical orientation. Some are more verbal in nature, while others rely more on performance aspects as criteria of intellectual ability. There may also be secondary handicapping conditions, as well as motivational or transitory factors, that influence a person's performance on an IQ test. Medical conditions (such as cerebral palsy) or emotional problems (such as low frustration tolerance, impulsivity, or an inability to pay attention) are among those factors that may affect a mentally retarded person's test scores.

There may also be discrepancies among different skills. Some mentally retarded persons are able to do performance-based tasks very well—some can perform a number of routine mechanical tasks quite well but have very poor verbal and other language-based skills, arithmetic skills, and abstract thinking skills. This may also take the opposite form, in which verbal and vocabulary skills might be well developed but gross and fine motor coordination and manual dexterity are poor.

Terms that refer specifically to the retarded person's ability to learn and need for care are frequently used, and they relate generally to the type of IQ categorization given above. The terms educable mentally retarded, trainable mentally retarded, dependent, and custodial are often used as global terms to reflect a person's level of competence. There may be gross discrepancies, however, between IQ and level of functioning. For example, a mentally retarded person may have a relatively high IQ yet be unable to tie shoelaces or dress or groom himself or herself. On the other hand, a person with a lower IQ might be able to perform fairly complex procedures such as cooking, cleaning, or even changing the oil on a car or repairing machines. These anomalies are a challenge to psychologists' understanding; one theory is that they may reflect damage to a part of the brain at birth or in early childhood.

Some mentally retarded people need institutional care or even extreme one-on-one assistance. Some are able, with considerable supervision, to live in community group homes. On the other hand, a number of mentally retarded people can perform simple repetitive tasks in a wide variety of settings. Some hold jobs wherein they are supervised closely by a foreman; others are employed in what are termed sheltered workshops. In these facilities, the mentally retarded may work assembling objects or help on projects in the community. Some mentally retarded people have other medical or psychological problems that require attention and considerable assistance; many have secondary handicaps such as cerebral palsy or epilepsy.

The mentally retarded person may also manifest many deficits in adaptive behavior in several areas. As the level of retardation increases, the level of deficiency in adaptive behaviors generally increases. Many retarded people do need to be fed, dressed, and groomed; some are incontinent. Mentally retarded individuals may also become lazy or withdrawn; in particular, this occurs if they are not being challenged but are left simply to watch television or listen to the radio. Severely and profoundly retarded individuals may show behavioral manifestations of retardation such as perseveration (repetitious rocking or repeated words over and over), drooling, poor attention to dress and grooming, and attention-seeking behaviors. Skills that were once possessed can also be lost; this is especially true of educational skills.

Applications

The gifted person apparently has more sophisticated thinking skills, an ability to process more information in a more rapid manner, and a greater ability to sift salient information from meaningless information than does the average person. The gifted person also seems to have a higher degree of insight. The three germane components of insight—selective encoding, selective comparison, and selective combination—have been deemed crucial factors in giftedness. Gifted people seem to encode (or learn) important material more rapidly, compare it to previously learned information quite easily, and then combine, synthesize, and integrate information more readily than less gifted individuals.

Howard Gardner, in his book *Frames of Mind: The Theory of Multiple Intelligences* (1983), wrote on another aspect of giftedness: the various types of skills, abilities, and talents that are possessed by artists, musicians, and others. Gardner hypothesized that there are six domains of intelligence: linguistic, musical, logical-mathematical, visual-spatial, bodily-kinesthetic, and interpersonal and intrapersonal. Different cultures emphasize different aspects of intelligence—people in Japan, India, and Australia, for example, place emphasis on different skills, abilities, and talents than do people in the United States. In the United States, it is not uncommon for talented children with exceptional thespian, public speaking, creative, or writing skills to be ignored; perhaps American society is unsure how to encourage and nurture those skills. Mentoring has been seen as one avenue toward the encouragement of those gifts (Shaughnessy, 1989).

Several explanations have been given as to why exceptionally intelligent people do not always achieve at a level equal to their potentials. Robert Sternberg (1986) postulated twenty reasons for this; among them are lack of motivation, lack of impulse control, lack of perseverance, using the wrong abilities, inability to translate thought into action, fear of failure, excessive self-pity, distractibility and lack of concentration, and inability or unwillingness to "see the forest for the trees." Sternberg and others believe that it is most important to look at what a person does with the amount of intelligence that he or she possesses rather than at the sheer amount of measured intelligence. Personality, motivation, and a host of other factors contribute to intellectual and cognitive success.

Sternberg also developed what he termed a "triarchic theory" of intelligence. He posits that IQ tests have changed very little since the beginning of the twentieth century, whereas Western culture and society have changed considerably. In his book *Beyond I.Q.: A Triarchic Theory of Human Intelligence* (1985), Sternberg discusses his three subtheories of intelligence—exponential, contextual, and componential—and further subdivides them into more specific aspects.

Some theorists (as well as many parents of gifted children) believe that special skills and training are needed to teach gifted children. There are master's degree and doctoral programs designed to train teachers to work with gifted students and high achievers. Some educators advocate grade skipping or independent study for gifted children. Some gifted children take college courses from local universities; others attend special camps or residential schools. One such school, the Hollingsworth School in Maine, only admits students with IQs of 160 or higher. Special summer programs for the mathematically or scientifically precocious are offered at The Johns Hopkins University and other major universities. There are also a number of national and international societies and groups for highly gifted and intelligent students.

The needs of the mentally retarded vary considerably, according to the severity of the retardation; these needs can be examined as they relate to the five categories of retardation noted earlier. Borderline individuals may be able to live independently, work in the community, travel within their town, cook, and clean their homes. They may be unable to do tasks such as filling out their income tax forms, however, that require some sophisticated mathematics and reasoning skills. Those people with mild mental retardation usually have more difficulty with academic tasks such as reading instructions on the job, filling out an employment application, or balancing a checkbook. They may not be able to perform complex tasks and may require a considerable amount of supervision on the job—if they are performing at a level that enables them to procure employment.

Moderately retarded individuals typically are able to work in a sheltered workshop, with much supervision and assistance. They may need assistance in grooming (bathing, shaving, hygiene, and so on). They may get lost in their own locality if they travel, may be unable to make changes, and may engage in inappropriate behavior.

The severely or profoundly retarded person has extreme difficulties functioning independently. Some may need to be fed; some may not have any language skills other than a few words, such as "mama," "dada," or "want food." Others need assistance in dressing or may wear pull-over clothes (with no buttons) and shoes that do not lace (as they cannot perform the fine motor skills necessary for lacing). These individuals may sit for long periods in front of the television and move only when prompted. Some have slurred speech and difficulties in communicating. Many are at least occasionally incontinent and require prompting and assistance with toilet behaviors.

Since the 1970's, there has been remarkable progress using behavior modification techniques to shape and reinforce behaviors that help the mentally retarded to function with minimal adult assistance.

Context

As society becomes increasingly sophisticated and complex, intelligence is of greater and greater importance in terms of human functioning. A computerized society requires advanced intellectual skills; moreover, with increasing automation, jobs that can be performed by people with impaired intellectual abilities become fewer. Those people who are borderline mentally retarded may have much greater difficulty functioning and obtaining employment. Schools and even preschool and kindergarten facilities screen children for learning problems or developmental disabilities. Many psychologists and educators believe that it is important for those who are mentally retarded or have intellectual or language delays to receive as much early intervention as possible. Others, however, suggest that such early labeling tends to bring about lower expectations and therefore less investment in the child. It is important that this debate among educators and parents be kept active.

There are a number of federal laws regarding the mentally retarded and the amount of services they are legally entitled to receive. Most special educators, for example, are aware of laws specifying that those in special education programs or with handicapping conditions are entitled to receive certain services and should be educated in the "least restrictive environment" possible. A multidisciplinary treatment team should be involved in creating a treatment plan that indicates specific goals and how they should be achieved. What constitutes the "least restrictive environment" is not clearly specified, however, and is often difficult to determine. Many handicapped people still do not receive all the benefits to which they are entitled by law. At the other end of the spectrum, there is very little legislation concerning gifted people and gifted education programs. Much more needs to be done in this area in order to assist the academically, artistically, and intellectually gifted.

Bibliography

Feldman, David Henry, with Lynn T. Goldsmith. *Nature's Gambit: Child Prodigies and the Development of Human Potential*. New York: Basic Books, 1986. Feldman presents a number of case studies of prodigies and their growth and development. One of the best books on the subject.

Gardner, Howard. *Frames of Mind: The Theory of Multiple Intelligences*. New York: Basic Books, 1983. Gardner outlines his conceptions of intelligence and his domains of talent. A classic book that outlines different types of intelligence.

Gottfried, Allen W., et al. *Gifted IQ—Early Developmental Aspects: The Fullerton Longitudinal Study*. New York: Plenum Publishing, 1994.

Li, Rex. *A Theory of Conceptual Intelligence: Thinking, Learning, Creativity, and Giftedness*. Westport, Conn.: Praeger, 1996.

Shaughnessy, Michael F. "Cognitive Structures of the Gifted: Theoretical Perspectives, Factor Analysis, Triarchic Theories of Intelligence, and Insight Issues." *Gifted Education*

International 6, no. 3 (1990): 149-151. Presents a perspective on how intellectually gifted people think and discusses research in this area. As psychologists increasingly study gifted children and adults, they must pay more and more attention to the way in which these individuals learn and process information.

_____. "Mentoring the Creative Child, Adult, and Prodigy: Current Knowledge, Systems, and Research." *Gifted Education International* 6, no. 1 (1989): 22-24. Reviews the process of mentoring with various special groups. As mentored people seem to do very well in life, it is important to study this process; this article provides a "how to" overview for the beginner.

_____. "What's New in I.Q.?" *Creative Child and Adult Quarterly* 10, no. 2 (1985): 72-78. This article outlines theories of intelligence. Presents a very good summary of the theories of Gardner, Sternberg, and other theorists in the field.

Sternberg, Robert J. *Beyond I.Q.: A Triarchic Theory of Human Intelligence.* New York: Cambridge University Press, 1985. An excellent book on reconceptualizing intelligence for the 1990's and beyond. It is heavy reading in places but is important for those people genuinely interested in understanding intelligence and Sternberg's theories.

_____. *Intelligence Applied: Understanding and Increasing Your Intellectual Skills.* New York: Harcourt Brace Jovanovich, 1986. Helps one understand one's intelligence and provides exercises to increase it; for those people who want to work at being more intelligent and using their skills optimally.

Wechsler, David. *Manual for the Wechsler Intelligence Scale for Children-Revised.* New York: Psychological Corporation, 1974. Contains information about the most widely used contemporary IQ test for children. This test has been revised, however, so many people will encounter the WISC-III.

Michael F. Shaughnessy

See also:

Creativity and Intelligence, 176; Intelligence: Definition and Theoretical Models, 321; Intelligence Tests, 333; Race and Intelligence, 495.